# ACQUAINTANCE WITH THE ABSOLUTE

# Acquaintance with the Absolute

*The Philosophy of Yves R. Simon*

ESSAYS AND BIBLIOGRAPHY

*Edited by*
ANTHONY O. SIMON

Introduction by James V. Schall, S.J.

FORDHAM UNIVERSITY PRESS
New York
1998

© Copyright 1998 by Fordham University
All rights reserved.
LC 98-19888
ISBN 0-8232-1751-5 (*hardcover*)
ISBN 0-8232-1752-3 (*paperback*)

Library of Congress Cataloging-in-Publication Data

Acquaintance with the absolute : the philosphy of Yves
  R. Simon : essays and bibliography / edited by Anthony O. Simon ;
  introduction by James V. Schall.
     p.   cm.
  Includes bibliographical references and indexes.
  ISBN 0-8232-1751-5 (hc). — ISBN 0-8232-1752-3   (pbk.)
   1. Simon, Yves René Marie, 1903–1961.   I. Simon, Anthony O.
B2430.S5464A24   1998
194—dc21                                                                          98-19888
                                                                                         CIP

Printed in the United States of America

For
Richard Marco Blow
George S. Stratigos
and
Meg Donohue Spitznogle
with gratitude and affection

# CONTENTS

| | |
|---|---|
| Editor's Note | ix |
| Acknowledgments | xv |
| A Brief Chronology | xvii |
| Introduction by James V. Schall, S.J. | 1 |

## Part I
## ESSAYS

| | |
|---|---|
| 1. Yves R. Simon's Metaphysics of Action<br>RAYMOND L. DENNEHY | 19 |
| 2. Yves R. Simon's Philosophy of Science<br>RALPH NELSON | 57 |
| 3. Yves R. Simon and the Neo-Thomist Tradition in Epistemology<br>JOHN F. X. KNASAS | 83 |
| 4. Yves R. Simon on Natural Law and Reason<br>RUSSELL HITTINGER | 101 |
| 5. Yves R. Simon on Liberty and Authority<br>VUKAN KUIC | 128 |
| 6. Practical Wisdom in the Thought of Yves R. Simon<br>ROBERT J. MULVANEY | 147 |

## Part II
## BIBLIOGRAPHY

| | |
|---|---|
| Yves R. Simon: A Definitive Bibliography, 1923–1996<br>ANTHONY O. SIMON | 185 |
| Indexes | 295 |
| Notes on the Contributors | 327 |

# EDITOR'S NOTE

YVES R. SIMON (1903–1961) was born in Cherbourg, France, the son of an industrialist, and was educated at the Lycée Louis-le-Grand, the Sorbonne, and the Catholic Institute of Paris. He studied natural science, economics, and medicine as well as philosophy and initially thought of pursuing a literary career. Despite being handicapped during childhood with tuberculosis of the bone, he completed his studies and began teaching in 1930. He began writing in his early twenties. Simon made a strong entry into the world of philosophy with an impressive list of articles on both theoretical and practical topics, followed by the publication of his first two books, *An Introduction to Metaphysics of Knowledge* and *Critique of Moral Knowledge*.[1]

During the last decade Yves R. Simon's fame as a master teacher and thinker has been greatly enhanced by the steady stream of posthumous books and articles as well as by the reprinting of many of his early works. He is once again teaching a new generation in the same renowned fashion, marked by great lucidity and the ability to explain profound and complex problems through the perceptive use of everyday examples.

Many philosophers and teachers are in agreement that Simon's writings could be read ten years ago or a decade hence with equal profit because they retain their modernity and contemporaneous value. A non-specialized philosopher by principle, Simon made major contributions in political philosophy, logic, ethics, philosophy of science, epistemology, and metaphysics, and wrote insightful texts on a variety of other topics.

He had a rare genius for friendship and was very devoted to his students—a devotion they fully returned. His mentor was Jacques Maritain, with whom he carried on a treasured forty-year friendship and collaboration. That relationship was notably preserved

---

[1] The French titles of these volumes are *Introduction à l'ontologie du connaître* (Paris: Desclée de Brouwer, 1934) and *Critique de la connaissance morale* (Paris: Desclée de Brouwer, 1934). An English edition of the latter is forthcoming.

by the publication of Simon's last public lecture, occasioned by the inauguration of a Jacques Maritain Center at the University of Notre Dame.[2] His philosophical thinking was formed by Aquinas, but unlike many other Thomists his thought went far beyond any narrow, strident Thomism. Educationally he felt "that on a college level not philosophy but man considered in the contingencies of his concrete existence should be the main subject of liberal studies."[3]

Before coming to the United States in the fall of 1938 as a Visiting Professor, Simon taught philosophy for eight years at the Catholic Institute of Lille, simultaneously directing a series of weekly public philosophy lectures at the Catholic Institute of Paris, where he regularly delivered his own papers. In addition, he was managing editor of the *Revue de Philosophie* and editor of two book series entitled *Cours et Documents de Philosophie* and *Les Beaux Voyages d'Autrefois*, published by Pierre Téqui. Simon was very active in political and cultural movements, frequently contributing to avant-garde as well as to conservative journals. For nearly two years during the 1920s he was active in Marc Sangnier's league of the *Jeune-République,* which supported Franco–German reconciliation and the League of Nations during the early years after World War I. Later he joined numerous committees dedicated to mediating the Spanish Civil War and aiding its refugees who were pouring into France. He was a prominent signatory of a series of important political and ethical manifestoes published during the 1930s. The most important and well-known of these manifestos was "For the Common Good," signed by fifty-two leading French literary, cultural, and political figures.[4]

Simon was also, along with Georges Bernanos, Emmanuel Mounier, Stanislas Fumet, Gabriel Marcel, François Mauriac, and others, one of the founding members of and a frequent contributor to *Temps Présent* (1937), the influential Parisian newspaper

---

[2] John Howard Griffin and Yves R. Simon, *Jacques Maritain: Homage in Words and Pictures* (Albany, New York: Magi Book, 1974), pp. 3–15.

[3] Ibid., p. 4.

[4] The original French edition was *Pour le bien commun: Les Responsabilités du chrétien et le moment présent* (Paris: Desclée de Brouwer, 1934). This manifesto was published on April 19, 1934 and had an important impact on the critical political affairs of the time. For the English edition see "For the Common Good: The Christian's Responsibility in the Present Crisis," trans. with an introduction by Bernard E. Doering in *Notes et Documents* (Rome), 5, No. 20 (1980), 1–20.

published after the suppression of *Sept,* its controversial predecessor. *Temps Présent* was to suffer a similar fate at the hands of the Nazi-controlled Vichy government. Having spent a year teaching in Germany during the early 1930s, he foresaw with an awesome precision where the Nazi policies would inevitably take Germany, France, and the world. His passionate reflections were laid out in articles and in three books written during the war: *The Road to Vichy, 1918–1938*; *The March to Liberation*; and the *Community of the Free*.[5] He believed that France had been defeated from within and that a major cause was that the French had lost their understanding of the meaning of authority in democracy and that conservatives had willingly yielded to fascism.

Once established in America, Simon continued his political writings in journals, newspapers, and books in defense of liberty, democracy, and the efforts of the Free French and the Allies. These books, written in French, were promptly translated into English; two of them were reprinted four decades later. Simon's analysis of the causes of social problems transcends the specific events to which he applied it. No philosopher in this century has demonstrated so lucidly how a free and ordered society depends on political liberty as a necessary complement to legitimate political authority.

In America he first taught philosophy for ten years at the University of Notre Dame before accepting an invitation from Chancellor Robert M. Hutchins to join the Committee on Social Thought at the University of Chicago. The Committee at the time (1948) consisted of members from diverse academic fields, including: John U. Nef, F. A. Hayek, David Grene, Peter H. von Blankenhagen, Edward A. Shils, Mircea Eliade, Marshall Hodgson, Frank H. Knight, James M. Redfield, and Otto von Simpson, and a host of lecturers such as T. S. Eliot, Jacques Maritain, and Marc Chagall. Simon's colleague in Chicago's department of political science, Hans J. Morgenthau, wrote that "he had a profound impact at both Schools and that . . . one is struck by one quality that distinguishes the whole of Simon's work: the combi-

---

[5] See the original French editions, *La grande crise de la République Française: Observations sur la vie politique des Français de 1918–1938* (Montréal: Éditions de L'Arbre, 1941); *La marche à la délivrance* (New York: Éditions de la Maison Française, 1942); and *Par delà l'expérience du désespoir* (Montréal: Lucien Parizeau, 1945).

nation of a profound understanding of the basic insights of Western philosophy with a vivid experience of the philosophical problems of the contemporary world. It is the interaction of these two factors which is at the root of Simon's originality and importance for contemporary philosophy."[6]

Simon also lectured widely in the United States, Canada, and Mexico. His Charles R. Walgreen Foundation lectures, delivered at the University of Chicago in 1948, were the basis for his best-known work in English, *Philosophy of Democratic Government*, published by the University of Chicago Press in 1951. It remains a classic work on the modern underpinnings of democracy, enduringly relevant to the current crises of American democracy and the problems critically facing the emerging democracies of Eastern Europe and the Third World. This book has been translated into six foreign languages from Japanese in 1955 to Polish in 1993, while the English edition remains in print after forty-seven years.

Maurice Cranston, writing from the London School of Economics in 1975, lamented that "the death of Yves R. Simon in 1961 at the age of fifty-eight robbed the Western world of one of its most original and distinguished political theorists."[7] As impressive as this statement is, Cranston could not have anticipated the full impact and enhancement of Simon's reputation resulting from the publication of additional posthumous works and the reprinting of his earlier books. Here is the current posthumous book list, with more in the offing: *A General Theory of Authority*; *The Tradition of Natural Law*; *Freedom and Community*; *Freedom of Choice*; *Traité du Libre Arbitre*; *The Great Dialogue of Nature and Space*; *Work, Society and Culture*; *Community of the Free*; *The Definition of Moral Virtue*; *The Road to Vichy, 1918–1938*; *An Introduction to Metaphysics of Knowledge*; *Practical Knowledge*; *Philosophy of Democratic Government*; and *Foresight and Knowledge*, to which must be added numerous translations of his articles from the French originals. Now with so much previously unavailable material finding its way into print, renewed scholarship of the range and interest

---

[6] See Hans J. Morgenthau's review of Simon's *Work, Society and Culture* in *The Annals of the American Academy of Political and Social Science*, 411 (January 1974), 229.

[7] Maurice Cranston, "Political Philosophy in Our Time," in *The Great Ideas Today* (Chicago: Encyclopaedia Britannica, 1975), p. 126.

expressed by the authors of this collection is possible. The expectation then is that these studies will not only introduce Simon to a new generation but also will encourage others to develop their own interest.

This collection of studies touches on but a few of Simon's major themes. The papers are presented in the hope that they will entice readers to take up Simon's original works. I have added an annotated "Yves R. Simon: A Definitive Bibliography 1923–1996" detailing books, translations, chapters in books, articles, selected book reviews, edited book series, manifestoes, archival materials, and selected works on Simon, with cross references and indices to facilitate the ever-increasing interest in and research on his thought. All these materials, including dissertations and theses, are available at the Yves R. Simon Institute. A vast collection of archival materials is also housed at the University of Notre Dame Hesburgh Library and Archives as well as in their Jacques Maritain Center. A number of other monographs on aspects of Simon's philosophy are currently at press and it is hoped that they will be followed in time by a suitable intellectual biography.

Unlike many philosophers, in the case of Yves R. Simon his life and his works were intimately linked. The "Philosopher of the Fighting French" was to become the "Philosopher of Democracy" and a "Philosopher's Philosopher," but, above all, one of the great teachers of our time.

ANTHONY O. SIMON
Director,
Yves R. Simon Institute
Mishawaka, Indiana

# ACKNOWLEDGMENTS

MY THANKS GO FIRST to the contributing authors of this volume. Their articles reflect not only their interest but a continuing judgment of the unique value of the philosophical thought of Yves R. Simon.

I am especially grateful to Jeanne Knoerly, SP program director at the Lilly Endowment, who made the research, editing, and publication of this book possible with encouragement and a supporting grant. The Homeland Foundation in New York also helped initially with a summer research stipend.

Professor Alasdair MacIntyre of Duke University and the Reverend Theodore M. Hesburgh, President Emeritus of the University of Notre Dame, kindly promoted the funding of this project through their supporting recommendations.

The compilation of the Yves R. Simon bibliography was greatly facilitated by help from Peter A. Redpath, Charles P. O'Donnell, Jean-Louis Allard, Joseph A. Buckley, and Thomas W. Brown, Jr., all of whom helped track down copies of rare items. From Canada Professor Ralph Nelson at the University of Windsor provided invaluable suggestions and assistance during the indexing of the bibliography. Michel Nurdin in Toulouse, France, graciously searched and discovered some unknown Simon texts and provided data from various Parisian libraries. Paul Christophe, a French historian, provided correspondence and political documents from the Simon files housed at his university archives in Lille, France. Dennis Wm. Moran, managing editor of *The Review of Politics* at the University of Notre Dame, once again graciously offered his editorial expertise and generous counsel throughout the manuscript preparation. My thanks also go to Robert Bonazzi who offered very creative last minute suggestions.

The hospitable availability of research staffs and the use of technical facilities at the libraries of the universities of Chicago, Notre Dame, Ottawa, Laval, and the Library of Congress were of particular assistance.

Mary Beatrice Schulte, executive editor of Fordham University Press, has left her careful mark on the final manuscript. I am deeply grateful to her for all her assistance.

In the end it was the support of my wife, Judith, and that of many friends to whom I owe an undischargable debt for all they did to help with this book.

# A BRIEF CHRONOLOGY

1903 Yves René Marie Simon was born in Cherbourg, France on March 14, 1903. His parents were Auguste Simon and Berthe Porquet dit la Féronnière. His father, an industrialist, was director of Établissement Simon Frères, the family's large farm implement manufacturing company in Normandy.

1919 Passes the Baccalauréat-ès-Lettres in Cherbourg.

1920 Enrolls at the Lycée Louis-le-Grand in Paris in the form "Rhétorique Supérieure" in preparation for the École Normale Supérieure.

1922 Receives his Licence-ès-Lettres in philosophy, Université de Paris (Sorbonne).

1923 Awarded Diplôme d'Études Supérieures de Philosophie, Faculté des Lettres, Université de Paris (Sorbonne). His thesis, *Mémoire sur Charles Dunoyer*, was directed by Célestin Bouglé.
Officially registers his doctoral dissertation topic at the Université de Paris (Sorbonne) on Pierre-Joseph Proudhon and simultaneously attends courses at the Institut Catholique de Paris.

1926 Begins several years of medical studies at the École de Médecine of the Université de Paris (Sorbonne).
Earns the Certificat d'Études Physiques, Chimiques et Naturelles from the Université de Paris (Sorbonne).

1928 Granted the degree of Lector Philosophiae from the Institut Catholique de Paris.

1929 Licentiate in philosophy, Institut Catholique de Paris.
Teaches at Heiligkreuz-Neisse, Nordost, Germany, during 1929–1930.

1930 Marries Paule Dromard in Paris. They have six children; four are born in France before the family's departure for the United States in the fall of 1938.
Accepts the chair of philosophy at the Institut Catholique de Lille. Simultaneously named director of public Thomistic lectures at the Institut Catholique de Paris, 1930–1938.

1932 Appointed Secrétaire Général (managing editor) of the *Revue de Philosophie*, published by Pierre Téqui, Paris, 1932–1938.

1934 Receives his Doctorate de Philosophie, Cum Singulari Prorsus Laude, from the Institut Catholique de Paris. Defends his doctoral dissertation on April 18 1934, before a board of examiners composed of F. A. Blanche, Daniel J. Lallement, Jacques Maritain, Georges Dwelshauvers, and Charles Eyselé. It was directed and approved by Émile Peillaube, Dean of the Faculty, and published as *Introduction à l'ontologie du connaître*.
Named editor of Cours et Documents de Philosophie, a philosophical book series published by Pierre Téqui, Paris, 1934–1938.

1938 Becomes director of a second book series, Les Beaux Voyages d'Autrefois, also published by Téqui.
Awarded a prize for his philosophical works by La Société des Sciences de Lille.
Leaves for the United States to become Visiting Professor of Philosophy at the University of Notre Dame and joins the regular faculty after the collapse of France.

1943 Teaches at and receives an honorary degree, Profesor Extraordinario, from La Universidad National de Mexico in Mexico City.
Appointed to the faculty of the École Libre des Hautes Études [New School for Social Research], New York, and continues to write articles for various Free French publications in the United States, Canada, and England.

1946 Elected to the Pontificia Academia Romana S. Thomae Aqvinatis *Diploma Cooptationis Causa* (Pontifical Academy of St. Thomas Aquinas) in Rome. First American citizen to be so honored.

1948 Leaves the University of Notre Dame and is appointed professor in The University of Chicago's Committee on Social Thought, by Chancellor Robert M. Hutchins. Among his colleagues at the Committee are John U. Nef (Economic History), David Grene (Classics), Peter H. von Blankenhagen (Archeology), Edward A. Shils (Sociology), F. A. Hayek (Economics), Otto von Simpson (Art History), Mircea Eliade (Comparative Religion), Marshall Hodgson, J. M. Redfield (Economics), and Frank H. Knight (Economics).

1961 Yves R. Simon dies in South Bend, Indiana, on May 11, 1961.

# ACQUAINTANCE WITH THE ABSOLUTE

# Introduction: Immanent in the Souls of Men
## *James V. Schall, S.J.*

> "The principal act of social life is immanent in the souls of men. It is a communion in some belief, love, or aversion. The principal part of our common good is contained within our souls."
>
> YVES R. SIMON
> *A General Theory of Authority.*[1]

I

In gathering together the bibliography of his many writings, we have available to us in this welcome volume a complete listing of Yves R. Simon's clear and incisive books, essays, and reviews, as well as materials about him, information that often we knew only in part. Many admirers knew of Yves R. Simon on authority, of course, and perhaps on free will and democratic government. We knew that he was a follower of St. Thomas, and of his relation to Maritain and Gilson, but we forget sometimes John of St. Thomas or Simon's writings on politics, World War II, science, metaphysics, and knowledge theory. Simon remains an education in himself as well as someone who critically transmits to us Aristotle and St. Thomas in the light of the various ways that they have been received, understood, or, too often, misunderstood during the past hundred years.

The struggle for the modern mind is a real one. The slightest error in understanding what reality is about, as Étienne Gilson

---

[1] Yves R. Simon, *A General Theory of Authority* (Notre Dame, Indiana: University of Notre Dame Press, 1980; repr. 1996), pp. 125–26.

once said, following Aristotle and St. Thomas, will appear eventually in an increasingly distorted form down the ages when other thinkers take up, in yet more dangerous ways, an idea that really did not hold in the first place. When an age goes wrong, it is important to have a thinker who understands why the mistakes are being made, in the light of a center that retains its own criteria and intellectual validity. Yves R. Simon can be for us this thinker who points directly to the center, to the first things, to the truths we would hold if we are to remain sane and honorable.

## II

Yves R. Simon thus must first be seen as a teacher who teaches us things we would not in all probability come across without him. Simon has some marvelous things to say about teaching and learning in *A General Theory of Authority*. He acknowledges that in the sphere of speculative truth, of how things are, not of what is to be done, authority is always substitutional, that, whenever possible, it ought to disappear in favor of argument and the clarity of knowledge. But this result does not mean that authority is not helpful or often necessary in order for us to proceed in theoretical life and, more so, in the life of faith. Most of the things we do in our practical life, we do because of authority; very few things do we work out for ourselves. We, most of us, do not know how engines work or how electrical door bells chime. It is enough for us to follow instructions, to let others know the design, the details. We take our automobiles to a mechanic, even though, should we choose, we ourselves might go to engineering school to learn how to repair cars. When it comes down to it, both for convenience and for time, we would rather act on the truth of authority than not act at all until we learn, say, how the engine works or how the door bell rings. Life is too short not to trust many authorities. The very common good in which we dwell means that we can rely on others to know some specialty that we do not know but take only on authority, on the testimony of someone who does know.

When I read this book about authority with classes of mine, I always stop, with some emphasis, at the passage in which Simon points out that there are, before any teacher, three kinds of students. There are those students who are in the classes mainly for grades, for looking good on their record, who really do not care about the matter at hand. Then we find those students who already know everything. Such students only have objections at class presentations. They are unwilling to allow other argument or experience to present a problem in the dimensions in which it is handed down to us and offered by the teacher. And, finally, we can find those students who are, to use Simon's felicitous phrase, "intelligently teachable," those who are capable and desirous of learning but do not know exactly how to approach their goal.[2] Consequently, students can and do save much time and energy by having a good teacher show them the way. "Teachable minds," Simon adds, "have the privilege of understanding that a provisional belief is often the best, or the strictly indispensable way, to science."[3] Thus, for Simon, authority is essential in practical matters, yet it is also of great usefulness and aid in speculative affairs, where it plays only a substitutional role.

When the task of teaching is completed, however, the truth that is possessed is not the private property of teacher or pupil, but some good, undoubtedly belonging to each, some common truth in which both teacher and pupil share because they both know. They both know, not what they conjured up by way of creating their own free first principles, but *what is*, what is given as the objects of their knowing powers. Our mind is *capax omnium*, yet it becomes all things only by actually knowing, or by believing when that is the only way open to us. Friendship and love themselves depend upon agreement in truth, on our capacities to live in the same universe, to have the highest things in common, and to know that we have them in common.

### III

Though he does not write in the "*Quaestiones*" form of Aquinas, we cannot help but be aware of the care that the French scholar takes in stating the position that he is disputing and clarifying.

---
[2] Ibid., p. 95.
[3] Ibid., p. 96.

Simon is never prolix. The famous French logical "clarity" is second nature to him. His order of thought and presentation is always obvious in manageable, coherent forms. Simon often needs to be read carefully again and again. Indeed, he is always worth reading again and again. Simon has a happy pedagogical facility of using vivid examples, particular instances in which the universal idea he is trying to elaborate exists, so that we can understand it and, in understanding it, remember it.

The very title of this book comes from a passage in *Philosophy of Knowledge*, in which Yves R. Simon remarked that "it is in the flux of a relation to sense qualities that [man] achieves his first *acquaintance with the absolute*."[4] Needless to say, this is a remarkable phrase, because it reminds us that all things are somehow bound together, that the fact that we are finite mortals does not also mean that we have no contact, through our being finite, with the Absolute. We human beings will not find a way to the Absolute that does not begin and proceed through the particular things that we know.

Who can forget—to take an example of Simon's capacity to teach through particulars, through examples—his various illustrations of the need for authority, in which he uses the happy example of the large family who consider together their upcoming vacation. The family members are intelligent and prosperous, virtuous and considerate of one another. The members are asked to suggest a place to spend their vacation, while remembering that they are a family, that is, they want to be together. They have a common good. It turns out, not surprisingly, that ten different quite pleasant and exciting possibilities turn up. The family cannot go to every place suggested and do not want to go their separate ways. Thus, someone, an authority, needs to decide which one of the many good choices will be selected. Once it has been chosen, the members see that it is also a good choice and one that meets the requirements of being in a family.

Reason by itself, then, far from "proving" what choice is the "best," proves only that all are good and desirable. As Simon points out in this model case, no lack of virtue or intelligence is

---

[4] Yves R. Simon, "An Essay on Sensation," in *Philosophy of Knowledge: Selected Readings*, ed. Roland Houde and Joseph P. Mullally (Chicago: J. B. Lippincott, 1960), p. 95; emphasis added..

to be found here. The more intelligent and the more virtuous we are, the more good selections there will be and, hence, the more we will need authority. Therefore, he concludes, in this one instance, at least, authority is essential. We do not violate but fulfill our nature, our rational nature, by following this decision of authority. Authority thus does not, as such, arise out of sin or a lack or deficiency of some sort, though it may be called in to meet these situations also.

Now, in using such an example, a single instance, Simon makes clear a subtle, complicated point about a very specific problem that arises in political philosophy itself. He explains authority to us in his own way. He spells out for us just what Aristotle meant when he said that man is by nature a political animal, a rational animal who needs authority to achieve more fully what is already given to be in reality. Of course, in characteristic thoroughness, Simon also notes the one limitation of his example: namely, that when everyone agrees, when there is unanimity, no authority is necessary. Simon, however, goes on to propose other examples and considerations to make his argument more clear, more definite, more to the point. But what I want to suggest here in the beginning is that reading Yves R. Simon, like reading Aristotle or Cicero, brings us before a philosopher who is a born teacher and who gives his students, his readers, the best sort of instances that enable them to grasp for themselves the intellectual point he is making. Such examples enable them to see that the philosophic point relates to their own experience.

## IV

Simon's uncanny capacity to relate speculative and practical philosophy, something touched upon in one way or another in each of the essays in this volume, can, again by way of example, be seen in his discussion of gift and of what we love when we love a person. Simon writes very beautifully on these profound topics. In examining experience, Simon simply denies that all things in us, including knowledge, arise from selfish or subjective motives, even though, to make another point, it is impossible that real goods do not in fact redound to our benefit. We cannot not wish for happiness, for this is what we are.

But what does it mean that something proceeds "by way of gift" and not by necessity, not by way of coercion?

> Such disinterestedness, which concerns both the content and the ways of action, originates in rationality, but inasmuch as it implies the actual transcending of the self by itself, it is traceable, in strict appropriateness, to the way of subsisting and to the way of acting which belong to a complete substance of a rational nature. In short, it is traceable to the personality.[5]

Here is recalled Boethius's famous definition of a person in a discussion of what it is we love when we love. The transcending of the self does not mean its destruction, but its completion. We are already, in these reflections, on the verge of the mystery of the Trinity as it is reflected in our personal and social lives. In the Trinity, the persons are relations, not somehow separate, autonomous entities. We are, each of us, created in the image of this very Trinity.

Simon thus wonders if it is some quality in the one loved that we rely on in our loving—say, beauty, intelligence, or riches. These qualities are real and do call our attention to others of our kind. He points out, however, that, in what Aristotle called true friendship, that most profound of topics, it is the person we seek, not merely the quality under which we first were drawn to our friend. The ultimate gift, paradoxically, is the gift of self, a gift that completes the self but does not destroy it. Friendship is between "person and person," not the qualities of the person. "The question of why one loves is best answered—if this can be called an answer—by pointing to what is unique and unutterable about a person."[6] This observation enables Simon to distinguish between the "object" of love and its "grounds." The object of love is really the person, what cannot be repeated in the universe.

Again we can see the charm of Simon's metaphysics, if I can put it that way; we can see how the clarification of the truth of things relates to our own acts and the understanding of what we are and how we are to live:

> Let us see in what sense friendship can make itself independent of its own grounds. Indeed, the only thing that human love cannot

---
[5] Ibid., p. 75.
[6] Ibid., p. 76.

do is create out of nothing the goodness, the desirability of its object. Divine love alone causes the beloved to be good, independent of any good antecedent to love. In order to be an object for the love of a creature, a thing must already be good: in that sense it is true that no one is loved or liked except for his qualities.[7]

But notice what is the result of this acute analysis of what the object of love is for finite creatures. It is not that when the initial motive or quality of love ceases—the example Simon uses is of a beautiful woman who loses her beauty because of smallpox—love ceases. "Under the worst of circumstances the excellence of human nature, considered in actual existence and in relation to its end, would still be a ground for loving a person without measure."[8] The particular good that is found in an individual person is itself likewise a good of society, of the capacity to acknowledge in each existing person the good that is actually there by virtue of its creation. The love "without measure" of the person furthermore grounds the stability of society by teaching us to understand why particular goods themselves are important.

V

A lively literature in political philosophy involves how Leo Strauss, one of the great thinkers of the twentieth century, understood his own intellectual vocation. Was he primarily a secret writer who devoted himself to philosophical things so that he could protect the claims of Jerusalem, or was he a philosopher who chose Athens for the highest way of life? Was his quest for truth by reason alone, for the whole, undertaken because reason and revelation were unable to resolve the question about the highest form of life? What are we to make of the modern claim that the life of action, the political life, of statesmanship, is itself the highest form of thought? Would it not be better to be a statesman, perhaps a philosopher-king? I sense in Raymond Dennehy's essay in this volume some light on how Simon himself responded to these considerations by the way he led his own life, a philo-

---
[7] Ibid., p. 77.
[8] Ibid., p. 78.

sophic life about practical things that itself led to metaphysics and indeed to revelation.

Strauss reviewed Simon's *Philosophy of Democratic Government*.[9] His review is especially interesting in light of Strauss's own opinion that the best form of government, which Simon argues is democracy, is, in Strauss's opinion, rarely, if ever, found in practice and if then, as a result only of historical accident, not of political "science." Strauss admired Simon's book in many ways and recognized that the modern temptation to "escape into anti-social dreams," as Simon called it, into an arbitrary ideology imposed on reality by politics and the political mind, was real enough in modernity. Strauss pointed out, however, that Simon seems to have thought that he was contributing to a development of democratic theory that was in the line of St. Thomas, but not adequately accounted for by either St. Thomas or his early modern followers like Cajetan, Bellarmine, or Suarez.

The transmission theory, whereby the people are the origin of political order and rule, holds that the people must transfer this original authority to a specific ruling body, whether monarchic, aristocratic, or popular. Simon wanted to argue that the transmission theory really meant that democracy was the natural form of political rule. Of this Strauss asks "why this classical implication escaped the notice of the classical Thomistic writers."[10] Strauss does not find Simon's argument about the earlier moral environment of the sixteenth and seventeenth centuries to be persuasive. Simon seems to think that what made the understanding of democracy as the best form of rule come about was the improvement in economic or technological conditions.

"I confess to a great reluctance to believe that 'our conscience has improved' on any important subject," Strauss observed in his review of Simon,

> or that we understand great thinkers of the past better than they understood themselves. I am inclined to assume that the classics of Thomism have given sufficient thought to the transmission theory to bring out all its necessary implications. I would therefore regard it wise to assume that the democratic spirit is a possible, but not a

---

[9] Leo Strauss, *What Is Political Philosophy?* (Glencoe, Illinois: The Free Press, 1959), pp. 306–311.
[10] Ibid., p. 308.

necessary, development of the transmission theory, a development favored by extraneous or accidental circumstances.[11]

By denying any real change in human nature and doubting the theory of progress by which some change in the actual human condition might have come about, Strauss notes that Simon was cautious to speak of possibilities, not necessary laws.

Strauss finds that Simon's treatment of technology parallels his treatment of democracy. Strauss is most careful, or "moderate," to use a favorite word of his. He thinks that Simon's argument for democracy as the best form of rule by nature needs qualification. Even when democracy is working in the best form that is theoretically proposed, it must be considered not the normal but a very rare and accidental thing. Political philosophy does well to be aware of the unusual conditions in which good forms of rule can exist. Thus, to expect too much of democracy could be dangerous in not preparing actual regimes for what they are most likely to face.

Charles N. R. McCoy likewise seems to have treated Simon's arguments for the natural superiority of democracy by nature with care. McCoy agreed with Strauss that direct democracy or pure democracy is not a natural form of rule, but, rather, the source or condition out of which any sort of rule arises. All good rule is intended for the good of all. But the form of rule has to be transferred by the prudential requirements of nature, that is, some definite and formal arrangement of authority is required. Simon, of course, seems to have argued precisely this point in his general theory of authority; that is, some positive body of rule needs to be selected, even if it is a democracy. Democracy still needs to be political, that is, it needs a formal structure to decide public issues.

McCoy wrote, in his memorable essay on "The Origin of Political Authority," that democracy is not a usual or normal form of rule, though it sometimes could happen. I will cite McCoy at length because he brings out the essence of the problem well:

> It is interesting that Professor Yves Simon presented Bellarmine's theory as allowing that the *respublica* can manage political power for itself. The opposite opinion, he said, "does not seem to be borne out by [his] text"—this despite the explicit statement that

---

[11] Ibid., p. 309.

"since the *respublica* cannot exercise this power for itself, it is bound to transfer it to one person or a few." At the same time, Professor Simon admitted that "in all cases in which Bellarmine can think . . . the duty to pursue the common good . . . entails also the duty to put it in the hands of a distinct governing personnel . . ." (*Philosophy of Democratic Government* [Chicago, 1951], p. 168).

If Bellarmine could not, as Simon acknowledged, think of any case in which the *respublica* can exercise political power for itself, how does Simon conclude that Bellarmine's theory allows for precisely that? It is, he told us, because "all that Bellarmine demonstrates is that the transmission of political power from the multitude to the distinct governing personnel is not a matter delivered to the free choice of the multitude *when*, as he put it, 'the republic cannot exercise such power for itself' (*ibid.*, 168; italics mine). But did Bellarmine put it quite that way? He said not '*when*' but '*since*' the republic, etc." "Since" it cannot, Bellarmine, of course, did not treat of the conceivable case when it could. Science does not treat of the accidental as such. Certainly it may be said that there is some conceivable case in which the *respublica* can exercise political power for itself—this is simply the unnatural but possible case. Again we might recall Aristotle's definition of the natural as that which happens always or for the most part. That it is natural for the *respublica* to exercise political power for itself is explicitly denied by Bellarmine.[12]

I bring up these somewhat obscure disputes about Simon's understanding of democracy and its philosophic grounding because the evolution of democracy seems to have been in the direction better described by Simon in his analysis of liberalism, as a philosophy allowing us to deny first principles of reason, than in his discussion of democracy as the most natural form of government.[13]

Strauss and McCoy thought that Simon's analysis of democracy as the natural form of rule stands outside the context of Bellarmine's classically grounded insistence that democracy is not the normal or most obvious application of political principle. This

---

[12] Charles N. R. McCoy, "The Origin of Political Authority," *On the Intelligibility of Political Philosophy: Essays of Charles N. R. McCoy*, ed. James V. Schall and John Schrems (Washington, D.C.: The Catholic University of America Press, 1989), pp. 52–53n11. See also McCoy's remark on Simon in *The Structure of Political Thought* (New York: McGraw-Hill, 1963), p. 206.

[13] See Simon's discussion of liberalism in *General Theory of Authority*, pp. 102–15.

difference does not mean that Simon thinks that direct democracy, in the rare historical instances when it does exist, does not need to organize itself into a formal ruling body when deciding public business; he does think that it should have a formal organization whereby it could rule itself. The issue is, rather, that even though democracy might sometimes, though rarely, be a possible form of rule, it was an exceptional form of rule, not really natural. Simon was, of course, writing during a period in which democracy was a general term for mixed, limited government based on popular selection of rulers, themselves limited constitutionally and morally. Simon's discussion of a liberalism that no longer considered itself bound by first principles of reason or even by its own rules takes us closer to the sort of worry about democracy that we are finding today.

If we look at Simon's discussion of direct democracy in *Philosophy of Democratic Government*, however, it is clear that he rejects any so-called Rousseauean "coach-driver" theory of democracy as a legitimate form of rule. He rejects this radical form because it does not allow a distinct governing personnel which is required by his own theory of authority and civil obedience. In examining Suarez, Simon does think that Suarez holds direct democracy to be a possible form of rule which does not require transmission of authority. However, even here, in Simon's view, democracy is subject to the requirement of a distinct governing body formally constituted. "Democracy never transmits the whole of transmissible powers," Simon affirms. "Every democracy remains, in varying degrees, a direct democracy."[14]

The direct democracy that Simon sees in every democracy, nevertheless, is not one that somehow is rooted in a pure people's-will thesis. Rather, it must be exercised in an organized way, formally constituted for governing purposes, for instance, in the election of leaders. As I read him, I do not think the concern that we find in Strauss and McCoy about Simon's misunderstanding the rarity of direct democracy is exact. When we examine the restrictions that Simon places on direct democracy, even when expressed in republican forms, it is clear that he is close to the concern of Strauss and McCoy that actual governments have the

---

[14] Yves R. Simon, *Philosophy of Democratic Government* (Chicago: The University of Chicago Press, 1951), p. 184.

obligation and authority actually to govern, even in their democratic aspects.

Let me cite two passages—one from the columnist Georgie Anne Geyer, the other from the Pope John Paul II—that illustrate, I think, the essence of the concern that Strauss and McCoy thought they found in Simon's interpretation of the transmission theory as meaning in modern times that democracy was the "natural" form of rule. Georgie Anne Geyer wrote:

> When they were designing America, the Founders drew a sobering distinction between our form of American representational democracy, where the people rule through the mediation of representatives, and what James Madison called "pure democracy," where the people supposedly rule directly. They concluded that "pure democracy" was too vulnerable to demagogues and characterized by cataclysmic shifts from anarchy to tyranny. Today we are already beginning to call pure democracy by its newer name, "direct democracy." One has to be incredulous that any candidate would be so callow or so ambitious as to seriously embrace or praise such a concept—and even more astounded if the American people allow it.[15]

These were also Simon's concerns about the coach-driver theory of direct democracy, which maintains that the sole purpose of government is, not to rule, but to fulfill the will of the people, no matter what it is.

And John Paul II, who has mentioned the problems of modern democratic theory in many of his recent encyclicals, wrote to a Conference on Religion and Secularism:

> Today however we would do well to consider another form of limitation on religious freedom, one which is more subtle than overt persecution. I am thinking here of the claim that a democratic society should relegate to the realm of private opinion its members' religious beliefs and the moral convictions which derive from faith. . . . But if citizens are expected to leave aside their religious convictions when they take part in public life, does this not mean that society not only excludes the contribution of religion to its institutional life, but also promotes *a culture which redefines man as less than what he is*? In particular, there are moral

---

[15] Georgie Anne Geyer, "Direct Democracy Demons," *The Washington Times*, February 9, 1996.

questions at the core of every great public issue. Should citizens whose moral judgements are informed by their religious beliefs be less welcome to express their most deeply held convictions? When that happens, is not democracy itself emptied of real meaning?[16]

After the refounding of political rule after World War II, when Simon wrote, democracy in practice has not retained the sort of grounding in natural law and political philosophy that he had proposed. Rather, a form of voluntarism, subject to nothing but itself, has more and more ominously characterized the democracies. Democracies have increasingly emptied themselves of any "real meaning," to use the Holy Father's term, and tended in the direction of the sort of direct democracy that Simon himself rejected most clearly in his analysis of Rousseau's political heritage.

## VI

That Yves R. Simon remains the excellent teacher and that his "pupils," if I might call them that, remain immanently teachable will be seen in each of the six essays in this volume. Russell Hittinger on law, Vukan Kuic on liberty, Robert Mulvaney on practical wisdom, Ralph Nelson on science, Raymond Dennehy on metaphysics, and John Knasas on epistemology—each demonstrates in his tightly reasoned presentation how the intellectual guidance of Yves R. Simon persists as a vital starting point for many a good scholar looking for the truth of things. Not only does the variety of topics illustrate the wide range of Simon's own interests but it also occasions opportunity to clarify further certain basic ideas or arguments left unclear or about which further scholarship can elaborate. What is striking in these essays, something I found surprising, is the degree to which we must consider Simon as a defender and articulator, not of the practical life, but of the speculative life.

This concern to connect Simon's renown in matters of practical reason with those of speculative philosophy thus seems to me to be what is behind Hittinger's careful elaboration of the place of eternal law in any full understanding of positive or natural law.

---

[16] John Paul II, December 7, 1995, *L'Osservatore Romano* [English], December 20–27, 1995, p. 7.

This is a delicate question, no doubt. An error about what is ultimately at issue can lead to the most serious intellectual consequences, consequences that Hittinger notes in the case of Justice Anthony Kennedy's position in the *Casey* decision where liberty means "the right to define one's own concept of existence, of meaning, of the universe, and of the mystery of human life."[17] Simon's discussion of liberalism (in *A General Theory of Authority*) had already, as I have mentioned, anticipated such an almost incredible result that, when espoused, undermines any objective order or truth or rule.

For those who are Catholic, there is a triple irony here as this position of everyone's defining his own philosophy was elaborated by a Catholic judge from a case involving a Catholic governor about an issue that is, as Hittinger shows, central to the natural law as developed in the Catholic tradition. Nothing better illustrates Gilson's remark about carrying error to its logical conclusion when left to itself than the *Casey* decision. We are fortunate to see a mind of Hittinger's caliber carefully spelling out the root of this problem within the tradition of Simon.

No doubt, Simon is most noted for his work in clarifying the nature of practical reasoning. Vukan Kuic, from the side of law, and Robert Mulvaney, from the side of the practical intellect itself, have spelled out much of the central reasoning that Simon followed and that will help unify the thought that he devoted to this most significant topic. It is characteristic of the Aristotelian tradition to address itself to all phases of science, indeed to the very nature of science itself. No doubt, most of the confusions in modernity about philosophy and revelation have some origin in current scientific theory. One of the great advantages of the French Thomist tradition was its willingness to address the nature and influence of science head on. Ralph Nelson's account of Simon's understanding of science presents a side of Simon that we might otherwise miss. No philosophical account of speculative or practical intellect in the Thomist tradition would be complete without considerable attention to the intellectual background to modern science. The presumption of some implicit or inescapable conflict is widespread. Nelson suggests how Simon approached

---

[17] See Russell Hittinger, "Et Tu, Justice Kennedy: The Real Story Behind the *Casey* Decision," *Crisis*, 10 (September 1992), 16–22.

this relationship and how science itself is to be related to the central tradition for which Simon stood, so that science and philosophy are not in opposition but supportive of each other.

John F. X. Knasas takes up another side of the problem of modern knowledge theory in his discussion of the tradition of realism. Knasas's is the one essay in this series that attempts to analyze what could be Simon's misunderstanding of epistemology. This essay is useful both in itself and as an example of the way Simon can still teach through efforts of his students to save the truth in his original position. Raymond Dennehy's insightful essay on Simon's metaphysics in a way fits into all the other essays in this volume. In a highly original and perceptive essay, Dennehy has made nothing less than a spirited defense of the contemplative life in the very process of explaining why Simon devoted so much of his attention, not to the theoretical life, but to the practical. If we recall that the old argument about the primacy of active or contemplative life is a controversy that recurs in differing forms throughout the history of philosophy, we will soon see the relevance of this particular discussion.

## VII

The ease with which good principles and ideas can slip into their opposite dangers, to conclude, brings us back to the subject matter of these various essays about the work of Yves R. Simon. The first line of political freedom is truth, the purpose of intelligence itself. Truth lies, as Simon implies, "in the souls of men." Each of these essays, in a particular way, make us aware that the practical intellect, the highest activity of which is politics, as Aristotle said, is itself rooted in the principles and reality of being itself, the object of our finite intelligence. What is remarkable about Yves R. Simon is the way he was able to carry a practical problem back to its proper theoretical root. Robert Sokolowski recently recalled the value of Simon's discussion of the useful place of authority even in speculative matters, of how the very principles of reason must themselves be protected and promoted by authority, ecclesiastical, academic, and political.[18]

---

[18] Robert Sokolowski, "Church Tradition and the Catholic University," *Homiletic and Pastoral Review* (February 1996), 30. Sokolowski is referring to the discussion in chapter 3 of *A General Theory of Authority*.

Simon's detailed concern with practical reason, art, technology, work, and science was itself something that led him to metaphysics. He realized that the common good must also be in our souls as a clearly understood and chosen truth that corresponded to the things that ought to be. The gift nature of reality, the abundance of reality that Simon saw to be also reflected in an economy and in human friendship, itself requires philosophical understanding. The essays in this book provide an introduction to and firm grasp of the highest things. The careful, clear reflections on Yves R. Simon that we see in these fine essays still stimulate and incite the good thinkers and "intelligently teachable" students we read here, men who manifest vividly to us the reward of reading Yves R. Simon.

# Part I
# ESSAYS

# 1
# Yves R. Simon's Metaphysics of Action
*Raymond L. Dennehy*

"To exist is not enough; *il faut agir.*"

Yves R. Simon

### Introduction

I use the word "action" in this essay's title in two quite different, but, as I hope to show, intimately related senses: *practical* and *metaphysical*. Permit me to explain. You will search in vain among Yves R. Simon's writings for a treatise devoted to metaphysics. Yet it is correct to say that "Simon's voluminous output deals mainly with three areas: political philosophy, metaphysics and ethics."[1] The point is that while he has works devoted to political philosophy and ethics and none to metaphysics, metaphysics remains both pervasive in and key to his thinking. He almost always turns to metaphysical theories and concepts to rationally justify or clarify topics in these other areas of philosophy. Thus Alasdaire MacIntyre correctly calls attention to the importance of Simon's metaphysics for understanding crucial concepts that he sets forth in *The Definition of Moral Virtue*.[2]

From the drift of his writings it is clear that Simon assigned huge importance to practical philosophy, but I think it hazardous to go further and say that he thought it more important than

---
[1] Yves R. Simon, *The Great Dialogue of Nature and Space*, ed. Gerard J. Dalcourt (Albany, New York: Magi Books, Inc., 1970), p. xiii.
[2] Alasdair MacIntyre, review of *An Introduction to Metaphysics of Knowledge* by Yves R. Simon, *American Catholic Philosophical Quarterly*, 65, No. 1 (Winter 1991), pp. 112–114.

metaphysics. My own assessment, which I hope to cinch below, is that he was primarily a metaphysician and that, had he not died at an untimely age, he would eventually have produced a work on metaphysics. I base it on three considerations. First, wherever Simon engages in metaphysical discourse, you find the sure hand of the master, along with an unmistakable enthusiasm and reverence for the subject. Second, as I noted above, metaphysics pervades his writings on practical philosophy. So frequently and easily does he resort to metaphysical principles as the final rational arbiter in matters ethical and political that you can hardly avoid the thought that being and its principles mark the place where his heart lies. Third, as I hope will be clear by the end of this essay, what makes his Thomistic metaphysics distinctive—his analysis of the concept of action—both parallels and interacts with his philosophical claims about the "active life," as that term is understood in everyday experience. Indeed, the interplay of metaphysics and practical philosophy displayed in his writings reveals an upward movement from practical philosophy to speculative philosophy and chiefly to metaphysics.

In Simon's view, contemplation is the ultimate justification for practical activity, for it is the most perfect activity. That is why I have characterized his metaphysics as a "metaphysics of action." It may well be that he spent so much time writing on ethics and political philosophy just to show that the important problems in these areas could not be addressed profitably without resort to their metaphysical underpinnings.

I divide the following exposition into two main parts, under the respective headings "Practical Metaphysics" and "Speculative Metaphysics." The first focuses on important examples of the way Simon uses metaphysics in his political, ethical, and socio-cultural writings; the second focuses on his metaphysics of action itself, calling attention to his unification of transitive and immanent activity under an analogous conception of action. The latter shows not only why he found it so easy to appeal to metaphysics in his writings on practical philosophy but also why, despite his interest in ethics and political philosophy, he regarded metaphysics as the highest form of natural knowledge and contemplation as the highest form of intellectual activity.

## Practical Metaphysics

*Democratic Equality and the Metaphysical Unity of Nature*

The problem of ascertaining the meaning of the democratic principle "All men are created equal" is understandably regarded as far more clearly a social and political problem than a metaphysical one. Since the time when Alexis de Tocqueville observed that its proper understanding would continue to bedevil American democracy, democratic theorists have struggled to interpret it.

The democratic commitment to human equality challenges its defenders to explain, in the face of widespread individual diversity, the sense in which all human beings are equal. Immediately identifying this challenge as a variant of the problem of universals, Simon draws upon Thomas Aquinas's solution. Simon himself is too shrewd an observer of human events, and too keenly aware of the vast distance that separates theory and practice, to underestimate the social and political significance of the problem. Yet he also grasps the necessity of addressing this "practical" problem from the standpoint of a clear understanding of the sense in which it can be correct to say that all men are equal. In this regard, he makes brilliant and original use of Thomas Aquinas's metaphysical theory of universals to unfold a concept of human equality:

> To ask whether men are essentially equal, in spite of all the accidents which cause inequality among them, is the same as to ask whether there is one human nature, common to all men. Anyone recognizes here a particular case of the problem of the universals, to which logicians used to dedicate much labor and ingenuity. Without a reminder, no matter how brief, of the principles commanding this issue, such expressions as "human nature," "the unity of human nature," etc., would never have a definite sense.[3]

What are the "principles commanding this issue"? To begin with, "universal" refers to a nature or essence that pertains to all individuals of a certain type but to no one of them in particular. When, for example, we say, "Betty is a human being," we do not

---

[3] Yves R. Simon, *Philosophy of Democratic Government* (Chicago: The University of Chicago Press, 1951), p. 197. See also the rev. ed. (Notre Dame, Indiana: University of Notre Dame Press, 1993), p. 197.

mean that the subject, "Betty," and the predicate, "human being," are convertible, since that would mean that any being that is a human being is Betty. But that is clearly false, for George is a human being also. Despite their respective individualities, Betty and George are equally human.

Simon enlists Aquinas's solution to the problem of universals to account for the fact that human beings are both the same and different. You can analyze a given concept all you wish and you will never find among its intelligible features either "individuality" or "universality." An analysis of the concept *human being* or *man*, for example, yields "such intelligible features as rationality, progressivity, sociability, morality, sensibility, life, corruptibility, etc., but never 'individuality' or 'universality.' "[4] The reason is that these are not features but "existential modalities."[5] Because no essence or nature is in itself either universal or individual, it can exist as one or the other depending on its existential state. In the actually existing human being, it is in a state of individuality since it is *this* or *that* human being; in the mind, i.e., as known, it is in a state of universality since the condition of knowability or intelligibility is freedom from the opaqueness of matter, which the mind achieves by a process called "abstraction."[6]

To say that human nature is a reality that is one and the same in all human beings is not to commit oneself to Platonism: "It is in the mind alone that human nature, or any human nature, possesses a condition of positive unity." In the real world, what are universal features in the mind exist in Betty in a way that is identical with the individual reality of Betty while they exist in George in a way that is identical with the individual reality of George. Despite this unity of nature, Betty and George are not identical with each other. This is possible, Simon observes, because, as John of St. Thomas noted, "two things each of which is identical with the same third thing are not necessarily identical with each other if the third thing is virtually multiple: 'But the universal nature is virtually multiple because it is communicable to several things; therefore, identity with it does not entail the identity of the individuals among themselves.' "[7]

---

[4] Ibid., p. 199.
[5] Ibid.
[6] Ibid., p. 200.
[7] Ibid.

Imagination is the bane of the aspiring metaphysician. You will get nowhere if you rely on imagination to grasp something that in itself is neither individual nor universal. But it is conceivable. What makes a nature or essence are the intelligible constituents of a thing, not universality or individuality. Despite the many points of inequality among human beings, they all have the same human nature and hence are identical in an "essential and fundamental sense."[8]

This appeal to the metaphysical theory of essence and Thomas Aquinas's account of how essence can be both individual and universal enables Simon to set forth a philosophy of universality that renders intelligible the way in which there is a brotherhood of men, natural rights, and equal justice for all. He rightly observes that no one can consistently be a nominalist and desirous of justice for all; the latter, after all, implies the reality of the unity of human nature. What he has done, in this regard, is nothing more than elucidate the metaphysics of The Declaration of Independence.[9]

It was noted above that Simon entertained a keen appreciation for the difference between the theoretical and the practical realms. This evinces itself in his application of the equality dictated by the unity of human nature. There are, he says, two kinds of egalitarian rules that spring from that unity. The first kind pertains to cases in which "the rule of justice is unqualifiedly egalitarian"; the second, to cases that require only "an egalitarian tendency."[10] These are cases in which inequality is not necessarily unjust. With regard to the first kind, the moral law that protects human beings against murder allows of no exceptions or qualifications: it is always wrong to directly kill an innocent human being. This moral law "expresses a necessity everlastingly belonging to the constitution of a universal essence."[11] Because the law has its ground in the human essence, it pertains to any human being *insofar as he or she is human*:

> The prohibition of murder is not relative to any of the aspects in which men are unequal but to features pertaining to the unity of human nature. Murdering an ignorant person is just as much a

---
[8] Ibid.
[9] Ibid., p. 201.
[10] Ibid., p. 202.
[11] Ibid., p. 203.

murder as murdering a well-educated person; education does not matter and degrees of education make no difference. Murdering a colored man is just as much a murder as murdering a white man; the law prohibiting murder is in no way relative to such contingencies as color or other so-called "race" features. Murdering a cancerous patient is just as much a murder as murdering a healthy person; it is not on account of health that murder is prohibited but on account of universally human features, common to healthy and to diseased persons. Murdering an unborn child is just as much a murder as murdering an adult man; the phase of life in which murder takes place is altogether incidental.[12]

It is just because what makes a being a human being are "essential features" that Simon can insist that the wrongness of murder does not depend on "the aspects in which men are unequal." Only the metaphysical theory of essence can make such a claim rationally defensible. Properties that are sensible or measurable admit of more or less: one individual is more or less intelligent, healthy, industrious, wealthy, etc., than another, but no one can be more or less human than another. Therefore, what applies to an individual man or woman because of what he or she is *essentially*, i.e., his or her *humanness*, applies equally to every human being.

This absolute sense of equality is the ground of the second kind of egalitarian rules, those that demand an "egalitarian tendency."[13] The delineation between the two forms of egalitarian rules testifies to both the Thomistic tradition of moderate realism that Simon's thought embodies and his above-mentioned sensitivity to the imperatives of the practical realm. It is characteristic of the zealot to see the essence of justice, say, so clearly, in all its absoluteness and universality, as to be completely intolerant of the *fait accompli*. Refusing to accept anything less than the immediate and unqualified embodiment of equality in society, he has been known to demand the razing of all existing political, social, and economic institutions in the name of the ideal of justice. Simon, in contrast, understands that, while the demands of fundamental justice are absolute, it is practically impossible to realize them at any given time. The reason is that the effort to attain perfect jus-

---
[12] Ibid.
[13] Ibid., p. 202.

tice in one area of social life almost inevitably produces injustice in other areas.

He illustrates the point with the following pertinent examples. Given the intrinsic evil of directly killing an innocent person, what is to be said about the historical fact that the members of the lower classes die at an earlier age than do the members of the upper classes? The causes of their earlier demise are clearly socio-economic, for they must work in more noxious, hazardous occupations and they lack access to good medical care. Admittedly, because the egalitarian dynamism flows from the unity of human nature, all members of society, regardless of socio-economic status, ought to enjoy equal protection from early death. Nevertheless, Simon remarks that that dynamism can often legitimately be limited and delayed: "If, for instance, in order to hasten the day when the death rate will be as low in the poorest section of society as it is today in the wealthiest, we had to suffer an enormously increased weight of bureaucratic organization, at the cost of a considerable amount of liberty, there might be a duty to accept, as on the battlefield, loss of life for the sake of liberty and community."[14] Simon is not thereby justifying maintenance of the *status quo*, as his use of the term "egalitarian dynamism" makes clear.[15] What he advocates instead is a commitment to fulfill, in a reasonable way, the political, social, and economic imperatives of the unity of human nature.

In doing so, he has rationally justified the democratic ethos "All men are created equal" by zeroing in on its ground, the metaphysical theory of essence; at the same time, he has displayed the caution and reserve that must be observed in its worldly realizations.

### The Metaphysical Ground of Natural Law Theory

In arguing for the foundation of moral law in nature, Simon enters upon a metaphysical analysis of the concept of nature. He finds three implications of that concept especially pertinent; to wit, *plurality, teleology,* and the *relation between beginning and end.* As will become clear shortly, *teleology,* or finality, is the most crucial

---
[14] Ibid., p. 206
[15] Ibid.

of these, at least in the sense that Simon finds its explication and defense necessary to arrive at the rational ground for moral obligation.

The rise of mathematics in science since Descartes has been accompanied by the replacement of the universe seen as *nature* for the universe seen as *extension*. This fits well with the imperatives of mathematics but collides with those of the traditional conception of nature. In terms of formal definition, a mathematical object may be called "essence, whatness, quiddity, etc.," but "we may not attribute to it a dynamism, a tendency to forge its way into a world of becoming. It does not grow; it is what it is by definition, by construction, instantly; it is possessed of its proper condition of accomplishment immediately and does not have to acquire it by growth."[16] That explains the difference in outlook between the botanist and the mathematician. For the botanist, plants grow and their mature stage is not the same as their beginning stage. Our expectations of their behavior imply the affirmation that they are entities and as such possess essences, quiddities, or whatnesses. Thus, granting the limitations of our knowledge of plants and other living things, we could hardly expect to be taken seriously if we claimed that maple seeds grew into oak trees. The poverty of our knowledge does not blind us to the fact that natural entities are what they are by virtue of their essences or natures. Each entity possesses a nature which confers it with its own law of progression.[17]

This brings us to the first of the three implications regarding the concept of nature that Simon finds important: *plurality*. Parmenides is the father of monism because he maintained that the universe is absolutely one, a unity. Change and plurality were, accordingly, illusions. This unity is a material oneness devoid of all qualities and motion. The only diversity it boasts are consequences of its parts' necessarily being external to one another. But this is to make all diversity quantitative. Simon notes that this is the universe of mechanism and, as such, places Parmenides in the same camp as Descartes. For although arguing that mind is

---

[16] Yves R. Simon, *The Tradition of Natural Law*, ed. Vukan Kuic, rev. ed. with a new introduction by Russell Hittinger (New York: Fordham University Press, 1992), p. 44.

[17] Ibid.

immaterial and therefore not extensive or quantifiable, Descartes regarded corporeal reality as pure extension, which for him meant *space*. Corporeal reality cannot therefore be called "nature," for "it is not a thing endowed with a constitutive identity by reason of which it would tend toward a state of accomplishment to be reached through a progression."[18] Because there are no natures in the Cartesian universe, stability must be guaranteed by appeal to an extrinsic agent, God. It is the divine immutability that ensures the stability of this universe. If the laws of motion do not follow necessarily from the essential nature of things, how is the science of physics possible? The answer is that God has decreed such laws.[19]

Simon here follows Aristotle's lead in arguing that the denial of plurality in nature leads to absurdity. Aristotle observed that it is an obvious fact that there is a plurality of physical natures. He also observed, however, that an obvious fact cannot be demonstrated; so it is impossible to resort to demonstration to refute someone who denies an obvious fact. The most you can do is show that the denial leads to absurdity. In the face of Parmenides's denial of plurality, Aristotle accordingly shows that monism consistently leads to Heraclitean flux, which is as much as to say that things are nothing. If all things are one, if they all have the same definition, then you have no alternative other than to embrace the doctrine of Heraclitus. "To be good" and "to be bad" will mean the same thing, as will "man and horse." Since this is to say that things both are and are not at the same time and in the same way, it leads to the conclusion, not that things are "one," but that they are nothing.[20] Simon converts this metaphysical argument into moral capital:

> to say that all things are one "in the sense of having the same definition" would entail that killing a horse and killing a man have about the same meaning. We have not demonstrated the fact that there exists a plurality of natures, but we have shown that denying such plurality entails unacceptable consequences. "Unacceptable," here, should not be understood practically or pragmatically or emotionally, but rationally. The thing rationally unacceptable helps

---
[18] Ibid., p. 45.
[19] Ibid., p. 46.
[20] Ibid.

to perceive an obviousness which happened not to be perceived directly.[21]

From this conclusion, Simon proceeds to a consideration of the second implication of the concept of nature, *teleology*. If there is nature, then there is a drive toward a state of fulfillment. This developmental process is an obvious fact of daily life: acorns become oak trees, infants become adults, etc. But despite its obviousness, biologists inevitably label the appeal to teleology as "primitive" or "anti-scientific." A major reason for this discrepancy is to be found, according to Simon, in that mathematics acknowledges neither natures nor final causes. Mathematical entities admit of no development or movement. Any development of a mathematical object occurs within our minds, for the "development" is no more than our explication of properties already implicit in it. That is why every science in which mathematics is the form and standard of method is incompatible with final causes.[22]

The challenge to natural law theory posed by the mathematicized view of the universe is not hard to spot. It is, in fact, the mechanistic universe of Descartes along with his polarized view of mind and corporeal things. If things lack natures or essences and are instead pure extension, then any meaning or purpose attributed to them must be imposed extrinsically by mind. This, says Simon, is the philosophical basis of *values*.

> When mechanism is associated with idealism, as it is in Descartes and in most modern philosophers . . . [,] we have *values* instead of natural laws. Apparently, it is after having played a role of enormous importance in the work of the economists that the notion of value has reached the foreground, the most brightly lighted place in ethical philosophy. A realistic notion of value is not impossible. . . . But in the actual history of modern and contemporary philosophy, values have generally been conceived as placed in things, imposed upon them, forced into them by the human mind. Assuming that we still retain a sense for the distinction between the right and the wrong, what else can we do if things have no nature and no finality of their own?[23]

Despite efforts by thinkers such as Kant to establish moral values objectively, the difficulty in freeing them from subjectivism

---

[21] Ibid.
[22] Ibid., p. 48.
[23] Ibid., p. 50.

springs from their origin in the mind as opposed to things. Simon's reference to economics is accordingly incisive. He notes that in schools of economics it is taught that a thing's value is decided, not by "its relation to good human life, but entirely by the willingness of men to pay a certain price for the possession or use of that thing."[24]

The third implication of the concept of nature, *beginning and end*, can be characterized as one more way of viewing the significance of both *nature* and *teleology*. *Beginning and end* pertain to both not only because *teleology* presupposes the incipient and mature stages of a thing but also because "nature," and its cognate "natural," are often taken to mean the incipient, native, or primitive stage as opposed to the mature and developed one. The "state of nature" described in Rousseau and Hobbes refers to a primitive, prepolitical state of mankind. But would we wish to say that this state is "more natural" than the civilized one? Simon would answer, "No." To appreciate his answer, all you have to do, he writes, is to consider the difference in living conditions in a major city before and after its destruction by a nuclear bomb. In the aftermath of destruction, the survivors would revert to a Hobbesian savagery, for ". . . there would be no mayor, no police, no courts, no administration, and the plundering of the wrecked houses would begin immediately."[25] Which state is more natural for human beings, the civilized or the savage? The answer should be clear from a brief reflection on the accomplishment of civilization. Consider a major city, like Chicago, where millions of people from all over the world live in harmony despite the fact that they often have good reasons to despise each other. Can it be denied that the state of civilization harmonizes far more with human nature than the state of nature does? Simon's own words on this head bring together the concepts of *nature, teleology,* and *beginning and end*.

> No doubt, a state of accomplishment is the most natural condition of a nature, for it is that toward which nature has been striving from the beginning and by reason of its identity with itself. Yet, in human affairs principally, the condition that nature is striving toward is not brought about by nature alone but requires such

---
[24] Ibid.
[25] Ibid., p. 52.

causes as understanding, crafts, arts, sciences, techniques, and above all, good will and wisdom.[26]

This passage encapsulates Simon's success in bringing to bear, unobtrusively but unmistakably, the metaphysical principles of *nature*, *plurality*, and *teleology* to explain what is "natural" about the natural law. But to see precisely how the explanation works, a couple of points stand in need of clarification.

First, the phrase "by reason of its identity with itself" refers to his argument for plurality in nature. Each natural entity has its own essence or nature; it is what it is and is not anything else. It accordingly strives to become more fully what it is; in an important sense, the maple tree is in the maple seed, for the growth from seed to tree is but an unfolding of what is already there: maple seeds do not grow into oak trees. Still, the tree is not in the seed in the sense in which the concept "interior angles equal to the sum of two right angles" is in the concept "triangle." The tree is not implied by or in the seed; the passage from the one to the other, from *beginning to end*, if you like, is a genuine development. This was Simon's point in distinguishing earlier between essence or nature as used in mathematics and as used, say, in botany: there is no dynamism or movement in mathematical entities, no teleology therefore, where there is in physical nature. Yet, because that development is an unfolding of an entity's potency to more fully actualize its nature, it is correct to say that the maple tree is in the maple seed from the beginning. Natural entities thus display a dynamism toward a certain completion just because of what they are, because of the identity of each with itself.

Second, the completion of an entity's natural tendency toward the fulfillment of its nature is natural. That is why Simon can argue that life in civilized society is more natural for human beings than life in a state of nature, even though one may wish to call the latter "natural" because it is spontaneous and unhampered by socio-political institutions. If human flourishing requires life in political society, then such a life cannot be regarded as "unnatural" just because it is "not brought about by nature alone but requires such causes as understanding, crafts, arts, sciences, techniques, and above all, good will and wisdom." Simply put: civili-

---
[26] Ibid., p. 53.

zation is "natural" because it is the environment necessary for the fulfillment of a human being's natural striving. Simon does not deny the appropriateness of calling the primitive and spontaneous "natural"; but he does point out that the spontaneous is not *ipso facto* the paradigm for the natural nor is the civilized and conventional *ipso facto* less natural than the spontaneous. Just as eyeglasses, although artificial, are not unnatural but are instead natural insofar as they facilitate the natural end of the eye to see, so civilization, although the work of human intelligence and deliberate execution, is natural because it makes possible continuing humanization.

*Final Causality: The Metaphysical Ground of Moral Obligation*

Perhaps the most striking and original application of metaphysical principle to natural law theory by Yves R. Simon is his use of final causality to ground the concept of moral obligation.

"[W]hat is the meaning of obligation under the law?" Simon immediately rejects the not uncommon but slavish answer that we obey the law because failure to do so results in punishment. The difficulty with this reason is that it makes obligation a mere matter of coercion or threat of coercion.[27]

But if not this, what? Simon fingers the ontological grounding of the natural law as the source of the problem of coming up with a satisfactory account of obligation. The principle of this grounding he expresses thus: "before natural law exists in our minds as a proposition it exists in things."[28] Such judgments as that it is better to live than to die, that mothers should nurture their children rather than abandon them, that it is better not to lie than to lie, etc., derive their objective rationale from the nature of things: "because man is a being, because a mother is a mother, because human beings are rational agents."[29] Our rational formulations of the moral law do not belie the fact that the work of reason is "a reason measured by things."[30]

If things, not reason, ground natural law, does this mean that it is embodied in things before anyone thinks of it? But how do you

---

[27] Ibid., p. 136.
[28] Ibid., p. 137.
[29] Ibid.
[30] Ibid.

get *obligation* out of *things*? Does not the very attempt imply that "the rational is controlled by the non-rational; the work of the reason, the expression of understanding, is controlled by things; the rational is controlled by the ontological?"[31]

The way out of this difficulty, Simon argues, is by appeal to the principle of finality and the existence of the divine intelligence. As the deists of the eighteenth century insisted, not only is there an order to physical nature that is guaranteed by God, but by analogy there is a moral order equally guaranteed by "Nature's God." There are an intellect and will that give an ultimate guarantee to things both physical and human. But this is to say that the realms of physical nature and morality are ultimately rational. What, then, does this make of the earlier claim that the natural law is grounded in *things*?

Simon's answer depends on the traditional distinction between the order of discovery and the order of reality, a distinction he prefers to look at in the context of three stages:

> First, natural law exists in our minds as a proposition. For instance, "Cheating in the execution of a contract is wrong by nature." But saying "by nature" we imply that natural law, before it is apprehended by the intellect, exists embodied in things; that is the second stage in the order of discovery. In the third stage, we are led to the recognition of an "author of nature" ... who is the legislator of nature. And thus the law which, *in the order of discovery*, exists first as a proposition in our minds, secondly as a way of being, thirdly and ultimately exists in the divine mind, where it takes on the name of divine law.[32]

These three steps solve the problem of moral obligation, but at the same time they constitute what is perhaps the strongest reason for opposing the natural law. If it is true to say that "obligation in natural law does not hold unless the natural law exists in a state which is actually prior, but which is ultimate in the order of discovery—'this law is an aspect of God,'"[33] it is also true that there is controversy over the claim that God exists.

The difficulty can be limned by briefly restating Simon's argument thus far: (1) the natural law exists in our minds as a rational

---
[31] Ibid., p. 138.
[32] Ibid., p. 139.
[33] Ibid.

formula; (2) but this formulation is based on the nature of things; the natural law is embodied in things before it is formulated in our minds; (3) things themselves cannot be the source of moral obligation; but this obstacle is surmounted by the inference from (2) that the nature of things is imposed and willed by a divine intelligence. What, asks Simon, is the gain in positing "a normative, regulating intellect behind the things and calling this the third stage itself?"[34] Why stop there, instead of continuing on to a regulating intellect behind the regulating intellect, etc.? In short, the difficulty with positing the divine intelligence as the rational ground for natural law obligation is the same difficulty as dogs any attempt to demonstrate the existence of God: where is the nonarbitrary point of closure? As Aquinas pointed out, there is no logical impediment in the thought of infinite series. You can conceive of infinite series of generative causes, for example, "the generation of an egg by a hen, and the growth of a hen out of an egg." In such a series, there is no rational necessity to arrive at an end; but that means there is no first cause (by definition of "infinite series") and thus no cause whatsoever.[35]

What Simon chooses not to address directly and explicitly with regard to this objection is that a logically unimpaired conception of an infinite causal series assumes that all the causal agents are of the same kind, that they possess the same nature and level of being. Because all the agents are essentially the same, no agent can do anything that any of the others cannot do and hence there is no rationale for closing the series with a first cause or, in the case under discussion, first intelligence. He does, however, address the matter indirectly with a footnote example, a classic one at that, to illustrate how an infinite series drives the first cause out of existence: "Imagine a painting being painted. There is a pack of hair, a ring of copper, a handle, and we call that a brush; behind the brush there is a painter. Now suppose the handle of the brush is a little longer. Do we still need a painter? Suppose the handle of the brush is indefinitely long. Well, we have driven the painter into inexistence, and we realize that nothing is being painted."[36] Simon's point is that the validity of the argument from the fact of

---
[34] Ibid., p. 140.
[35] Ibid., pp. 140–141.
[36] Ibid., p. 141.

obligation to the existence of God has the same logical structure as the other arguments that proceed from a given fact of experience—motion, efficient causality, contingency and necessity, degrees of being, and the order of the universe. Not only do they all start with experience but they arrive at the necessary existence of "a first cause which is pure act or being, itself subsistent in its own right."[37]

The intelligence accordingly implied by the fact of moral obligation escapes the charge of arbitrariness because it is not simply one more addition to the length of the handle to the painter's brush. It is rather a being of a higher nature and level of being; it is pure being, pure act, self-subsistent being; and, as such, it can do what no other being or agent possesses the ontological wherewithal to do: stand as the ultimate intelligence and will, the source of all nature and order.[38]

Here Simon introduces a concept that exerts a profound and pervasive influence on his philosophy: the identification of "to be" and "to think" (or "to know"). This identification explains why the divine intelligence is truly the First Intelligence; why once it is arrived at, there is no need to seek an intelligence beyond it. With that achievement, the rational ground of natural law obligation is vindicated:

> In our scheme of natural law existing—in the order of discovery—first in our minds, secondly in things, and thirdly as an aspect of God, the distance between the second and third stages is of minor relevance, even if not completely irrelevant. What is decisive is whether or not we have to reach a stage where "to be" and "to think" are one; here the problem disappears and the obligation is explained. What is relevant is to understand what condition should be satisfied that the third stage will be better than any intermediary placed between it and the second stage, that it should be final; that condition is the identity of "to know" and "to be."[39]

Simon knows that he hereby presupposes a good bit of metaphysics and natural theology; but his professed aim is merely to "out-

---
[37] Ibid.
[38] Ibid.
[39] Ibid., p. 142.

line" the argumentation, which he regards as "conclusive and accordingly . . . [capable] of strict exposition."[40]

Central to this "outline" is the identification in the Supreme Being of "to be" and "to know." You can make a nominal distinction between them, but that is all. Valid distinctions can be drawn between God's understanding and God's will, between his understanding and his love. Granted, they are not real distinctions but only distinctions of reason as, for example, is that between twice six eggs and one dozen eggs and one dozen eggs and the square root of 144 eggs. Although all three refer to the same thing, we are able to distinguish each from the others by regarding it in terms of a diverse aspect. These different intellectual perspectives determine why the distinctions are merely rational and not real.[41] In contrast, "between the 'to be' of God and the 'to think' of God there is no distinction whatsoever; it is like two names designating exactly the same thing. And it is this identity of being and knowing that stops the regression to infinity in our search for the ground of obligation under the natural law."[42]

Thus, in answer to critics who find the idea of a being "outside" nature as the regulator to be arbitrary ("Why stop there? Why not a regulator of the regulator, etc.?") and therefore as engendering an infinite regress which drives the ground of obligation into nonexistence, Simon makes the following point. A being in whom "to be" and "to think" are identical is of its very nature the source of all regulation. Positing it as the ultimate intelligence and will is hardly arbitrary. Such a being must be outside nature, for, by definition, it cannot be part of nature. The things of nature lack the identity of "to be" and "to think"; otherwise they would be ultimate and unlimited, which they clearly are not. On the contrary, they are contingent, changeable, and multiple.

To sum up, Simon has used the metaphysical principle of finality, and that principle's presupposition of the identity of 'to be' and 'to think' in God, to rationally justify moral obligation: "The acts of order in the universe and the facts of obligation under natural law, i.e., that our reason bows before things, both require

---
[40] Ibid., p. 140.
[41] Ibid., pp. 143–144.
[42] Ibid., p. 144.

rationally a transcendent First Being in whom 'to be' and 'to act' and 'to think' are one and the same."[43]

*Final Causality and Culture: The Antagonism Between Humanism and Science*

Simon does not limit his discussions of final causality to moral obligation. He has written a trenchant piece on the consequences that the exclusion of final causality from the social sciences has had for Christian humanism.

He begins with the observation that the influence of Saint-Simon on the social sciences is still with us. Saint-Simon believed that the imposition of scientific method on society would usher in the "Golden Age," which the poets assumed had been lost in our distant past.[44] His school entertained a rosy picture of the influence that the science of nature had upon society. Whereas governments had previously seen their task as the exploitation of human beings, the "scientific enlightenment" focused attention on the industrial transformation of physical nature. This produces a loss of interest in human exploitation. The government of persons would thus give way to the administration of things.[45]

The application of science to society itself would accordingly achieve the following salutary results: it would replace authority with impersonal exactness. Ignorance causes social disunity over ways and means. Were it not for the practice of empowering some men to make decisions that bind everyone, society would be paralyzed by this disunity. Because the social sciences show what means lead to what ends, authority becomes unnecessary. Science alone dominates since the interpreters of nature will supplant lawmakers. The scientific reorganization of society will also bring peace. The cause of war is the desire of some human beings to dominate others. But by facilitating the development of industry, science makes human association more desirable than domination.[46]

Simon calls attention to three arbitrary assumptions of this phi-

---

[43] Ibid., p. 145.
[44] Yves R. Simon, *Practical Knowledge,* ed. Robert J. Mulvaney (New York: Fordham University Press, 1991), p. 138.
[45] Ibid.
[46] Ibid.

losophy. First, it excludes contingency, because science lacks the methodological wherewithal to accommodate it; contingency must thus be regarded as irrelevant to the understanding of social affairs. Second, it assumes that the deterministic patterns that apply in the physical sciences can be applied to the social sciences; this is incompatible with free will. Third, this philosophy is driven by the unbridled optimism of the eighteenth century. The promulgation of demonstrated scientific truth, by teaching and persuasive preaching, will be accepted by the public and the need for coercion will evaporate.[47]

This rosy vision of the way science was to usher in a new age of human progress was shattered by the events of the twentieth century. It is no longer widely believed that people trained in the sciences are the best leaders. Instead, new emphasis has been placed on the importance of a humanistic education. Simon attempts to clarify the meaning of "humanism" by calling attention to two importantly different uses of it: humanism as an *attitude* and humanism as a *culture*.

> As an attitude it is characterized by respect for all men and confidence in the ability of mankind to accomplish good things in *this* world. It is not necessarily optimistic, but it is necessarily confident. And if a friend of man expects great things of his fellow men, but only in the other world, he cannot be described as a humanist.[48]

> With regard to humanism as a culture, a few historical references make up an adequate substitute for a definition. We know very well what we mean when we set in opposition the Scholastics and the Humanists of the time of Erasmus or when we say that the French writers of the seventeenth century had a strong background of humanistic education. Again, if I say that a certain professor is a good humanist but by no means a philosopher, everyone will understand me perfectly.[49]

It is important to keep these two different uses of "humanism" in mind since Simon switches back and forth between them as he deems appropriate. He probably has both in mind when he writes that, far from believing that science and technique lead to wisdom

---

[47] Ibid., pp. 138–139.
[48] Ibid., p. 139.
[49] Ibid.

and order in the world, we are inclined instead to fear that a technical culture is incompatible with "attitudes that foster the understanding of man, cooperation, and brotherhood."[50]

As an example, Simon cites the drive of scientific method to understand things by analysis of data. This means reducing things from wholes to parts. A mind theoretically trained in this manner has difficulty understanding persons and things as wholes. This limitation applies as much to philosophy as to the sciences.[51] It is also the case, that despite the importance of the analytical approach, thinkers so trained do not acquit themselves well when thrust into the world of action as, say, citizens or statesmen. Simon expresses reservations even when it comes to programs of humanistic studies that lay great emphasis on philosophy and theology. For example, these disciplines might garner so much of the curriculum as to rule out the possibility of a thorough set of humanistic studies: "the program might not be conducive to the understanding of men under the conditions of totality which are decisively significant in all social relations. A philosopher must grant that, when there is need for an holistic approach to human realities, philosophy has no further claims on the student's time."[52]

Alongside our age's humanistic predilections, Simon notes the presence of an antithetical psychological state. Scientific knowledge enshrines man's power over nature. The efficiency and regularity of technique contrast with the disorder that comes from man. Not only progress but order becomes an ideal in society. Only human behavior continues to be disorderly. This discontinuity breeds a resentment among the members of society. Why, we ask, cannot people who are special to us behave with the exemplary order and dependability of machines? It is in the new patterns of regularity that Simon sees important ways in which contemporary totalitarianism differs from past tyrannies: "We feel that there is in mankind something that ought to be crushed. A highly developed technical environment has given birth to a particularly frightful kind of misanthropy."[53]

---

[50] Ibid., pp. 139–140.
[51] Ibid., p. 140.
[52] Ibid., p. 141.
[53] Ibid., p. 142.

The Renaissance gave birth to both an important humanistic culture and the modern interpretation of nature. The latter's rejection of final causality caused humanism its most serious problems. On the one side stands the scientific interpretation of the world which could not be further removed from the universe of natures. The new world cannot be called a nature, for it is simply extension or space. Insofar as man has "tendencies, desires, purposes, and meaningful activities," he finds himself isolated in this new world.[54]

> This [new] science is a mathematical reading of the physical world. As far as its form is concerned, it is mathematical, and consequently foreign to the study of final causes. . . . The exclusion of finalistic notions results from the nature of mathematical abstraction. Objects treated mathematically have lost the relation to existence that desirability implies. As Aristotle says, there is no goodness in mathematical entities. Mathematical sciences are good, but mathematical objects are not. You may fall in love with mathematics—many people do—but you cannot fall in love with the square root of minus one.[55]

The rapidly growing success of the mathematical interpretation of nature dichotomized the world of culture. On the one hand, there is the physical world, devoid of finality and intelligent order; on the other, there is the human world, bursting with tendencies and goals, such as the erasure of ignorance and suffering, the attainments of longer life and world peace. The principle of finality remained secure as long as the culture retained a clear vision of the natural law and the metaphysical conception of human dignity. But the allurements of a social science that addressed mankind as successfully as physics addressed nature led to the former's adoption of scientific method and, with it, the disavowal of "unscientific prejudices," chief of which was explanation by final causes. The results have been disastrous:

> In contemporary atheism, the non-finalistic pattern is applied, regardless of the cost, to the totality of human affairs. Not only physical nature, but also mankind and its history have become a tale told by an idiot, signifying nothing. An all-embracing picture of absurdity expresses the last word of a mechanistic philosophy

---
[54] Ibid.
[55] Ibid., p. 143.

which has grown into a violent negation of all that humanism values. In some respects existentialism is an effort to achieve decency in a world whose meaninglessness extends to human actions.[56]

It would be a serious misconstrual of Simon's thought to suppose that the above examples of "applied metaphysics" are mere opportunistic metaphysical interventions. They stand, instead, as testimonies to what it means to say that metaphysics is a universal science. "Being" refers to *that which is*, either actually or possibly. Because all things are reducible to being, it follows that everything is governed by the principles of being: act and potency, essence and existence, efficient and final causality, etc. Ethical and political theories accordingly presuppose metaphysical theories. Final causality, so important, as we have seen already in Simon's thought, exerts a commanding influence in his ultimate metaphysical interpretation of human events and aspirations. That is doubtless why his discourses on modern culture's abandonment of the Aristotelian view of the universe as *nature* in favor of the Cartesian view of it as *space* attains the status of an *idée fixe* in his writings.[57] As there is no room for final causality in the Cartesian universe, so there is no meaning or direction in it; in short, there is no intelligibility. But, for Simon, the intelligibility of things and events in the material universe is real because the term of completion for which they strive is real, namely, the pure actuality of God. He thus claims contemplation to be the highest and noblest of all activities and sets out to prove it in what must surely be one of the most brilliant, incisive, and exhaustive investigations of the notion of action in modern literature.

## Speculative Metaphysics

Simon's metaphysics of action emerges from his investigation of the metaphysical foundations of knowledge. Standing squarely in the philosophical tradition of moderate realism as espoused by Aristotle and Thomas Aquinas, Simon insists that the starting point of any constructive theory of knowledge must be the prin-

---

[56] Ibid., p. 144.
[57] For example, *Practical Knowledge*, pp. 142ff., *Tradition of Natural Law*, chap. 3, and esp. all the chapters of *The Great Dialogue of Nature and Space*.

ciple that knowledge is objective.[58] It is this principle, specifically, that inspires his investigation of the meaning of action. He notes that passivity follows from potentiality. Pure passivity equals pure potentiality. But potency negates knowing. The law of potentiality dominates created beings, for "they are only what they can be."[59] That is why knowing shines forth as so remarkable an activity. Beings possessing the capacity to know can literally become what they cannot be existentially. What can account for this exception to the rest of nature? "It is knowledge as superexistence that triumphs over the potentiality of being and provides certain creatures with an opening upon the infinite not available to the rest of nature."[60] The antinomy comes down to this: passivity is the principle of subjectivity and limitation. A form received by a purely passive being is inevitably constrained by the potentialities of that being. The result is a subjective embodiment of that form because, although the receiver becomes other than it was, that change is confined to its capacity to receive it. Simon's point can be illustrated thus: a family crest etched in a gold finger-ring is impressed on a wax tablet. The impression changes the tablet to the extent that it is now something that it was not—the bearer of a crest. The wax tablet cannot, however, be the crest as it exists in a gold ring. On the contrary, it is the crest to the extent that the potencies of the wax allow the wax tablet to be it. That is what Simon means by saying that passivity is the root of subjectivity and limitation. The wax tablet's potential for being other than what it is is confined to its own limited capacities for being.

But cognition is entirely different. The knower becomes the other "as one could not be";[61] it becomes the other *as other*. In short, knowledge is objective. Now, if subjectivity and limitation follow from passivity, which is to say, from potency, their opposites, objectivity and openness on the infinite, must follow from activity.

> The objectivity of knowledge thus clearly presupposes activity on the part of the knower. A subject can be united objectively—not

---

[58] Yves R. Simon, *An Introduction to Metaphysics of Knowledge*, trans. Vukan Kuic and Richard J. Thompson (New York: Fordham University Press, 1990), pp. 1–10.
[59] Ibid., p. 39.
[60] Ibid.
[61] Ibid., p. 40.

subjectively—to a form only if he actively participates in that union. This absolute exclusion of potentiality, which in God is the root of his omniscience, is imitated in the created knower by what is his most characteristic and vital activity. A knowledge resulting from pure passivity would be an absolute contradiction, a fictitious potentiality that denies itself. Cognition is action as well as existence.[62]

Simon thereby concludes that in order to understand the act of cognition, a metaphysical investigation of action is necessary: "But precisely because knowledge appears not only as a unique sort of existence but also as a particular activity totally without parallel in the physical world, our next step must be a thorough review of the general theory of activity."[63] And this is necessarily a metaphysical investigation, because the immanent activity of knowing carries us into a domain of law different from that of the material world—"the laws of being as being."[64] Toward this end, Simon proceeds by way of a four-level definition of "action."

The first and most conspicuous manifestation of action is the phenomenon of change. There are three forms of change: (1) as taught by revelation, an event in which there is "total change that has no subject that affects the term of the change in the whole of its being"—to wit, Eucharistic transubstantiation;[65] (2) substantial change; and (3) accidental change.[66] Examples 2 and 3 show that whatever changes requires for its change a reality distinct from itself that is the source of the change.[67] Clearly, if the thing changing does not change into a state that it possesses by its very nature—that is, in other words, a state identical to itself—then the sufficient reason for the change must be some agent other than itself. Thus change requires the actual exercise of efficient causality. As the change unfolds, we see that the proper subject of the action is, not the agent, but the patient. The change pertains to the patient in a substantial sense and to the agent only in a modal sense.[68]

---

[62] Ibid.
[63] Ibid., pp. 40–42.
[64] Ibid., p. 46.
[65] Ibid., pp. 42–43.
[66] Ibid., p. 43.
[67] Ibid.
[68] Ibid., pp. 43–45.

Yves R. Simon, age 9. Cherbourg, summer 1912. All photographs are courtesy of the Yves R. Simon Institute.

School of Medicine, University of Paris, 1926. Simon is directly above and behind the man with glasses and folded arms in the lowest standing row.

Simon in Paris, 1920s.

Simon in Cherbourg, 1930.

Simon at the University of Notre Dame, 1940.

Simon hunting on his mountain farm in New Mexico, 1955.

Simon in his study, South Bend, Indiana, 1950.

Simon in 1958.

Simon in 1959.

Change, however, is only one kind of action. Although all our knowledge begins with sensible experience and our knowledge of being thus begins with sensible being, the intellect grasps the truth that being is not by its nature confined to the sensible world, as it proceeds from a knowledge of sensible things to the knowledge of being as being. The latter is the domain of the laws of being; these laws do not advert to whether or not the being possesses sensible qualities or undergoes change. Here is universal, transcendent knowledge, for the laws governing being as being apply to everything that is being, which is to say, all things. Here we arrive at the knowledge of the source of actuality, not just of sensible, changing things but of all things that are not absolutely identical with themselves: "As long as the being under consideration is not identical with its act, a source distinct from it is required, regardless of whether we are dealing with the imperfect actuality of change or with the actuality of the perfection of being."[69] Because no finite being can claim its existence to be identical with itself, it is clear that efficient causality operates on all beings, save God, regardless of whether the subject is in act by change or by some other way. Since action consists in the actual exercise of efficient causality, it need not be identified with change. Indeed, the act of creation most perfectly expresses the idea of efficient action:

> There is not a trace of change in the purely conserving action by which God keeps the creature in existence, the just soul in the state of grace, and generally maintains realities united to one another that are not one by identity. What happens at the beginning of things, at the very instant when the nature that does not possess existence by itself arises out of nothingness? Well, here not only is action unaccompanied by any change, but it is also unaccompanied by any kind of reception, there being nothing to receive it. . . . No longer involving either change or reception, action here becomes pure production, that is, efficiency elevated to unconditional freedom.[70]

This first definition of action is not comprehensive, for Simon notes that it does not extend to immanent action. That form of action, for example, knowing, produces nothing and leads to no

---
[69] Ibid., p. 46.
[70] Ibid., pp. 46–47.

term distinct from itself. Because actions such as seeing and contemplating produce nothing, immanent action cannot be an exercise of efficient causality.[71] Our tendency to set the contemplative and active ways of life in opposition shows a spontaneous hesitation to call immanent activities "action." Only by analogy, therefore, will it be possible to embrace both transitive and immanent action under a "general, transcendental definition of action."[72]

The second (transcendental) definition of action requires the division of being into act and potency and this invokes the use of analogy. What this definition will highlight is that whether activity is transitive or immanent, it always ends as a terminal act. The metaphysician proceeds both analytically and synthetically. He proceeds analytically by going from the multiplicity given by perception to the abstract and simple notion of being. He proceeds synthetically by going from the notion of being to an understanding of the multiplicity and complexity of the sensible world.[73] The second to the last step in the analytic regression (the first step is the affirmation of the principle of non-contradiction, "Being is not nonbeing") and the first step in the synthetic progress is the division of being into act and potency. By means of the analytic reduction, the idea of act is arrived at by an analysis of the fact of action. When we regard the realities proper to the transcendental order of being in act, we immediately think of transitive activity not only because we are accustomed to it but also because it expresses itself with a special force. Thus, we get a clearer understanding of the transcendental notion of being in act by "the workman's hammering, the scientist's conclusion, the lover's delight in the possession of the beloved object."[74] Nevertheless, whether the action is immanent or terminal, it always ends in a terminal act.[75]

But if transitive and immanent activity are united in the idea of terminal act, they are not the only things that have a terminal act. For existence, too, has a terminal act. A thing can do nothing if it does not exist, but even when existing, it perfects itself, actual-

---

[71] Ibid., p. 49.
[72] Ibid., p. 50.
[73] Ibid.
[74] Ibid., p. 51.
[75] Ibid., pp. 51–52.

izes the potency of its nature by action. What is the significance of existence as a terminal act and action as a terminal act?

The answer begins with a consideration of the notion of being. The metaphysician's formal object of investigation is being as being. Nothing in that idea either affirms or denies imperfection. That is how the idea leads to God. Implying no limitation, being as such leads to perfect being, God, for a being free of all limitation and imperfections exists by pure identity with itself, with being. Such a being is infinite being. From the premise that being of itself implies no imperfection or limitation, then how are we to account for limited being? If being implies neither imperfection nor limitation, then clearly it cannot limit itself. Nor can it be limited by something outside itself, for outside being there is nothing and nothing cannot limit anything. What accounts for limited being, then, must be potency. In other words, what limits a finite being is the duality in it of potency as well as act. Finite beings are an admixture of being and nonbeing, of being in act and being in potency. There is in them a real distinction between essence and existence; their essence does not imply existence. A finite being is not being; rather it *has* being.[76]

The above shows why Simon is at such pains to delineate the respective senses in which action and existence are terminal acts: "Any subject lacking being by identity has reality only by virtue of its participation in existence; but in the created essences the gift of existence always leaves a residue of potentiality."[77] Truly, an existent being is more valuable than a merely possible being; a hundred actual dollars is more valuable than a merely possible one hundred dollars, but existence adds nothing to the essence of the thing it brings into existence.[78] Existence and activity can accordingly be distinguished as terminal acts in the following way. Existence actualizes specific possibilities, essences, to be: "Existence is not *this* or *that*, a particular kind of thing; it is what causes things to be set outside of nothingness."[79] Simon does not mean that the act of existing is univocal; on the contrary, it is analogical, for it actualizes an essence's possibility to be according to the specific

---

[76] Ibid., pp. 53–55.
[77] Ibid., p. 55.
[78] Ibid., pp. 55–56.
[79] Ibid., p. 57.

structure of that essence. His point is to bear in mind that the differences among things come not from existence but from their respective essences.[80]

We learn what a thing is and therefore what its possibilities are by observing its operations. We thereby see that every finite being, owing to the duality within it of act and potency, has two levels of potency. The first is its potency to be; the second is the potency inherent in its specific type of essence to become more fully what it already is by nature. The first potency is actualized in existence; the second, in activity. All of which leads Simon to a more precise definition of action "*as the terminal act that fulfills the active nature in accordance with its specific constitution.*"[81]

Simon sees this second definition as merely foundational to the construction of a complete notion of action; by itself, it does not clarify that notion. A genuinely comprehensive definition of action requires a second look at the earlier analysis of thought as spontaneously expressing itself in experience. For the one thing that characterizes all action, whether transitive or immanent, is *emanation*. Here, then, is his third (transcendental) definition of "action": "born in the womb of the acting nature, action may be said to be an *emanating terminal act,* in an 'AB' (from) relation to the potency which it fulfills."[82] This definition decisively distinguishes the terminal act of action from the terminal act of existence. The latter clearly does not emanate from a being's nature for the obvious reason that until existence actualizes that nature, there is nothing from which to emanate. So whereas action is a terminal act that stands in an "AB" relation to the potencies of the acting nature, existence is "the terminal act that fulfills any nature through a special 'IN' (in) relation."[83]

This illumination of action does not, however, show whether emanation expresses itself identically in transitive and immanent action. A closer scrutiny of the notion of emanation is therefore dictated. The result of this scrutiny will be Simon's fourth (transcendental) definition of action.

He begins by observing importantly different kinds of emana-

---

[80] Ibid.
[81] Ibid., p. 58.
[82] Ibid., pp. 60–61.
[83] Ibid., p. 61.

tions. First, there are some purely logical emanations which defy any distinction among the emanating effect, the source of the emanation, and the emanation itself. Such emanations apply only to the activity of God; in all other beings, emanation, rather than identical with the being, is accidental to it and hence is really distinct from the nature whence spring the action and the acting being's existence. Second, there are real emanations that have no ontological dependence, to wit, those of the divine procession. As we learn from revelation, the person of the Son proceeds really from the person of the Father and the person of the Holy Spirit really proceeds from the Father and the Son, without any relation of dependence or subordination among the three divine persons.

Having noted the above exceptions, Simon addresses the third kind of emanation, which is to say, all other kinds of activity, and calls attention to their common denominator: every activity displays a relation of efficient causality. A grasp of the significance of this fact entails an unfolding of the meaning of "the efficient cause of action itself."[84]

Analysis reveals that two realities, effect and action, can emanate from the terminal act of an efficient cause. The effect flows from its cause by means of a transitive action; the latter is the intermediary through which the effect travels from its source in the agent to its term. But because the action produced by a finite being is not identical with that being's nature, it requires the intervention of a being whose action belongs to it by pure identity. This dependency on an external being for acting has the same rationale as the dependency of a contingent being on a necessary being for its existence.[85]

In contrast to transitive action, immanent action in itself implies no term distinct from itself. For one thing, it has only one emanating reality: namely, action; and for another, the efficient cause of this reality can only be the acting subject. What Simon means by the second of these considerations is simply that immanent actions, such as knowing, desiring, and choosing, are, as we shall see below, so intimate to the agent acting as to make logically impossible the performance of a particular immanent action by any other agent. For such actions are self-identical with the agent,

---
[84] Ibid., p. 62.
[85] Ibid., pp. 62–63.

unlike transitive actions, which are not: others besides me can write an essay on Thomas Jefferson, file an accident report if I am unable to do so, etc., but nobody can say for me "I know," "I love her," "I choose to resist the temptation," etc. For then the "I" would have an entirely different meaning. Thus, Simon writes: "Immanent action proceeds really from its subject, on which it depends and to which it is bound by what we have called an 'AB' relation."[86] Yet, an examination of the dependence, direct emanation, and "AB" relation shows that they are intimately bound up with efficient causality. But what sets this manifestation of efficient causality apart from its manifestation in transitive action is that the efficient act and immanent act it produces are identical. What thinking and choosing "produce" cannot be distinguished from those acts themselves.[87]

All of which leads Simon to formulate the fourth and final definition of action: "*a terminal act emanating by way of an efficiency with which it is identified without necessarily being absorbed in it.*"[88] He finds this definition in harmony with common-sense assessments. We apply the term "active" to those whose lives are devoted to producing effects because, from a formal standpoint, transitive activity alone counts as efficiency. Nevertheless, we also apply the term "acts" to the operations of thought and will because they too are produced by efficient causality. Again, we are more apt to say that decision-making is an act than that acquiring knowledge or desiring things is. The reason is that, in choosing, the agent is the efficient cause of his or her determination in two ways rather than one; the first by nature, the second by freedom. And even in matters of cognition, we take the difference between active and passive behavior as a way of establishing degrees of involvement. After all, the soul asserts itself as the efficient cause of its cognitive activity to the degree that it activates that activity and to the extent that the will moves the intellect.[89]

Having established the ways in which transitive and immanent activity can be embraced by the single term "action," Simon finds their union nonetheless troubling. In the end, he concludes that,

---

[86] Ibid., p. 63.
[87] Ibid.
[88] Ibid.
[89] Ibid., pp. 63–64.

although efficient causality pertains to both kinds of action, they still display differences so significant that their unity can only be described as "imperfect and analogical." No generic unity is possible between an act ordered to the production of something other than itself and an act that is identical with its product. The two kinds of action cannot therefore be subsumed under a univocal concept: "Transitive action is efficiency. But even though it includes efficiency, immanent action is not efficiency; it belongs to the category of quality."[90]

The singular nature of immanent activity leads Simon to infer that immanent activity is more than a quality; it is a special kind of disposition. It qualifies as a quality because it occurs entirely within the acting subject. The way a person thinks and chooses determines from within whether he or she is good or bad, sad or happy, while thinking, choosing, and desiring imply the possession within the person of an intentional being; but this is to say that he or she thereby enjoys an existence, on the intentional level, that is qualified by the object. Simon says it is the specific kind of quality known as a disposition because it possesses the characteristics of immateriality and freedom from potentiality. Knowing, for example, is an immaterial operation, so that immanent activity cannot be identified with any quality that depends on materiality. And because it is a terminal act, immanent activity also stands apart from any quality that implies potentiality.[91]

By "disposition," Simon means *"the supreme ordering of the dynamic parts of a vital faculty in relation to its end actually possessed."*[92] Consider, for example, the scientist whose attention is directed to the game of bridge he is playing. He is capable of thinking of any number of subjects, including the scientific theorizing to which his intellect is disposed. As a scientist, he possesses the habitus for scientific thought; at the moment, it is not utilized, but it is nevertheless an actual state, a real disposition that will exert its influence as soon as he decides to focus his attention on a scientific object.[93]

From the above analysis, Simon concludes that immanent ac-

---

[90] Ibid., p. 64.
[91] Ibid., pp. 66–67.
[92] Ibid., p. 70.
[93] Ibid.

tivity is "a wondrous union of two antinomic characteristics."[94] The first is that knowing is a particular kind of qualitative perfection, a disposition. "Disposition" is the key word here. The only change that occurs in the knowing faculty when it knows is that its potentialities are arranged in an order that enables it to know. Granted, alongside this arrangement there is the intentional object, but, by nature of being a purely formal sign, it neither changes nor is changed by the noetic faculty. Nevertheless, it is impossible to find a contact "more radical and penetrating than the knowing mind with its object." Here Simon doubtless has in mind that knowing consists in the knower's actually becoming the known, achieving perfect identity with it, while still remaining himself. Hence he calls knowing "a masterpiece of interiority."[95]

The importance of the notion of immanent activity in Simon's thought emerges quite clearly from his discussion of "motionless activity." The notion clarifies our understanding of the relation between activity and change. While the concept of efficiency does not necessarily imply the concept of mobility, the concept of transitive action does imply the concept of change. The subject of transitive action is the recipient of the latter's effect, not its producer. It is thus an imperfect being dependent for its completion on the termination of the action being exercised on it. But when that happens, the action recedes into the past. Transitive activity is exercised only on what is incomplete: one does not begin construction on an already existent house. "Thus transitive action appears necessarily related to imperfect being to the extent that it is imperfect—which is the very definition of change."[96]

In contrast, immanent activity escapes the clutches of mobility. Having arrived at a truth, the intellect does not abandon its knowledge of it, as a workman must necessarily abandon his work once it has been completed. Similarly, the heart does not cease loving the beloved once it has possessed it. Thus contemplation and joy transcend time because they transcend change. The fact that human intelligence must resort to discursive thinking and the fulfillment of human desire requires effort—both forms of

---

[94] Ibid.
[95] Ibid., pp. 70–71.
[96] Ibid., p. 71.

transitive activity—has nothing to do with immanent activity but is instead a consequence of the imperfection of our spiritual faculties. We must resort to discursive thinking or reasoning because we are diminished intellectual substances; we desire the good only because we do not possess it fully. But these accompanying transitive requirements bear only an accidental relation to knowing and loving: "Stripped of these accidental perfections, knowing is the act of a perfect subject and so is loving."[97]

Simon is not content to end his investigation of action with the notion of immanent activity, for he sees that it is a form of actuality and thus that the latter is appropriately regarded as *life* or *vitality*. Here what he offers us is a reflection on Thomas Aquinas's discussion of the concept of a perfect life according to the principle *"vivere viventibus est esse,"* to live in a living thing is to be. Simon's distinction between "life" and "vitality" is stipulative, in the sense that, although the two terms are synonyms, he clearly wishes to use "vitality" to indicate a higher form of "life."

A thing is alive if it has the capacity to impose change upon itself. This capacity forms a hierarchy, as the spectrum of living things shows that animals have a greater capacity to change themselves than plants do, human beings a greater capacity than animals. But, given that immanent activity is not the same as change, for change is a transitive activity, Simon wishes to speak of the behavior of beings capable of immanent activity as a different kind of actuality. Hence he prefers to use the term "vitality" rather than "life" with regard to beings capable of immanent activity. To return to the spectrum of living things: angels have a greater capacity for self-actualization than humans do, but God alone enjoys absolutely perfect and infinite actualization; in him alone are being and intellect identical. Plants and animals are self-moving, self-actualizing, but not in a proper sense, for their actions are completely predetermined and do not originate from a center of immanent activity. Human beings move themselves in the proper sense, in that their activity flows from an interiority, an immanent activity of knowledge, love, and freedom. The reason that neither human beings nor angels can be said to be perfectly self-moving is that they are not completely the cause of their determinations. Human beings act out of knowledge and choice; but to know

---
[97] Ibid., p. 72.

they must have a predetermination to know, i.e., the natural desire of their intellect; moreover, they are dependent for their knowledge on external, material things: the material object of the human intellect is the essence of sensible being. To choose we must already be by nature inclined to desire the good in itself; otherwise there would be no reason for us to choose one way rather than another and thus no reason to choose at all. Angels are not dependent on external things for their knowledge, but they are noetically dependent nonetheless, for their knowledge is infused in them by God.[98]

All of which shows that creaturely action needs divine premotion. But God alone is self-sufficient since He is completely self-actualizing: His being, nature, and intellect are identical with each other. Of the spectrum of life, actuality, and vitality, Simon accordingly writes:

> Thus the idea of life, originally derived from the observation of material nature, appears to leave behind the whole created world to acquire a unique meaning in God. Actually, however, what we learn when we thus reach the summit of the hierarchy of life is that our idea of life, already turned metaphysical and analogical, must undergo a further purification based on an even more profound analogy. The first of living beings offers us no grip on the notion of causality that turns back upon itself. God is not the cause of His perfections, since His perfections are not really distinct from His being. To give expression to its first and supreme analogate, then, we need to rework our idea of life. If to live means to bring about change in oneself, or to confer upon oneself some kind of actuality, then, we come to realize, it is He Who possesses every actuality by identity with His own being, activity and goodness Who is life itself, and everything else is by comparison as if it were dead.[99]

The infinite distance separating creatures from the divine perfection does not, however, belie the uniqueness of the creature that is human. Simon makes this clear in pointing out that the superiority of cognitive life over vegetative life is incalculably greater than the superiority of vegetative life over inanimate nature. Vegetative life belongs in the same category as inanimate

---
[98] Ibid., pp. 80–81.
[99] Ibid., pp. 81–82.

nature in this important sense: namely, that its activity, like that of inanimate things, takes place or occurs entirely within the order of physical nature and in all its functions is limited by that nature. "By contrast, cognition presupposes that the being endowed with it has access to an order of existence transcending the limits set to its existential capacity by its constitutive idea. And this access gives birth, with the appearance of understanding, to something marvelously resembling divine infinity."[100]

In the first part of this essay, I claimed that the identification of "to be" and "to think" ("to know") exerts a profound and pervasive influence in Simon's philosophy. The justification for that claim should now be clear. The identification of "to be" and "to think" ("to know") lies at the heart of his metaphysics of action. He has argued that immanent activity, the paradigm of which is cognition, is the perfect form of activity. By showing that all action is an analogue of the supreme perfection of God, in whom being and action completely identify with each other to produce the absolute perfection of life and activity, Simon has set forth the ultimate rationale for the subordination of transitive action to immanent action, for the superiority of speculative activity over practical activity, for contemplation over all other activities. This rationale is a causality that is at once efficient, final, and exemplary:

- *Efficient* because it is the "premotion" without which finite beings would never come into existence since there would be no first terminal act, to wit, the act of existing to actualize their potential to be.
- *Final* because its second terminal act, the act by which it strives to actualize the potentials conferred by its essence through action, presupposes an antecedent intellect who instills the creature with the initial impulsions of its peculiar nature and faculties: in order to choose, the will must first be ordered to the good; to know, the intellect must first be ordered to the intelligible. We have already seen in the first part of this essay Simon's invocation of the principle of final causality to explain how the natural law reconciles moral obligation with its grounding of moral rules in the nature of

---

[100] Ibid., p. 84.

things: in themselves things cannot be the source of obligation, for things are not legislators. But to talk of mere things is to create an idealization, an *ens rationis*. The intelligible patterns displayed by the actions of natural entities, indeed the very fact of acting for an end, without which they would not act at all, necessitates the reality of a being in which "to be" and "to think" are identical.

- *Exemplary* because, as noted above, God, in his absolutely perfect being, thereby exemplifies the absolutely perfect immanence and thus the absolutely perfect action. Creaturely action is accordingly the secondary analogate of the divine action. The former derives not only its being and intelligibility from the latter but its paradigm as well.

Simon's analysis of action can be characterized as a kind of "flow chart" which depicts action as an ascending dynamism with ethics and socio-political activity deriving their final validation from, and leading to, the higher forms of immanent activity, ending in the absolutely perfect life and creative self-knowledge of God.

## Conclusion

I hope to have supported my opening claim that Yves R. Simon was primarily a metaphysician. But how does this square with the fact that so many of his writings address subjects that belong under the heading of practical philosophy? There is the obvious and undoubtedly correct explanation that he had an abiding interest in ethical and socio-political subjects in themselves. I suggest a second explanation. Simon had a profound appreciation for the importance of work. Here "work" is used in his sense, as applying broadly to the activities of engineers and technical workers of all kinds, social workers, civil servants, politicians, psychiatrists, teachers, priests, and intellectual workers—e.g., mathematical physicists and other pure researchers—as well as manual workers. Although willing to exclude those who only contemplate, he added that because a considerable amount of effort is needed to reach the point of contemplation, "not even professors of philosophy need be absolutely excluded from the general category of workers."[101] He wrote of the necessity for the life of culture of maintaining an harmonious balance between work and contemplation.

For one thing, he feared what he called the "flower-like culture," by which he meant a culture based on freedom from work. Not only does it exclude the vast majority of people from the life of culture; but a leisure class is always in danger of losing its connection with reality. What is needed, Simon maintained, is a theory of culture that has its roots not in leisure but in work in its broadest sense. This sense includes moral, social, and intellectual work in addition to technical and manual work The former and the latter kinds of work exert a mutually beneficial influence. An ideal of culture that is based on freedom from work would undermine the culture by leading to "subjectivism, arbitrariness, and an attitude of frivolous aversion to nature and its laws." Simon accordingly argued for the importance of making knowledge of truth rather than possession of culture our guiding ideal: "if truth is sought according to its own laws and to its own spirit, culture also will be attained. Everything is in perfect order if the factors of refinement, flexibility, and charm spring from what is strong and determinate and of itself hard."[102] He was persuaded that by making possible a "collaboration between all kinds of technical work and fine arts," we can develop a culture with a contemplative ideal. The stupendous advancements of modern technology make the realization of that goal all the more plausible by increasing the worker's options.[103]

This mutual dependency that Simon sees between work and culture parallels a mutual dependency in his thought between transitive and immanent activity and thus between practical philosophy and metaphysics. The following text of his says it all:

> [I]t is impossible not to be struck by a widespread aversion to scientific forms in philosophy, theology, and human affairs—briefly, in the realms characterized by the predominance of mystery. . . . What is lacking in our relation to mystery is neither earnestness nor abundance of ideas, it is the rigor of the scientific spirit. There

---

[101] Yves R. Simon, *Work, Society, and Culture*, ed. Vukan Kuic (New York: Fordham University Press, 1971; rev. 1986), p. 17.
[102] Ibid., p. 187.
[103] Ibid., pp. 187–188.

are things which will never be accomplished by "tragic sentiment of life," "immersion in history," "experience of death," "esprit de finesse," "cultural refinement," "esthetic sophistication," "our cultural heritage," etc. Those things are clarity in the statement of questions and principles, firmness in inference, rational evidence of conclusions, appropriateness in prediction, integral preservation of past developments, lucid order; and the unique defense against error that rational forms alone can provide.[104]

Just as contemplation, the activity that carries us into the realm of mystery, requires discursive thinking or problem-solving—what Simon means by "intellectual work"—so the pursuit of metaphysics depends upon a well-ordered life, which, in turn, requires just and reasonable socio-political institutions. It all comes down to the human condition, to what Maritain called the glory and the misery of the human person: we are not pure intellects but integral composites of spirit and flesh, rationality and animality. We have seen above Simon's brilliant portraiture of action, showing why transitive action is the most immediately important demand in our lives. Its importance is not unqualified, however; it is instrumental. We have no choice but to negotiate with the world of matter in all its change and mobility in order to attain the freedom of immanent action and the more perfect life it offers.

I put to you that Simon was primarily a metaphysician, but spent most of his energy writing on ethics and socio-political subjects because he keenly appreciated the "work" that was needed to reach the promised land. His plan is all there, in Chapter Two of *The Metaphysics of Knowledge*.

---

[104] Yves R. Simon, Foreword to *The Material Logic of John of St. Thomas*, trans. Yves R. Simon, John J. Glanville, and G. Donald Hollenhorst (Chicago: The University of Chicago Press, 1955; repr. 1965), pp. xxii–xxiii.

2

# Yves R. Simon's Philosophy of Science

*Ralph Nelson*

AT THE BEGINNING OF THE TWENTIETH CENTURY a critical examination of science, particularly of physical science, was prompted by the theory of relativity, quantum theory, and other discoveries in physics. It brought into question much that had previously been considered as valid. A kind of revolution had occurred. The leaders of what was called the critique of science were mainly, though not solely, French. For a similar kind of critical examination was also going on in Germany.

Along with this development, there were attacks against philosophical idealism coming from a number of different quarters, such as the return to realism in Britain with Russell, Moore, and Whitehead; the resurgence of realism in the United States, and the emergence of realist metaphysics in France.[1] Among the realists were to be counted the Thomists.

Now, if we combine these two preoccupations, the critique of science and the revival of realism, we can understand the aims and achievements of Jacques Maritain and Yves R. Simon as practitioners of the philosophy of science from a realist perspective. Simon always acknowledged what he owed to his teacher which is clear in the notable essay he devoted to Maritain's philosophy of the sciences at a time when he was about to offer his own important contribution to this domain.[2] But it is not my intention

---

[1] On this development, see I. M. Bochenski, *Contemporary European Philosophy*, trans. Donald Nicholl and Karl Aschenbrenner (Berkeley: University of California Press, 1956) and Étienne Gilson, Thomas Langan, Armand A. Maurer, *Recent Philosophy: Hegel to the Present* (New York: Random House, 1966).

[2] Yves R. Simon, "Maritain's Philosophy of the Sciences," added as chapter IV to Jacques Maritain's *Philosophy of Nature*, trans. Imelda C. Byrne (New York: Philosophical Library, 1951), pp. 157–182.

to trace the influence of the master on the student; my intention is to elucidate Simon's contributions to the philosophy of science when he speaks, not as an interpreter of the thought of others, but in his own name.

This examination proceeds through three stages: (1) Simon's reflections on the various aspects of the philosophy of science prior to the publication of *Foresight and Knowledge*;[3] (2) the character and main themes of *Foresight and Knowledge*; and (3) Simon's reflections on the social sciences in the period from 1944 to 1961. His mature observations were about an apparent subfield of science that had been alluded to briefly before the publication of *Foresight and Knowledge*, yet had not been taken up in that treatise, principally because of its theoretical orientation.

Initially, it is important to locate Simon's endeavors within the context of French philosophy in the twentieth century. It is my contention that Simon and Maritain, of course, must be located in that context and movement if one is to fully grasp what they are trying to do in the critique of science. More specifically, I think Simon should be situated at the confluence of French philosophy of science and Thomism. To illustrate this I will refer to a significant study of contemporary French philosophy by Isaac Benrubi that was published about the time that Simon published a paper on the theory of facts in philosophy and science, in the same year as Maritain's great work *The Degrees of Knowledge* first appeared in print.[4]

In a chapter devoted to the philosophy of science, entitled "La critique de science," Benrubi says the representatives of this discipline are "scientists and mathematicians who from the viewpoint of this or that science try to bring out the limits of scientific precision and rigor in each of them and, consequently, the role and

---

[3] This is the title of the edited translation by Ralph Nelson and Anthony O. Simon (New York: Fordham University Press, 1995) of *Prévoir et savoir: Études sur l'idée de nécessité dans la pensée scientifique et en philosophie* (Montreal: Éditions de l'Arbre, 1944).

[4] Isaac Benrubi, *Les sources et les courants de la philosophie contemporaine en France*, 2 vols. (Paris: Félix Alcan, 1933). Maritain's work was published in 1932; the standard translation is *Distinguish to Unite, or, The Degrees of Knowledge*, trans. Gerald B. Phelan (New York: Charles Scribner's Sons, 1959). See also the *Collected Works of Jacques Maritain*. VII. *The Degrees of Knowledge* (Notre Dame, Indiana: University of Notre Dame Press, 1995).

power of the mind in the cognitive task."⁵ It is an odd description, because it seems to emphasize that the philosophy of science is not specifically something that philosophers do, but something that scientists do, unless we are to consider philosophers as included in the class of *savants*. Among the principal figures examined by Benrubi are earlier writers like Bernard, Cournot, Tarde; and contemporary figures such as Duhem, Milhaud, Meyerson, Poincaré, Goblot, and Bachelard. (When Copleston deals with French philosophy of science in 1977, he mentions André Lalande, not Edmond Goblot, and recognizes the stature of Bachelard as one of the main exponents of the philosophy of science in France. Most of Bachelard's major works had been published in the interim.⁶)

It is remarkable that the longest section in this part of Benrubi's study is the space allotted to Émile Meyerson, the one in this group who exercised the greatest influence on Maritain and Simon and, by all accounts, is reckoned to be a philosophical realist. However, the space allotted to Thomism in Benrubi's two-volume work is relatively brief.⁷ The author, having noted Maritain's criticism of Bergsonian philosophy, focuses on the design of *Réflexions sur l'intelligence et sur sa vie propre* as "a Thomistic prolegomena to any critique of knowledge."⁸ In retrospect, this highlighting is perspicacious, for *Réflexions* is related to *The Degrees of Knowledge* to a considerable degree as Kant's *Prolegomena to Any Future Metaphysics* is related to *The Critique of Pure Reason*. Only *The Degrees of Knowledge* had not yet been published when Benrubi completed his manuscript. There are good reasons for seeing that formidable work as continuing in the line of the critique of science, if science is taken in a broad non-positivistic sense. Simon's major treatise in the philosophy of science is, as he

---

⁵ Benrubi, *Les sources et les courants de la philosophie contemporaine en France*, 1:325.

⁶ Frederick Copleston, *A History of Philosophy. IX. Modern Philosophy: From the French Revolution to Sartre, Camus, and Lévi-Strauss* (New York: Doubleday, 1977).

⁷ Benrubi, *Les sources et les courants de la philosophie contemporaine en France*, 2: 939–951.

⁸ Ibid., 939. The reference is to Jacques Maritain, *Réflexions sur l'intelligence et sur sa vie propre* (Paris: Nouvelle Librairie Nationale, 1924), p. 77.

will say in a letter he addressed to Maritain, "a seed in the furrow of *The Degrees of Knowledge*."⁹

We now turn to Simon's writings prior to the publications of *Foresight and Knowledge*. Simon makes his debut as a philosopher of science in a paper that appeared in the *Revue de Philosophie* in 1932, whose title literally translated is "The Experimental Preoccupations of Philosophers and the Notion of a Philosophical Fact," more simply translated as "Philosophers and Facts."¹⁰ Subsequently, in a number of essays and in two major monographs, Simon elaborated a number of themes clearly relevant to the philosophy of science. Four of these themes will be discussed here: the typology of facts, the notion of critical realism, the system of the sciences, and the status of the philosophy of science within the system. To avoid needless repetition, since much material that appeared between 1932 and 1944 is incorporated in *Foresight and Knowledge*, I shall concentrate on material that either is not dealt with at length in that treatise or furnishes a background understanding of what Simon was about when he brought forth a sort of culmination to his earlier inquiries.

I begin with Simon's "general theory of facts," also called "a typology of facts."¹¹ His main purpose is to show the analogous character of the notion of a fact, that is, to show that amid a shared meaning—the role of the fact as a kind of starting point; "in each case there is an absolute"¹²—there are significant differences between and among a vulgar fact, a scientific fact, and a philosophical fact. He is particularly keen, I think, on showing the difference between a scientific fact and a philosophical one. It may be the case that a fact may be considered to be a principle—

---

⁹ In a letter dated October 6, 1944, in the unpublished correspondence between Yves R. Simon and Jacques Maritain in the archives of the Yves R. Simon Institute, Mishawaka, Indiana.

¹⁰ Yves R. Simon, "Les préoccupations expérimentales des philosophes et la notion de fait philosophique," *Revue de Philosophie*, n.s. 3 (May–June 1932), 267–289. Gerard J. Dalcourt did the translation and is the editor of Yves R. Simon, *The Great Dialogue of Nature and Space* (Albany, New York: Magi Books, 1970), pp. 139–160.

¹¹ Simon, *Great Dialogue of Nature and Space*, chap. 8, "Philosophers and Facts," p. 158, "general theory of facts"; and Yves R. Simon, "La science moderne de la nature et la philosophie," *Revue Néoscolastique de Philosophie* (Louvain), 39 (1936), 77, "a typology of facts."

¹² Simon, *Great Dialogue of Nature and Space*, chap. 8, "Philosophers and Facts," p. 146.

"the awareness of facts is the first step in scientific research,"[13] but then it must be seen as distinct from a principle in the sense of an axiom. (No doubt, one of the reasons for Simon's low view of pragmatism as a theory of knowledge stems from its denial of both facts and first principles. Charles Sanders Peirce was quite explicit on this point.[14])

Common sense may involve "a rudimentary philosophy,"[15] but the facts of common understanding require philosophical refinement. There are "some philosophical facts which can be established only through the technical elaboration of an experience."[16] Even though the sensation may be the same for the scientist and the philosopher, the facts are different, as when the philosopher may see a meter reading and not know what it means, or notice a spot on the skin and not know that it is a symptom. Influenced in this regard by Henri Bergson, Simon makes a very strong argument against the philosophical position that would adopt scientific facts as its starting point.[17] No more than the scientist can begin by taking the philosophical formulation of facts can the philosopher simply take over scientific facts without sacrificing the integrity of the inquiry. However, "one of the functions of the philosophy of nature is to sort out the

---

[13] Ibid., p. 160.

[14] Simon considered pragmatism to be one of the greatest threats to theoretical thought. The following passage may indicate why he was of this opinion. "It is false to say that reasoning must rest either on first principles or on ultimate facts. For we cannot go behind what we are unable to doubt, but it would be unphilosophical to suppose that any particular fact will never be brought into doubt" (Charles Sanders Peirce, "The Logic of 1873," in *Collected Papers of Charles Sanders Peirce* VII, ed. Arthur W. Birks (Cambridge, Massachusetts: Harvard University Press, 1958), 7.322, p. 189).

[15] Simon, *Great Dialogue of Nature and Space*, chap. 8, "Philosophers and Facts," p. 155.

[16] Ibid., "Philosopher and Facts," p. 154.

[17] Henri Bergson, *Creative Evolution*, trans. Arthur Mitchell (New York: Modern Library, 1944), pp. 212–214. While Simon shares many of Maritain's critical views of Bergsonian philosophy in his review of the second edition of *La philosophie bergsonienne* in the *Revue de Philosophie*, n.s. 2, No. 3 (May–June 1931), 281–290, in other places he is much more positive about Bergson, accepting the idea that a basic intuition is at the foundation of any great philosophy, the contribution that Bergson makes to psychology in his analysis of two kinds of memory, the importance of *The Two Sources of Morality and Religion* to moral philosophy, and a feeling that Bergson was moving away from the philosophy of universal mobility in his last book. See *Great Dialogue of Nature and Space*, pp. 72, 73, and 110.

philosophical meaning of facts discovered by the scientist—when they have a philosophical bearing."[18] While it might be expected that new facts will affect the development of a philosophy of nature, Simon believes that "the empirical material of metaphysics is provided entirely by common experience."[19]

Now, without using the term, Simon is embarked on a critical approach to knowledge. In the two monographs, and companion pieces, *Introduction to Metaphysics of Knowledge* and *Critique de la connaissance morale*,[20] Simon reveals his affinity with Jacques Maritain's approach in *The Degrees of Knowledge* by adopting as his own Maritain's conception of critical realism.[21] He refers to "the well-established principles of critical realism."[22] He observes "how we necessarily begin the critique of knowledge on realistic grounds,"[23] and he expresses his views on the role of critique in the following passage: "It is granted that a complete *critique* of knowledge presupposes a fully developed *theory* of knowledge. But without an initial critique, however summary and sketchy its statement of the value of knowledge may be, any theoretical treatment of knowledge is bound to be incoherent, making a sound critique in turn forever impossible."[24]

It has not been unusual to find philosophers, and not only neo-Kantians, who assert that the only authentic voice of science is idealism. The critical realism of Maritain and Simon in its awareness of the prevalence of this attitude is intent on countering it.

---

[18] Yves R. Simon, "Philosophy of Science," *Revue de Philosophie*, n.s., 6, No. 1 (January 1935), 64. This is not an essay written in English but a review article on Fulton J. Sheen's book of the same title. Fortunately for our purposes, Simon goes beyond an examination of Sheen's views alone. It provides him an opportunity to state his own perspective.

[19] Simon, *Great Dialogue of Nature and Space*, chap. 8, "Philosophers and Facts," p. 161n8.

[20] Yves R. Simon, *An Introduction to Metaphysics of Knowledge*, ed. Vukan Kuic and Richard J. Thompson (New York: Fordham University Press, 1990) and *Critique de la connaissance morale* (Paris: Desclée de Brouwer, 1934). I have been kindly given access to Vukan Kuic's as yet unpublished translation of the latter book and I have used his title.

[21] Maritain, *Degrees of Knowledge*, pp. 71–135 on critical realism. For concerns about the label, if not necessarily the content, of Maritain's realism, see Étienne Gilson, *Réalisme thomiste et critique de la connaissance* (Paris: J. Vrin, 1947), pp. 46–48.

[22] Simon, *Metaphysics of Knowledge*, p. 22n32.

[23] Ibid., p. 33.

[24] Ibid., p. 38.

The reception given to Émile Meyerson's research can be understood in terms of his realist bent. After having briefly discussed Meyerson's ideas in *Philosophy of Nature*, Maritain goes on to give a general assessment of Bachelard's contribution in this area. Perhaps Maritain understated the extent to which Bachelard's *The New Scientific Spirit* was a modification, rather than a rejection, of Meyerson's position, but he does note that Bachelard's "work seems to incline overmuch toward idealism."[25] Furthermore, Maritain says, "I am convinced that only the Thomist theory of the *ens rationis* allows the ideality of the knowledge of nature to play its part (an immense part) without spilling over into idealism."[26] In the only reference I have found to Bachelard in Simon's writings he seems positive about Bachelard's book on space.[27] Moreover, he raises an interesting question about Bachelard's polemics against the realists. Any reader of Bachelard is bound to wonder about the denotation of the term "realists," for in some instances he refers to very obscure figures and in others—I am thinking in particular of *The Philosophy of No*—he castigates naïve realists without mentioning their names.[28] In a notable utterance made during a defense of Maritain's political philosophy, Simon had wondered who the personalists alluded to were, and what were their names. Here he wonders who the realists are. Add to that the frequent qualification of these people as naïve

---

[25] Maritain, *Philosophy of Nature*, p. 70. Frederick Copleston, of course, was aware of much more of Bachelard's work than Maritain's at this time, and is more tentative about Bachelard. "But the latter's [Bachelard's] view of modern man as projecting or creating an extremely abstract world of relationships, in which materialism is left behind or at any rate transformed, might perhaps be given an idealist setting, if one wished to do so" (*History of Philosophy* IX, p. 291).

[26] Maritain, *Philosophy of Nature*, p. 70.

[27] Yves R. Simon added a note to Émile Callot's review of Bachelard's *L'expérience de l'espace dans la physique contemporaine* (Paris: Félix Alcan, 1937) in the *Revue de Philosophie*, 8, No. 4 (July–August 1937), 355. It seems to me that a contrast between Simon and Bachelard might begin by focusing on the notion of the experimental absolute in Simon's philosophy of science and the notion of the epistemological obstacle in Bachelard's. It may well be that the former takes something to be an ultimate point that would be construed as an obstacle by the latter. Another point of comparison would be the role played by mental constructions in the respective philosophies. Bachelard often speaks as if science were about a human creation rather than a human discovery. Such a view would be repugnant to the realist.

[28] Gaston Bachelard, *The Philosophy of No*, trans. G. C. Waterston (New York: Orion Press, 1968).

and a natural suspicion arises that it concerns straw men. Are we to believe that all idealists are sophisticated?

As to the background philosophy of the sciences, Kant, as is well known, stressed "the constructive or synthetic activity of the mind."[29] Simon comments: "The stubborn adherence to an idealistic justification of positive science conflicts in striking fashion with the spontaneous realism of scientific thought."[30]

In dealing with the reality of scientific objects, the realist should keep in mind certain critical principles. While human thought is capable of grasping reality, it never does so in an exhaustive way. The concept of reality is an analogous term implying diversity and differences in degree. Moreover, understanding reality requires the recognition of the role of beings of reason (*entia rationis*) in the knowing process and of the fact that some of the objects of thought are not real beings, but beings of reason.[31]

The *Metaphysics of Knowledge* is complemented by *Critique of Moral Knowledge*, as theoretical knowledge is complemented by practical. The latter work surveys the distinction between theoretical and practical knowledge, truth, and judgment. Furthermore, Simon, once again following Maritain, distinguished between theoretically-practical and practically-practical knowledge. He refers also to moral philosophy and Christian ethics. The last two chapters examine the relation between moral philosophy and the social sciences.

There are good reasons for taking as a reference point in this analysis a famous book written just after the turn of the century and often re-edited since; the latest edition, the sixteenth, was published in 1971. I refer to Lucien Lévy-Bruhl's *La morale et la science des moeurs* (*Moral Theory and the Science of Morals*).[32] Lévy-

---

[29] Simon, "Maritain's Philosophy of the Sciences," p. 169.

[30] Ibid.

[31] This is a paraphrase of the critical principles set down by Simon in "La science moderne de la nature et la philosophie," 71.

[32] Lucien Lévy-Bruhl, *La morale et la science des moeurs*, 15th ed. (Paris: Presses Universitaires de France, 1953). I have followed the translator of Jean Cazeneuve's *Lucien Lévy-Bruhl* (New York: Harper & Row, 1972), Peter Rivière, in rendering *la morale* as "moral theory." In "La philosophie bergsonienne," Simon counters Lévy-Bruhl's main thesis: "There is no science of moral facts without value judgments, because it is the very essence of a moral fact to be evaluated as good or evil, to such an extent that we cannot know what it is if we remain ignorant of what its worth is" (p. 288).

Bruhl's aim is to replace moral philosophy by the science of morals. Moral philosophy in this context is understood to be a study both theoretical and normative. Just as the philosophy of nature was supposedly replaced by the science of nature, so should moral philosophy by replaced by an objective study of human nature. In contrast to moral philosophy, the research will be theoretical and non-normative.

Subsequently, on the assumption that this project is successful in formulating laws—we are dealing here with a Comtean conception of social science—the possibility of a rational moral art involving the application of science to behavior becomes feasible. The art is completely contingent on the successful formulation of laws, and, if that fails, there can be no rational art. Like Descartes, awaiting the success of the grand design, we may have to be satisfied with a provisional morality, more appropriately a provisional moral art, for the time being. In fact, what Lévy-Bruhl concludes, given the state of the science of morals, is that it can only be said now that the rational art remains a *desideratum*.[33]

The term "moral science," be it noted, at least in certain cases is ambiguous. If the Aristotelian notion of moral science is normative and practical, the term "moral science" was used in the nineteenth century, and even in the twentieth century in France, to designate human or social science. For instance, John Stuart Mill discussed the logic of the moral, that is, the social sciences in his famous treatise on logic.[34]

Now, Simon would agree that a moral philosophy is a normative discipline, though not, as Lévy-Bruhl insists, a purely theoretical endeavor. On the contrary, as I have mentioned earlier, moral science is a theoretically-practical kind of knowledge. Furthermore, Simon goes to some pain to discern the various levels of practical knowledge, from science to *prudentia*. He believes that the aspiration for a theoretical social science is a delusion, that whatever knowledge is produced by the various forms of social inquiry serves, and is subordinated to, moral philosophy. The at-

---

[33] Lévy-Bruhl, *La morale et la science des moeurs*, p. 256.

[34] See John Stuart Mill, *A System of Logic Ratiocinative and Inductive*, 2 vols. (Toronto: University of Toronto Press, 1974). Book VI is entitled "On the Logic of the Moral Sciences." Raymond Aron in a book originally published in the 1930s refers to the social sciences as moral sciences: *La sociologie allemande contemporaine* (Paris: Presses Universitaires de France, 1966), p. 91.

tempt to make social science more than an autonomous domain—but an independent one—is considered a misconception of its function. From an examination of sociological claims in general, Simon proceeds to deal with specific social sciences, including under this heading economics, history, political science, as well as sociology seen as a part, not the whole, of social science. We do not find in these chapters a complete examination of the status of social science. Indeed, it will be some time before Simon offers a more complete systematic treatment of this issue.

Further developments in regard to articulating the various epistemological levels of moral philosophy are to be found in the collection *Practical Knowledge,* where it is poignant to realize that Simon's reflections continued literally to the end of his days, as witnessed by his correspondence with Maritain in 1961. There are also passages in the translation of John Poinsot's *Ars Logica* in which Simon takes issue with the conception of moral philosophy contained therein.[35] The theme reiterated throughout Simon's moral reflections is that moral philosophy is essentially theoretically practical knowledge.

The third theme emphasized during the first stage concerns the relation between two aspects of physical knowledge. There are no doubt some Thomists, mainly interested in metaphysics, who are willing to surrender the philosophy of nature. This is perhaps based on the grounds widely held among historians of science that the emergence and development of the physical sciences in the seventeenth century definitely established the obsolescence of a distinct philosophy of nature. While in Newton's case it seems to be a matter of identifying the new science as a philosophy of nature, in reality it was generally thought that a replacement had emerged. On the other hand, there were those, again attaching themselves to Thomism, who rejected a duality within the first level of abstraction, holding what might be called the unbroken

---

[35] *The Material Logic of John of St. Thomas,* trans. Yves R. Simon, John J. Glanville, and G. Donald Hollenhorst (Chicago: University of Chicago Press, 1965), p. 592n34. The significance of using John Poinsot rather than John of St. Thomas is that it takes the author out of the shadow of St. Thomas and deals with him in terms of his own contribution to philosophy and semiotics. For an account of the relationship of semiotics and philosophy see the introductory essay by John Deely in the special issue of the *American Catholic Philosophical Quarterly* devoted to John Poinsot: 68, No. 3 (Summer 1994), 259–275.

unity thesis. This was expressed in different ways—for instance, by considering the science of nature merely a dialectical extension of the philosophy of nature—hence, continuity was safeguarded.[36]

Now, Simon is aware of "the homogeneity of *physica*" in ancient philosophy.[37] However, he believes that progress in physical investigation forces us to recognize the distinction between the philosophy of nature and the science of nature in "a great movement of differentiation."[38] The grounds for this differentiation consist in the fact that in each case there is a different resolution of concepts, in ontological factors, on one hand, in phenomena, on the other. Furthermore, the definitions employed are different in the two cases. For instance, consider the way in which the human is defined in philosophy and in zoology.[39] Following Maritain, he terms the one ontological and the other empiriological (which includes the empiriometric where measurement is paramount, and empirioschematic where it is not). The common basis is that both deal with mobile being, though in ways that would lead to seeing them as discontinuous investigations.

Simon knows that this differentiation thesis runs counter to what might be called "ontological integralism."[40] He sees this tendency among certain Thomists who refuse to allow the notion of a non-philosophical science of nature. In their eyes either modern science is bad philosophy or its achievements are somewhat trivialized. They deny that a non-ontological approach can attain any intelligibility apart, of course, from integration into a philosophy of nature. In criticizing this stance, Simon argues that the science of nature does attain intelligibility, even though that intelligibility has to be understood in terms of the methods, definitions, and concept resolution proper to an empiriological discipline. It is, after all, physical knowledge, though clearly of a different kind from that found in the philosophy of nature. An expression of

---

[36] Vincent E. Smith refers to "the Laval School" where empiriological physics is taken as a continuation at the dialectical level of the demonstrative science that is true philosophy (*Philosophical Physics* [New York: Harper & Brothers, 1950], p. 178). The continuation thesis was also upheld by the River Forest school.
[37] Simon, "Philosophy of Science," p. 61.
[38] Ibid.
[39] Ibid., p. 59.
[40] Simon, "La science moderne de la nature et la philosophie," 68.

what Simon called "ontological integralism" persists in Thomist circles and continues to reject what we have called the differentiation thesis.[41]

If Simon tends to get vehement about any of the various positions that so-called Thomists have taken in regard to the philosophy of nature, it is surely the epistemological system that he associated with the Philosophical Institute of Louvain. From its inception under Cardinal Mercier until, let us say, the treatise on epistemology by Fernand Van Steenberghen, and allowing for inevitable variations on its themes by individual philosophers, the Louvain School has advanced a systematic account of the sciences that Simon found completely unacceptable, both as Thomistic and as sound philosophy. In an address given at Louvain and subsequently published in 1936 he seems to beard the lion in its den. "Until quite recently modern Thomists had the habit of incorporating the philosophy of nature in metaphysics, under the names of cosmology and psychology. It is needless to point out that this assimilation of philosophical physic into metaphysics cannot for a moment be upheld in the perspective of the teaching of Saint Thomas."[42]

This infidelity—and there is little doubt it is that, or eclecticism, became a tradition with the Louvain School in philosophy as is evident in the conclusions of Van Steenberghen's well-known book on epistemology. In it there are four general divisions of human inquiry: epistemology, positive sciences, metaphysics, and philosophy of the sciences. Metaphysics is divided into general

---

[41] Benedict Ashley, O.P. expressed this position when he said: "The whole of man's effort to understand the natural world forms one integrated enterprise and flows from one single *habitus* of the intelligence" ("Does Natural Science Attain Nature or Only the Phenomena?" in *The Philosophy of Physics*, ed. Vincent E. Smith [Jamaica, New York: St. John's University Press, 1961], p. 81. That Ashley's views have not changed is evident in his essay, "Thomism and the Transition from the Classical World-View to Historical Mindedness," in *The Future of Thomism*, ed. Deal W. Hudson and Dennis W. Moran (Notre Dame, Indiana: University of Notre Dame Press, 1992), pp. 109–121. See also John C. Cahalan's review of *The Problem of Evolution* in *The New Scholasticism*, 49 (1975), 350–362.

[42] Simon, "La science moderne de la nature et la philosophie," 68. Simon also discusses this confusion in an historical context when he observes that "Today we consider it a paradox that Thomists have ever accepted a division of philosophy which was initiated by Wolff, consolidated by Kant, popularized by the Eclectics of the school of Cousin, and was fundamentally at variance with that upheld by Saint Thomas" ("Maritain's Philosophy of the Sciences," p. 159).

and special, and special metaphysics encompasses cosmology and anthropology (within which psychology is located)—in Van Steenberghen's words: "If in our scheme, we leave aside the positive sciences, we get a synthesis of the philosophical sciences, or philosophy in the broad sense, which embraces epistemology, metaphysics and the philosophy of science."[43]

Finally, in this preliminary stage, we arrive at Simon's formulation of the philosophy of science in the system of the sciences. After having noted the deleterious effects of the Louvain School, the time is ripe to set out a definition of the critique of knowledge or, as more commonly known, the philosophy of science. "We believe that the part of knowledge which takes scientific knowledge as its object is only metaphysics itself in the exercise of its critical function. As to the philosophy of nature, its object is nature and not the science of nature."[44]

This succinct definition should be kept in mind when reading the Foreword to the translation of John Poinsot's *Ars Logica*. The point at stake is the status of meta-logical inquiries, that is, inquiries about logic itself. Simon asserts, "the fact that reflection on logic itself . . . in an Aristotelian and Thomistic version of the sciences, belongs not to logic but to metaphysics."[45]

It may not be immediately obvious to the reader of *Foresight and Knowledge* what kind of book it is. Only later on in the long first chapter does Simon finally identify the perspective in which the book has been conceived and executed. "The critique of knowledge studies the relation of the idea to reality, its truth value and the kind of truth it involves. . . . The critical point of view is predominant throughout the present study."[46] When Simon translated the first chapter he decided to render *la critique* as "the philosophy of science," clearly indicating that the two were synonymous. So the reader should expect to enter into a reflective study that presupposes knowledge of the science of nature, the philosophy of nature, and metaphysics. Simon is quite explicit on this point.

---

[43] Fernand Van Steenberghen, *Epistemology*, trans. Lawrence Moonan (New York: Joseph F. Wagner, 1970), p. 276.

[44] Simon, "Philosophy of Science," 62.

[45] *Material Logic of John of St. Thomas*, trans. Simon, Glanville, and Hollenhorst, p. xvi.

[46] Simon, *Foresight and Knowledge*, pp. 38–39.

He selects as the central focus of the treatise the problem of determinism, causality, and chance. There have been a number of far-fetched interpretations of the implications of the famous principle of indeterminacy, including Lucretian-like inferences concerning free choice, so that it becomes expedient to sort out the various meanings of determinism and indeterminism. In a manner similar to his treatment of the typology of facts, Simon examines how determinism is to be understood in the three different conceptual systems: the philosophy of nature, the philosophy of science, and physics. If there is a crisis of indeterminism, it is not specifically a philosophical crisis; it is a crisis in physical science. For determinism in physics is "conceived as a possibility of certain and exact prediction,"[47] and whatever may be the case in macrophysics, it has turned out that there is a problem in microphysics. Simon wants to emphasize that there are no implications in this for the issue of free choice; nor does he believe that the principle of indeterminacy has serious implications for theoretical philosophy. Still this crisis in physical science provides a good opportunity to re-examine concepts of causal explanation, of chance occurrence, of probability, and of the way in which scientists rely, and must rely, on substitutes for causal explanation in statistical laws.

Now, some might suppose that a treatise published fifty years ago is bound to be out of date, particularly in a domain where so many contributions have been made in the interim, namely, the very influential writings of Karl Popper and the New Philosophers of Science, such as Imre Lakatos, Thomas S. Kuhn, Paul Feyerabend, and Stephen Toulmin. Isn't a pre-Popperian treatise, to consider just one item, bound to be obsolete? The remarkable characteristic of *Foresight and Knowledge* is that it has avoided many of those features that tend to mark a book as a product of a certain time, place, and milieu. No doubt, the amount of attention devoted to logical positivism, or logical empiricism, is one such mark, but most of the work displays an intellectual freshness, even though a number of contemporary issues, such as the concern with inductive and deductive logic, are not addressed in it. It should be judged by the number of perennial issues, such as those concerning determinism, causality, and explanation that are ex-

---

[47] Ibid., p. 39.

amined. Although the attention once paid to logical positivism has subsequently been turned toward Popper, the reaction to logical positivism presupposes some acquaintance with it, as a dialectical movement requires knowledge of both thesis and antithesis. How otherwise can we understand Popper's falsification thesis than as a logical criticism of the verification thesis of the Vienna Circle?

Simon begins by contrasting two conceptions of philosophy: a type which he refers to as literary philosophy and his own conception of philosophy which stresses its kinship with science. In the chapter on Epistemological Pluralism, Simon, in dramatic contrast to the positivists, says: "In our view, whoever wants to work out a theory of the relations between philosophy and the sciences should above all take note of the scientific character of philosophy and understand that metaphysics, which is the archetype of all philosophical thinking, is at the same time purely and simply the archetype of all scientific thinking."[48] Somewhat earlier, in *The March to Liberation*, he refers to himself as "a man of science by profession."[49]

The author of a treatise in the philosophy of the sciences, if not an actual practitioner of scientific research, must deal with the frequent charge that philosophers are given to making judgments about scientific matters when they have little or no acquaintance with its practice, a notion that if consistently pursued would exclude all but practitioners from becoming involved in a metascientific discourse. In any case, Yves R. Simon was no armchair philosopher without direct acquaintance with the sciences, having devoted several years of his life to the study of them. We know that Simon not only studied the sciences, but, over and above his attachment to his philosophical vocation, even attended medical school in Paris—a fact that leads us to believe that the remark in the text about "being out of his depth" is autobiographical.[50] So we are not surprised when Simon says of the philosopher and the scientist, "we belong to the same breed."[51]

---

[48] Ibid., p. 90.
[49] Yves R. Simon, *La marche à la délivrance* (New York: Éditions de la Maison Française, 1942), p. 10. The translation is *The March to Liberation*, trans. Victor M. Hamm (Milwaukee, Wisconsin: Tower Press, 1942).
[50] Simon, *Foresight and Knowledge*, p. 21.
[51] Ibid., p. 5.

In discussing the relations between philosophy and science, Simon stakes out a middle ground between two tendencies in contemporary philosophy. He supplies no examples of that literary philosophy he excoriates, but I suspect the phenomenon he had in mind is more prevalent now than when he made his reflections. An entire constellation of philosophers have become indistinguishable from sophisticated literary critics. I think particularly of the writings of Jacques Derrida in France and of Richard Rorty in the United States. For them there is no kinship between philosophy and science. If it is granted that science is about explanation, philosophy at best is interpretation, and then we have to discover what domain of interpretation is appropriate for philosophers, as opposed to biblical scholars, historians, and literary critics. If indeed philosophy is reduced to interpretation, yet has no specific domain, it is little wonder that there is much talk that philosophy has lost its identity, that it is coming to an end.

There is a way of relating philosophy to science by asserting that philosophy comes out of, or derives from, science. This is the way of Willard Van Orman Quine. "The philosopher's view is inevitably an extension of the scientist's. There is a continuity, if not an actual unity, of science and philosophy."[52] Simon does not believe that philosophy is derived from science any more than he believes that science is derived from philosophy. Even though he refers to the philosophy of scientists as "philosophy within science"[53]—meaning, I take it, the tendency of scientists to raise philosophical issues—he is clearly of the opinion that some scientists do it better than others, and, no doubt, some do not do it very well at all.[54] He articulates a middle way between identification of the Quinian sort, philosophy is something scientists do, and the assertion of a total dissimilarity between philosophy and science. Philosophy and science are distinct; they are akin; they should not be separated. A simple way of stating the similarity would be to emphasize the common search for explanations.

---

[52] Alex Orenstein, *Willard Van Orman Quine* (Boston: Twayne, 1977), pp. 152–153.

[53] Simon, *Foresight and Knowledge*, pp. 43–48.

[54] In the unpublished correspondence, Jacques Maritain expressed some difficulty with the notion of philosophy within science. "I don't understand your philosophy within science very well. I rather think as Adler does that it is a kind of pre-philosophy of common sense on which science rests, but which does not enter into its texture." Letter dated 6 March 6, 1939.

Once that kinship is accepted, one is in a position to note the different ways in which the two proceed in this search. The differences are striking whether it concerns definition, determinism, causation, or concept resolution. Prior to the publication of *Prévoir et savoir*, as I noted earlier, Simon had distinguished two paths to a knowledge of physical reality: an ontological path and another form following an empiriological or empiriometric path.[55] When naturalists define the human being using the cephalic index, its upright posture, and the curvature of the vertical column (the spinal column), they do not furnish ontological definitions of the human, but an empiriological definition.[56]

As to determinism, Simon indicates that the term assumes different meanings depending on the system that is at stake. There are three different systems: that of common sense, that of science, and that of philosophy.[57] In like manner, if explanation means providing reasons or causes, we should not expect the same kind of explanation in philosophy and in science. On the one hand, there is the philosopher's quest for proper causes; on the other hand, the principle of causality undergoes a transformation, often expressed in terms of necessary and sufficient conditions.[58] Indeed, in the positivist scheme of things, conditioning is completely substituted for the idea of causation. However, to surrender the idea of causation is to give up the idea of explanation itself. Similarly, the attempt to convert the relation of causation into one of functionality in physical science would lead to the disappearance of the reality of physical change itself.[59] In conjunction with the analysis of causation, Simon notes as well the distinction between essential laws and statistical laws.

Finally, a distinction has to be made between the ways in which concepts are resolved in an ontological inquiry and in an empiriological one. Simon states the contrast very succinctly: "Every pos-

---

[55] Simon, "Philosophy of Science," 59.
[56] Ibid.
[57] Simon, *Foresight and Knowledge*, p. 39. I have made a distinction between systems, in the broadest sense, and conceptual systems, in a precise sense.
[58] Ibid., p. 20.
[59] Yves R. Simon, "Causality and Indetermination," Lecture 16, February 26, 1959. This is from an unpublished transcript of a series of lectures given at the Committee on Social Thought at The University of Chicago in 1959. See Alfred North Whitehead, *An Introduction to Mathematics* (New York: Oxford University Press, 1958), pp. 107–109.

itive scientist is on the wrong track when he uses a term whose meaning cannot be reduced to observable data. Every philosopher is on the wrong track who uses a term whose meaning cannot be reduced to being; the primary datum of the intellect."[60] There is, then, a reduction to sensory evidence and a reduction to rational evidence.

It is opportune now to reiterate that *Foresight and Knowledge* is the result of the confluence of the two streams of Thomism and of French reflection on science from Auguste Comte to Émile Meyerson. In stressing the ongoing need to refute idealism, Simon repeats his commitment to philosophical realism, critical realism. However, despite the emphasis on the critical approach as dominant, a noted phenomenologist, Aron Gurwitsch, insisted on referring to *Prévoir et savoir* as an example of naïve realism, a rather trite form of idealist put-down.[61] Gurwitsch believed that there was a linkage between phenomenology and the philosophy of science espoused by Ernst Cassirer. Another instance of a realist/idealist standoff involves Émile Meyerson and Gaston Bachelard. According to the author of a study on Bachelard, Meyerson was considered as the anti-model.[62] Simon has provided a framework for a fruitful comparison between realist and idealist conceptions of science in "An Essay on Sensation."[63] In regard to what he refers to as the experimental absolute, he suggests that the role of sensation, imagination, understanding, and construction be

---

[60] Simon, *Foresight and Knowledge*, p. 75.

[61] Aron Gurwitsch's review of *Prévoir et savoir* is in *Philosophy and Phenomenological Review*, 7, No. 3 (March 1947), 339–342. It is comforting to realize that according to Bachelard, there are nave idealists too. See *L'activité rationaliste de la physique contemporaine* (Paris: Presses Universitaires de France, 1951), p. 10.

[62] Jean-Claude Margolin, *Bachelard* (Paris: Seuil, 1974), p. 66. See also René Poirier, "Autour de Bachelard épistémologue," Colloque de Cerisy-la-Salle sur le thème Gaston Bachelard 1970 (Paris: Union Générale d'Editions, 1974), p. 17.

[63] "With due allowance for the voluminous parts played by interpretations and constructions, the analysis of scientific facts brings forth a core of existential decisiveness by reason of which the facts can be called the *experimental absolute*. In this existential decisiveness, we recognize the crucial *difference* brought forth at the beginning of this paper, the immense qualitative difference between sensing an object and imagining it (no matter how vividly) or understanding it (no matter how clearly and distinctly), or constructing it (no matter how elaborately)" (Yves R. Simon, "An Essay on Sensation," in *Philosophy of Knowledge: Selected Readings*, ed. Roland Houde and Joseph P. Mullally [Chicago: J. B. Lippincott, 1960], p. 95).

considered in the constitution of scientific knowledge. He has already commented on the role of construction, that is, the employment of *entia rationis*. The key question becomes what happens "if the experimental absolute is unqualifiedly negated."[64]

The second stream consists of French reflection on science, the importance of investigations by Comte, Poincaré, Duhem, and Meyerson. Comte assigns as the goal of science not explanation, but mere prediction, human utility rather than the cognition of truth. Meyerson, on the contrary, maintained that formulating laws, general facts, was insufficient to explain phenomena.[65] Despite whatever reservations Simon had about Meyerson as a philosopher, and several times these reservations are voiced in *Foresight and Knowledge*, this emphasis on explanation accounts for Simon's consideration for him.

Of course, it would be a distortion of Simon's explorations in the philosophy of science to see them as parochial, French parochial. It was the French perspective in which he was educated, but the reader will note the use he makes of Erwin Schrödinger and Max Planck, of Philip Frank and Werner Heisenberg. Note also the use of Whitehead and Eddington.

An issue that particularly preoccupied the French school since Comte has been that of explanation and prediction in science. Meyerson's influence on Simon has already been noted. Perhaps more than any other chapter in the treatise, "Science and Systematic Knowledge" specifically addresses the connection between foresight and knowledge. Though brief, it indicates the direction a more complete treatment might fruitfully pursue. Comte, it is argued, has confused science and systematic knowledge. Corresponding to each of these kinds of knowledge is a kind of prediction. However, while "the prediction of phenomena is one of the essential functions of science,"[66] "concrete prediction is outside of the realm of pure science,"[67] though it is what systematic

---

[64] Ibid.
[65] "We prove that the principle thus put into play, the principle of lawfulness (*légalité*), is not enough, that science attempts equally to *explain* phenomena, and that this explanation consists in the identification of the antecedent and consequent" (Émile Meyerson, *Identity and Reality* [New York: Dover Press, 1962], p. 10).
[66] Simon, *Foresight and Knowledge*, p. 66.
[67] Ibid., p. 67.

knowledge is about, searching as it does for a practical solution. This is tantamount to saying that the pertinent contrast is between theoretical prediction and prediction related to practice. Stephen Toulmin in *Foresight and Understanding* makes a similar point when he says that "science is certainly not a matter of forecasting alone, since we have to discover also explanatory connections between the happenings we predict."[68] He rejects what he calls "the predictivist account of explanation"[69] and shows instances where explanations may not involve forecasting at all. Toulmin then emphasizes the disjunction of explanation and prediction, sometimes identified, while Simon wants to distinguish two different notions of knowledge to which characteristic forms of prediction correspond.

Turning from problems that arise in Comtean positivism to an examination of logical positivism, more precisely the Vienna Circle, Simon discusses its doctrines at a moment of its growing ascendancy in North America, which turned out to be an important phase in the history of the philosophy of science rather than a lasting school.

Although there were aspects of the new empiricism (or logical positivism) which Simon was bound to view negatively—notably the characterization of metaphysics—his approach to the Vienna Circle is positive, albeit critical, in that he seeks to learn what contribution its representatives have made to our understanding of scientific knowledge. In this regard, he devotes more attention to the lesser-known Hans Hahn than to the well-known Rudolf Carnap.

Concentrating on the new empiricism as a theory of meaning, Simon discusses semiotics and sign functions. He reflects on the process of concept resolution, the empiricist postulate and the exclusion of metaphysics, the relationship between observation and theory, and the pragmatic conception of truth endorsed by the new empiricism.

Insofar as logical positivism maintains that only positive science can furnish true knowledge it is a brand of monism or, some

---

[68] Stephen Toulmin, *Foresight and Understanding: An Inquiry into the Aims of Science* (New York: Harper Torchbooks, 1963), p. 16. See also his *Return to Cosmology: Postmodern Science and the Theology of Nature* (Berkeley: University of California Press, 1982).

[69] Toulmin, *Foresight and Understanding*, p. 23.

might prefer, a brand of reductionism. It is obvious at this stage that Simon adheres to an epistemological pluralism. I would relate his comments in the fourth chapter to two discernible tendencies in modern Thomism—which is not to imply that there are not others—concerning the philosophy of nature. On one hand, there is a school of metaphysics in which the philosophy of nature is completely ignored. The issue of its status vis-à-vis metaphysics is never discussed. On the other hand, there is another school or tendency which indeed asserts the importance of the philosophy of nature, but refuses to accept the notion of an autonomous science of nature. Therefore either metaphysics absorbs the philosophy of nature or the philosophy of nature absorbs any other approach to the study of nature. It is apparent that Simon has a place for both an ontological and an empiriological knowledge of nature. Moreover, metaphysics again is a distinct form of knowledge.

The last two chapters contain companion pieces in the knowledge of nature: the first concentrates on the various definitions of physical knowledge, the second on the epistemological confusion in contemporary psychology. The former treats the issue of what we know through perception and what we conceptualize. It is corrective of a certain conception of perception, such as the Berkeleyan, with its failure to distinguish between *per se* and *per accidens* perception. Because of its brevity, the fifth chapter should be read in conjunction with Simon's "An Essay on Sensation."

In the recently published *The Definition of Moral Virtue*, based on lectures Yves R. Simon gave at The University of Chicago in 1957, there is a passage that helps us understand the place that the chapter on knowledge of the soul has in Simon's work as a philosopher.

> Let us admit that psychology is a poorly organized discipline and one whose disorderliness does not seem to be diminishing. Were I a little younger, I would consider dedicating my life to improving the situation, because the science of the soul is so important for morality.
>
> But sometimes I wonder if it is not already too late.[70]

---
[70] Yves R. Simon, *The Definition of Moral Virtue*, ed. Vukan Kuic (New York: Fordham University Press, 1986), p. 64.

This essay on the epistemological nature of psychology, which appeared in *Gants du Ciel*, No. 5, 1944, provides an introduction to that project envisaged by Simon but never completed. It is a starting point. It is not constitutive epistemology in the Kantian sense but a reflective one, that is, it surveys the state of the discipline in order to clarify the problems, eliminate false leads, identify areas requiring further development, and, finally, point out the interconnections. Simon's essay is timely in the absence of an undisputed and unified science of psychology commanding the support of competent persons. It is not dated, because he sticks to the issues and does not dwell on personalities. There are no references to twentieth-century psychologists in the text. However, it is easy to supply topical references to illustrate a point, whether it be Sigmund Freud, Jean Piaget, or B. F. Skinner. Take, for instance, the attack on philosophical psychology. In Freud's case, there was a constant effort to completely divorce psychology from philosophy, which he distrusted, even though some would say that there is an implicit or disguised Freudian philosophy. In Piaget's case, there is a vehement polemic against philosophical psychology in his book *Sagesse et illusions de la philosophie* (1965).[71] It seems clear that Piaget would not acknowledge any positive contribution to psychology in the writings of Maine de Biran, Bergson, Sartre, or Merleau-Ponty, to mention just the better known. Philosophy might be "wisdom" in Piaget's sense, but that is far from being a compliment since "wisdom" is not "science." In the case of B. F. Skinner and his efforts to go beyond freedom and dignity, there is a perfect exemplification of that technology extended to human beings so aptly described by Simon. Yet, in spite of scientistic confidence, the identity crisis in psychology persists.

If one is neither to reject philosophical psychology out of hand nor to dismiss the claims of positive psychology, it is necessary to make appropriate distinctions, such as the distinction between theoretical and practical psychology and between applied psychology and moral psychology. Yet, having done that, Simon shows that an analysis of individual cases reveals that applied and moral psychology are complementary.

---

[71] Jean Piaget, *Sagesse et illusions de la philosophie* (Paris: Presses Universitaires de France, 1965).

Simon's contribution to the task of "improving the situation" did not end with the epistemological essay. It is important to note his treatment of moral psychology. I recall years ago reading Aquinas's examination of human acts in the *Summa Theologiae* and thinking that this was a kind of moral psychology. However, that was not then, nor is it now, a common term. In Rawls's *A Theory of Justice*, and again in *Political Liberalism*, there is a section on moral psychology which seems to be about moral learning. A recent study by an English philosopher, N. J. H. Dent, *The Moral Psychology of the Virtues*,[72] seems more to the point; following G. E. M. Anscombe and analytic philosophy, it examines psychological concepts particularly relevant to ethics. Now, Simon not only talked about moral psychology but also developed a number of concepts that are characteristic of it, such as the notion of practical reasoning, free choice, knowledge by inclination, and virtue (based on the important distinction between habit and *habitus*). Again, *The Definition of Moral Virtue* brings out the significance of Simon's contribution from the viewpoint of both method and content.

Much has been done, through the efforts of scholars like Vukan Kuic and others, to publicize the political philosophy of Yves R. Simon. Much remains to be done in developing a moral psychology with a Thomistic inspiration. In the project of developing such a systematized approach, Simon's writings could well furnish the basis and starting point.

Psychology, in Simon's view, is "a part of the science of nature."[73] It is not a social science. Since nowhere in *Foresight and Knowledge* is there an examination of the social sciences as such, it would be useful to look at some of Simon's reflections in an essay first published in 1953 and recently reproduced in *Practical Knowledge*.[74] The essay entitled "From the Science of Nature to the Science of Society" attempts to show why the natural science model is not an appropriate one for social science. At the first stage when the notion of social science emerged, the project was

---

[72] N. J. H. Dent, *The Moral Psychology of the Virtues* (Cambridge: Cambridge University Press, 1984).

[73] Yves R. Simon, *Practical Knowledge*, ed. Robert J. Mulvaney (New York: Fordham University Press, 1991), p. 128.

[74] Ibid., pp. 115–136. The essay originally appeared in *The New Scholasticism*, 27, No. 3 (July 1953), 280–304.

to produce "a science of society patterned after the science of nature."[75] Were such a science developed, its applied side would be social engineering, just as applied natural science is engineering. Then, at a later stage, Max Weber introduced the notion of value neutrality. Weber's argument entails the independence of social science from morality. The riposte to this conception, trenchantly stated by Leo Strauss, is that moral considerations enter into the very context of social inquiry. They are essential to understanding social, that is human, facts. Simon's own response to the Weberian notion of ethical neutrality is to counter Weber's distinctions with one of his own, that between nature and use. For instance, because psychology is a natural science, meaning that it is concerned with nature, not use, "the principle of ethical neutrality holds in psychology."[76] But it is quite different when considerations of nature and use are inseparable. Simon concludes that "facts pertaining to the life of human society seem to be of such character that a philosophy of man is necessarily at work in the reading of their intelligibility."[77] This seems clearly to be a rejection of an independent social science, presumably a theoretical discipline. Consequently, the relation of social philosophy to social science is in no way comparable to the relation of the philosophy of nature and the science of nature. It might be comparable were one to conceive of social philosophy and social science as both theoretical inquiries; Simon denies that either of them is theoretical. Together they fall under the heading of practical knowledge.

Clearly, much more needs to be said about the epistemological status of the social sciences. If Simon wants to accentuate their practical side, as when he says "that the practical task of social science is to give prudence access to a more enlightened condition,"[78] he nevertheless has always conceded that the social sciences proceed in a theoretical mode, which means that they are

---

[75] Simon, *Practical Knowledge*, p. 119.

[76] Ibid., p. 128.

[77] Ibid., p. 132.

[78] Yves R. Simon, *The Tradition of Natural Law: A Philosopher's Reflections*, ed. Vukan Kuic, rev. ed., Introduction by Russell Hittinger (New York: Fordham University Press, 1992), p. 85. I have examined similar aspects of Jacques Maritain's philosophy in "Maritain's Account of the Social Sciences," in *From Twilight to Dawn: The Cultural Vision of Jacques Maritain*, ed. Peter Redpath (Notre Dame, Indiana: University of Notre Dame Press, 1990), pp. 143–153.

concerned with understanding and explanation. The point must be that the knowledge obtained through social inquiry is not an end in itself, for the social sciences should serve human goals. Philosophers of science like Karl Popper, as well as social science positivists, who conceive of the social sciences as purely theoretical, objective knowledge, hold that the applied side of social science theory is appropriately called social engineering. This seems logical if the analogy with physical science is maintained, for applied science is just another name for engineering. Since Simon has been extremely critical of the concept of social engineering, of the replacement of practical reasoning by technical, or at least the confusion of the two, his rejection of the notion that social science is pure theory makes not only an epistemological point but also a moral point, the concern with the manipulation of human beings.

So there are several reasons for Simon's position, and these reasons are understandable and commendable. Nevertheless one learns little about the kind of knowledge that has been acquired in the social sciences or the kind of knowledge that is likely to be disclosed by social science inquiry. Are we to look for the formulation of laws, not in a Comtean sense, but in the senses articulated in *Foresight and Knowledge*? What about the use of mental constructions in social inquiry, the Weberian ideal-types, for instance? What about the empiriometric approach, like survey research, in addition to empirioschematic research? We must conclude that the answers to these questions would require us to extend the basic concepts of the philosophy of science so lucidly stated by Simon to a critique of social knowledge, while accepting the conclusions concerning the liaison between social science and moral philosophy.

Without in any way denying the need for a more intensive exploration of the themes already uncovered in this realist philosophy of science, let me conclude by identifying two research projects that would constitute the greatest tribute to Simon's achievement in this field, the continuation of his work. Simon recognized, with some regret, that much more could be done in the study of psychology as a discipline to overcome the present disorder. Perhaps he was offering someone an invitation to take up that heavy task. The other research project would fill the gap that I see in Simon's rather concise commentary on the condition of the social sciences. In keeping with Simon's early treatment of moral knowledge, I suggest the title, the critique of social knowledge. However, if such a critique were to succeed, it would have to endorse Simon's contention, in opposition to Lucien Lévy-Bruhl, that the social sciences are not independent of moral philosophy.

3

# Yves R. Simon and the Neo-Thomist Tradition in Epistemology

*John F. X. Knasas*

I

I was originally asked to contribute a piece for this volume on Yves R. Simon and the neo-Thomist tradition. But since by training and temperament I am oriented more to speculative matters, I quickly, and with permission, abstracted from Simon's work in morals and political philosophy and focused on his *An Introduction to Metaphysics of Knowledge*.¹ My intent here, then, is to assess Simon's epistemological stance, with emphasis on the liaisons with Simon's fellow epistemologists in the neo-Thomist tradition.

By that tradition I mean the tidal wave of Catholic philosophizing that rolled forth from Pope Leo XIII's *Aeterni Patris* (1879). In that encyclical Leo exhorted Catholic philosophers to return to the way of philosophizing found in the Church Fathers and in the great medieval theologians, especially St. Thomas Aquinas. For these thinkers, their religious faith functioned as an extrinsic guide to their thinking.² One can compare this guidance

---

¹ Yves R. Simon, *An Introduction to Metaphysics of Knowledge*, trans. Vukan Kuic and Richard J. Thompson (New York: Fordham University Press, 1990). The work was Simon's doctoral dissertation at the Institut Catholique in Paris and was originally published as *Introduction à l'ontologie du connaître* (Paris: Desclée de Brouwer, 1934).

² "Those, therefore, who to the study of philosophy unite obedience to the Christian faith are philosophers indeed; for the splendor of the divine truths, received into the mind, helps the understanding, and not only detracts in nowise from its dignity, but adds greatly to its nobility, keenness, and stability. . . . A

to mathematics textbooks that at the back contain answers to problems. Evidently already having the answers helps a student to learn mathematics. Likewise, a believer's already having answers to many philosophical questions is not a hindrance but a help to doing philosophy.[3]

Even though *Aeterni Patris* recommended Aquinas for a way of philosophizing rather than for any special Thomistic doctrines,[4] the encyclical's effect was a resurgence in Thomistic studies which crested through the 1930s and into the 1950s.[5] Whether by intention or by accident, the Second Vatican Council marked an end to the revival, at least as far as wide commitment on the part of Catholic institutions of higher learning.

Simon belongs to the heyday of neo-Thomism. To prepare for a discussion of him, I will sketch the main lines that formed in neo-Thomist epistemology. Because Aquinas's philosophical theism appeared to demonstrate God from the existence of material things really other than ourselves, and because modern philosophy disparaged our cognitive ability to attain these divine effects, neo-Thomists expended huge efforts to defend epistemological realism. These defenses took two main forms. During the peak of the neo-Thomist revival, the reigning defense was the *a posteriori* form. In the *a posteriori* defense, material reality makes itself known in sensation. Reality can do this in two ways. First, reality

---

wise man, therefore, would not accuse faith and look upon it as opposed to reason and natural truths, but would rather offer heartfelt thanks to God, and sincerely rejoice that in the density of ignorance and in the flood-tide of error, holy faith, like a friendly star, shines down upon his path and points out to him the fair gate of truth beyond all danger of wandering" (*Aeterni Patris*, in *One Hundred Years of Thomism: Aeterni Patris and Afterwards—A Symposium*, ed. Victor B. Brezik [Houston: Center for Thomistic Studies, 1981], pp. 181–182).

[3] Unbelievers will object that this extrinsic guidance of reason by faith is simply a bias and prejudice. My response is that the value of the practice of "Christian philosophy" is best judged by its fruits. In that respect the vitality and depth of philosophy in the Christian Middle Ages is awesome. Gilson has forever set the record straight.

[4] See Armand A. Maurer, "Gilson and *Aeterni Patris*," in *Thomistic Papers* VI, ed. John F. X. Knasas (Houston: Center for Thomistic Studies, 1994), pp. 94–96.

[5] Even among Catholics, the typical reaction to this revival is that it was a Thomistic ghetto. But merely a scanning of major neo-Thomist authors and periodicals reveals a constant dialogue with secular philosophies of all kinds. Neo-Thomism has considered the opposition far more than the opposition has considered it, and yet neo-Thomism is called narrow!

can make itself known immediately, so that the really other is the direct object of sensation. As will be seen, at least by intention Simon, Maritain, and Gilson are all members of this camp. Second, reality can make itself known mediately, so that the direct object of sensation is the subjectively existing effect of the real material thing.[6] I refer to both immediate and mediate epistemological realism as *a posteriori*, because the basic content of knowledge derives from outside the knower. The knower is a *tabula rasa*.

Beginning with the Belgian Jesuit Joseph Maréchal in the golden era of neo-Thomism but picking up steam in the 1950s with the work of Karl Rahner and Bernard Lonergan, there was the *a priori* defense of epistemological realism. In the *a priori* defense, knowledge of real material things is again mediated. But the mediation is not in and through a subjective factor engendered by those material things themselves. Rather, the mediating factor derives from the knower alone. The mediating factor is part and parcel of the knower. It is *a priori*, and with respect to this factor the knower is not a *tabula rasa*. Obviously indebted to Kant's transcendental philosophy but also claiming Thomistic texts in its behalf,[7] the *a priori* defense of epistemological realism has become known as "Transcendental Thomism."

The actual workings of these defenses are not as pure as their authors may intend. Various weaknesses in one defense are rehabilitated by an appeal to a move in another defense. We will see one key instance in Simon's and Maritain's direct realism. To prepare for it I want to linger on Transcendental Thomism.

II

As mentioned, the Transcendental Thomist defends the realistic content of sensation through the introduction of an *a priori* medi-

---

[6] For neo-Thomists in this vein, see Étienne Gilson, *Thomist Realism and the Critique of Knowledge*, trans. Mark A. Wauck (San Francisco: Ignatius Press, 1986), and Kenneth T. Gallagher, *The Philosophy of Knowledge* (New York: Sheed & Ward, 1964), pp. 103–119.

[7] For cited Thomistic texts and an evaluation, see my "Transcendental Thomism and the Thomistic Texts," *The Thomist*, 54 (1990), 81–95, and "Transcendental Thomism and *De Veritate* I, 9," in *Thomistic Papers* VI, ed. Knasas, pp. 229–250.

ating factor. For example, just as an object's precise length becomes apparent when the object is placed up and against a ruler, so too the objectivity of the content of sensation becomes apparent when that content is appreciated up and against the knower's *a priori* mediating factor. This *a priori* mediating factor is the dynamism of the human intellect to a term variously described as Infinite Being (Maréchal), absolute *esse* (Rahner), and the notion of being (Lonergan).[8] Obviously crucial is the knower's confidence in the non-distortive nature of the *a priori* mediating factor. For instance, a crooked ruler will show an object to be of such and such a length, but this apparent length will not be the object's real length. How do we know that the *a priori* factor in knowledge is not more like the crooked ruler than the straight ruler?

Transcendental Thomists reply in a number of ways. I want to mention two. First, in a philosophical vein, they appeal to the mediating factor's ineluctabililty. Even the very doubt of it presupposes the mediating factor, and so the doubt reduces itself to incoherence. For example, I can question a ruler's straightness, because I can compare it to the standard. The ruler is one thing; the standard is another. But where the ruler is ineluctable, it becomes the standard and any distinction is lost. In that case, how can one "question" the ruler? This reply is called the retorsion or performative self-contradiction defense of realism.

In my opinion, one can make the case that objectivity remains the nagging issue. The skeptic can admit that the mediating factor is ineluctable. His concern arises from a familiarity with less encompassing mediating factors, for example, the crooked ruler. This more relative mediating factor acquaints the skeptic with the ideas of something standing outside the mediation and of the factor placing the thing in a different light. Mediating factors can be limited and distortive. Why may the ineluctable mediating factor not be distortive also? Hence, the ineluctability may well be indicating how we have to think rather than how reality must be.[9]

Second, Transcendental Thomists appeal to the authority of Aquinas. They cite Aquinas's example of furnishing an "indirect

---

[8] For sketches of these positions, see my "Intellectual Dynamism in Transcendental Thomism: A Metaphysical Assessment," *American Catholic Philosophical Quarterly*, 69 (1995), 17–23.

[9] Ibid., 23–25.

proof" of the principle of non-contradiction. In dealing with the deniers of the principle, Aquinas, commenting on Aristotle, says that refutation is achieved provided that the one denying "signify something by a word." If so, then "there is straightway found to be something definite and determinate which is signified by the term distinct from its contradictory."[10]

In reply, two comments. Aquinas also grounds the principle in and through an abstractive understanding of the notion of being. The principle is true, because it follows the notion of being which has in turn been derived through abstraction from the real. For Transcendental Thomism, however, retorsion is the sole means of establishing the principle.

Second, it is anachronistic to understand the indirect proof of the principle as applicable to a Kantian whom Transcendental Thomists are trying to beat at his own game. In the Aristotelian and Thomistic debate, the deniers of the principle are still all realists. They may dispute with Aristotle and Aquinas about the nature of the real, viz., "Is the real contradictory or not?" Yet they agree that thinking is determined by the real. This residual realism enables Aquinas to catch the deniers in self-contradiction. All that is required is that the deniers say something meaningful. In other words, if thinking is determined by the real, then to employ words to say something definite is to admit that something definite exists. Everything is not its opposite, and so the principle is affirmed. Contrariwise, if the real is the contradictory, it is not definite and so thinking itself should not be.

The Kantian denies this realism consisting in the conformity of thought to reality. The Kantian admits only that thinking is determined by thought itself. As a result, performative self-contradictions in thinking point to what may be exigencies in thought alone. There is no manifest way to go beyond thought to the real.

III

Simon definitely intends to be an *a posteriori* Thomist. Sensation is the source and basis for all our concepts. Simon remarks, "As

---

[10] *In IV Meta.*, lect. 7, n. 611; trans. John P. Rowan, *Commentary on the Metaphysics of Aristotle* I (Chicago: Henry Regnery, 1961), p. 248.

*the actuality of physical existence existing intentionally,* empirical knowledge supports in intentional existence everything that can exist intentionally. . . ."[11] Moreover, the notion of being derives from an abstraction, though an intensive rather than extensive one.[12] Unlike a Transcendental Thomist for whom the intellect is by its nature already a case of knowledge and not a *tabula rasa*, Simon understands the intellect as a pure condition for knowing. All the intellect's content, even its basic concept of being, derives by abstraction from sensation.

Furthermore, among the two noted kinds of *a posteriori* neo-Thomists, Simon intends to be a direct realist. He expresses this direct realism as the truth of sensation. He says,

> If it is true that the senses are basically indefectible with respect to their proper objects, and if every object of sensation, as an object of experiential knowledge, envelops actual physical existence, then it follows that *the act of sensing has to be made such as to reach the actual existent without error.* Any theory of sensation, therefore, that does not preserve before all else the notion of a knowledge made to reach external reality *as it is* will be at fault.[13]

That in sensation the knower is the really existing other is so true for Simon that sensation becomes a challenge to the principle of identity.[14] According to the principle, a thing is what it is. Hence, the principle would seem to exclude a direct realism in which the knower is not itself but something else. In a moment I will look at how Simon attempts to deal with the challenge. Suffice it to say here that his intended answer involves no retreat from direct realism.

In sum, in virtue of his abstractive interpretation of intellection and his position that sensation confronts the knower with the really existing other, Simon is an *a posteriori* neo-Thomist of the

---

[11] Simon, *Introduction to Metaphysics of Knowledge,* p. 87.

[12] Ibid., p. 53.

[13] Ibid., pp. 89–90. Also, "But actual existence would not admit of indirect ascertainment: it could not be inferred or believed in, if it had not first been grasped directly. At the basis of all our cognition of things existent, possible or fictitious, there is an act which implies in essential manner the physical presence of its object" (Yves R. Simon, "An Essay on Sensation," in *Philosophy of Knowledge,* ed. Roland Houde and Joseph P. Mullally [Chicago: J. B. Lippincott Company, 1960], p. 65).

[14] Simon, *Metaphysics of Knowledge,* p. 6.

direct realist stripe. I have only the profoundest sympathies with his stance. But I do have a worry. In my opinion, the subsequent elucidations Simon provides unintentionally compromise him. I have in mind his reply to the principle of identity challenge engendered by his direct realism of sensation. Simon begins by claiming that the principle applies only to physical existence, not to the intentional existence that characterizes the knower.[15] Simon explains intentional existence this way. In knowledge the knower becomes the thing known thanks to the "idea."[16] The idea is described as follows. First, the idea is a "reality" distinct from the thing itself yet nevertheless a "likeness" of the thing. Second, accordingly, the idea has "two faces." Simon explains: "By its own natural being, it is distinguished from the thing that it represents, and it goes forth as such to rest in the soul as an accident in its subject, constituting a composite, like a form joined to matter. But it is by its intentional existence that the idea accomplishes its primary function, which is to become the object of knowledge. In fact, the idea is the object itself existing intentionally."[17] Third, to illustrate this twofold status of the idea, Simon quotes from Aristotle and Aquinas on the memory image.[18] Both compare the memory image to a painting. A painting is not only something in itself, and so can be contemplated, but also a likeness of something else. Like the painting, the memory image can also be considered just as existing in the memory or as the likeness of something else.

The comparison of memory images (and hence ideas) to pictures seems to be a clever move to explain the direct realism of sensation without violation of the identity principle. I find that some pictures, but not all, by the impressionist Claude Monet possess the ability to transport me to the actual scene itself. For example, gazing at his *L'Église sur la Falaise* (Church on the Cliff, 1882), I suddenly am "there." I "feel" the air and the light, "hear" the wind through the vegetation. This remarkable "inten-

---

[15] Ibid., p. 10.
[16] "In the knowing subject, as was said before, either the thing known must be present in its own reality, or it must be re-presented there somehow. In the latter case, clearly, that by which the thing is known must be a reality distinct from the thing itself, and we call that reality a likeness or an idea" (ibid., pp. 14–15). In note 22 Simon clarifies that he is using "idea" so generally that ideas will be in external sensation as well as in intellection.
[17] Ibid., p. 17.
[18] Ibid., p. 17n24.

tional" capacity possessed by some artistic works is the common stock of our memory images. They all effect a transportation to the thing itself.

Unfortunately, Simon's comparison of all ideas with memory images is debilitating to and disastrous for his direct realism of sensation. For all the transportation to the thing itself, memories are not self-validating. They can and should be checked out with the record, e.g., as attorneys have done using videotapes in cross-examining witnesses in the O. J. Simpson trial. On a basis like this, we build up a trust in our memories and a confidence that the vividness of the thing to which memory images transport us is an "objective" transportation. For all its pleasant vividness, the intentionality fails by itself to assure us of objectivity. Likewise, Monet's painting would still perform its magic even if it were simply made up. But part of my enjoyment of it is the knowledge that what it depicts was real.

So, if memories are not self-validating and yet are taken as illustrative of all ideas, even those basic ones of sensation,[19] then the intentionality of sensation will never be validated. The accurate intentional functioning of these ideas of sensation will have to be accepted on faith. An implicit admission of the difficulty seems found in Simon's chiding remark that under pain of solipsism, construed as analogous to egotism, we "must treat ideas as noth-

---

[19] Simon's analogical use of memory images to understand what is going on in sensation is expressed in places other than *An Introduction to Metaphysics of Knowledge*. For example, "Aristotelianism is the philosophy which places ideas not only in the intellect, the memory and the imagination, but also in the external senses. . . . the Aristotelian *eidos* is an idea and belongs to the distinct world of entities that images and concepts exemplify more clearly. . . . Human knowledge purely and simply remains unexplained so long as there is no answer to the question, 'How did sense impressions get there?' The Aristotelian answer is that just as remembering is made possible by two-sided realities that are called memories, so sensation is made possible by another instance of these two-sided realities whose primary function is not to be but to represent, and which are, in one way, states of the psyche and in another way are the object that they stand for" ("Essay on Sensation," pp. 74–76). Then from Simon's "To Be and to Know," *Chicago Review*, 14, No. 4 (Spring 1961): "What holds for 'memory' also holds for such terms as representations, images, concepts, ideas, notions, and those *immaterial* or *intentional* forms that Aristotle, as recalled, places in the external senses" (p. 94); "The text on the sense as 'that which is receptive of the sensible forms without the matter' means, among other things, that Aristotle places ideas not only in the understanding . . . , and in the memory . . . , and in the instinct . . . , and in the imagination . . . , but also in the external sense" (p. 96).

ing more than objective means that alone can lead us to [knowledge]."[20] If ideas are self-validating, why this need to scare by an appeal to solipsism? Likewise, "this ascetic requirement of our intelligence, bound by its own law that alone can lead us to objective knowledge, is just like the denial of oneself that leads to God."[21] Again, I have difficulty avoiding the impression that at bottom Simon is claiming for our ideas a speculative faith analogous to religious faith. Such an interpretation is understandable in light of my claim that as described by Simon our ideas are not self-validating.

Defenders of Simon will insist that my difficulty stems from a common misunderstanding of the two-sidedness of ideas. What is unique about these twin facets is the epistemological primacy of the intentional facet. First one knows things, then one knows the idea, not vice versa. This correction solves any doubts about the realist nature of knowledge. In his own words, here is Simon:

> a two-sided entity may still be a thing. What determines an entity's belonging to the genus of being called, in the words of Cajetan, "the intentions of things, their sensible or intelligible forms," is not its two-sidedness; it is a certain primacy of the existential order. In terms of existence, an idea is not first of all a distinct kind of being; it primarily is one with the thing that it represents; it has no being of its own save as needed for its representative function. A memory is both the event remembered and a psychological disposition. But this psychological disposition is not just a thing representative of another thing. *Primacy, here, belongs to the objective way of existing which is that of the event remembered.* No bridge has to be built, for the memory, as disposition of the psyche, is not known first: what is known first is the remembered event. The disposition of the psyche is a means rather than an object of knowledge, except in the secondary process of psychological reflection.[22]

---

[20] Simon, *Metaphysics of Knowledge*, p. 20.
[21] Ibid., p. 21.
[22] Simon, "To Be and to Know," 99. Also, "In the whole theory of knowledge, there may not be any problem more significant, doctrinally and historically, than this: are ideas representative things, like photographs, paintings, and sculptures, or are they a distinct kind of entities, defined by the primacy of representing, defined by the primacy of objectivity, defined by the primary function of bringing about objective rather than matter–form unions, defined in short, by the primacy of objective over natural existence?" (ibid., 95). The point is reiterated in "Essay on Sensation," pp. 71–72.

With all due respect to Simon, the difficulty remains. I will not dispute the primacy of the objective in our ideas. My problem is that unlike Simon, for whom this primacy removes any bridge problem—even for the memory—I find this primacy congruent with the need for validation. Again, if the Simpson trial has taught us anything, it has taught us that memory images, for all their intentionality and ability to transport us to something else, are not self-validating. If they were, we would never bother to check them out against the historical record. With memory images, intentional primacy does not render validation otiose. Finally, if the play of intentionality in memory images is considered paradigmatic even for sensation, then the validation issue is quite legitimately extended to sensation. On this account there does appear to be a bridge problem.

Simon insists that the crucial issue is not the two-sidedness of ideas but the correct epistemological ordering of the sides. Primacy must be accorded to the intentional or objective side. But because of my above-stated difficulty, I find that a two-sided notion of ideas is the problem. Once one realizes, even secondarily, that ideas have a side other than the objective or intentional side, it becomes fair to ask if the idea's objective side is accurate. A two-sided idea cannot be self-validating. Certainly, its two-sidedness *distinguishes* it from a one-sided real thing. To be self-validating, doesn't the idea have to be simply and totally something belonging to the real thing itself?

If my reading of Simon is correct, it leads to the realization that what Simon describes as the idea cannot, properly speaking, be basic. The cognitive species that are fundamental must be of a different nature from Simon's understanding of them. I grant that some ideas function like the memory images Aristotle and Aquinas describe. But for all its vividness the intentionality involved here is insufficient to do justice to the demands of an immediate realist epistemology. Again, on the model of memory images, ideas are not self-validating. What kind of idea is needed for this epistemology I will explain shortly. I want to consider first a possible defense of Simon taken from the "critical realism" of Jacques Maritain's *The Degrees of Knowledge*. Simon's own book is replete with Maritain references.

## IV

Maritain expresses his critical realism in terms of an undeniable unity of the real "thing" and the "object" of thought. But for purposes of critique, it is crucial to realize that the starting point is the unity of the real as possible and the object of thought. Here are some expressions of this:

> In fact, the intellect, in virtue of its own proper activity, perceives that necessary law of all possible being in an actual (and contingent) existent grasped by it through the sense. . . . But for critical reflection it is well to give distinct consideration to the primary datum (revealed by psychological and logical analysis) of the intellectual perception as such. And that is why we say, . . . with R. Garrigou-Lagrange, that awareness of the irrefutable certitude of the principle of identity as the law of all possible being is part of the first conscious (philosophical) grasp that constitutes the starting point of critique.[23]

And also:

> Starting from that certainty [that the intellect's first apodictic and absolutely irrefragable certitude has to do with possible extramental being of which it knows in an entirely and eternally certain and necessary way that insofar as it is, it is not nothing] [the intellect] reflexively confirms for itself ("justifies" to itself) the veracity of sense and its own certitude of the existence of the sensible world. Thus, it is nonsense to posit (as is constantly done) the problem of the import of intellectual knowledge by bringing into question, as real being other than the ego, not, first of all, possible extramental being, but only the existence or non-existence (in act) of the sensible world.[24]

If I understand him, Maritain's position is astonishing. As noted in the first quote, Maritain admits that the intellect draws the principle of identity (and the notion of being that it expresses) from actually existing things given in sensation. In short, the intel-

---

[23] Jacques Maritain, *Distinguish to Unite, or, The Degrees of Knowledge*, trans. Gerald B. Phelan (New York: Charles Scribner's Sons, 1959), p. 92n1. See also the new edition of this book in *The Collected Works of Jacques Maritain*. VII. *The Degrees of Knowledge* (Notre Dame, Indiana: University of Notre Dame Press, 1995).

[24] Ibid., p. 102n2.

lect abstracts the principle. However, for purposes of initiating a critique of knowledge, this abstractive origin can be put aside. The critique should begin just with the "intellectual perception as such." For simply at that point we already know that we are in possession of an object that holds at least of the possibly real. This undeniable feature of the intelligible object illustrates the unbreakable unity between thing (as at least possible) and object. The principle of identity is more than subjectively necessary; it expresses what anything must be if it is to be an actual being. How does Maritain's thinking defend Simon's position on the objectivity of the ideas of sensation? To see the connection, one must turn to the second Maritain quote. Maritain says that from our certitude about the real as possible, we can reflexively confirm the veracity of sense. Maritain leaves unelaborated the reflexive justification. My best bet as to what he was thinking is this. The objectivity of our ideas of sensation is no difficult matter, because we already know that our idea of being is true for all possible real being. But we can grasp something true of all possible real being only by taking it from some actual real being. Now, being is taken from the object of sensation. Hence, the object of sensation is an actual. In sum, the unity of thing and object on the intellectual level is used reflexively to confirm the unity of thing and object on the sense level.

My problem with Maritain's exercise of critical realism concerns its first part, viz., the unity of thing and object on the intellectual level. In the absence of a perceived abstractive derivation of the notion of being from some actual existent—i.e., just with the intellectual perception as such—how do I know that I am dealing with anything objective at all, even the real as simply possible? Might the notion be expressing simply an ineluctable way of thinking? Maritain fastens on this ineluctability to justify the principles of metaphysical wisdom and to show that idealism is an absolute impossibility. But ineluctability is also true for the merely *a priori*. It is no sure-fire sign of realism. Maritain's move is strikingly reminiscent of the retorsion or performative self-contradiction defense of the Transcendental Thomists and has all the noted shortcomings thereof.[25]

---

[25] At ibid., p. 74, Maritain appears to interpret Aquinas's argumentation at *In IV Meta.*, lect. 6, as a case of retorsion. In "The Problem of Thing and Object

As far as the objectivity of intellectual knowledge goes, there is no substitute for abstraction. Unless the notion is seen in the real as given by sensation, a division between thing and thought will be thinkable. In this respect, Gilson in his *Thomist Realism and the Critique of Knowledge* appears to speak more correctly. In the last two chapters, Gilson repeatedly defends realism by portraying the intellectual apprehension of being as an abstraction, the apprehension of the universal in the particular given by sense. Speaking of classical realism, Gilson asks: "Is it so difficult, then, to understand that the concept of being is presented to knowledge as an intuitive perception since the being conceived is that of a sensible intuitively perceived? The existential acts which affect and impregnate the intellect through the senses are raised to the level of consciousness, and realist knowledge flows forth from this immediate contact between object and knowing subject."[26]

Gilson identifies the grasp of a notion's objectivity with the grasp of its abstraction from the sensible real. For Maritain the objectivity of the notion of being is independently recognizable.

---

in Maritain," *The Thomist*, 59 (1995), 22–27, John C. Cahalan defends realism with two clever arguments supposedly "derived" from Maritain. Both arguments use "object" for the term of a knowledge relation where "knowledge" includes sensation. The arguments attempt to demonstrate that objects of awareness are more than "objects." The first argument begins with my awareness of my awareness of X. It then asks what X is. Even though X is appearing as an object, the argument claims that I can know that X is more than an object. Why? If I deny it, then when I cognitionally step back into my awareness of X, I will once again have an awareness of my awareness of X. If I try to step into my second awareness of X, I again have an awareness of my awareness of X. An infinite regress is begun in which the nature of awareness is in truth described as an awareness of an awareness of an awareness of, *ad infinitum*. There is no object for the awareness to be of. Having an object of awareness, therefore, must mean having more than an object. In the second argument, Cahalan says, ". . . when A thinks B, if that which is thought were nothing more than 'that which is thought,' there would be nothing thought, even potentially. The description of something as 'that which is thought' (that is, as an object) must imply that the term of a knowledge relation possesses, in itself, characteristics other than being the term of a knowledge relation." I have two comments. First, Maritain's defense of the realism of sensation seems to be along the line given in note 24, above. This line correlates with neither of Cahalan's arguments, Second, both Cahalan's arguments seem to work only presupposing an awareness of infinite power. Only such an awareness could actualize argument one's infinite regress or argument two's total description of B as an object and so vaporize the object. But any awareness without infinite power would seem to be at least provisionally in front of an object.

[26] Gilson, *Thomist Realism*, p. 206.

The intellectual perception as such suffices. No reference to being's abstraction from sensible things need be considered. According to Gilson, "if you feel that abstraction should not presuppose its object, it would be far better to stop treating it as an abstraction, since there is no longer anything from which it could be abstracted. Make it the idea of some Cartesian thought, but do not try to play two tables at one time."[27]

V

So I return to my earlier point. To do justice to the immediate realist understanding of sensation, one cannot always be knowing through ideas that are like memory images. For all their intentionality, memory images are not self-validating. What would a self-validating idea be?[28] It would present the thing itself not because the idea represents the thing but because it is the thing. In other words, what is in the knower is numerically identical with what is in the known. It is the genius of both Aristotle and Aquinas to explain how such an idea is possible. Using Aquinas, I want to sketch that explanation.

Of Aquinas's works, the *De veritate* contains the greatest concentration of texts on cognitional species. But introductory to the entire discussion is an early text detailing the nature of cognition. In *De ver.* II, 2c, both sensory and intellectual knowing are characterized as ways in which the finitude of individual creatures is overcome. For characteristic of the knower is that the known is in some way in the knower.[29] Within the parameters of a presumed hylomorphic understanding of bodies, the text goes on to describe the manner of this containment.

---

[27] Ibid., p. 193. For another excellent presentation of abstraction as the validation of our concepts, see Robert J. Henle, *Method in Metaphysics* (Milwaukee: Marquette University Press, 1980).

[28] Cf. "Working toward an explanation of what is absolutely initial in mental development, working toward an intelligible interpretation of the first relationship between the mind and physical nature, is the most indispensable, as well as the most difficult part of the philosophy of sensation." Simon, "Essay on Sensation," p. 73. Of course, Simon's explanation is the "two-sided" idea previously mentioned.

[29] ". . . quia secundum hoc a cognoscente aliquid cognoscitur quod ipsum cognitum aliquo modo est quod cognoscentem" (Marietti ed., p. 27).

And because the forms and perfections of things are determined through matter, something is knowable insofar as it is separated from matter. Whence it is also necessary that that in which the perfection of such a thing is received be immaterial. For if it were material, the perfection would be received in it according to some determinate being. Hence, it would not be in it as it is knowable, namely, as the existing perfection of one thing is in another.

To understand how the known exists in the knower, one must understand how the form of the known is received by the knower. Crucial for this reception is immateriality. Since matter individuates, material reception of form engenders an individual only specifically like the agent. To have a reception of form that engenders the very individual, the reception of form must be without matter. What this means, positively speaking, Aquinas explains elsewhere. Immaterial reception of form is possible because of the "amplitude" of the knower's own form.[30] Because the knower's form is not completely sunk into its matter, it retains the "space" to receive into itself the very form of the thing known.

Aquinas's talk of the knower's form having amplitude and extendedness over matter may sound metaphorical and arbitrary. But its warrant lies in the thought that in a hylomorphic body, one has only matter and form. If in hylomorphic composites that are knowers the matter is unable to take on the determination of the known, then by process of elimination the knower's form must have the capacity. This concluded-to capacity is what the word "amplitude" is trying, perhaps too spatially, to express. In other words, the key to understanding knowledge is *formal* reception of form. Such reception, unlike material reception, allows the received form to remain numerically identical with the form of the known.[31] Through such reception, the known itself becomes present in the knower.

---

[30] "Natura autem rerum cognoscentium habet maiorem amplitudinem et extensionem" (*S.T.* I, 14, 1c; Ottawa ed., p. 91b).

[31] "The form into which the percipient or knower is brought by the efficient causality is the same individual form that actuates the child in real life. It is not just specifically the same, as is human form in child and parents. It is individually the same form, actuating both child and percipient in two different ways of existing. It makes the percipient *be* the individual that exists in reality"(Joseph Owens, *Cognition: An Epistemological Inquiry* [Houston: Center for Thomistic Studies, 1992], pp. 41–42). Also, "From this viewpoint there is reception of

The above is Aquinas's initial description of cognitional *species*. If it is correct, it obviously brings out a problem in the standard translation of *species* as likenesses. That translation could lead one to think of cognitional *species* along the lines of the memory image model with the noted problem for realism. The standard translation of *species* by "likeness" needs to be taken up in the light of the thought that form as formally received is not set up as something numerically distinct from the form of the real thing.

In sum, in cognition we know the really existing thing. As Aquinas remarks at *De ver*. II, 2c, to be knowable means "*existens perfectio unius, est nata esse in altero.*" Such knowledge is possible, because we become the real existent through information by its form.[32] Aquinas's position is perfectly compatible with my ignorance of being known by someone else. Even though it is the real existent me who exists in that person's cognition, no continuity of matter exists. In fact, the lack of continuity is the very condition for my existence in someone else's cognition. Hence, I am not in someone's cognition as my hand is in a heated oven. The continuity of matter in the second case ensures that the oven's action upon my hand is felt by me. The lack of material continuity in cognitive becoming obviates such self-knowledge even while it ensures my very presence in the knower.

---

form into form instead of form into matter. The result is that the one and the same form makes the sensible particular thing exist both in the real world and in the percipient" (ibid., pp. 42–43).

[32] In accord with Aquinas's metaphysics in which something is "a being" by virtue of its act of existence (*esse*), the previous discussion of cognition can be supplemented to include not only a reception by the percipient of the thing's form but also of the thing's *esse*. In the context of creation, Aquinas describes *esse* as both formal and received: "Cum enim dico esse hominis, vel equi, vel cuiuscumque alterius, ipsum esse consideratur ut formale et receptum" (*S.T.* I, 4, 1, ad 3m; Ottawa ed., p. 24a). I see no reason to prevent an extension of these metaphysical thoughts on *esse* as formal and as received into an explanation of cognition. Hence, "In that object [of sensation] there are the quidditative and existential factors. As impressed passively on the sentient power both those aspects enter into the actuation of the faculty" (Joseph Owens, "Judgment and Truth in Aquinas," ed. John R. Catan, *St. Thomas Aquinas on the Existence of God: Collected Papers of Joseph Owens* [Albany: State University of New York Press, 1980], p. 42. The distinct grasp of the *esse* would still be reserved for the intellectual act of judgment. In other words, on the sense level one would know "an existing thing"; on the intellectual level one would know "a thing *with* existence." See my "The Fundamental Nature of Aquinas's *Secunda Operatio Intellectus*," *Proceedings of the American Catholic Philosophical Association*, 64 (1990), 190–202.

Nor does Aquinas's requirement of immateriality for both sensation and intellection confuse these activities. The amplitude of form over matter can be accompanied either by continued contact with the knower's matter or by a separateness from the knower's matter. The former scenario would reductively ensure that the received form continues to be singularized and so is productive of sensation. The latter case would allow the received form to escape the bonds of singularization and account for intellection.

I would be remiss not to mention that Simon is well-acquainted with the above Thomistic passages as well as parallel ones both in Aquinas and in Aristotle. Not only are Simon's expositions of them masterful,[33] but they even include the conclusion on which I have insisted, viz., something of the *thing itself* is in the knower. For example, Simon takes pains to explain Aristotle's remark that sense receives "without the matter" the form of the thing sensed. One must understand that left behind is not only the matter of the thing acting on the sense but also the material type of existence the received form has in the sensed thing.[34] In other words, the sensing subject *qua* sensing does not receive within its own matter the form of the sensed thing. Only this twofold understanding of "without the matter" ensures that in sensation the form is united to its subject "without undergoing any modification,"[35] and that we have a union that "leaves untouched the identity of the things united,"[36] so that they are, as

---

[33] Simon, "Essay on Sensation," pp. 74–75 and n. 27; "To Be and to Know," pp. 86–88.

[34] "What distinguishes reception by the sense from the common way of receiving, St. Thomas goes on to say, is the special relation which obtains, in the case of sense, between the form that is received and the subject that receives it: in an ordinary reception, the relation between the form received and the receiving subject is the same as the relation that obtains, in the agent, between the same form and the agent's matter. Thus, together with the form itself, an ordinary reception involves the communicating of a certain relation between form and bearer, of a certain mode pertaining to the existence of the form in its subject [e.g., when a cold body placed near a warm body becomes itself warm, heat exists in the same way in either body]. It is this way of being of the form in its subject which is not communicated by the action of the sensible upon the sense, for in the thing the sensible form possesses a physical way of being, whereas in the sense it exists in an intentional and spiritual way" (Simon, "Essay on Sensation," pp. 74–75*n*27).

[35] Simon, "To Be and to Know," p. 87.

[36] Ibid.

Averröes remarked, "face to face,"[37] and that the idea is the "sensory quality itself."[38] I take these remarks to mean, as I have noted, that in sense the received form is numerically identical with the form of the really existing thing. But doesn't this incisive analysis make the introduction of the "two-sided" idea a non sequitur? Any way you turn it, the received form remains the form of the thing. A "two-sided" idea seems more appropriate for a *species expressa* than for the *species impressa* of sense. As totally the other, the received form is self-validating. Nowhere does it reveal its own side which would introduce a concern with its intentional accuracy.

## VI

In conclusion, Simon's general epistemological position represents the future of Thomism. The *a priori* form of Thomistic realism remains unable to make the case for itself both philosophically and textually. On the other hand, weaknesses in Simon's position are open to remediation. Problems caused by overextending the memory image model to all ideas, even those of sensation, can be solved without resorting to the questionable moves of Maritain's "critical realism." Rather, using recent work on Aquinas's epistemology, one can expound another and more fundamental idea to ensure the immediate realism of our basic activity of sensation. This more fundamental idea would be the very form of the real thing in the formal amplitude of the knower. The sensor becomes the really other without loss to itself and goes on to cause the really other as the term of its act of sensation. Finally, there opens up a clear path to the abstractive grounding of the objectivity of concepts.

---

[37] Ibid., p. 86.
[38] Simon, "Essay on Sensation," p. 75*n*27.

# 4
# Yves R. Simon on Law, Nature, and Practical Reason
*Russell Hittinger*

I

In his 1958 LECTURES at The University of Chicago, later published under the title *The Tradition of Natural Law: A Philosopher's Reflections* (1965), Yves R. Simon remarks that the subject of natural law "is difficult because it is engaged in an overwhelming diversity of doctrinal contexts and of historical accidents. It is doubtful that this double diversity, doctrinal and historical, can so be mastered as to make possible a completely orderly exposition of the subject of natural law."[1] A "thorough analysis of natural law," he goes on to say, requires "an elaborate technique and sharp philosophical instruments."[2]

But to what should the instruments be applied? What is a theory of natural law a theory of? In the first place, natural law can be regarded as an issue of propositions that are first in the order of practical cognition. On this view, a philosophical account of natural law endeavors to bring into focus those "reasons for action" antecedent to reasons yielded through practical deliberation and judgment. In the second place, natural law can also be regarded as an issue of nature or human nature, in which case natural law is not only a problem of the logic and epistemology of practical reason, but also a problem of how practical reason is situated in a broader order of causality. Finally, natural law can be

---
[1] Yves R. Simon, *The Tradition of Natural Law: A Philosopher's Reflections*, ed. Vukan Kuic rev. ed., with an Introduction by Russell Hittinger (New York: Fordham University Press, 1992), p. 5.
[2] Ibid., p. 15.

approached not only as order in the mind or in nature, but as the ordinance of a divine lawgiver.

Simon held that all three foci—law first in propositions, law first in things, and law ultimately in the mind of a divine lawgiver—provide distinct grounds for philosophical reflection.[3] For this reason, the study of natural law cannot be a simple endeavor. Even apart from complications of history and the great variety of doctrinal contexts, the subject is inherently multifaceted. Philosophers who have focused variously, if sometimes myopically, on natural law chiefly as a problem of moral epistemology, or of nature, or of divine legislation can claim to address some legitimate piece of the subject. As we will see later, Simon insisted that all three foci need to be integrated.

At the same time, he understood, and indeed warned his students of, the difficulties that beset the philosopher who would try to give a full and proper account of natural law. Some of the difficulties are philosophical, about which we will have more to say in due course. Others, however, are extra-philosophical, arising from practical problems in institutions of law, politics, and culture. It is at least paradoxical that the persistent sociological and political sources of interest in the concept of a natural law also tend to militate against full and proper philosophical accounts of the subject. Doctrines are cut and trimmed to serve practical ends of institutional justice—and of course to remediate injustices. Undeniably, the rhetoric of natural law and natural rights has proved to be a powerful and sometimes very effective tool in debates over politics and law. There is hardly a movement of social justice in American history that has not been activated, often on more than one side of the issue, by a concept of natural law.

Despite the fact that modern philosophy has steadily eroded the theoretical grounds for natural law in nature or proceeding from the mind of a divine legislator, we find more rather than less exuberance for framing debates in the language of natural law or natural rights. Simon worried that the concept of natural law would be reduced to its function as a practical tool—in short, that natural law, especially in its modern setting, would become increasingly more difficult to separate from ideology. Therefore, before we turn to Simon's philosophical reflections on natural law, we

---

[3] Ibid., p. 145.

should discuss his assessment of these extra-philosophical contexts.

## II

Simon refers to the "eternal return" of natural law thinking.[4] The idea of a natural law is irrepressible, because it arises from experience rather than from philosophical doctrines and debates. Moral and legal philosophers exercise their analytical tools on an idea that is rather sturdily shaped in the course of practical affairs. In its most rudimentary form, the idea of natural law arises from the contrast between what is right by nature and what is made right by convention or contract.

Thomas Aquinas summarizes a millennium of legal dicta in pointing out that what is due to a person in the order of justice can issue from two different sources.

> First by the nature of the thing [*ex ipsa natura rei*], as when a man gives so much that he may receive equal value in return, and this is called "the natural right." In another way a thing is adjusted or commensurated to another person, by agreement, or by common consent [*ex condicto, sive ex communi placito*], as when a man deems himself satisfied if he receive so much. This can be done in two ways: first by private agreement [*per aliquod privatum condictum*], as that which is confirmed by an agreement between private individuals; second, by public agreement [*ex condicto publico*], as when the whole community agrees that something should be deemed as though it were adjusted and commensurated to another person; or when this is decreed by the prince who is placed over the people, and acts in its stead. And this is called "the positive right."[5]

Some things are owed to persons because of the very nature of the thing; other things are owed to persons because of tacit or explicit agreements, or because of the determination of a legislator that such and such be the case.

The idea of a *ius naturale* expresses the conviction that not all

---
[4] Ibid., p. 4.
[5] Thomas Aquinas, *Summa Theologiae*, II–II, q. 57, a. 2.

terms of justice are artifactual.[6] What is right is not exclusively the creature of what is "made" to be right. It is true, of course, that some theorists, notably Thomas Hobbes, have challenged the ontological grounds of this distinction. Prior to the political covenant establishing the authority of the sovereign there is no obligation, for by natural right "every man has a Right to every thing; even to one another's body."[7] In *De homine*, Hobbes explains:

> Politics and ethics (that is, the sciences of just and unjust, of equity and inequity) can be demonstrated *a priori*; because we ourselves make the principles—that is, the causes of justice (namely, laws and covenants)—whereby it is known what justice and equity, and their opposites injustice and inequity, are. For before covenants and laws were drawn up, neither justice nor injustice, neither public good nor public evil, was natural among men any more than it was among beasts.[8]

Hobbes's denial of the traditional concept of *ius naturale* includes two propositions: (*a*) that all moral norms of justice are conventional; and (*b*) that these conventions are nothing other than the artifacts of positive law—or, as Hobbes has it, the commands of the sovereign.

But it should be noted that most of his successors, who could be classified in some broad way as legal positivists, have retreated from directly assailing the distinction between *ius naturale* and *ius positivum*, preferring instead to defend the autonomy of positive law and its logical independence from requirements of morality. Even if they reach the same result, it is one thing to deny *ius naturale* (which is to say that nothing is owed to persons prior to contract or statute), and quite another thing to hold that the *ius positivum* is (legally) valid whatever its moral properties.

---

[6] "The Philosopher here calls justice political or civil from the usage the citizens are accustomed to, but the jurists call the right political or civil from the cause [*juristae autem nominant ius politicum vel civile ex causa*], viz., that some city has decreed for itself. . . . Political justice then is properly divided by means of these two, for the citizens use justice to the extent that it is imparted to the human mind by nature and to the extent that it is posited by law [*eo quod natura menti humanae indidit, et eo quod est positum lege*]" (Thomas Aquinas, *In V Eth.*, lectio XII, no. 1017).

[7] Thomas Hobbes, *Leviathan*, I §14.

[8] Thomas Hobbes, *De homine*, 10.5.

H. L. A. Hart, for example, emphasizes that the celebrated "separation thesis" between law and morality only asserts that a norm can be legally valid and at the same time morally unjust; the thesis does not, however, suggest that society does not have a moral reason or even obligation to change the law.[9] After all, modern positivism in the English-speaking world began as a movement to reform the penal laws. The positivist bid to sharpen our perception of the difference between what law is and what law ought to be only reinforces the pre-philosophical intuition that the right (or the *ius*) is not merely artifactual, and that what is "made" to be right by legal enactment may not be morally right.

Here, our business is not to examine, much less refute, all the species of conventionalism and positivism. We are interested in Simon's remark about the "eternal return" of natural law thinking. It returns because theories that would deny it face the daunting challenge of explaining away the notion that there are things to be distributed and owed to persons on grounds other than those made by positive ordinances.

Whenever a polity finds itself debating which laws ought to be made or changed, some distinction between the moral and the legal terms of justice is presupposed. The presupposition, however, is usually brought to mind in the context of a problem that forces a polity to doubt the justice of a custom or positive law.[10] Wherever war exists, or the maldistribution of economic resources, or political despotism, or disputes that attend the litigation of rights—in short, wherever a serious imperfection is perceived in human practices and institutions—questions leading to natural law will emerge. If we take historical experience as our guide, it is difficult to imagine a legal or political culture in which such questions would never arise.

---

[9] See H. L. A. Hart, "Positivism and the Separation of Law and Morality," *Harvard Law Review*, 71 (1958), 593–629; and Neil MacCormick, "Natural Law and the Separation of Law and Morals," in *Natural Law Theory: Contemporary Essays*, ed. Robert P. George (Oxford: The Clarendon Press, 1992), pp. 105–133.

[10] Simon, *Tradition of Natural Law*, pp. 112–116. For a discussion of the way the problem of natural law is disclosed in the contrast between nature and custom, see Robert Sokolowski, "Knowing Natural Law," in *Pictures, Quotations, and Distinctions* (Notre Dame, Indiana: University of Notre Dame Press, 1992), chap. 14.

Indeed, the persistence of various concepts of natural law in modern politics is due in no small part to the material fact of the abundance of rules that have no other proximate source than human decree. In pre-modern society, law resided chiefly in a customary order. Legal officials periodically attempted to codify the customs, and, of course, to apply them. But the law was more grown than made. In such case, the contrast between nature and convention is more difficult to draw, for the customs not only have no distinct origin in terms of legislative pedigree, but also constitute a kind of second nature. In modernity, however, there is virtually no area of human conduct that is not regulated by public law, particularly by administrative law.

Although it is a virtue of a modern legal culture that citizens and legal officials can discreetly trace a rule to a human mind, for that very reason the positive law is rendered more rather than less vulnerable to a critical contrast between nature and legal convention. The more positive, as it were, a system of positive law, the more we can pinpoint "official" responsibility, and the more we can use moral reasoning to make or unmake the law. If it is a paradox of written law that seeking to make the pedigree and meaning of laws clearer tends to provoke doubts and debates over how texts are to be interpreted, it is also a curious upshot of the law of modern states that, in relying so heavily upon positive law, the "law" appears inherently changeable and, where changeable, amenable to moral criticism and emendation. When we add to this picture the enormous power of modern states, we can understand why the idea of natural law is perhaps more prominent today than it was in previous cultures which had a more favorable intellectual and religious climate for the notion of natural justice.

In *The Tradition of Natural Law* Simon sets out "to see the difficulties where they are and to puncture a few myths."[11] He worries that the problem of natural law in our times is not so much the need to defend the idea against its cultured critics as the need to prevent it from being ensconced in ideologies formed under the practical pressure of responding to the various intellectual and institutional felonies of modern life.

---

[11] Simon, *Tradition of Natural Law*, p. 13.

Our time has witnessed a new birth of belief in natural law concomitantly with the success of existentialism, which represents the most thorough criticism of natural law ever voiced by philosophers. Against such powers of destruction we feel the need for an ideology of natural law. The current interest in this subject certainly expresses an aspiration of our society at a time when the foundations of common life and of just relations are subjected to radical threats. No matter how sound these aspirations may be, they are quite likely to distort philosophic treatments. For a number of years we have been witnessing a tendency, in teachers and preachers, to assume that natural law decides, with the universality proper to the necessity of essences, incomparably more issues than it is actually able to decide. There is a tendency to treat in terms of natural law questions which call for treatment in terms of prudence. It should be clear that any concession to this tendency is bound promptly to cause disappointment and skepticism.[12]

Simon observes that natural law is a "subject of direct, intense, daily, and tragic interest to all sorts of people whose philosophic tools may well be primitive."[13] For this reason, he proposes that "when the theory of natural law seems to be commonly accepted and works as a factor of agreement, there are good reasons to suspect that it is embodied in an ideology."[14] By "ideology" Simon means a "system of propositions" that refers not so much to any real state of affairs as to the "aspirations" of a society at a certain time.[15] In political debates, doctrines of first things are liable to be reduced to policy aspirations regarding things quite contingent. In a situation marked not only by diminishing moral and cultural consensus, but also by the reduction of authority to the ever-expanding apparatus of the state, there exists a climate favorable to natural law as a solvent for moral crises.[16] For what else is "natural" law than a body of moral premises untainted by the human will and by the vagaries of political compromise?

For Simon, the "great example" in American history of

---
[12] Ibid., p. 23.
[13] Ibid., p. 14.
[14] Ibid., p. 66.
[15] Ibid., pp. 16–17.
[16] In *Practical Knowledge*, Simon contends that one of the reasons for the immoderate expectation with respect to any kind of moral theory is the "breakdown of tradition" (Yves R. Simon, *Practical Knowledge*, ed. Robert J. Mulvaney [New York: Fordham University Press, 1991], p. 97).

"timely aspirations" assuming the "language of everlasting truth" is the nineteenth-century debate over slavery.[17] Everyone wanted the problem resolved. But the crisis involved exceedingly complicated social, economic, and political compromises, not to mention the legal issues concerning how the positive law of the Constitution distributed shares of authority to deal with the problem. As the controversy escalated, what began as a legal accommodation of slavery on pragmatic grounds became a "universal law" for some Southern apologists. What was once acknowledged to be solely the creature of positive law—the right to property in slaves—became in the opinion of Justice Taney in *Dred Scott v. Sandford* (1857) the most natural and inflexible of rights. Of course, both sides invoked natural law and the authority of the Declaration of Independence.[18]

History is replete with examples of natural law used for the purpose of defending a political, economic, or social status quo. Arrangements of prudence are made to look like the dispensations of nature. Simon points out, however, that in modernity appeals to a natural order of justice are usually made "against constituted authority."[19] Modern discourse of natural law and natural rights tends toward a "belligerent universalism." Indeed, in the courts of a constitutional polity as relatively stable as the United States the government(s) are repeatedly sued by individuals who claim to possess a certain status, goods, or liberties prior—even superordinate to—the terms of justice "made" by the state or "made" by parties at private law. Whether the issue concerns race, gender, age, or a miscellany of lifestyle concerns, it is widely believed that things are owed *ex ipsa natura rei*, by the nature of the thing itself.[20]

---

[17] Simon, *Tradition of Natural Law*, p. 17.

[18] In the twilight of his life Jefferson Davis insisted that the Southern case for the original Constitutional order depended all along not merely on the written Constitution but also on natural law. In the final pages of his apology for the Confederacy, Davis invoked the Declaration of Independence with respect to "the inalienable rights of man," and wrote that the demise of the South augured the demise of the more universal cause "of the natural rights of man." Davis was speaking here not of any natural right to hold slaves, but of a right to political self-determination (Jefferson Davis, *The Rise and Fall of the Confederate Government* II [New York: De Capo Press, 1990], chap. 57, p. 645).

[19] Simon, *Tradition of Natural Law*, p. 8.

[20] For a sense of how many different kinds of issues are discussed today under the rubric of "natural law," see my "Liberalism and the American Natural Law Tradition," *Wake Forest Law Review*, 25 (1990), 429–499. For a consideration of

In our time, no contest over natural justice has proved more controversial than abortion, where we find natural law and natural rights invoked once again on both sides of the argument. In 1991, on the eve of the Senate hearings on the nomination of Clarence Thomas to the Supreme Court, Senator Joseph Biden took the position that the Judiciary Committee explore whether Judge Thomas held a "good" or "bad" theory of natural law. A bad theory of natural law, on Biden's view, would seek to expound a "code of behavior . . . suggesting that natural law dictates morality to us, instead of leaving matters to individual choice."[21] A good theory, on the other hand, would support rights of immunity against government on matters of personal sexual conduct and abortion. Senator Biden's remarks, of course, were made with a kind of naïve simplicity. But they are useful for illustrating Simon's point about ideology. For Biden, the true and false are to be seen as nothing other than the good or bad outcomes of applying a particular concept of natural law.

One year after the nomination of Judge Thomas, the Supreme Court made yet another bid to settle the abortion issue by issuing what is perhaps the strongest and unqualified statement of natural right in our judicial history. With respect to the word "liberty" in the due process clause of the Fourteenth Amendment, the authors of the joint opinion explain that: "At the heart of liberty is the right to define one's own concept of existence, of meaning, of the universe, and of the mystery of human life. Beliefs about these matters could not define the attributes of personhood were they formed under compulsion of the State."[22] To be sure, this dictum might include a kernel of truth. It is by nature, not merely by custom and positive law, that human persons have a competence to make morally responsible choices, and to constitute their character by so doing. For the sake of argument, we might stipu-

---

whether natural law requires judges to settle disputes about positive law on grounds of natural law, see my "Natural Law in the Positive Laws: A Legislative or Adjudicative Issue?" *The Review of Politics*, 55, No. 1 (1993), 5–34.

[21] Senator Joseph Biden, "Law and Natural Law," *The Washington Post*, September 8, 1991. Senator Biden, it can be recalled, voted against the confirmation of Robert Bork, among other reasons, because Bork expressly rejected judicial uses of natural law. Against Bork, Biden declared: "I have certain inalienable rights because I exist. . . ."

[22] *Planned Parenthood of Southeastern Pennsylvania v. Casey*, 112 U.S. Supreme Court, S.Ct. 2791, at 2807 (1992).

late that some zone of decision-making belongs, of right, to human persons. An order of positive law presupposes that principle. But so stated, the proposition requires much more specification if anything is to be resolved about the justice or injustice of abortion. Unfortunately, the judicial use of such rudimentary propositions about natural rights is expected to stop a debate precisely where it has to begin: namely, with carefully drawn specifications of concepts, both in terms of moral and in terms of legal reasoning. Indeed, if consistently applied, the Court's dictum would guarantee a natural right to immunity against virtually any positive law that peremptorily binds the individual to conform his action to the state's definition of things—including the Court's own resolution of disputes.

Of course, since it is one of the tasks of positive law to "hold men together, organize their cooperation, bring about uniformity in the behavior of indefinitely many individuals," Simon notes that "it is highly desirable that these formulas should command the assent of all persons concerned or most of them. We must, accordingly, expect the jurists to evidence an eagerness to keep away from issues on which minds are irretrievably divided."[23]

Simon characterizes the problem as a kind of "antinomy." On the one hand, the positive lawyer is concerned with explaining the relationship between the *determinatio* of the positive law and its moral premise(s). In varying degrees, positive law secures unanimity of action; yet unanimity of action cannot be created wholly out of the cloth of positive law, for positive laws (again in varying degrees) presuppose consensus about some principles and facts of the moral order. Hence, to the extent that the positive lawyer regards his work as explaining the relationship between law and morality, he is liable to ignite philosophical disagreements—the more remote the linkage between absolutely first premises of morality and the law or policy at hand, the more likely that the explanation will be disputed.

On the other hand, insofar as the positive lawyer is immediately interested in governing the community, rather than merely explaining a set of entailments for action, he frequently must abstract from these areas of disagreement. Prudential compromises will have to be made. The positive lawyer, then, could be tempted to

---

[23] Simon, *Tradition of Natural Law*, p. 65.

use the rhetoric of natural law to split the difference. That is to say, he will insinuate (often in the language of natural rights) an order of moral necessity that undergirds the law, even though (*a*) the law at issue really rests upon quite contingent premises and facts, or (*b*) no such moral consensus really obtains within the political community, or (*c*) no such consensus would obtain if the rhetoric were connected to the philosophical issues which are being glossed over.

### III

Simon's uneasiness about the ideological face of natural law discourse is meant to foster caution rather than skepticism about natural law. He concedes that a "philosophy unaffected by any ideological feature would involve a degree of perfection that human affairs do not admit of."[24] As he says, "for a thorough analysis of natural law an elaborate technique and sharp philosophical instruments are needed." What are the philosophical issues which tend to be submerged in the practical and institutional discourse? Simon pinpoints at least three sets of issues: (1) the relation of law to practical reasoning; (2) the ways that law differs from authority and individual prudence; (3) and the lingering, difficult issue of whether order in the human mind or in nature constitutes in some non-metaphorical manner a natural "law."

"Practical science," he wrote, "is pledged to reconcile the opposite features of intelligible necessity and contingent determination."[25] In the sphere of the contingent, where reason must judge and choose amid a welter of options, the perfection of practical reason is exemplified in the cardinal virtues, primarily in prudence. Here, the attunement of the intellect and will to objects cannot be reduplicated, or even completely communicated, by way of general propositions and injunctions. If we ask the prudent agent to explain with the clarity of abstract, general terms the *ratio* of his deliberation, judgment, and choice with respect to the contingent singular, the answer will disappoint.

In the sphere of necessity, however, law plays a principal role

---

[24] Ibid., p. 22.
[25] Simon, *Practical Knowledge*, p. 41.

in directing practical reason. In contrast to prudence, law has the opposite, though complementary, traits of necessity, generality, and publicity. In matters of law-making, we might not expect the clarity of a demonstration, but we do expect a fair degree of clarity in the order of communication. Those to be governed by a law must know what it is, and those responsible for enforcing and adjudicating it must be able to cognize and debate it in public settings. Although law must be treated analogically, one can say that "the more a law is universal, natural and impersonal, the more it has the character of a law."[26] Law, Simon says, "is a premise rather than a conclusion."[27] To the extent that the premises represent what is universal and necessary, the more they bespeak the character of law.[28] "Law is more at home in the realm of necessity. If any law is so grounded in a necessary state of affairs as to be unqualifiedly immutable, this is a law in the most excellent sense of the term."[29]

The concept of natural law, in both its authentic and its ideologically distorted senses, derives from the notion of "prior premises" of action—prior, that is, to terms of action which are constructed by practical reason, either in its individual office of prudence or in its more public office of laying down positive laws.[30] Those absolutely prior were traditionally called the "first precepts" or "common principles" of the natural law, which are always reasoned from rather than to; while those derived as implications of the first precepts were called "conclusions" or "secondary precepts."[31]

From a first premise, it might be possible to generate a demonstration of what is entailed in a particular matter of action—at least for those minds prepared to understand and give assent to a train of argument. So, from the premise that we must always act in accord with the good of life, the practical reason can draw the conclusion that murder is wrong. The more proximate the conclusion to the premise, the more likely the mind will give assent to the entailment.

---

[26] Yves R. Simon, *A General Theory of Authority* (Notre Dame, Indiana: University of Notre Dame Press, 1962; rev. 1980), p. 20.
[27] Simon, *Tradition of Natural Law*, p. 85.
[28] Simon, *General Theory of Authority*, p. 20.
[29] Simon, *Tradition of Natural Law*, p. 84.
[30] Ibid., pp. 86, 129, 151.
[31] *S.T.* I–II, qq. 94, a. 2; 95, a. 2.

The inferences from premises that have a high degree of certitude are usually expressed in the form of negative precepts or injunctions. These express "acts wrong by essence."[32] Traditionally, these have included such acts as murder, adultery, and theft.[33] No external circumstance, no subjective element of motivation, can ever make these acts right, for they are inherently inapt for bringing about justice. They are said to be contrary to nature, or wrong by the very nature of the case.[34] As for natural law in the mind, Simon notes that only a few moral problems are resolvable into necessities expressed by first precepts. These would be problems amenable to the negative precepts which can be stated universally and are always relevant to specific choices, circumstances and other complications notwithstanding.

The natural law "is known by way of inclination before it is known by way of cognition."[35] The distinction between knowledge *per modum inclinationis* and *per modum cognitionis* is taken from Thomas Aquinas.[36] Lest the distinction be misconstrued, it should be noted that it expresses a difference, not between intellective and non-intellective acts, but rather between two ways of know-

---

[32] Simon, *Tradition of Natural Law*, p. 146.

[33] See, for example, the papal encyclical *Veritatis Splendor* (1993), § 52: "The 'negative precepts' of the natural law are universally valid. They oblige each and every individual, always and in every circumstance. It is a matter of prohibitions which forbid a given action 'semper et pro semper,' without exception, because the choice of this kind of behaviour is in no case compatible with the goodness of the will of the acting person, with his vocation to life with God and to communion with his neighbor. It is prohibited—to everyone and in every case—to violate these precepts. They oblige everyone, regardless of the cost, never to offend in anyone, beginning with oneself, the personal dignity common to all."

[34] As Aristotle said, adultery is an act that admits of no "mean"; which is to say that adultery is something that cannot be done well or ill. Morally considered, it cannot be done at all, which is to say there is no authentic prudence about the act (*Nicomachean Ethics*, II.6, 1107a15).

[35] Simon, *Tradition of Natural Law*, p. 132.

[36] "A man may judge in one way by inclination [*per modum inclinationis*], as whoever has the habit of a virtue judges rightly of what concerns that virtue by his very inclination towards it. Hence it is the virtuous man, as we read, who is the measure and rule of human acts. In another way, by knowledge [*per modum cognitionis*], just as a man learned in moral science might be able to judge rightly about virtuous acts [*de actibus virtutis*], though he had not the virtue. . . . The second manner of judging belongs to this doctrine, which is acquired by study [*per studium*], though its principles are obtained by revelation" (*S.T.* I, q. 1, a. 6, ad 3).

ing: knowing something because of a connatural avidity for an end, in contrast to enjoying a term of knowledge by virtue of reasoning it out.

Thomas used this distinction between connatural and reasoned-out knowledge for more than one purpose. He used it to explain how an agent having a virtuous inclination to right acts "knows" the rectitude of a virtue differently from someone who knows it from an outsider's perspective, by dint of having figured it out.[37] He also used it to explain what happens at the other end of the spectrum of cognition from acquired habits.

Some terms of action are understood by exercising one's nature. For example, one does not know that life and bodily integrity are good, and worth pursuing, by argument. Indeed, it is hard to imagine what kind of argument could make such knowledge known *ab initio*. Thomas usually summarizes this most rudimentary knowledge of terms of action as the natural assent "to be, to live, and to know"—and this is nothing other than the tripartite scheme of integral goods that are expressed by the first precepts of natural law.[38]

As Thomas proposed, the inclinations are the *seminalia* or "seeds" of both the common principles of law and the virtues.[39] Both the order of precepts and the order of virtue stem from the order of inclinations. These inclinations are the first way we recognize both the objectives of action (the good of life, friendship, etc.) and, in a simple and uncomplicated manner, the actions that are congruent with those objectives. Before a rational creature moves himself through acts of practical reasoning and measuring, God moves the human intellect and will by instilling a

---

[37] "Now, rectitude of judgment is twofold: first, on account of perfect use of reason; second, on account of a certain connaturality with the matter about which one has to judge. Thus, about matters of chastity, a man after inquiring with his reason forms a right judgment, if he has learned the science of morals, while he who has the habit of chastity judges of such matters by a kind of connaturality" (*S.T.* II–II, 45.2).

[38] See *S.T.* I–II, q. 10, a. 1. In II–II, q. 34, a. 1, Thomas speaks of these three integral goods in the course of answering the question whether it is possible to hate God: "Moreover some of His effects are such that they can nowise be contrary to the human will, since 'to be, to live, to understand,' which are effects of God, are desirable and lovable to all."

[39] *S.T.* I–II, q. 51, a. 1.

principle of natural movement. This is what Thomas called *lex indita,* or instilled law.[40]

But the knowledge furnished by these inclinations is not sufficient either for a body of law or for fully practical judgments about action. As premises given to cognition via the inclinations, they need to be spelled out in the form of conclusions, applied to individual cases, and eventually complemented and made effective through determinations of positive law. Simon points out that considerable time can elapse between what is grasped by affective connaturality and what is understood in the way of explanatory reasons.[41] The first premises of natural law are not always clear either in the psychological sense[42] or in the sense of what can be communicated by demonstration.[43] Hence, we can see why debates about natural law are more difficult than debates about positive laws. As premises of action, positive laws command a less vigorous assent, but (as long as they are artfully framed) evince considerable propositional clarity; the elementary precepts of natural law, on the other hand, generate strong assent, but are relatively less "clear." And whereas a positive law can be located along a train of other propositions, allowing the mind to reason back and forth, the first precepts of natural law are always reasoned from.

It is a mistake, then, to look to the absolutely first premises as terms of a conclusion about difficult issues in morality. The vigorous assent given to first principles is not to be confused with the consent of many minds to the conclusion of an argument that proceeds, at least tacitly, from those principles. Those whose job is to win consensus in the public arena (policy-makers, lawyers, political officials) need to be on guard against trying to reduplicate through arts of persuasion those modes of assent and consent which stem from nature.

Simon understood that the concept of natural law has always been Janus-faced. From one point of view, it presents the notion of premises of action prior to the constructions of practical reason.

---

[40] *S.T.* I–II, q. 90, a. 4 ad 1.
[41] Simon, *Tradition of Natural Law,* p. 158; see also Simon, *Practical Knowledge,* p. 34.
[42] Ibid., p. 77.
[43] Ibid., p. 133.

This theme is typically brought into view when we notice a problematic contrast between what is right by nature and a convention that seems wrong or unjust. The mind moves back, as it were, to things that are first. From a different point of view, however, we can consider how to make the natural law effective. Here, the chief theme is not reconnecting a convention to a first principle, but using a first principle to create a convention. Although considerable attention is given to the first theme, Simon was more interested in the second.

Simon notes, "[n]ot every rule of human action is a law."[44] If rationalism is the price paid for reducing all the premises of action back into first principles, legalism is the price paid for trying to depict all the operations of practical reason as laws. In the *Summa Theologiae*, Thomas remarks that a rule of action, such as what appears in the first premise of a practical syllogism, is a necessary condition for the exercise of prudence. The human mind is a measured measure: it can actively measure action only if it is first measured; and it is first measured by law, though of course not first by positive law. When Thomas speaks of the natural law as our "participation" in the eternal law,[45] he not only means that we participate in an order of law by receiving and knowing a law; he also means that from the divine exemplar the human mind can go on to do something more: namely, to be "provident for itself and others."[46] The knowledge of things for an end is in God called providence, in human agents, prudence.[47] Prudence is not merely obedient and receptive, but also creative.[48]

But there is more than one species of prudence. Thomas mentions individual, domestic, and political (or jurisprudential) prudence.[49] When practical reason deliberates and measures an act, it can be said to act lawfully (in reference to a primordial rule), but

---

[44] Ibid., p. 86.

[45] *S.T.* I–II, q. 91.2.

[46] Ibid.

[47] *S.T.* q. 22.1; I–II, q. 19.4.

[48] "Again men receive from divine providence a natural capacity for rational judgment, as a principle for their proper operations. Now, natural principles are ordered to natural results. So, there are certain operations that are naturally suitable for man, and they are right in themselves, not merely because they are prescribed by [positive] law" (Thomas Aquinas, *Summa contra Gentiles*, III, 129 [3]).

[49] *S.T.* II–II, q. 47, a. 11.

its measures are not necessarily laws. Legislative prudence aside for a moment, human prudence exhibits traits quite different from those we ordinarily associate with law-making. Simon writes:

> [I]t is the privilege of prudence to deal with the singular and to answer unprecedented questions. Prudence is often defined by this privilege: this is perfectly fitting as long as we realize that answering general questions is also a proper function of prudence whenever, by reason of contingency, the general answer cannot be logically connected with any essential necessity. But at this point the psychological situation is almost inevitably obscure. When the answer of prudence is relative to strictly singular circumstances, it can be put in print without much danger of confusion; all understand that they are presented with a case history. On the contrary, when the question answered by prudence has a character of generality, its treatment normally assumes a systematic and doctrinal form which may, if we are not on our guard, deceptively imitate the ways of science.[50]

In matters of practical reason, Simon emphasizes the difference between legislative reason, which issues the premises for action, and practical reason in the strict sense of the term, which regards action as the conclusion of its discourse. The "conclusion of the practical discourse implies, in the most essential fashion, a trait opposed to the rational character of law": right reason in the singular and contingent matter of action.[51]

The function of law as a premise and the fully practical judgments of action by an individual are not reducible to each other. A traffic code, for example, posits certain binding directives for a multitude as to how vehicles are to be operated. However, if such a code is to bring about uniformity of action, it cannot regulate every singular action, in every contingent circumstance, for every single driver (considered in his singularity). Good positive law is under the imperative to achieve adequate generality, and it is precisely this virtue of legislative reason that can prove to be a vice if it is confused with other operations of practical reasoning, in which generalities are never adequate to concrete judgments. The positive law is no substitute for the myriad of intelligent judgments that have to be made on the part of drivers. On the other

---

[50] Simon, *Practical Knowledge*, p. 31.
[51] Simon, *Tradition of Natural Law*, p. 83.

hand, if there is to be any common order in this regard, individual judgments and actions must be brought under general rules. "The principle of government law," Simon contends, "is subject to such precarious conditions that, if it were not constantly reasserted, it soon would be destroyed by the opposite and complementary principle, viz., that of adequacy to contingent, changing, and unique circumstances."[52]

The first premises of natural law are the foundation for both prudence and legislative prudence, but differently. Legislative prudence is under the burden of ordering a multitude of agents, according to general classes of actions, with a level of publicity and communicability that is rarely appropriate to individual prudence. In other words, the way positive laws are related to natural law overlaps with, but is not exactly the same as, the way individual prudence stands toward those first premises. Now, both species of prudence share common premises. The moral law forbids murder and theft regardless of the distinction between species of prudence, for whether one ought to steal or murder is not a question of prudence. But when we move beyond the question of acts that are adjudged wrong by their nature to consider acts adjudged right, there can be a considerable difference between the measuring to be done by positive law and the measuring of individual prudence. On this score, Simon was concerned that the proposition (i) that *practical reason is ultimately rooted in a law* would be conflated with the proposition (ii) that *all practical measures are laws*. If conflated, it would seem to follow not only that natural law gives birth to positive law, but also that all moral discourse is essentially legal discourse—not merely lawful, but legal as well.

What marks off the sphere of legislative prudence? Let us return for a moment to what marks off prudence from first premises of action. If there is a per se order of necessity between an act and an end, there is no issue for prudence. The negative precepts of the natural law, for example, express such relations of acts and ends. Prudence comes into its own when there is something contingent or variable about the relation. Thomas held that "practical reason not only apprehends but causes,"[53] and where there is something variable or indeterminate in the relation of acts to

---

[52] Ibid., p. 84.
[53] *S.T.* II–II, q. 83, a.1.

ends, we can say that reason rather than nature is (proximately) causative of the act.

The ends of being, living, and knowing win our natural assent; as such, we do not need to deliberate and to issue a command in order to move toward these ends.[54] Although interpreters have been vexed by the Ulpinian dictum at the outset of the *Institutes*, that the *ius naturale* is "what nature teaches all animals," there is a relatively simple and plausible way to construe the dictum.[55] When the Roman governor goes to Asia Minor, he understands that the ordinances of Roman positive law are not needed to move the inhabitants to copulate, procreate, and educate the young. Nor is the competence of man and woman to engage in such acts solely the creature of positive law. No doubt, commands of law or custom might be required for a myriad of details pertaining to these acts and ends. Individuals will deliberate and command themselves with regard to particulars. By the same token, it would be ludicrous to think that the ordering of acts to ends in this regard is caused by positive law, or that it is in any primary sense an artifact of practical reason.

Thus, on the question of whether prudence is from nature, Thomas argues: "Now the right ends of human life are fixed; wherefore there can be a natural inclination in respect of these ends. . . . some, from a natural inclination, have certain virtues whereby they are inclined to right ends; and consequently they also have naturally a right judgment about such like ends. But the means to the end, in human concerns, far from being fixed, are of manifold variety according to the variety of persons and affairs."[56] As Simon contends, the more the right option is found among a welter of contingencies, and the more the right option is expressed in its very singularity, the more it expresses the rectitude characteristic of prudence. Once we move beyond the things that are known and desired naturally, acquired habits of intellect and will are needed for picking out the right relation and for rectitude of will in the choice.

Legislative prudence also deals with the variable and contingent

---

[54] Although considerable deliberation might be required for the choosing of these goods in particular contexts.
[55] *Iustiniani Institutiones* 1.2, cited by Thomas at *S.T.* I–II, q. 94, a. 2.
[56] *S.T.* I–II, q. 47, a. 15.

in relations between acts and ends. It differs from individual prudence insofar as law-making establishes a rule of action for a multitude of agents. It is widely agreed that one of Simon's chief contributions is his distinction between authority and law. Because these two notions are interrelated, they need to be sorted out. Let us begin with what they have in common. Given a field of indetermination with regard to things to be done communally, the question is how to achieve unity of action.[57]

Simon writes: "Now unity of action depends upon unity of judgment, and unity of judgment can be procured either by way of unanimity or by way of authority; no third possibility is conceivable. Either we all think that we should act in a certain way, or it is understood among us that, no matter how diverse our preferences, we shall all assent to one judgment and follow the line of action that it prescribes."[58] Of course, the unanimity of judgment has some basis in nature, reason, and custom prior to the application of authority or positive law. Thus, in extreme situations, such as when the community is threatened, individuals are often quickly mobilized to see what needs to be done in concert.[59] Here, unanimity rests upon common inclinations and habits, and consensus about the common terms of action is readily achieved—usually, however, only temporarily. Given any sizable community, beginning perhaps with the tribe, "unanimity is a precarious principle of united action whenever the common good can be attained in more than one way."[60] Whenever there is a plurality of "genuine means," the community cannot rely simply upon the "fortuitous" intersubjective, affective attunement of wills.[61]

Simon observes that law and authority differ, among other respects, in their manner of directing action. "[W]hereas law is attracted by an ideal of rational impersonality, acts of authority tend toward a state of concreteness involving the personalities of men,

---

[57] For a clear exposition of Thomas's understanding of the derivation of positive law from natural law, see John Finnis, *Natural Law and Natural Rights* (Oxford: The Clarendon Press, 1980), pp. 281–290.

[58] Yves R. Simon, *Philosophy of Democratic Government*, rev. ed. (Notre Dame, Indiana: University of Notre Dame Press, 1993), p. 19.

[59] Ibid., p. 29.

[60] Simon, *General Theory of Authority*, p. 40.

[61] Ibid., p. 45.

and all the contingencies to which human wills are subject."[62] Or, as he puts the same distinction elsewhere: "[A]uthority and law evidence opposite intelligible tendencies inasmuch as the more a proposition is expressive of necessity, the more it participates—other things being equal—in the character of law, whereas there is nothing in the concept of authority that expresses aversion to contingency."[63]

Given the plurality of ways that united action can be achieved, the exercise of moral authority can be very effective, precisely because it is not encumbered by the somewhat artificial contrivances and offices of positive law. Governance by authority thrives on our perception of the personal virtues and skills of a person, which seem to have a promptness and adequacy to the situation. We can think, for example, of the collective consent to the despot because he appears to be "the man of the moment." Governance by law, on the other hand, has the trait of "rational impersonality."

While legislation always requires competent authority, authority does not always require a juridical office. There is no principle that absolutely forbids a community from being organized around an authority who gives particularized commands rather than general standing laws. Whenever a judgment has to be supplied, the authority supplies it. In its ideal form, such an order resembles what Aristotle called "animate justice."[64]

Thus, when some matter of common interest must be decided, the dispute or problem is taken to whoever has virtue or charisma that commands the respect of those to be governed. At first glance, this would seem like a reasonable procedure. Whoever has virtue has the requisite habit of attunement to the contingencies of action. His animated virtue is more apt to reach the right result than the inanimate directives of general standing laws will. In *A General Theory of Authority*, however, Simon points out that when an authority gives directives, out of the saddle as it were, the political order can be called "authoritarian." Rather than distinguishing in some clear institutional way between individual, familial, and political dictates of prudence, the executive powers

---

[62] Ibid., p. 20.
[63] Simon, *Tradition of Natural Law*, p. 83.
[64] *Nicomachean Ethics*, V.4, 1132a22.

are permitted "to manage the concrete circumstances by connecting the conclusions of their choice with premises that have no other source than their good judgment, since no positive enactment ever gave these premises any juridical existence."[65]

The precepts of natural law are realized in the contingencies of human action in more than one way. The task of being provident for oneself, for small, affective communities, and for a city require significantly different uses of practical reason. The precision and clarity of the judgments derived from natural law in one case are not necessarily appropriate to the others. Prudential rules of action for an individual require little in the way of art, for the end of action is not a product external to the agent. Prudential rules of action for a family are secured chiefly through common affection, and the main art is education by way of rhetoric. But the rules of action appropriate to a city not only depend on the ability to see what is right and useful, but are secured especially by the ability to artfully create external institutions which govern a great multiplicity of acts and agents.

Political prudence causes a harmony of action from a distance, as it were. When it is tailored to the model of individual or familial prudence, the goods it seeks to secure are usually endangered. Indeed, it is characteristic of political prudence to "make" artificial limits on its own effort to make natural law effective. In a host of ways, including rules of evidence in criminal proceedings, limited terms of office, and requirements that ordinances be written, political prudence prudentially limits itself for the sake of the common good. Many of the limits characteristic of a system of positive law would be inappropriate, if not destructive, of prudence in individual and familial settings.

Given these important differences between individual, familial, and political prudence, Simon thought that the problem of natural law is best discussed not exclusively as a regression to first premises, but prospectively toward the distinct ways that the first premises are made effective.

## IV

There is, however, one philosophical problem concerning natural law that Simon thought required the regression to first principles.

---

[65] Simon, *General Theory of Authority*, pp. 48–49n11.

It is one sufficiently difficult as to incline even the metaphysician "to economy of words on the subject."[66] Why call natural law "law"? Simon insisted that the issue of God's existence is unavoidable once we raise the problem of the natural "law" in the order of being. "There are a hundred reasons for opposition to natural law," he remarked, "but this is one of them and at certain times it may be the strongest: obligation in natural law does not hold unless the natural law exists in a state which is actually prior, but which is ultimate in the order of discovery—'this law is an aspect of God.' "[67]

In yet another passage, he writes:

> There is no question of denying the connection between the problem of natural law and the problem of God. But it is not easy to show precisely what this connection is. One may wonder whether the study of moral nature and of natural law is a way to the knowledge of God or whether the knowledge of God must be had before the proposition that there exists a natural law of the moral world is established. We may be able to show that the truth is better expressed by the first part of this alternative. . . . But from this logical priority in the order of discovery it does not follow that the understanding of natural law can be logically preserved in the case of failure to recognize in God the ultimate foundation of all laws.[68]

Let us recall the *definitio legis* given by St. Thomas. It is the framework for Simon's reflections. Something is called law if it is an ordinance of reason, for the common good, made by a competent authority, and promulgated.[69] Simon notes that this is a nominal definition, gathered from the way we ordinarily speak about law.[70] In the order of names, it should be clear that we first speak about the familiar traits of positive law. While it is obvious that in the path of discovery we start with the data of positive law, this surely will not suffice for reaching a real, rather than a provisional or merely nominal, definition of natural law. For any alert philosopher, the following problem comes to mind. It is perhaps true that positive law has antecedent premises. Positive laws are *deter-*

---

[66] Simon, *Tradition of Natural Law*, p. 28.
[67] Ibid., p. 139.
[68] Ibid., p. 62.
[69] *S.T.* I–II, q. 90.
[70] Simon, *Tradition of Natural Law*, pp. 70ff.

*minationes*, inasmuch as they render determinate what is left indeterminate. This cannot begin from scratch, for something has to be made determinate.

A traffic ordinance, for example, enjoins motorists to drive on the right-hand side of the road. Thus, in the fashion of all laws, something is taken out of the sphere of prudence, and is made binding by virtue of the legal ordinance. Yet there is nothing in the nature of the thing itself—driving on this or that side of the road—that imposes any moral necessity on our choices. This would seem to be a clear of case of something that is made just simply by being posited.[71] Presumably, the legal posit is connected, though not reducible to, moral obligations to act in accord with the common good, to obey properly constituted authority, etc. It is not so clear, however, that the antecedent moral premise(s) should be called law. If the moral premises are to be called "law" without equivocation or metaphor, they have to satisfy, in some analogous fashion, all four traits of law, including the legislative point of origin in a lawgiver. To summarize: it is one thing to say that laws are like premises; it is quite another thing to propose that all premises of action are laws. What is called natural "law" leaves a question about the ontological ground of the name.

Simon maintains that the resolution of this problem involves at least two things. First, it is necessary to distinguish between what is first in the order of discovery and what is first in the order of being. For natural law to be "law" it is not necessary for the order of knowledge that the moral norms or *iura* be immediately cognized as effects of some ultimate legislative act. Rather, what is first in cognition would have to include some evidence that, upon inquiry and reflection, leads the mind to assent to the existence of a first, legislative cause. In short, there would have to be grounds for a traditional *a posteriori* inference leading the mind from things to God.

Simon surely recognized the difficulty here. In the first place, Thomas himself attempted no such formal argument in the ques-

---

[71] As Thomas quotes Aristotle: "in the case of the legal just, it does not matter in the first instance whether it takes one form or another, it only matters when once it is posited" (*S.T.* II–II, q. 57, a. 2, ad 2, citing *Nicomachean Ethics* V.7, 1134b20.

tions on law. The eternal law, in relation to which the natural law is defined,⁷² is itself defined *supposito quod mundus divina providentia regatur . . . quod tota communitatis universi gubernatur ratione divina*, that is to say, granting that the world is regulated by divine providence and that the entire community of the universe is governed by the divine mind.⁷³ Thomas assumed that this supposition had been verified elsewhere in the *Summa*. In the second place, Simon understood not only the difficulty posed by textual loose ends in the tradition, but also the inherent difficulty of convincing minds tutored by modern philosophy to grapple with the problem as anything other than one concerning the order of propositions in the mind. He commented that if the order of propositions is examined in view of order in things, the next move is made more favorable. "In our scheme of natural law existing—in the order of discovery—first in our minds, secondly in things, and thirdly as an aspect of God, the distance between the second and third stages is of minor relevance, even if not completely irrelevant."⁷⁴

Second, the definitional effort will require a logic of analogy. Precisely what kind of analogy is a difficult matter, for in constructing the analogy it will be necessary that the primary analogate cannot turn out to be positive law, even though that is where one has to begin. If, at the end of the day, positive law stands as the primary analogate, then the moral premises can be called law only by the logic of extrinsic attribution. So, for example, food can be called "healthy" only because it is a cause of health in the body. Properly, however, the property of health can be predicated only of the body. In the case of law, this would mean that law can be properly predicated only of positive law.

Take away the relation of the moral norms to positive law, and you remove the ground for speaking of those premises as laws—not indeed in the order of names, for in this order we move from the name "law" in reference to positive law, to the name "law"

---

⁷² In *S.T.* I–II, q. 91.2 ad 1, Thomas insists that the natural law is not diverse from the eternal law. Laws are said to be different according to the active principle, which is the legislative reason. Therefore, the eternal and natural laws are not different laws. In I–II, q. 91, Thomas seems to admit of only two different laws: namely, those traceable to a human mind (temporal laws) and those traceable to the divine mind.

⁷³ *S.T.* I–II, q. 91.1.

⁷⁴ Simon, *Tradition of Natural Law*, p. 142.

in reference to its moral antecedents. There is no question that in this order of naming the notion of moral law is dependent upon the notion of positive law, which is in this restricted sense the prime analogate. But with respect to priority and dependence in the order of being, Simon saw very clearly that the logic of extrinsic attribution will save some of the appearances, but will not rescue natural "law."[75] Although he did some closely reasoned work on the logic of analogy, Simon did not systematically apply it to the problem of the definition of natural law.[76] Rather, he suggested that there ought to be an argument from obligation to God,[77] and that not only the order of names and legal usages concerning natural "law" but also the very structure of political authority presuppose at least the *de jure* possibility of a complete metaphysical grounding.[78]

What does it matter whether the prior moral premises of positive legislation are called "laws"? Simon writes:

> The depth of this difficulty is clearly seen when we once again point out that natural law, in the very meaning of that expression, exists ontologically before it exists rationally in our minds; it is embodied in things before it is thought out, thought through, understood, intelligently grasped. Plainly, it is because natural law is first embodied in things that we declare such and such an action to be right, and such and such an action to be wrong, under circumstances which may have to be defined with great attention and particularity. And here we find ourselves face to face with the real problem of obligation. It is clear what happens if we stop here. If we stop here, the last word does not belong to the reason, the last word does not belong to that which is intelligent. The last word belongs to things.[79]

---

[75] Ibid., pp. 69–70n. On the theological part of the problem generally, and on the analogy of attribution particularly, see my article, "Natural Law as 'Law'" (*American Journal of Jurisprudence*, 39 [1994], 1–32. But the most complete examination of the problem in Thomas is Stephen L. Brock's "The Legal Character of Natural Law According to St. Thomas Aquinas," Ph.D. Dissertation, University of Toronto, 1988.

[76] The preliminary work that Simon did can be found in his "On Order in Analogical Sets" (*The New Scholasticism*, 34, No. 1 [1960], 1–42).

[77] Simon, *Tradition of Natural Law*, pp. 14, 142.

[78] Simon, *Philosophy of Democratic Government*, p. 167. But see also his comment at p. 154 on Leo XIII's encyclical *Diuturnum* (1881).

[79] Simon, *Philosophy of Democratic Government*, p. 137. For a useful discussion of this passage, see the review essay by Steven A. Long, "Yves R. Simon's Approach to Natural Law," in *The Thomist*, 59, No. 1 (January 1995), 125–135.

The legality of natural law inevitably raises some of the most profound issues of philosophy and theology. Once we see the need to appeal to some standard or measure of action other than those rules posited by the human mind, we are poised to ask questions about first things. These questions are as interesting as they are difficult. Simon believed that if the last word about moral order belongs to the human mind, it will be difficult to surmount the ancient challenge of Protagoras that the human mind is a measuring measure, measured by nothing but itself. If this were so, then perhaps the political order can rest on nothing more than the rules of "rational" artificers who endeavor to make their decrees "fair" according to a set of procedures which are themselves artifacts of human practical reason. Yet, there is also something unsatisfactory about the notion that the last word belongs to things—to an order of nature that is somehow "there," bespeaking no ordering intelligence. If this were the case, the traditional concept of natural law would have to be reduced to the so-called laws of nature—to lower "laws" which express structural rather than moral or properly legal limitations on human rule-making. The question is whether the political and legal cultures founded in modernity on convictions about a "higher law" have closed themselves to the inquiry into first things.

# 5

# Yves R. Simon on Liberty and Authority

*Vukan Kuic*

YVES R. SIMON was not a political scientist or even primarily a political philosopher. But he was a profound thinker and, faithful to the tradition of Western philosophy, he understood well the need for continuous re-examination of mankind's political experience from a philosophical point of view. His *Philosophy of Democratic Government* is a complete treatise of politics, realistic both about the past and about the future. It exposes historical myths and warns against undue optimism about the spontaneous progress of democracy. For instance, one can find there a thorough explanation of the various meanings of the so-called divine right doctrine as well as of the multiple meanings of popular sovereignty and the consent of the governed. This essay, however, drawing also upon other works by Simon, will deal only with a very specific subject that may be said to represent his most significant contribution to contemporary political philosophy: namely, his explanation of the complementariness of political liberty and political authority.

I

There are two major keys for the understanding of this central part of Simon's political theory. One is his explanation of free choice as superdetermination; the other, his explanation of the good of society as a moral good. Though derived from classical political philosophy, in Simon's hands these concepts allow us to perceive new meanings in their sources at the same time as they help us sort out modern views.

Perhaps the best-known current classification of teachings on political liberty is Isaiah Berlin's distinction between Hobbesian "negative" and Rousseauean "positive" interpretations.[1] But if this seems too simple, there is also Mortimer J. Adler's more elaborate scheme. Adler identifies the following main conceptions of freedom: "circumstantial freedom of self-realization," "acquired freedom of self-perfection," "and natural freedom and self-determination." In addition, he presents "political liberty" as a special variant of circumstantial self-realization and something he calls "collective freedom" as a special variant of acquired self-perfection.[2] Berlin, who never mentions Simon, would have trouble placing him. Adler, who gives Simon a prominent place in his book, groups him together with Aquinas, Locke, Montesquieu, and Jacques Maritain. Yet Simon's own classification of views of freedom differs from both Berlin's and Adler's.

Thus, the "gratuitous act" beloved of existential literature is, according to Simon, the perfect literary expression of a theory found in a variety of philosophical, moral, scientific, and psychological contexts which, from the consideration that causal or deterministic processes are predictable, infers that unpredictability is the real measure of our freedom.[3] In other words, one basic view of freedom is that it is something akin to accident or chance, lacking a firm cause, undetermined. Simon's example from existential literature is the unpremeditated murder of a perfect stranger taken as a proof of one's absolute freedom. But the same basic notion may be found also in its more moderate and socially acceptable versions. A good example would be the claim by a respected judge and popular writer that "the spirit of liberty is the spirit which is not too sure that it is right."[4] While this may pass as a conventional public expression of democratic tolerance, one is entitled to wonder whether it captures the core meaning of personal freedom. For where do we actually find the most unmis-

---

[1] Isaiah Berlin, "Two Concepts of Liberty," in *Four Essays on Liberty* (London and New York: Oxford University Press, 1969).
[2] Mortimer J. Adler, *The Idea of Freedom*, 2 vols. (Garden City, New York: Doubleday, 1958, 1961).
[3] Yves R. Simon, *Freedom of Choice*, ed. Peter Wolff, with a Foreword by Mortimer J. Adler (New York: Fordham University Press, 1969; repr. 1987, 1992), p. 157.
[4] Learned Hand, *The Spirit of Liberty*, ed. I. Dillard (New York: Alfred A. Knopf, 1952), p. 190.

takable examples of whatever we call freedom, free choice, free will, liberty? Is it in perplexed, irresolute, weak-willed, and highly suggestible people? Or in persons in firm control of their images and emotions, who know what they want, and who will not be deterred from their goals? As Simon sees it, "Persons who are at the summit of human energy hold that death itself is an accident which cannot affect their relation to the really important ends of human life."[5] Thus, contrary to what would follow from some of those well-intentioned theories, it is Patrick Henry who had the spirit of liberty; Hamlet suffered from the lack of it.

When we act on pure impulse or hesitate to do anything because we are not sure what is right, we only delude ourselves in thinking that we are free. Action for the sake of action no less than any state of uncertainty, vacillation, suspense, ambiguity, timidity, bewilderment, vagueness, confusion, etc., is the exact opposite of freedom. It makes as little sense to equate human freedom with indeterminism as to describe the sometimes indeterminate and unpredictable behavior of individual atomic particles as being "free."[6] The opposite of indetermination in the human world is, not determinism, but free choice, which, according to Simon, "proceeds not from any weakness, any imperfection, any feature of potentiality on the part of the agent but, on the contrary, from a plenitude of being and an abundance of determination, from an ability to achieve mastery over diverse possibilities, and from a strength of constitution which makes it possible to attain one's end in a variety of ways."[7]

Hence, freedom does not come cheap. It cannot be attained either by "letting it all hang out" or by flipping a coin. To become a free person who will lead a free life, each of us needs to work very hard to acquire many qualities of character called vir-

---

[5] Simon, *Freedom of Choice*, p. 158. "In the heroes and the saints the sense for freedom is accompanied by a sense of the unique worth of irrevocable decisions. The literary characters who seek mobility in order to avoid decisions do almost exactly the contrary of what the heroes and the saints do. They would be without prestige and without imitators if the cultivation of passive indifference did not procure a cheap substitute of freedom to intellectuals who no longer have any sense of freedom" (ibid., p. 122).

[6] Yves R. Simon, *The Tradition of Natural Law*, ed. Vukan Kuic (New York: Fordham University Press, 1965; repr. 1967; rev. ed. 1992), pp. 55–58. The 1992 edition contains a new introduction by Russell Hittinger.

[7] Simon, *Freedom of Choice*, p. 153.

tues. That these qualities are not so easy to define and admit of degrees does not affect their being indispensable for enabling us to make free choices. For we shall be able to do so in exact proportion to our charity, courage, temperance, justice, and prudence, which alone can keep us from choosing wrongly.[8]

For depth of insight, this ancient view of freedom has still to be matched by anything that specifically modern psychology, ethics, or political theory has to offer. As stable states of character which practice and habit have turned into second nature, as it were, virtues guarantee their own performance. A temperate person will always act temperately and will not be swayed by temptation to make exceptions. To have prudence backed by all the other virtues means, then, not only to know what is right but actually to do the right thing, regardless of any difficulties that would have to be overcome. This, according to Simon, is true free choice of which all persons are capable who have achieved self-government. In other words, far from even resembling indetermination, freedom *is* super-determination.

II

The second key to Simon's theory of complementariness of liberty and authority, his concept of the good of society, can also be appreciated best on his own terms. For instance, in a book surveying theories of the public interest, Virginia Held identifies three major historical positions as follows: the "preponderance theories" of Hobbes, Hume, and Bentham; "the public interest as common interest" theory of Rousseau (with variations by Pareto, Arrow, Buchanan, and Tullock, etc.); and the "unitary conception," which she traces from contemporary writers such as C. W.

---

[8] Yves R. Simon, *Philosophy of Democratic Government* (Chicago: The University of Chicago Press, 1951; repr. 1961, 1977), pp. 21–30. There is now a new revised edition with a detailed index and the author's corrections (Notre Dame, Indiana: University of Notre Dame Press, 1993); Yves R. Simon, *A General Theory of Authority* (Notre Dame, Indiana: University of Notre Dame Press, 1961; repr. 1980, 1990), pp. 36–38; Simon, *Tradition of Natural Law*, pp. 154–155; Yves R. Simon, *Work, Society, and Culture*, ed. Vukan Kuic (New York: Fordham University Press, 1971; repr. 1986), pp. 173–174. See also Yves R. Simon, *The Definition of Moral Virtue*, ed. Vukan Kuic (New York: Fordham University Press; 1986; repr. 1989), esp. chap. 5.

Cassinelli and Richard E. Flathman, by way of Marx and Hegel, all the way back to Plato and Aristotle.[9] Held does not mention Simon at all, but whether she knew of him or not makes little difference, for his theory fits none of her categories. Moreover, lumping Marx and Aristotle together, or Plato and Aristotle, on the basis of their conceptions of the common good would never do for Simon.

According to Simon, besides the notorious "greatest good of the greatest number," there are two other historically significant interpretations of the good of society which he denounces as counterfeits. In one, the good of society is conceived after the pattern of a work of art and is represented as something external to its members. In the other, the good of society is represented as a mere means to the good of individuals. A popular example of the first of these views would be the pyramids of Egypt, but far more insidious instances are found in the theories of the transcendent state from Plato to Hegel. In this model, the state is conceived as a kind of masterwork of art, and because there is special satisfaction in handling its "material," that is, beings endowed with intelligence and freedom, both men of action and political thinkers are attracted to it. "Just as the most modest teachers of history derive a sense of exaltation from a secret identification with heroes whose prowess they narrate to school boys," Simon remarks, "so political thinkers derive enthusiasm from identification with the molders of cities and states."[10] What we have to recognize is that the good of the city so conceived is exclusively its own good which not only permits but requires that the lives, liberties, and the pursuit of happiness of its members be sacrificed to it. Indeed, with all the qualifications that would have to be added, Plato's *Republic* may be said to be the original example of such a false common good and Machiavelli's *Prince* its best-known modern version.

But misunderstandings of the nature of the good of society spring also from sincere preoccupation with the good of the individual and justifiable suspicions with regard to the morality of politicians. Reacting against the unitary, transcendent, or "artis-

---

[9] Virginia Held, *The Public Interest and Individual Interests* (New York: Basic Books, 1970).
[10] Simon, *Tradition of Natural Law*, p. 93.

tic" conceptions of the state, some thinkers go to the other extreme and deny that the so-called common good can ever be anything more than a means to the good of the individual. A very clear statement of this position is supplied by Friedrich A. Hayek, who, addressing the question of whether government should use its power of taxation to finance such services as the care of the disabled and the provision of roads, writes:

> It is not to be expected that there will ever be complete unanimity on the desirability of the extent of such services, and it is at least not obvious that coercing people to contribute to the achievement of ends in which they are not interested can be morally justified. Up to a point, most of us find it expedient, however, to make such a contribution on the understanding that we will in turn profit from similar contributions of others toward the realization of our own ends.[11]

Lest Hayek's position be confused with a particular political ideology, it should be pointed out that such nominalist denial of the *reality* of the common good is entertained also by some thinkers at the opposite side of the political spectrum. Harold Laski, for instance, once put it this way: "The surrender we make is a surrender not for the rights of *society* regarded as something other than its members but *exactly and precisely* for men and women whose totality is conveniently summarized in a *collective and abstract noun*."[12] Also, as Christian Bay from still another political position would have it, "man himself is the only end," and "maximization of every man's and woman's freedom—psychological, social, and potential—is the only proper first-priority aim for the joint human effort that we call political."[13]

---

[11] Friedrich A. Hayek, *The Constitution of Liberty* (Chicago: The University of Chicago Press, 1960), p. 144. Hayek is also one of those who cannot distinguish lawful authority from coercion. See ibid., p. 37: "True coercion occurs when armed bands of conquerors make the subject people toil for them, when organized gangsters extort a levy for 'protection,' when the knower of an evil secret blackmails his victim, and, of course, when the state threatens to inflict punishment and to employ physical force to make us obey its commands."

[12] Harold Laski, *Liberty in the Modern State* (New York: The Viking Press, 1949), p. 39 (emphasis added); quoted in *Tradition of Natural Law*, p. 106, where Simon remarks that "the nominalistic mind is as unable to grasp the reality of a community as it is unable to grasp the meaning of a universal nature."

[13] Christian Bay, *The Structure of Freedom* (Stanford, California: Stanford University Press, 1958), p. 390.

The main reason why some political writers risk statements so contrary to what has to be granted if liberty and democracy are to make any sense is obviously their concern for the freedom and well-being of the individual. They do not want real people absorbed into an "abstract" society or crushed and pushed around by an equally impersonal state. But while this is an understandable motive, it is by no means clear that making the individual an end unto himself is the answer to the problem. Certainly, offering society itself as a means will not do, especially if that "society" is nothing but other men and women who compose it. Thus, while this notion of the good of society as a means for the good of the individual may save appearances, so to speak, it also suggests a kind of Ptolemaic perversion of political experience.

Still, the fault with modern individualism may not be so much its streak of egoistic hedonism as its misreading of human needs. True, we need others to survive, and we use others as they use us for our own ends. But we also need our fellow human beings gathered in society in order to become what is in us to be, and that ultimately means giving to others, not taking from them. The philosophy of individualism grossly underestimates what Simon calls our other-centered needs. For instance, what other use is there for love, strength of character, wisdom, or any other real and lasting human accomplishment, except to give of it freely? Indeed, as Simon specifically notes, "when the tendency to act generously is frustrated, it becomes the most redoubtable of antisocial drives, for people would rather stand physical destitution than be denied opportunity for disinterested love and sacrifice."[14] Everybody has been talking about alienation for quite some time now. However, rather than any of the ordinary deprivations suffered by everyone at one time or another, its deeper cause may well be the lack or restrictions of opportunity to contribute to society.[15]

## III

To represent the good of society as a mere means to the good of the individual, then, is as wrong as to represent it as a work of art,

---

[14] Simon, *General Theory of Authority*, p. 26.
[15] Simon, *Work, Society, and Culture*, pp. 83–86.

i.e., a thing external to its individual members. The nature of society, as Aristotle said, is indeed to be a plurality. That does not mean that the political community does not exist as a unit, has no life or meaning as a whole, and that it must ultimately be subordinated to its parts. The political association is a real whole without which its parts, its members, would not be what they are. Consider that even the greatest man or woman, besides living but a short time, can excel at best in two or three fields of endeavor out of an indefinite number of accomplishments required by society to produce what we call civilization and culture. Without society there would be no "common heritage of mankind," no science, no mathematics, no art, no morality, and probably no mankind. That is why, contrary to all the theories that want to deny it, the common good of society is greater than any individual good. Realistically and honestly, we need to recognize that, as Simon puts it, "beyond the satisfaction of individual needs the association of men serves a good unique in plenitude and duration, the common good of the human community."[16] It is precisely when we thus recognize the political community as a real, rational, and moral being with an autonomous good and purpose of its own that we are able to see, again with Aristotle, that this community must be a community of the free. The self-government of its members is not only a part of the common good of the political association; it is also an essential precondition for its attainment. Translated into an "operational" statement, this mutual relation between people's individual freedoms and their common good as members of the political association may be rendered in a simple formula as follows: "Autonomy makes authority necessary and authority makes autonomy possible."[17]

Beyond its "negative" conception, in which liberty is *defined* as absence of authority (usually confused with coercion), the opinion that sets liberty and authority in opposition to each other needs to be traced to a more general "deficiency theory of government." This theory, according to Simon, holds that authority's one and only function is to deal with what is, can go, or goes wrong.[18] The most famous example of "the deficiency theory of

---

[16] Simon, *General Theory of Authority*, p. 29.
[17] Simon, *Philosophy of Democratic Government*, p. 71.
[18] No contributor either to *Authority: Nomos* I, ed. Carl J. Friedrich (Cambridge, Mass.: Harvard University Press, 1958; repr. Westport, Conn.: Green-

government," is, of course, the Marxist doctrine of the withering away of the state, which stipulates that when the class struggle comes to an end, the government of persons will be replaced by the administration of things, and political authority and coercion will be things of the past.[19] Interesting variants expressed in equally pithy language can be found in the celebrated *Federalist Number 51*, where Madison declares that "if men were angels, no government would be necessary,"[20] and in Thomas Paine's statement that "society is produced by our wants and government by our wickedness."[21] One must not, however, confuse the deficiency theory of government with Marxism or with the liberal position describing government as a necessary evil. Fascists, for instance, would never admit that the state could be evil; on the contrary, they exalt it as the greatest good. Yet, their main reason for wanting the strongest possible political authority is also represented by a deficiency, namely, the conviction not only that men are not angels but also that they are not created equal either. What the proponents of the deficiency theory of government typically fail to consider is the possibility that political authority may have more than one legitimate function. They blame it all, so to speak, on what is wrong with human nature or society, which coincides nicely with their tendency to identify authority with coercion and thus keep it in irreconcilable opposition to liberty (except in the totalitarian variants where the two are made one by definition). But what if political authority had in fact several functions? Would that not introduce the possibility that "to govern" does not have always to mean "to coerce," and that in some of these functions authority and liberty might actually be complementary? Practically alone among contemporary writers to ask such questions about authority, Simon, by answering them in the affirmative, provides us also with some very sound arguments in defense of liberty.

---

wood Press, 1982), or to the symposium on "The Crisis of Authority," *The Southern Journal of Philosophy*, 7, Nos. 2–3 (Summer and Fall 1970), makes any use of the concept of "deficiency theory."

[19] Friedrich Engels, "Socialism: Utopian and Scientific," in *Marx and Engels: Basic Writings on Politics and Philosophy*, ed. Lewis S. Feuer (Garden City, New York: Doubleday, 1959), p. 106.

[20] *The Federalist* (New York: Modern Library, 1950), p. 337.

[21] *Common Sense*, in *The Writings of Thomas Paine* I (New York: G. P. Putnam's Sons, 1894), p. 69; quoted in Simon, *Philosophy of Democratic Government*, p. 4.

As was his wont, Simon begins with a simple example which commands general assent. Political authority may be a controversial subject, but everyone is more or less agreed on the meaning of parental authority. Before they can take care of themselves, children must be ruled and guided by their parents for their own good. Their own powers being underdeveloped and inadequate, children depend on the experience, the reason, and the will of their parents, often enough for their physical survival as well as personal development. The acknowledged characteristics of parental authority, then, are that while it aims at the good of the governed, it is by its very nature substitutional and pedagogical. No matter how hard it may be to evaluate actual cases, we all agree that when parents use their children for their own ends they are abusing their authority, which also happens when parents fail to teach children self-government.[22]

Now, political government, too, has a "parental" function: straightening things out, keeping them from getting worse, punishing law-breakers, etc. The question is whether all political government is of this sort, namely, basically substitutional. The deficiency theory of government assumes so, which leaves it no choice but to exclude the need for political authority from an ideal human condition. But is it really true that if men were angels government would not be necessary?

To find out, Simon proposes a model of a perfect self-governing community. This community is perfect because we assume that all its members are both intelligent and well-intentioned; there is among them neither ignorance nor ill-will to cause authority to step in. Moreover, being self-governing, this model avoids confusing the problem of authority pure and simple with the related but distinct problem of governing personnel. What Simon wants to know is how political decisions are made in such a community, and he finds its choice rather simple. This perfect community can arrive at its decisions either by unanimity or by authority; there is no third way. Either all members agree on what should be done, or some must accept the others' decision. For instance, shall they drive on the right side of the road or on the left side? It may not matter which, but if they are not unanimous,

---

[22] Simon, *Philosophy of Democratic Government*, pp. 7–19; Simon, *General Theory of Authority*, pp. 133–134.

they have to settle it by way of authority. This will be the case even if only a single person wants it the other way or if they all decide to flip a coin. All decisions pertaining to common action must be decided either by unanimity or by authority.[23]

So introduced, our inquiry into essential functions of political authority moves now to estimating the chances of a perfect community's arriving at decisions by unanimity rather than by authority. Would men if they were angels tend to be unanimous on what to do as a group? Simon's complete answer comes in two parts. On the one hand, if the action to be decided upon by this "angelic" community is uniquely determined, all members should indeed know exactly what must be done. In such a case, any difference of opinion or reluctance to go along would be a sign either of a failure to understand what is at stake or of a failure of the will to act, both of which are excluded from the model by definition. But if, on the other hand, the action to be decided upon by this ideal community is not uniquely determined and there is an actual choice of courses open to them, no amount of intelligence or degree of civic virtue can ever guarantee that they will be unanimous. In this case, even the perfect members of an ideal community must let authority decide exactly which course of action to take. Faced with a choice of means, in other words, even angels would have to resort to authority.

Simon's final argument nicely illustrates the thoroughness of his approach. Unanimity being logically impossible in the face of an actual choice of several equally suitable courses, the question of whether common action calls for authority becomes now a question of whether the assumed conditions, i.e., absence of deficiencies, would allow for a genuine plurality and equality of these courses. Suppose we had a choice among, say, $a$, $b$, $c$, and $d$. With more information about these options, should it not be possible ultimately to pick one that is demonstrably the best? Modern social science appears to aspire eventually to be able to provide such demonstrable solutions on the pattern of the modern natural sciences. But as social science is far away from fulfilling this aspiration, one may perhaps still wonder why exactly should improved knowledge of human behavior and social processes be expected

---

[23] Simon, *Philosophy of Democratic Government*, pp. 19–35; *General Theory of Authority*, pp. 47–50.

to reduce all policy options, in all cases, to a single, demonstrably best solution? For all we know, in the human world, as contrasted with natural processes, things can be otherwise than they are, and it has never been proven that the principle of causality that helps us understand nature also explains everything about society.[24] Thus, it is not at all obvious that progress in the science of society must point "beyond freedom." Indeed, taking notice of "the theory, so common among social scientists, that if social science were complete and ignorance totally routed, liberty would disappear together with our hesitancies, our trials and errors, and our arbitrariness," Simon speculates that there must be "more than one social scientist, having remained intuitively, emotionally, and morally dedicated to liberty," who wish at the bottom of their hearts "that social science should always be so imperfect as to leave plenty of room for trials and errors and for the arbitrariness of individual preference."[25] Behold the truth that sets the social scientist free from philosophical and methodological bondage to natural science.

As an example of real choice among equally suitable courses of action, Simon invites us to consider the case of a family planning a vacation.[26] If they are poor, ignorant of places to go, and in bad health to boot, their choice is clearly limited, if indeed they have a choice. Under these circumstances, they would probably have to stay at home or, at best, impose on some relatives living in the country nearby. If the family is rich, in excellent health, and familiar with all the nicest vacation spots in the whole world, their choices become practically infinite. At the same time, of course, there is also far less chance that this family will be unanimous on where to go and, consequently, if they are to go there together, the decision will have to be reached by resort to authority, be that of the father, mother, majority vote, or drawing straws.

It is the same situation at other levels of social experience. All other things being equal, a rich, educated, technically advanced nation has more options in regard to any number of policies than a poor, backward, primitive, so-called developing nation. Indeed,

---

[24] See John Searle, *The Construction of Social Reality* (New York: The Free Press, 1995), for a provocative discussion and distinction between social and natural processes and the understanding of them.

[25] Simon, *Freedom of Choice*, pp. 157–158.

[26] Simon, *Philosophy of Democratic Government*, p. 31.

it may be stated as a general law that such things as destitution, ill health, weakness, uncertainty, ignorance—in a word, any deficiency—contribute directly to restrict choice and cause dependence on determined means, while such things as abundance, good health, assurance, achievement, knowledge—including social sciences—are by contrast factors that clearly contribute to the widening of our choices. Simon puts it this way:

> [A] society enjoying a supremely high degree of enlightenment would, all other things being equal, enjoy much more choice than ignorant societies and have to choose among many more possibilities. It would not need authority to choose between two courses of action, one of which is bound to lead to disaster, since by hypothesis, knowledge would rule out illusory means. But it would need authority, more than ever, to procure united action, for, thanks to better lights, the plurality of the genuine means would have increased considerably. The function of authority with which we are concerned, i.e., that of procuring united action when the means to the common good are several does not disappear but grows, as deficiencies are made up; it originates not in the defects of men and societies, but in the nature of society. It is an essential function.[27]

What we need perhaps to add here is that the only way to set liberty in opposition to this kind of authority would be to define freedom as having one's way at all costs at all times without ever giving anyone, including oneself, any reasons for one's behavior. If we think of political liberty as self-government as well as free participation in the government of the community, we have an entirely different situation. The choosing by political authority, by government, among several equally suitable courses of common action becomes then a process that, far from checking anyone's freedom, necessarily complements the liberty of all. From this point of view, acceptance of the policy chosen to promote the common good, rather than an act of submission, becomes an act of free choice and an opportunity to participate in that promotion. Indeed, what about the principle of the consent of the governed? In a regime where the government need not ask for it, there is no problem. However, if the political system is said to rest on the consent of the governed, authority obviously must

---
[27] Ibid., p. 33.

complement liberty, because ultimately there is no way of giving consent except freely. So, if there is no such thing as genuine consent, there can be no such thing as free government, and with the illusion of freedom we should by all means give up dignity too.[28] For the supreme test of the complementariness of liberty and authority, however, we must go beyond common action, which is a mere means to it, and confront squarely a question pertaining directly to the very end of society, that is, its common good. What are the respective functions of liberty and authority in the willing or intention of that end? What exactly does each contribute to its realization? If they are shown to need each other, are there any limits to their complementariness?

That liberty needs authority is, despite various qualifications, a proposition commonly accepted by most political theorists and conveyed by such familiar expressions as "ordered liberty" or "liberty under law." What may be said to be among Simon's original contributions is not just his showing the obverse—namely, that authority needs liberty too—but proving it precisely in relation to the end or purpose of the political community, which makes them both "most essential" to it. Again, only a few would want to deny that practically speaking, in the real world, political authority is needed both to make sure that public business is taken care of and to ensure protection of individual liberties. But what Simon has worked out is a theoretical proof that this holds true especially under ideal conditions from which all deficiencies have been removed and in which alone *both* liberty *and* authority can come fully into their own. Considering that the question of how much power government really needs in modern society has of late been competing on theoretical grounds with the question of how much individual liberty a viable democratic society can really afford, this seems a most welcome clarification indeed.

---

[28] Criticizing B. F. Skinner's *Beyond Freedom and Dignity* (New York: Alfred A. Knopf, 1971), Arnold Toynbee exposes the general fallacy of the attempts to turn social science into a natural science as follows: "A technology of human behavior would be practicable only if it were true that behavior is wholly determined by heredity and environment and if it were also true that techniques could be devised for manipulating human beings' genetic endowment and their social setting. But if human freedom is truly an illusion, no human being would be free to plan and carry out the requisite biological and social 'engineering.' The blind cannot lead the blind" (*Center Magazine* [Santa Barbara, California] [March–April 1972], 62).

To take Simon's example that most closely approximates the model of a perfect self-governing community, in which the essence of authority is obscured neither by substitutional functions related to deficiencies nor by the problem of distinct governing personnel (and in which unity in diversity as a requirement of the common good is perhaps most easily grasped), let us imagine a small college with a faculty who double as the governing board of the institution. The faculty is composed of an English teacher, a Latin teacher, a philosophy teacher, a history teacher, and a mathematics teacher, all of whom are decent people, quite competent in their respective fields and exceptionally dedicated to their school. As such, they are all naturally strong individuals, but there is a particularly pronounced difference in the attitudes of the Latin teacher and of the teacher of mathematics. The latter is a person of great skills and a reputation for objectivity which he enjoys. At faculty meetings, it is usually he who mediates between opposing views, while seldom saying anything that could be interpreted as if he were partial to mathematics. By contrast, of the Latin teacher they say that if he had his way, he would convert every youngster into a Latin scholar, regardless of how ignorant his students might remain in mathematics, modern languages, and even Greek. The Latin teacher is the campus character, the subject of many jokes, and often a somewhat disrupting influence at faculty meetings. Indeed, at times one is tempted to call into question the genuineness of his dedication to the school's overall good. But that, according to Simon, could be a mistake. Among the motives for this man's behavior, a keen sense of service to society is not the least plausible. This old scholar's passionate attachment to his subject need not mean necessarily that he overdoes the importance of classics and ignores that of mathematics. As Simon sees it, his attitude could also mean a passionate attachment to the overall good not just of the school but also of the society at large, which, all other things being equal, would be a better society if a only a few people in it knew Vergil than if Vergil were entirely unknown. Society is well served by such individuals.[29]

Generalizing from this and other examples, and with the help of an important distinction between "formal" and "material" in-

---

[29] Simon, *Philosophy of Democratic Government*, pp. 45–46.

tention of the common good, Simon carefully pulls together the final arguments for the complementariness of liberty and authority as follows. Citizenship in a free society includes willingness to subordinate one's own private interest to the good of society (e.g., loyal faculty members put the interest of their school first). The common good of society may be intended formally without being intended materially (e.g., school loyalty is not the same as commitment to a specific curriculum). Loyal citizenship guarantees the intention of the common good formally considered, not the intention of the common good materially considered (e.g., there is nothing wrong with the Latin teacher's institutional loyalty despite his strong advocacy of his subject). The intention of the good of society materially as well as formally considered is the business of public reason and public will (e.g., the specific curriculum is decided by the whole faculty acting as the governing board of the school). Finally and decisively, the common good of society would actually be harmed if everyone were to be preoccupied with it not only formally but also materially; in a material sense, particular persons ought to tend to particular goods precisely because the excellence of particular goods is an essential part of the common good (e.g., the school cannot afford too many members like the mathematics teacher, minding the public business more than their own, for then the instruction in individual subjects would inevitably receive reduced attention at the expense of the students' overall education).[30]

Now, most people would probably agree that this kind of division of labor, as it were, between government and private citizens is desirable as well as logical and realistic. But what the reader needs to be reminded of is that the model upon which Simon shows these qualities to be so is an ideal model free from all deficiencies and capable, therefore, of revealing the innermost, essential, irreducible connection between political authority and political liberty. There is not, nor can there ever be, such a thing as literally totalitarian government. Everyone knows full well that there is no such thing as absolute freedom. Out of these more or less self-evident truths, political theorists have been extracting compromises variously favoring one or the other, but seldom renouncing the underlying belief that by their very natures, so to

---

[30] Ibid., p. 48.

speak, authority and liberty are opposed to each other. What Simon manages to show is that while the conflict between liberty and authority is indeed unavoidable in practice, political authority as such and political liberty as such rather than canceling each other need each other to grow and develop properly. The problem is that being so contrary to the received opinions, his proofs require some effort to be recognized. They appear to be paradoxical, in the sense that while saying that liberty and authority are complementary appears contrary to experience and common sense, the statement can be shown to be true. In fact, Simon's is but a version of the basic assumption of classical political theory which defines man as a rational *and* political animal. Where Simon departs from the classics, however, is in his use of that definition to defend democracy as the best regime. Thus, Mortimer J. Adler puts it rather well when, praising Simon's stand on liberty, he writes, "we can see here that the existence of political liberty is indispensable to a government's having an essential, and not merely a substitutional, authority; for essential authority inheres only in the laws or institutions of a self-governing people."[31]

### IV

The point that remains still to be clarified is why Simon is vaguely suspected of being on the side of authority. His general theory of government shows that especially under ideal conditions free of deficiencies the good of the political association requires the closest cooperation between authority and liberty, and thus he has no trouble envisaging an expansion of authority accompanied by a simultaneous expansion of liberty. But when he asserts this by saying that "the more definitely a community is directed toward its common good and protected from disunity in its common action, the more perfect and more free it is,"[32] some take this statement as favoring authority. In part, the blame for giving such an impression can be traced to Simon's condensed style. But there is another reason for such misreading of Simon's contribution, which illustrates with particular clarity Hannah Arendt's com-

---

[31] Adler, *Idea of Freedom*, v. I, p. 345.
[32] Simon, *Philosophy of Democratic Government*, p. 141.

plaint that the reason we no longer understand the idea of freedom is that we no longer understand the meaning of authority.[33] It is a complaint that illuminates also the apparently deepening confusion in the debates about the theoretical as well as political intentions of the American Founders. Is the Constitution itself a charter of liberty, or do we depend for the protection of our rights more specifically on the Bill of Rights? Though Simon cites the American Founders only occasionally, his counsel for political practice is not much different from the constitutional theory of *The Federalist*. Thus, he is particularly concerned with how to protect both liberty and authority in a democracy, where political conflict between them is the hardest to manage. He writes:

> The illusion of the democratic transformation of the state is completely dissipated when it is understood that, in order to save society from state absolutism it is not enough to incorporate into the structure of the state a system of checks, balances, and constitutional guarantees. Not even the ultimate check constituted by the control of the people over the governing personnel suffices; this control may not be genuine and it may also become the accomplice of state absolutism, for the passions which make for absolutism may get hold of the people itself, even though to its disadvantage. In democracy as well as in nondemocratic polities, the absolutism of the state must be held in check by forces external to the state apparatus. This does not mean that the guarantees procured by democratic forms are held ineffective or unimportant; they are important but would soon disappear if they were not supplemented by external institutions.[34]

While there is little that is original in Simon's view about these external institutions needed to safeguard liberty, especially in a democratic state, his demand for them in a sense supplements his "federalist" theory with the antifederalists' insistence on a Bill of Rights. Simon's list of rights includes freedom of religion, of speech, and of the press; it includes the private school, the independent labor union, the autonomous cooperative, and, finally, private property. He does not expect these institutions to work without a high ratio of failure, but he does not allow that because "freedom of the press may easily produce public immorality, slan-

---

[33] See "What Was Authority?" in Friedrich's *Authority*, p. 81.
[34] Simon, *Philosophy of Democratic Government*, pp 136–137.

der, hateful strife, skepticism, the dissolution of the community spirit," freedom of the press should be abolished. Likewise, even though independent action by labor unions may on occasion endanger national economy, national defense, and public health, if the right to strike is abolished, liberty, for Simon, "is gone and death is coming."[35]

A more affirmative position in defense of constitutional liberties seems hardly possible, and one wonders again how Simon's critics ever got the idea that his political theory contains an "excessively restricted notion of freedom." Simon conceives of freedom as super-determination, self-government, and free choice, and makes the most essential function of authority, that is, the intention of the common good, ultimately depend on full exercise of individual liberties. He insists on an absolute right to strike and calls liberty "a divine name." Yet, some readers remain unconvinced. Why? Because most of us not only harbor deep-seated suspicion of all authority but also are accustomed to think of freedom as indetermination. The subtle tenacity of these common prejudices is poignantly revealed in an otherwise favorable review of Simon's *Freedom and Community* by Thomas A. Spragens, Jr., who reproaches Simon for failing fully "to assimilate the deep epistemological humility in the realm of moral knowledge that is so basic to the rationale of constitutional democracy."[36] Surely, the question of whether "epistemological humility" actually supports constitutional democracy cannot be considered closed to debate. And if the question remains open, Simon's unconventional approach may well provide a needed counterweight to mere repetition of received opinions. Among political philosophers of our time, Yves R. Simon stands out as a distinguished defender of liberty. He is such not the least because he never faltered in his conviction that "all our real freedom is contained within the limits of our knowledge of truth."[37] His success in producing also a very good theory of authority need not be traced any further.

---

[35] Ibid., p. 139.

[36] Thomas A. Sprangens, Jr., *The American Political Science Review*, 62, No. 2 (June 1969), 561–562.

[37] Yves R. Simon, *Freedom and Community*, ed. Charles P. O'Donnell (New York: Fordham University Press, 1968), p. 4.

# 6
# Practical Wisdom in the Thought of Yves R. Simon

*Robert J. Mulvaney*

YVES R. SIMON (1903–1961) was one of the greatest modern students of the ancient virtue of practical wisdom, called φρόνησις by Aristotle and *prudentia* by his commentators in the Middle Ages, such as Thomas Aquinas. Simon's interest in this issue was both theoretical and practical. He was concerned with the role of practical wisdom in resolving major moral problems, particularly in social and political philosophy, such as the problem of freedom and authority in a democracy. He was also concerned with profound foundational problems underlying virtue, particularly those in moral epistemology. Simon recognized that the seventeenth century's epistemological revolution had given some of these questions radically new directions. The reconstruction of knowledge we associate with figures like Descartes had momentous repercussions, not only in the foundations of mathematics and natural science, but in moral and political philosophy, in the psychology of the human act, and in basic metaphysical positions as well. Modern ideals of a unified science, the triumph of the deductive method, and the mechanical interpretation of nature were involved in this revolution. They constitute some of the elements in a rich concept of "modernity." At least one utterly new chapter came to be written in the history of Western civilization: "The Social Sciences." The concept of practical wisdom tested the power and efficacy of these modern departures, and its epistemological foundations challenged much of the mainstream of modern thought. Simon realized all this with uncommon clarity and introduced a kind of urgency into the re-examination of Aristotle and Aquinas as modern dogma began to bear fruit in twentieth-century social and political experiments.

Simon's interest in these matters is evident from the earliest period of his life and dominates his thought to the last. One of his first books, *Critique de la connaissance morale* (1934), examined the epistemology of ethics.[1] Its table of contents reveals the essential range of Simon's thinking on the central problems of moral knowledge which concerned him throughout his professional life and which found their final form in the posthumous *Practical Knowledge*, published in 1991.[2] Those contents include themes such as "Practical Wisdom," "Understanding, the Disciple of Love," "Moral Philosophy," "Practically Practical Knowledge," "Christian Ethics," and "The Notion of Political Science." These topics constitute the constellation of Simon's perennial concerns and are developed and enriched by the great works of his maturity. Every major writing of Simon's devotes some attention to practical wisdom and its epistemological underpinnings. These are not merely cursory allusions, or embellishments over some perpetual and haunting pedal point. Rather, they throw the central message into bolder and brilliant relief. The most instructive of Simon's major writings in this regard, in addition to the two mentioned above, are his 1940 Aquinas Lecture, published as *Nature and Functions of Authority*, his *Philosophy of Democratic Government*, the posthumous collections *Freedom of Choice*, *A General Theory of Authority*, *The Tradition of Natural Law*, *Freedom and Community*, *Work, Society, and Culture*, and *The Definition of Moral Virtue*.[3]

---

[1] Yves R. Simon, *Critique de la connaissance morale* (Paris: Desclée de Brouwer, 1934). An English translation is being edited for publication.

[2] Yves R. Simon, *Practical Knowledge*, ed. Robert J. Mulvaney (New York: Fordham University Press, 1991).

[3] Yves R. Simon, *Nature and Functions of Authority* (Milwaukee: Marquette University Press, 1940; repr. 1948); *Philosophy of Democratic Government* (Chicago: The University of Chicago Press, 1951; repr. 1961, 1977, 1992; rev. ed. Notre Dame, Indiana: University of Notre Dame Press, 1993); and the posthumous collections *A General Theory of Authority* (Notre Dame, Indiana: University of Notre Dame Press, 1962; rev. 1980; repr. 1990), later editions contain an expanded index and a new introduction by Vukan Kuic; *Freedom of Choice*, ed. Peter Wolff (New York: Fordham University Press, 1969; repr. 1987, 1992); *The Tradition of Natural Law*, ed. Vukan Kuic (New York: Fordham University Press, 1965; repr. 1967; rev. ed. 1992), the revised edition contains a new introduction by Russell Hittinger; *Freedom and Community*, ed. Charles P. O'Donnell (New York: Fordham University Press, 1968); *Work, Society, and Culture*, ed. Vukan Kuic (New York: Fordham University Press, 1971; rev. 1986) and the more recent *The Definition of Moral Virtue*, ed. Vukan Kuic (New York: Fordham University Press, 1986, repr. 1989).

In this essay I present a sketch of the development of Simon's thought on the virtue of practical wisdom and a detailed account of the contents of his major treatment of this issue as found in *Practical Knowledge*. Before I proceed to these principal themes, an account of the nature of practical wisdom in Aristotle and in Thomas Aquinas will be useful. My ambitions at this juncture must be modest. I cannot adequately situate their theories of practical wisdom within a general moral theory, or even within their theories of virtue. I must begin midstream, so to speak, and refer the reader ignorant of Aristotle's ethics or of Thomas Aquinas to more general treatments. I shall begin, therefore, with Aristotle and Aquinas, pass on to Simon's 1934 book and then to the posthumous collections still appearing, and conclude with his 1991 *Practical Knowledge*. Although I cannot hope to approximate either Simon's depth of thought or his rhetorical polish, this introduction may attract the reader to Simon's work itself. An overture is no substitute for the opera, but it should make us want to see the curtain rise.

## Aristotle and Aquinas

Few notions in the history of moral philosophy will be as difficult for the modern reader to understand as the classic doctrine of practical wisdom. It has no name in modern languages. "Prudence" will not do (although I shall occasionally use it in this essay), standing as it does in common usage for self-interested cunning, the polar opposite of a wise regard for the interests of all. In that sense "prudence" is probably a vice, or amoral at best, the pseudo-virtue of self-interest. Practical wisdom in its ancient signification also implies an antithesis to modern illusion about the identity of theoretical and practical knowledge. Since the seventeenth century, knowledge has often been conceived as subject to a uniform methodology whereby the mind operates identically on any object whatsoever, whether it be the sciences, the emotions, society, law—the whole range of theoretical and practical cognitive activity. Aristotle, on the other hand, saw a great gulf fixed between the realm of science and the realm of human action. His epistemology of "formal objects" requires that knowledge be specified in terms of real differences in the world and not some purported identity in the knower. A world divided into the changeless and the changeable demands two irreducible kinds of knowledge, theoretical and practical. Logic, mathematics, the empirical sciences, and theology are part of the unchanging world of theoretical knowledge. The person possessing theoretical understanding in its full depth and range is the "theoretically wise person" (the σόφος), or even the "philosopher." The person with practical understanding and good judgment in personal, domestic, and civic affairs is the "practically wise person" (the φρόνιμος). Within the practical realm Aristotle makes an important distinction between "art" (τέχνη) and practical wisdom. Both are directed to the changing experience in human knowledge, but the arts are specified by a product, something effected in the outside world. Practical wisdom, in contrast, is specified by an action, something realized internally, something done rather than made. Practical wisdom is "right reason in things done," a virtue of good deliberation, judgment, and choice.

This theory has important psychological ramifications. First, the human soul has its theoretical and practical employments as well as the emotional and sensitive life it shares with other animals. When we think practically, both morally and technically, those mental activities are not reducible to a set of formal logical or scientific operations. The syllogism, cornerstone of Aristotle's logic, has no parallel in practical reasoning. It does have an analogous, almost metaphorical structure, in what has come to be called the "practical syllogism." Human decision has three aspects resembling the major premise, the minor, and the conclusion of a well-formed argument. The major premise is the general rule, duty, or principle governing a specific choice, the goal to be attained. The minor premise adds consideration of the means to be employed in realizing the goal or performing the duty involved. The conclusion is the action performed. Practical wisdom is the virtue of human thinking in this process. Unlike the theoretical syllogism, the practical syllogism is marked throughout by change and contingency. The rule might be otherwise, the means to the end might be otherwise, and the action performed might be otherwise. Human action is conditioned by the peculiarities of time and space embedded in the situational circumstances of human life, in the "mystery of matter," one might say. At the same time, practical knowledge corresponds to the formal and intelligible dimension of the action. One may meaningfully call practical wisdom the "hylemorphic" virtue. That does not make ethics in any crucial sense subject to abstractive intelligence. It simply means that human action, despite its intense particularity, is nevertheless ultimately subject to some kind of rational principle, the λόγος spoken of in Aristotle's definition of virtue. But this is the rational principle of the practically wise person, not that of the scientist or philosopher. Metaphysically, as well as psychologically and epistemologically, practical wisdom is radically dissimilar to scientific theoretical understanding. It is a wisdom which is not science.

Thomas Aquinas stood on the shoulders of Aristotle, but his great treatise on practical wisdom (*Summa Theologiae*, II–II, 48–57) shows a student who has surpassed his teacher. All the major points of Aristotle's theory are maintained but deepened, extended, and ramified as perhaps only a saint could have done. I cannot survey the full range of Aquinas's contribution, but a few elements are particularly relevant to Simon's story. The first great "footnote" Aquinas adds to Aristotle's account is his vastly more complicated model of the human act. For Aristotle the "practical syllogism" was a relatively simple affair, consisting of only three distinguishable elements. By Thomas Aquinas's time the doctrine of will, developed by Augustine and others from exigencies deep within the structure of Christian revelation, introduced a far more subtle dimension to the role of appetite in rational life. The role of will is felt no more strongly than in the conclusion of the syllogism, the point at which our deliberations become activated. Aquinas saw as clearly as anyone that the final movement of the mind is choice, not rational judgment, making the will the ultimate determinant of action. This introduces a quite un-Aristotelian dimension into deliberation, since it is possible for the will to move against it for good or ill, even given an optimal degree of deliberative rationality. In fact, Simon dwelt on the surprising feature of the necessity for the will to terminate deliberation in conformity with the movements of settled moral virtue. Deliberation can proceed *ad infinitum*. What prevents us from ignoring the appropriate moment of action in the interest of "completing" our deliberation? The answer can only be a virtuous will acting as a kind of substitution for the potentially endless deliberations dictated by the particularities of human choice.

The insistent role of will in Aquinas's moral psychology makes some elements of practical wisdom more pronounced and more astonishing. Among these we may single out "command" (*imperium*): that moment in the conclusion of the practical syllogism when deliberative rationality issues its order. It may be thought that the imperative function would have been assumed by Aquinas's enriched notion of will. (It might even be thought, as some seventeenth-century Aristotelians had it, that at the moment of action "art" fulfilled the deliberations of practical reason.) But Aquinas insists that at the moment of action itself, practical reason has an imperative function. The command given to the will and suitable to the action about to be performed is a work of reason and "informs" the action as its intelligible element. No one, not even Jacques Maritain, saw this imperative function of practical wisdom more clearly than Simon did. It makes his *Practical Knowledge*, particularly Chapter One, a philosophically thrilling adventure.

Let me point to two applications of this theory of command. One is in Aquinas's theory of law. However indebted Aquinas may have been to Aristotle for some elements of "natural justice," the treatise on law (*Summa Theologiae*, I–II, 90–108) owes its inspiration more to Stoic and Roman legal sources than to Greek thought. In the Stoic tradition in particular, the rational dimension of law dominates. Aquinas is heir to this anti-voluntaristic conception of law and repeatedly stresses its ultimate rationality. "Command" is shared by law and practical wisdom and constitutes the conceptual justification for a theory of continuity between law and the final deliberative act. I shall instance again and again the fruitfulness of this link in Simon's work. Law for him is a work of deliberative rationality, and themes of practical understanding are relevant everywhere. A second consideration revolves around the social and political dimension of practical wisdom. Unlike "prudence," practical wisdom for Thomas Aquinas is a public as well as a private virtue. It commands individual choice, but it also commands the choices of social groups. It therefore suffuses institutional structures, families, local, national, and international governments. Given a theory of the interconnection of the virtues, it forms the intelligible element in the public role of the moral virtues including justice, courage, and temperance. Simon's preoccupation with political philosophy brings with it a continuous consideration of the role of practical wisdom in conceptions of authority and political decision-making.

Finally, Aquinas's perception of the contingency of moral action is no less intense than Aristotle's—more so, in fact, given a theology of the radical dependence of all things upon God's creative act. The Book of Wisdom says, "uncertain are our foresights," and Aquinas recognizes that the deliberative reason has throughout, and certainly at the moment of action, potential for catastrophic miscalculation. The practically wise person at the moment of action needs "solicitude," a kind of healthy anxiety over the future, in order to issue commands at the right time and in the right place. But, here again, the well-ordered will can "substitute" for the limitations of reason and make appropriate "use" of the materials of action, fulfilling the demands of moral law where full understanding is kept from us.

## The Development of Simon's Thought

The development of Simon's thinking on practical knowledge, from his early *Critique de la connaissance morale* to the posthumous collections now in print, shows a striking and pronounced continuity. Many of the mature themes and positions are found in his earliest works. His mature works contain important differences of detail, and in marginal notes to his own copy of the *Critique*, Simon alludes to confusions in the earlier work. But the basic doctrine is changed in few important points. The essential difference between theoretical and practical knowledge is affirmed right from the beginning as consisting in the qualification of the latter by the twin and complementary notions of finality and the primacy of judgment.[4] The essential centrality of the final cause provides the necessary movement in matters of practice, and the anteriority of judgment over concept marks the specific object

---

[4] Simon, *Critique de la connaissance morale*, p. 11.

of practical knowledge as such.[5] This teleological and existential orientation of Simon's early text entails further profound differences between theoretical and practical knowledge. Practical knowledge, for one thing, is embedded in the concrete and singular.[6] In Aristotelian terms, the singularity of such judgments (not their imperative character) puts great constraints on their intelligibility. For Aristotle, only the universal is properly an object of science, because only the universal is constituted by formally abstract concepts or ideas. The objects of ethics, on the other hand, are contingent, concrete, and singular. The problem is only apparent, however, since the ultimate goal of moral knowledge is not simply knowledge for its own sake but knowledge conjoined with action, that is to say, knowledge that directs virtuous actions.[7] This direction suggests a motion toward the concrete and relieves the persistent cognitive impenetrability of singular actions.

This brings with it another essential element of Simon's theory: the union of practical understanding with a well-ordered will which ensures the proper perfection of both the act performed and the moral judgment made.[8] This is sufficient to produce the certitude necessary to perform virtuous actions, or to fulfill moral judgments in action. This does not deny a proper intelligibility to some items in ethics. There is such a thing as moral science, a kind of knowledge which concerns moral essences and universals.[9] However, this simply heightens the radical differences between ultimately practical judgments and those more or less remote from the business of acting itself. Only the prudential judgment makes contact with the utterly singular, the point of contact between all more or less theoretical judgments about ethics and the moment when action begins.[10] Simon frequently uses the terms introduced by Maritain, "speculatively practical knowledge" and "practically practical knowledge." Maritain maintained this distinction because of a lack of clarity on the nature of moral knowledge in both Thomas Aquinas and John of St. Thomas.

---

[5] Ibid. p. 13.
[6] Ibid. p. 21.
[7] Ibid. p. 31.
[8] Ibid. p. 39.
[9] Ibid. p. 53.
[10] Ibid. p. 54.

This distinction in itself is a subtle one for many, but Simon's concern is even more particularized: the specification of the ultimate practical judgment in its relationship to "practically practical knowledge." As we shall see in Chapter Three of *Practical Knowledge*, Simon continued to view this late in his life as an extremely important issue in moral epistemology, one which served, among other things, to specify the judgments of the practically wise person as distinct from all forms of social science.

Although Simon established the principles of his theory of practical knowledge in his early *Critique*, their rich employment in his social and political philosophy remained for his mature works. Many books for which Simon is justly renowned, such as *Nature and Functions of Authority, Philosophy of Democratic Government*, and *A General Theory of Authority*, are not fully intelligible without analysis of his more foundational position on practical knowledge. In his 1940 Aquinas Lecture, *Nature and Functions of Authority* (his first book written in English), the virtue of practical wisdom appears almost instantly in its political dimension and in its proper directive role. Any resolution of the apparent antinomy of liberty and authority, Simon insists, must be offered by the practically wise person, because issues of liberty and authority are inextricably embedded in concrete action. This theme has the quality of a keynote and is often strikingly repeated. An investigation into the philosophical foundations of the problem of authority "in no way overlooks the indispensability of the prudential inquiry."[11] "No ethical science, no casuistry will teach the head and the subject what they must do, in reference to singular circumstances, to maintain the just relationship between authority and liberty."[12] The link between practical wisdom and authority is a definitional one: "Authority is an active power, residing in a person and exercised through a command that is through a practical judgment to be taken as a rule of conduct by the free-will of another person."[13] The language of practical knowledge suffuses this definition and serves as a warning to those who might entertain *a priori* and authoritarian interpretations of authority. Since authoritative pronouncements are sufficient to guide conduct, we

---

[11] Simon, *Nature and Functions of Authority*, p. 4.
[12] Ibid.
[13] Ibid., p. 6.

must remind ourselves again and again that such judgments are "inevitably obscure."[14] "Command," analytically contained within the concept of authority and an integral element of the virtue of practical wisdom, is to be contrasted with all forms of coercion and persuasion. These are mere "instruments of authority" not to be "identified with authority as such."[15]

Simon makes greatest use of the theory of practical wisdom within the context of his distinction between substitutional and essential functions of authority. Authority has an essential function in public life, because the unity of action demanded in society is incapable of a thorough theoretical analysis. Practical knowledge, embedded in an infinitely complex set of circumstances, and requiring action as its end, not knowledge alone, is incapable of the kind of "intersubjectivable" certainty scientific knowledge possesses. A shift of focus in the theory of conformity of a mind and its object leads from a focus on the thing or reality in the world to the good will. All knowledge has truth as its end, but the measure or standard of truth in practical judgment is, not reality as it is, but the will as it ought to be. One can speak of true practical judgments when they are in conformity with a well-ordered will. In spite of the contingency of action and the infinitely complex demands made upon choice, we can speak of "a steady principle of indefectible truth" analogous to, but not reducible to, scientific canons of truth and certainty.[16] The theoretical elements in knowledge within the practical order remain merely probable, but the practical elements can be true and certain "as a rule of direction."[17] The possibility of mutually exclusive (not to say contradictory) prudential judgments, each of which enjoys practical truth, requires that members of the community agree upon one of these judgments as the rule of action. For this to occur authority is necessary.

Simon's theory of authority rests firmly upon his theory of practical knowledge. Characteristics of practical deliberation (not "defects") make authority necessary in a social group. In fact, although Simon will make this point only later, authority is one

---

[14] Ibid., p. 4.
[15] Ibid., p. 8.
[16] Ibid., p. 25.
[17] Ibid.

feature of the ultimate practical judgment in its social or political role. Authorities make commands, but they do so with the virtue of appropriate wisdom, that is, practical wisdom, not because of some special ability to deduce practical truth or because questions of action are amenable only to acts of will. Simon's theory of authority is compatible with autonomy and wisdom among subjects, as well as within the head, and unifies the separate acts of moral judgment appropriate to societal elements, families, local governments, nations, etc. Simon's position has characteristic ramifications in practice, not just in political theory.

Simon's *Philosophy of Democratic Government*, published in 1951, amplifies and gives more felicitous expression to many themes of his Aquinas lecture. The term "affective knowledge" is introduced[18] to express the continuity between practical judgment and dispositions of the will. This alone can bridge "the gap that no argumentation can bridge."[19] The morally good person cannot even express clear reasons for coming to this or that ethical decision. "Unlike scientific judgment, practical judgment, for the very reason that it is ultimately determined by the obscure forces of the appetite, does not admit of rational communication. It is, as it were, a secret."[20] The contingencies involved are wrapped in the "unique implications of human history."[21] The unique determination of actions to be done can therefore be found in no science and in no "expertness."[22] Virtuous inclinations of the will, interconnected with the deliberations and commands of practical wisdom, can alone be decisive.

The relationship between will and practical understanding is one of Simon's central topics in his *Traité du libre arbitre*, which appeared the same year as *Philosophy of Democratic Government* (although a partial English translation, *Freedom of Choice*, was not published until 1969). Simon makes the central point that the practical understanding and the will have a relationship of formal as well as final causality. "The practical judgment causes the act of the will not only by proposing an end for it but also by consti-

---

[18] Simon, *Philosophy of Democratic Government*, p. 23.
[19] Ibid., p. 24.
[20] Ibid.
[21] Ibid., p. 27.
[22] Ibid., p. 279.

tuting its form."[23] It is an act of knowledge that makes a given choice a choice of such and such a kind. It *specifies* it. Appetite can be rational not only because it is guided by reason, but also because reason functions metaphysically as an element of the choice itself. Nowhere is this relationship more significant than in the act of command, since command offers the formal principle in the ultimate act of choice, the actual deed performed.

At the same time one must not grant efficacy to pure and simple acts of knowledge. The formal cause moves nothing, although it renders what is moved intelligible. The will is the motive power toward some good, and therefore the will "brings it about that a certain practical judgment terminates the deliberation and constitutes the decision."[24] Deliberation of itself can proceed *ad infinitum*, since the conditions in which action takes place are necessarily infinitely complex. How, then, can a deliberative process be terminated? One might argue that only the external and non-rational circumstances of time and place can terminate deliberation, a dimension of situationalism that lends that theory peculiar force. But Simon argues that, because the will firmly adheres to the good, considered universally or particularly, it can be an agent in ending deliberation. The will is "superabundantly" determined by the good in such a way that it can fruitfully curb the indeterminacy of deliberative rationality. Theoretical analysis of contingent circumstance can yield only probabilities and can always leave the door open for further deliberation. The reduction of contingency to *a priori* or deductive rationality is also impossible, since this effectively denies the reality of contingency. But a doctrine of will properly compensates for the natural discursiveness of practical thinking and offers determination by the "heart" which makes a final judgment of choice possible: "This and only this is to be done."

*A General Theory of Authority*, completed before Simon's death but published only afterward, offers what Professor Vukan Kuic has called Simon's "last word" on authority, the theme raised so brilliantly in the Aquinas lecture discussed above and continued in *Philosophy of Democratic Government*. But the work also contains the full catalogue of themes essential to the articulation of Simon's

---

[23] Simon, *Freedom of Choice*, p. 98.
[24] Ibid., p. 148.

bedrock theory of practical knowledge in the social and political arena: (1) the necessity of unity in practical judgment as a condition for unity in community action; (2) the insufficiency of demonstrative logic in practical judgment; (3) the need for a well-ordered will as the analogue of reality in judgments of practical truth; (4) the interconnection of the virtues; (5) the irrelevance of distinctions between political and individual wisdom where the question of appetite is involved.

These pages contain striking elucidation of Simon's theory of authority and its distinction from law. Although it is not improper to speak of the authority of the legislator, and of derived formulas such as "government by law," law by its nature is general and possesses the character of a premise. Authority, on the other hand, is equally at home in contingency and the particular, in the "uttering of practical conclusions."[25] Alternatively, the concept of command is ambiguous. It can stand for the general binding power of abstract law, or for the immediate judgments preceding the accomplishment of some action. In the first case the command is less determined and therefore more "necessary." In the latter case the situational contingencies of the act fully determine the command. In the case of political action especially, the role of authority is fully felt and the place of command is fully appropriate.

The word "command" is missing from this definition of authority in *A General Theory of Authority*, and from the statement of authority's "most essential function,"[26] but it is used elsewhere, most tellingly in this explicit statement: "The ultimate answer to the practical question is a command, i.e., a judgment so related to action as to constitute its form."[27] And again in a related footnote we find: "The *ultimate* practical judgment is a sheer command."[28] I shall consider this at greater length, along with the knotty questions of the relation between imperative judgments and other forms of practical propositions. Simply put: Simon clearly links the question of authority to the theory of command as it operates in the conclusion of the practical syllogism. His extended work

---

[25] Simon, *General Theory of Authority*, p. 48n11.
[26] Ibid., p. 57.
[27] Ibid., p. 81.
[28] Ibid., p. 81n1.

on practical knowledge completes his foundational work on authority.

Simon's loyal adherence to Aristotle shows the greatest evidence of a need for completion in his posthumous *The Tradition of Natural Law*. Thomas Aquinas, however much he may be philosophizing *secundum mentem Aristotelis*, produced the great treatise on law, not his Greek teacher. "Aristotle was not expansive on the subject."[29] Simon's comments on practical knowledge are thus developed most clearly against the background of Aquinas, who insists, against all forms of legal voluntarism, that law is a work of reason. One may ask how rationality of law relates to practical knowledge. Simon's response is blunt: "Thus, considering this trait of law, viz., its being a work of the reason, let it be said that the conclusion of the practical discourse implies, in the most essential fashion, a trait opposed to the rational character of law."[30] This passage, imprecisely understood, seems to conflict with the theory that practical knowledge is a function of practical reason. However, Simon does not mean that the final judgments of practical understanding are "irrational," but that the character of universality and necessity proper to law are not found in acts of practical wisdom and that the gap between law and action may be large. He also means that practical wisdom enters into the development of law itself. The rationality of law does not demand its *a priori* derivability from first principles. It can be built up inductively as well. And it can be produced by the collective wisdom of generations of morally virtuous legislators. In Simon's understanding of the term, practical knowledge, however opposed it may be to some features of law, is fully operative in the legislative process itself.[31]

The contrast between prudence and "art" is developed at length in *The Tradition of Natural Law*. Simon works with the same concept of art as exercised Socrates in his great dispute with Thrasymachus and as surfaces time and again in political theory, especially since the Renaissance. Is political community to be understood as a production of the creative intelligence or of the good will? Are aesthetic criteria to be employed in judging the

---

[29] Simon, *Tradition of Natural Law*, p. 131.
[30] Ibid., pp. 82–83.
[31] Ibid., p. 86.

worth of a given social or political system, or are moral criteria to be used? The problem is keen, especially in the rationalistic climate that thinks of reason on a purely theoretical or geometric model. If there is no specific definition of practical reason irreducible to natural or social science, then one might argue that the only alternative must be to conceptualize political life (and individual life, for that matter) as an artistic product. An economy of principle might lead the theorist to assert that some form of art concludes the deliberations of the political philosopher, since it is art that produces objects in the world. Simon does not minimize this theory's powerful appeal, and he agrees that art may play an instrumental role in political wisdom.[32] But all art is indifferent regarding internal moral considerations or "human use."[33] The arts are concerned only with external products, "works" of art, and the artist's skill can in fact be used against the specific goals of his art. The arts need a virtue to make the artist a better person. The arts in themselves cannot do this; they can only make the artistic product better. If political life is merely the effect of some art, it can have "nothing to do with what goes on in the heart of men."[34] Political wisdom is not reducible to an art but is a form of practical wisdom that is necessarily connected with the moral virtues. To argue otherwise is to confuse works of imagination with acts of practical understanding. It can make us admire the elegance and efficiency of political structures, and divert us from the more problematic and experiential difficulties of suiting a given political structure to real human needs. Political community is, therefore, ideally governed by the virtuous and practically wise person rather than the philosopher-king who can have only theoretical knowledge, or the expert at "statecraft" who can be concerned only with the external trappings of political association, not with its internal life.

An extraordinary and intimate relationship exists between Simon's theory of practical knowledge and his enthusiasm for democratic political procedures. In *Freedom and Community*, he considers how the line between individual and community concerns may be drawn. "The last word will belong, in each concrete

---

[32] Ibid., p. 93.
[33] Ibid., p. 94.
[34] Ibid., p. 95.

case, to prudence (and one of the desirable effects of a system of checks and balances is to insure the proper consideration of the pros and cons in the deliberation)."[35] Practical wisdom dictates the "last word" in matters of decision, individual and social, because to it belongs the ultimate and decisive judgment: "such and such is to be done." The reference to checks and balances is revelatory and points to the contrast between deliberation and judgment in the practical syllogism as it is reflected in the constitutionally sanctioned separation of legislative from judicial power in a republican form of democracy. This coincidence could be called a dramatic instance of the "cunning of practical wisdom." Aristotelian moral epistemology was likely not on the minds of the Founding Fathers, but it is institutionally embodied in the structures they established. It would be tempting to reflect on the peculiar way in which practice precedes theory in American life, but this cannot be the place for it.

Simon's intense concern with concrete human activities is nowhere more evident than in the posthumous collection *Work, Society, and Culture*. His ardent critique of the social sciences is most felt in this work, as is his corresponding insistence on establishing a unique place in the analysis of social life for a wisdom that is both practical and in no sense a science. Here, too, Simon the cultural philosopher asks whether culture can be defined only by the bare necessities of intellectual virtue (he uses the scholastic term *habitus*) or whether it must also be understood in terms of superabundance and freedom from need. Taking his cue from Aristotle's fivefold division of the intellectual virtues, Simon argues that only practical wisdom is inaccessible to the possibility of "free expansion."[36] The sciences can be motivated by idle curiosity and the arts by an infinite range of possible representations, but practical wisdom is determined by the specific and incommunicable act to be performed. One and only one action is appropriate in given circumstances: "Under any and all conceivable circumstances, it is necessary to do that which is right, and, even though the decision may be to relax or to abstain from action, I do not see in prudence as an intellectual habitus any possibility of escape into the world of free development."[37] Practical wisdom introduces a

---

[35] Simon, *Freedom and Community*, p. 87.
[36] Simon, *Work, Society, and Culture*, p. 173.
[37] Ibid., p. 174.

seriousness into practical affairs which incriminates the so-called art of statecraft. It is an integral element of both individual and social culture. But it is dominated by such a precise mesh of the useful and the necessary that analogies with the sciences and the arts are invariably flawed. Since Simon ultimately holds for an integration of work and leisure within a fully developed notion of culture, it is clear that although all the intellectual virtues have work-like characteristics, practical wisdom is most amenable to work. Simon partly defines culture by a concept of "moral work."[38]

*The Definition of Moral Virtue* originated as a set of lectures given at The University of Chicago in 1957 and was published in 1986. It has considerable timeliness, given the renewed interest of philosophers in an ethics of virtue. Although the focus is on the moral virtues, not the intellectual virtues, practical wisdom is not ignored. In fact, along with *Practical Knowledge*, the most recent addition to the Simon corpus, *Moral Virtue* constitutes a compendious introduction to Simon's thinking on virtue in general.

The intense contextualism of practical wisdom which occurs throughout Simon's account of the virtue is present in his account of Aristotle's theory of intellectual virtue:[39] "But in an unprecedented situation, which may be so constituted by the mere fact that there has never been a person exactly identical with my own self, as well as by the historical uniqueness of the circumstances in which I find myself at that particular moment, there are no answers to be found in any book. To know what I should do here and now, I must rely on the judgment of practical wisdom."[40] It may be helpful to describe this position as a kind of prudential personalism, because the role of the deciding agent is so crucial. This is not relativism or moral skepticism, however, because moral judgments are given objectivity by their link with moral virtue and with the dispositions of the heart and inclinations of the will. "Formally" intellectual and "materially" moral, practical wisdom integrates the intellectual and affective realms and produces a holism of human perfection which alone seems adequate to deal with radical novelty in moral experience.

---

[38] Ibid., p. 185.
[39] Simon, *Definition of Moral Virtue* pp. 96–98.
[40] Ibid., p. 96.

The interconnection of the virtues, the theory that a person possessing one of the virtues possesses them all, is put to good use in these pages. The reason the judgment of the practically wise person may be trusted is that the answer given "will be the right answer only if that person is fully just and respectful of his neighbor's property, temperate and in control of his appetites, and courageous enough not to be afraid of the danger involved, one way or the other, in whatever judgment is handed down by his practical wisdom, by his prudence."[41] The reference to courage is striking, suggesting a willingness to accept the consequences of error in practical judgment, a vast new dimension of the virtue of courage, given the difficulties of decision-making in the modern world. The grain of truth in existential commitment may be understood not simply as the engagement of the free will but also as the integrated bravery of a just agent.

The "personalism" of Simon's position (not to be confused with uses of that term in modern idealism) is beautifully expressed by his insistence that the "rational principle" Aristotle specified as the ultimate determinant of the mean between extremes is further specified as "that principle by which the man of practical wisdom would determine it."[42] If any sense is a "sixth" one, it is the practically wise person's sense that a given action is right or wrong. Simon vividly compares this sense with the statement "I smell a rat." It has olfactory analogues. The practically wise person discerns the concrete performability or avoidability of a given action not through a deductive or inductive process, or a purely intellectual intuition, but through a kind of practical intuition compounding the full range of moral and intellectual virtues.

Although there need not be one and only one "objective answer" in a moral situation,[43] there is such a thing as "prudential objectivity."[44] This objectivity is in no sense theoretical or logically derivable from first principles. It is conveyed to the object by the virtuous subject and established or determined in league with the set of moral virtues possessed by the prudential agent. "It is I who must determine what is to be done: but if I possess

---
[41] Ibid., pp. 97–98.
[42] Ibid., p. 109.
[43] Ibid., p. 110.
[44] Ibid., p. 111.

the virtue of prudence, I will subjectively make my decision be the right one."[45] There is some truth in Kierkegaard's position that "truth lies in subjectivity,"[46] but it is clear that the language of subject and object does not suit the reality in question. Simon's ethics is not dualistic and rejects antitheses of subject and object. Rather, "prudential objectivity" is reducible to the unity-in-multiplicity of the virtues, their interconnectedness.

"[A]ll moral virtues are knotted together in prudence."[47] Simon reveals the true relationship between our moral and prudential qualities in this striking metaphor. They are not reducible to each other (for instance, they are not all species of wisdom); nor are they reducible to some other quality (the existentialist's self-determining free act, for instance). Nevertheless, they are ineluctably interinvolved, the knot of the moral life. Although a knot may have separate strands, only the knot has any moral strength, only the knot binds distinguishable moral abstractions into inseparable moral realities. The knot of moral and prudential virtue is the *e pluribus unum* of the moral life. No moral virtue is complete without practical wisdom; nor is practical wisdom possible without the moral virtues.

## Practical Knowledge

I have considered the role practical wisdom and its cognate terms play in the range of Simon's writings in ethics and moral epistemology. The most recent collection of papers devoted to this topic is *Practical Knowledge*, published in 1991. Some of these papers were published during Simon's lifetime; others were edited from his manuscripts and notes. Taken together they comprise the most thoroughgoing analysis Simon gave of the concept of practical wisdom, and I shall examine the work in some detail. It is fair to say that in most of Simon's other writings on this subject, practical wisdom is discussed within some other context, that of moral virtue, for instance. Here I turn directly to an account of practical wisdom in itself and look at the form of virtuous action by exam-

---

[45] Ibid., p. 117.
[46] Ibid., pp. 110, 118.
[47] Ibid., p. 127.

ining Simon's most sustained account of it, especially his altogether unique position on the element of command, the ultimate practical judgment.

Chapter One of *Practical Knowledge* is an edited version of an article entitled "Introduction to the Study of Practical Wisdom," which originally appeared in *The New Scholasticism* in 1961. It introduces Simon's maturest treatment of practical knowledge by considering what he calls "the ultimate practical judgment," indistinguishable in his mind from what classically was called "command" (*imperium*). Simon's published works contain repeated attention to this notion, but nowhere is the theme more fully developed than it is here. The issue is extremely difficult to understand fully, especially given centuries of dualistic thinking about the relation of thought and action. Simon begins with an instance of deliberative reasoning in a social context, recalling that adequate deliberation is always dialogical and requires mutually supportive counsel. A sportsman is considering whether to take part in a risky mountain-climbing expedition. Simon remarks that such deliberation takes on quite a different character as the sportsman approaches the moment of action. One may speak of a wide range of cognitive activities anterior to the moment of decision involving scientific or quasi-scientific investigation, memory, and the play of authority. However, when the sportsman reaches the crisis of action, a new deliberative element appears: "The ultimate degree of practicality is attained by the judgment which, except in the case of interference by some external force, cannot not be followed by action. Such is the *command* that a sportsman gives himself when he walks toward his companions and declares that he is ready to go."[48]

What is the relation between "command" and action itself? "This judgment, metaphorically described as touching action immediately, is in a direct, proper, and unqualified sense the *form of action*. Therefore it is as practical as action itself."[49] The formal identity of a command and the action directed by it holds great problems for Cartesian and post-Cartesian metaphysics. But its commonsensical conformity with ordinary modes of practical expression is not more problematic than understanding how a single

---

[48] Simon, *Practical Knowledge*, p. 3.
[49] Ibid.

event can have both causal and teleological accounts. If I open the door to let the cat out, I can explain the sequence of events both mechanically and intentionally. If both explanations are true and complementary, then why may I not understand each moment of that decision as involving complementary specifying forms? The door remains a door, turning on its hinges, conforming to relevant laws of nature. But it is equally an instrument of my choice, conforming to analogous laws in the domain of choice and decision. The command is formally identical with the action itself, just as the action can be analyzed in terms of more than one kind of causality. Although we primarily associate the concept of form with non-ethical explanation, this custom involves no definitional necessity. Formal explanation is also appropriate in the realm of practice not merely at a remove from action but also at the moment of action itself: "when the distance between thought and action is nil, when thought has come down into the complex of human action to constitute its form, it is described as practical in an absolutely appropriate sense."[50]

The inscissible conjunction of the ultimate practical judgment and the action to be performed, analogous to the unity of matter and form in a natural object, suggests that practical knowledge is achieved synthetically rather than analytically. Action has the character of a whole, and practical thought is "governed by a law of completeness,"[51] involving the motions of appetite and will as well as of reason and understanding. Practical wisdom is the completion or perfection of practical reason, but this perfection is present "perfectly," so to speak, only at the moment of action itself. The command presents us with perfectly realized practical knowledge, characterized by "decisiveness and completeness."[52] The synthetic nature of the ultimate practical judgment, linking practical thought decisively with action, can be elucidated further by the concept of "use." We have seen the differences between art and practical wisdom on this score. The artisan, craftsman, or technician can turn art to any use he or she pleases, for good or for ill. But practical judgment is so bound up with action itself that where the judgment is sound, the use must be humanly good.

---

[50] Ibid., p. 4.
[51] Ibid., p. 8.
[52] Ibid.

A practically wise person cannot make poor use of wisdom, and the action conformable to practically wise deliberation must itself be of good use. In scholastic language, "use" as an act of the will in the conclusion of the practical syllogism must be good when the ultimate practical judgment is made truly.

The problem of truth claims in matters of practical reason is highly controverted. There is, first, the sifting of factual claims from evaluative ones. Conformity with states of affairs can suffice in determining factual claims even in practical deliberation. This is a relatively straightforward view, and perhaps involves the concept of truth in a "primary and unqualified way."[53] But another kind of truth, "practical truth," is crucial to understanding fully Simon's theory of the ultimate practical judgment. This is a truth "of direction . . . a truth which does not consist in conformity to a real state of affairs but in conformity to the demands of an honest will, in conformity to the inclination of a right desire."[54] This "truth of direction" supplies certainty in practical decisions. It makes a "command" "true."

The intimate connection of practical wisdom and action through command requires the interaction of moral virtue. A balance between the probabilities established by deliberation and the need to make decisions under some degree of uncertainty leads to the role of will in the actual determination of certainty in practical knowledge. This doctrine of "judgment by inclination" implies "affective knowledge."[55] There is a necessary connection between affect and judgment in practical knowledge, one that provides the ultimate answer, the "yes" or the "no." The word "intuition" can be used, provided it is understood in the Aristotelian sense of νοῦς πρακτικη and not in the sense of the understanding of first moral principles. The person of concrete and practical intuition can determine at the last instant what action is to be performed, not because of some divine knowledge of the particular, but because, as a person of good will, he or she can with grace determine the appropriate course.

The inherent complexity of this view of prudential judgment leads Simon to argue for its "incommunicability."[56] A given prac-

---

[53] Ibid., p. 12.
[54] Ibid., p. 13.
[55] Ibid., pp. 17ff.
[56] Ibid., pp. 23ff.

tical judgment may be objectively certain and necessary and yet known only to the agent making the judgment. "The incommunicability of the last practical judgment results from the affective and non-logical character of the act which determines this judgment."[57] This language recalls positions Simon maintained as early as *Nature and Functions of Authority* which rejected intersubjectivity as a characteristic of the practically wise act. This is perhaps Simon's most "existential" position, recalling Kierkegaard as quoted in *Moral Virtue*. We act alone and in solitude in an important sense of these terms. It is significant that this circumstance does not more often cripple resolve. But shared inclination and, importantly, the need for united action when the common good is at stake mitigate the relevance of individual circumstance in some actions.

Explanation is only peripherally important in moral action. Moral obligations must be fulfilled but not necessarily understood.[58] This is perhaps more obvious in matters of political wisdom where fulfillment of authoritative commands is a necessary feature of the virtue, but it is also the case in individual decisions that fulfillment enjoys priority over understanding. Simon reiterates his firm conviction that neither philosophers nor moralists can substitute their proper forms of knowledge for the wisdom of the prudent person. Neither "speculativo-practical" nor "practico-practical" disciplines can fulfill all the functions demanded of the virtue of practical wisdom. There is a radical asymmetry between understanding and fulfillment. The affective factors necessary to the latter are only contingently involved in the former. Simon speaks to this point with telling conviction: "Accordingly, we may expect generations and centuries to elapse between the achievement of affective connaturality and the understanding of the reasons why actions are right or wrong. It is even perfectly conceivable that mankind should end its career in this world without having clearly perceived, in all cases, the reasons why what we hold to be right is right, and what we hold to be wrong is wrong."[59] The moral universe is profoundly mysterious, more so even than the world of nature. Even so, it is not necessary that

---

[57] Ibid., p. 24.
[58] Ibid., pp. 26ff.
[59] Ibid., p. 34.

we should understand what we should do; but it is necessary that we do what we should do. This is not to say that blind obedience is preferable to explanation. Merely fulfilling the law misses the uniquely human dimension which is explanatory, "animated by an aspiration toward the most rational modalities of fulfillment."[60] This is not moral skepticism but the position that our science is only asymptotically related to practical truth. Throughout our vigorous efforts to build knowledge in ethics, we must continue to do what is right.

The concluding section of Chapter One introduces us to the great issues concerning the nature of moral philosophy constituting the theme of Chapter Two. We move from the level of action to that of understanding, to Simon's "meta-ethics." The issues Simon develops here and in the next chapter are of critical importance, since he faces not only the classical and medieval need to distinguish practical wisdom from science in general but the more timely need to distinguish practical wisdom from the social sciences. This involves articulating the concept of "moral science" and developing a subtle and complex taxonomy of sciences, disciplines, and other forms of knowledge in the practical realm.

The contrasting figures of Socrates and Aristotle form an illuminating introduction to the range of issues at this juncture. Socrates represents the general tendency in the history of thought to make knowledge a sufficient condition of good moral actions. This identity of knowledge and virtue largely constitutes Socratic "intellectualism." Aristotle, on the other hand, insists that "improved manners are the proper effect of an action exercised upon the desires of men by such methods as exhortation, inspiration, habituation, example, and coercion."[61] The point of writing treatises on ethics and developing a moral science lies in the self-sufficiency of understanding itself. We come to know something for its own sake. Theoretical knowledge is an end in itself, whether the knowledge be of nature or of morals. The legacy of Aristotle's critique of Socrates on the meaning and function of moral knowledge lies in the twin vocation of moral philosophy as directive (qua "moral") and theoretical (qua "philosophy"). The tensions created by the synthesis of these ideas produce the

---
[60] Ibid., p. 37.
[61] Ibid., p. 44.

confusions dogging the history of moral philosophy but also its glory. In our time they raise the thorny problem of the relationship between psychology and moral philosophy. The issue was somewhat clearer in ancient times. Aristotle's *De anima* is a work in the theory of human nature. It is related only by indirection to the work of the moral philosopher. In modern times, psychology has taken on many new forms and conflicting ambitions. In some ways it blends almost imperceptibly into philosophy; in some ways it remains resolutely continuous with physical science. Simon insists that moral philosophy is necessarily distinct from psychology in its practical employment, as well as in theory. Psychology directs action only through the medium of "art" and not practical wisdom. Its techniques are infinitely closer to theoretical science than practical wisdom could ever be.[62]

It is *human use* which distinguishes moral philosophy from all other forms of theoretical knowledge (including psychology). Human use renders a discipline intrinsically practical, whether we speak of ultimate practical judgments or the more general questions involved in moral science. In terms of the distinction between analytic and synthetic methodologies developed in Chapter One, moral philosophy shares an analytic dimension with theoretical knowledge (and therefore is not "totally practical"), but it also shares a synthetic character with ultimate practical judgments.[63] In this sense it directs action *"from a distance"*[64] by examining moral essences and making judgments such as: "courage is a virtue," "one must be courageous," etc. These judgments are at a vast remove from the contingencies of actual conduct, but they are clearly normative and intended to guide conduct. Virtue is the more significant factor in moral choice, because it governs fulfillment, but there is an important sense in which an essentially practical discipline can have a theoretical or philosophical dimension. We may call such moral philosophy a "theoretically practical science."[65] We may distinguish such a science from a purely (i.e., non-directive) theoretical account of moral issues such as moral psychology or, at the other end of the spectrum, from the non-

---
[62] Ibid., pp. 47ff.
[63] Ibid., pp. 52ff.
[64] Ibid., p. 54.
[65] Ibid., p. 55.

scientific and yet generalized opinions of "moralists" and from the practically wise determination of actions to be performed absolutely here and now. Such a "prudence" is utterly practical on the one hand and utterly non-scientific on the other.

The synthetic nature of judgments regarding human use brings Simon to a position of great importance in the overall logic of his moral position, one that places him surprisingly close to some central themes in Kant's ethics. To state it generally, although somewhat obscurely, *"judgment enjoys priority over concept."*[66] The analytic tradition in science even in Plato and Aristotle, to say nothing of modern philosophers such as Descartes, claims that concepts enjoy some absolute logical priority over judgments. Judgments are strings or chains of concepts linked according to certain rules of combination. Simon, while willing to grant this account in non-teleological domains, insists that judgment comes first in the practical order and that concepts are abstracted from judgments. Thus, "Thou shalt not steal" is primary, whereas concepts of embezzlement, burglary, and grand larceny are abstracted from such judgments. They are not the analytic building blocks out of which such judgments are derived. Kant's statement in the realm of theory that concepts are derived from the judgmental structure of the mind was in error, but the *a priori* synthesis found in the realm of practical reason is closer to the truth. The connection is not exact, because finality is found in nature as well as in the structures of practical reason. The necessary character of moral knowledge is therefore not derivable from a logic of concepts, but is established by considerations of finality which in turn demand theoretical procedures involving the antecedence of concept over judgment.

The contrast between moral philosophical statements and the judgments of the practically wise act is sharp, extending to the concept of truth itself. The truth of moral philosophy as a theoretical science is established by conformity with a real state of affairs. The practical decision is true because of conformity with right desire or a good will. The relationship between theoretical statements and practical judgments is contingent; "leaky argumentation"[67] can nevertheless lead to certainty in the act because

---
[66] Ibid., p. 61.
[67] Ibid., p. 70.

practical wisdom is governed by considerations other than theoretical tightness. In the theoretical arena, such leaky argumentation is intolerable. Moral science is governed by the canons of science, not by the need to act well.

Rampant concern with moral certainty is a dominant characteristic of our times. A crisis of communication exists which makes the arguments of moral philosophy more needed than in past ages to support the conclusions of the practical understanding. The virtues are in crisis, and the kind of decisiveness they once lent to moral decision-making can no longer be taken for granted. The figure of Socrates is instructive: he uniquely and independently challenged received patterns of virtuous behavior and demanded they be tested in the crucible of logical argumentation. We live in another kind of Socratic age which subjects our virtuous dispositions themselves to critique. The justification of these dispositions must be by way of philosophical argument. It will not do to justify the virtues by claiming they are the dispositions of virtuous persons. Communicability in the moral order demands renewed attention to the arguments of moral philosophy. Many issues in contemporary ethics taken as settled, such as infanticide, require renewed attention to rational justification. Mere inclination no longer suffices: "The times of exclusive dependence upon judgment by inclination are gone forever."[68] This does not mean that virtuous inclinations are to be replaced by *a priori* argumentation. Rather, the need for virtuous inclinations itself, as a philosophical thesis, needs renewed justification. Fulfillment, whether in matters of social or individual ethics, cannot be satisfied with blind adherence to virtuous inclinations. Perhaps more than ever before, a rational account of the decisive command is required.

Considerations of the gulf between practical commands and the intelligible necessities of moral philosophy lead Simon in Chapter Three to re-examine the issue of "practically practical science" raised in his 1934 *Critique*. Here Simon is thinking, not of the philosopher or the practically wise person or the social scientist, but of the older and hallowed tradition (especially in France) of the moralist. The issue in Jacques Maritain's terms is whether there exists, between the moral philosopher's purely theoretical

---

[68] Ibid., p. 74.

accounts and the ultimate, virtue-laden judgments of the practically wise person, a unique science of the moralist, sharing the proper intelligibility of the theoretical sciences and, at the same time, proximate to action in such a way that it can be called properly "practical." Simon insists that such "practically practical science" is not truly a science, at least in Aristotle's understanding of that term. It lacks the essential combination of explanation and certainty that define a science. On the contrary, if the discipline in question provides some analytic connection with principles, it is a theoretical science. If, on the other hand, its certainty is established by conformity with well-ordered appetite, it is a practical wisdom. This is to deny neither that moralist writing is unique nor that it falls somewhere between moral philosophy and prudence. Moralists are neither engaged in a scientific enterprise nor proximately directive of conduct. Their efforts deserve some other name. In our range of studies they possess a uniqueness analogous with history.

This issue is elaborated by reference to the moral dimension of the problem of "Christian philosophy."[69] The relationship between philosophy and theology is no less problematical than the relationship between philosophy and empirical science or between philosophy and literature. However, the relationship between moral philosophy and moral theology is profoundly more difficult because of the necessary complexities of moral experience in general. Actions that might be universally frowned upon in the state of nature, such as ascetic practices, might be morally correct under the sway of revelation. The interconnection of the moral virtues in such a context will entail the further and infinitely greater complexity of interconnecting the divine virtues. Moral philosophy in the condition and state of revelation must be deftly subordinated to theology, not replaced by it or identified with it, in order to be "adequately taken."[70] Simon concludes this discussion by reiterating today's greater urgency to articulate as rationally as possible the theoretical goals of moral action and the concrete decisions made by moral agents. Traditional moral beliefs that are under heavy siege and appeals to authority or to a range of virtues themselves criticized will not suffice in communi-

---

[69] Ibid., pp. 87ff.
[70] Ibid., p. 95.

cating moral truth. Moral theology does not render particular judgments more scientific than they are, although it is knowledge reinforced by revelation. Moral theology may be concerned more with fulfillment than with explanation itself, with the amplitude of moral virtue, and therefore with affective certainty, than with the explanation of moral rules, principles, and decisions. Simon is not sure here, perhaps because he does not consider himself a theologian: "perhaps theology, in its practical part, is concerned more with fulfillment than with explanation. This remains to be seen."[71]

In a letter to Simon dated February 22, 1961, Jacques Maritain alludes to an important detail in Simon's concept of practical wisdom, when he distinguishes the "last practical judgment" from the *imperium*. "It does not say: 'Do this!' it says: 'Here is what is to be done!'"[72]

Simon's response is important to understand fully his theory of practical judgment, particularly in its concrete social and individual embodiments. He even refers to *A General Theory of Authority* at this point, indicating how central his understanding of command is to some of his most cherished philosophical positions. "I would call 'command' the non-propositional speech by which I order myself to do the thing which, according to the last proposition, ought to be done!"[73] In other words, the command preserves the full practical intelligibility of any other practical judgment. It is not itself an act of will, however much it may require synthesis with a well-ordered will to be effective. "Of the command, I would not hesitate to say that it is as practical as action itself. . . . I am tempted to conclude that I still can say the same of the ultimate practical judgment. This judgment, because it is the completely determinate form of the action is as practical as action itself."[74] The command, not the so-called "judgment of choice," is the ultimate practical judgment, and the virtue of practical wisdom continues into the action itself. Simon saw more fully than anyone of his time the need to close the gulf between thought and action, a dualistic hypothesis out of harmony with

---
[71] Ibid., p. 99.
[72] Ibid., p. 108.
[73] Ibid., p. 111.
[74] Ibid., pp. 111–112.

classic moral teaching. But this can be done only by stressing the identity of judgment and command at the moment of action. Indeed, this is the true depth of the doctrine of "command" and a signal contribution of Yves R. Simon's to the understanding of practical wisdom.

In the fourth chapter of *Practical Knowledge* Simon returns to one of his favorite themes, the limitations of modern social science when applied to human action. Social science is a strictly modern phenomenon. Ancient attention to questions of economics and politics was exclusively in terms of practical wisdom (one finds the term occasionally used in the plural—"prudences," like "sciences"). The relationship between theoretical science and action is closer in modern times, particularly in the phenomenon of technology. It has what Simon styles a "demiurgical" quality.[75] Given its huge success, modern science was bound to be applied to the formerly forbidden realm of moral action. The eighteenth century brought ambitions to establish a "physics of human nature" which could employ the methods of natural science in the direct manipulation and improvement of human affairs, whence came the modern sciences of psychology, economics, and political science.

These new social sciences, although principally related to such goals as the mastery of nature and the increase of general happiness, were in important details "value-free." The link with virtue demanded by the classic account of practical wisdom was ruled out, *a priori*, by an account of human behavior modeled on physics. The mathematical analysis of nature required by the new science had demanded and slowly achieved the exile of the final cause from the realm of explanation. The social sciences required an analogous development. More slowly but inevitably, the final cause was dismissed as a feature of social explanation as well. In Aristotelian terms, this is the genesis of the modern value-free social science. In practical terms, it involved bracketing the social scientist's value system in his or her investigation and as thoroughgoing a determinism as possible in the account of human affairs. At the same time the social sciences generate values themselves. For instance, statistical studies of the divorce rate in industrialized cultures lead surreptitiously to the claim that divorce may now be

---

[75] Ibid., p. 118.

"right." Experience gradually becomes normative, establishing a new fact/value relationship: facts generate values and are methodologically immune from them. The relevance of social Darwinism is obvious, as is a general characterization of modern experience in terms of laws of progress.

A finalistic interpretation of nature can make use of observational and statistical tools and yet discern value in the universe, including the universe of human nature. Thomas Aquinas develops his theory of natural law on an observation of order, in this case "the order of human inclinations."[76] But this approach is logically posterior to the methodological analysis of nature in general in terms of teleological considerations. Simon thinks that, if we are to interpret human nature finalistically, we must first interpret physical nature finalistically.[77] The relevance of these observations to the status of practical knowledge becomes obvious when we consider that practical decisions depend intimately upon the well-ordered will for their truth. Applied to the issue at hand, intelligibility of social processes may be determined by considerations of value. The supposedly commonsensical distinction of facts and values turns out to be predicated on an unexamined dualism. There corresponds in social analysis something akin to "theoretically practical science" at some elementary analysis of social theory where value considerations are irrelevant. But at the level of social fact, the conclusion, so to speak, of the social practical syllogism governing policy or action, values (virtues, really) are intimately relevant to understanding the fact in question.

The opposition of the social scientist's deterministic methodologies to the concept of free will implied in value decisions is a canard, since free will itself is not antithetical to the concept of causality. A free will is a kind of cause at the furthest remove from chance events, "superdeterminate rather than indeterminate."[78] It follows that an investigation into conditions of free choice will enhance our causal account of the social fact or situation and augment its intelligibility. The existence of a value-free fact in the moral domain (the "order of use") is a chimera. However possible it may be to establish a hard and fast line between science and

---

[76] Ibid., p. 124.
[77] Ibid., p. 125.
[78] Ibid., p. 129.

philosophy in the world of nature, when it comes to social philosophy the line becomes fuzzy indeed. It looks as though philosophical considerations concerning human nature and morality enter everywhere into our science of social life.

The theme of social science's shortcomings ("illusions") links the conclusion of Chapter Four with Chapter Five. The social sciences, begun in an almost pre-Socratic climate of enthusiasm and naïveté, have rendered many classic social and political values superfluous. For instance, if methods of science are applied to human affairs, authority in decision-making is no longer necessary, and a personalized government is reduced to a more or less efficient technical bureaucracy. Three questionable presuppositions make this fundamental move possible: (*a*) social nature is not specifically marked by contingency; (*b*) correlatively, the causal order is uniform whether nature or humankind is at issue, and there is no causal significance to a doctrine of free will; (*c*) the promise of science leads to a thoroughgoing optimism and faith in human progress. Given the catastrophes of twentieth-century experience, some reassessment of these claims is in order. It may be that a pre-social scientific humanism holds more promise for social betterment than modern social science itself. The sciences and to a degree philosophy itself proceed by the analytic method. But human betterment is holistic and synthetic in its demands. Programs of higher education offering too great an emphasis on philosophical studies are in danger of losing this irreducible and all-important humanistic perspective. But the greater danger lies in the illusions of progress and human perfectibility set before us by social sciences obsessed with technical success. Sometimes the failure of individual instances to conform to our predictive norms results in "a particularly frightful kind of misanthropy,"[79] in which mechanical efficiency finds itself stalled by recalcitrant human choice. Human affairs cannot be analyzed without reference to free choice and finality. To do so is to render them peculiarly meaningless. Perhaps this explains the phenomenon of modern existentialism, "an effort to achieve decency in a world whose meaninglessness extends to human actions."[80]

The possibility of a "humanistic" counterattack to the social

---

[79] Ibid., p. 142.
[80] Ibid., p. 144.

scientific project raises the thorny problem of the persistent historical tension between Christianity and humanism. Thomas Aquinas holds that the doctrine of Original Sin wounds nature itself, not merely the supernatural and preternatural condition of humankind before the fall. Nevertheless this wound is not total. Human nature is fallen, not corrupted, in Aquinas's tradition. This theory leads not to the pessimism of Pascal, the logical alternative of a too-lofty conception of human nature itself, but to a kind of meliorism. "It is not altogether impossible to cause what is just to be strong: it is only very difficult."[81] The optimism represented by Pascal's view of uncorrupted nature and reinforced by the heady successes of the social sciences leads, when challenged by the catastrophes of the twentieth century, to a new pessimism, or to what Simon prefers to call "disappointed optimism."[82] This in turn produces melancholic and misanthropic casts of mind, the polar opposite of the "confident humanism" to which a more balanced, more experiential view of human nature should lead us. Not even all Christians share this confidence; many, infected with pessimism, surreptitiously join with the disappointed optimists of the eighteenth-century mold. The poles meet, but the truth lies in the middle.

Is there something essential to the conflict between humanism and Christianity, or are we speaking simply of historically determined accidents? Theologically there can be no necessary conflict, because Christian faith holds as a matter of dogma the existence of a person whose nature was both divine and human. Historically the integration of a humanism centered on the classics of antiquity within a generally Christian system of values, although subject to constant tension, was an instance of realized Christian humanism. But as humanism became increasingly secularized, for instance in the eighteenth and nineteenth centuries, the opposition of humanism to Christianity became more and more an obvious cultural *a priori*.

Is there any chance in our own time, given its disaffections with linear progress, of some fresh synthesis of humanistic and Christian ideals? Simon suggests that a reinvigorated theory of natural law may show the way. He echoes his earlier account of

---
[81] Ibid., p. 146.
[82] Ibid.

relationships among various levels of moral science, suggesting that "the knowledge of natural law is firmest and most lucid when it is associated with faith in God as cause of the supernatural order."[83] The movements of the heart, so absolutely necessary to the practical judgment, are also de facto required in more general moral utterances. It is here that natural law (by itself deductively related to its conclusions) must employ the illumination provided by faith. Incidentally, a modern Christian humanism could employ for pedagogical reasons a wider range of materials from specifically Christian sources now ruled out by both the antiquity of the Renaissance and its contempt for medieval civilization. The opposition will then be not between Christianity and humanism but between humanism and the technical culture spawned by twentieth-century scientific optimism. However, the inevitability of this opposition entails grave practical consequences since humanism by definition cannot abstract from the realities of historical processes. Some accommodation to the salutary effects of modern technical process will be necessary to any form of humanism, Christian or otherwise. The solution lies in subordinating technical culture as an instrumental means to the demands of a full humanism. The painter's brush has some intrinsic value, but not much. It is overwhelmingly validated by the painter's skill and goals. The totality of the technical civilization fostered by modern natural and social science can be similarly separated from its originating causes and used as an instrument to fully humanize all persons.

The problem is still not easily solved. The "weight of the instrument"[84] may frustrate every effort to instrumentalize technical culture totally. Here, as so often in Simon's ethics, a mere judgment of the subordination of instrument to goal will not suffice. Moral truth is measured by correspondence with virtuous inclination. Simon concludes that the decisive virtue will be a supernatural one, the spirit of poverty. "In the relation of the human to the technical, we keep our instruments under control insofar as we remain free from attachment to things inferior to man."[85] A program in humanistic studies which is faithful to the demands of

---

[83] Ibid., pp. 151–152.
[84] Ibid., p. 155.
[85] Ibid.

Christianity on the one hand and to humanism on the other, and adequate to the need to subordinate modern technical culture, will include some attention to the masterpieces of Christian mysticism.

## Conclusion

What Jacques Maritain called the majesty and poverty of metaphysics thus finds a fitting analogue in practice with its combined injunction to pursue a thoroughly human wisdom along with mystical literature and the counsels of perfection. As such, Yves R. Simon's lifetime consideration of practical wisdom, culminating in his book *Practical Knowledge*, has both intense contemporary relevance and a profound continuity with the past. Simon saw more clearly than any of his contemporaries the way in which practical wisdom unifies and systematizes a theory of virtue and law. He also saw how the resultant synthesis could fill the huge theoretical hole in modern thought and culture caused by the abandonment of practical wisdom in favor of an uncritical social scientific project. The modern dualism of science and ethics with its accompanying dichotomization of knowledge and freedom and of mind and body has many roots. One of them is the insistence that knowledge follow a single methodology and principle of order. However compelling this ambition may be in the natural sciences and in those human sciences properly contiguous with natural science, the methods of moral inquiry and decision-making must follow other paths. Theory and practice are simply different in origin and in goal. But the temptation of a modern scientific culture is at most to give lip service to this distinction and to preserve the hegemony of theoretical science by reducing its practical derivatives to technique. Simon's critique of the conflation of theory and practice has to be understood as entailing a correlative critique of the conflation of practice and art. Unless proper limits are set to science, art, and prudence, institutional, social, and individual life will continue to suffer the crises we are so familiar with in technology, bureaucracy, mass education, and the simple day-to-day problems of living well. The recovery of practical wisdom and its total philosophical context is a pressing and overarching need of our times.

# Part II
# Bibliography

# Yves R. Simon:
# A Definitive Bibliography, 1923–1996

*Compiled and Annotated by
Anthony O. Simon*

Contents of the Bibliography:

| | | | |
|---|---|---|---|
| I | 100–118 | Books | 186 |
| II | 150–156 | Translations | 203 |
| III | 200–225 | Parts of Books | 205 |
| IV | 300–413 | Articles | 212 |
| V | 500–551 | Selected Book and Article Reviews | 236 |
| VI | 600–609 | Series Edited by Yves R. Simon | 245 |
| VII | 700–865 | Selected Works on Yves R. Simon | 246 |
| VIII | | Addenda and Forthcoming | 280 |
| IX | 900–905 | Manifestos and Allied Publications | 282 |
| X | | Archival Materials | 289 |
| Bibliographic Index | | | 295 |

# I
## Books

100  *Introduction à l'ontologie du connaître*\*
Collection ⟨Bibliothèque Française de Philosophie⟩ (Troisième Série)
Paris: Desclée de Brouwer, 1934. Pp. 232
Reprinted: Dubuque, Iowa: William C. Brown, 1965. Pp. 232.
   This edition is now distributed by Irvington Publishers, New York (1995).
Contents:
   1. La nature et la connaissance
       Être et connaître
       La chose et l'idée
       Véracité
   2. Connaissance et activité
       Objectivité et activité
       Le fait du changement: Première définition de l'action
       Notion de l'activité immanente
       Seconde définition (transcendantale) de l'action
       Troisième définition (transcendantale) de l'action
       Quatrième définition (transcendantale) de l'action
       Action et qualité
       Activité immobile
       Vitalité
   3. L'expérience et la pensée
       Nécessité d'une connaissance expérimentale
       La passivité du sens et l'action immanente de connaître
       La naissance de l'idée
       La pensée et l'expression intérieure du pensé
       Connaître la vérité
       Le progrès et la pensée

---

\* In print, reprinted, or available in another source as indicated.

100.1 English edition of 100
*An Introduction to Metaphysics of Knowledge*\*
Edited and translated by Vukan Kuic and Richard J. Thompson
New York: Fordham University Press, 1990. Pp. vii + 180
New York: Fordham University Press, paperback edition, 1990. Pp. vii + 180.
Contents:
Translators' Preface
1. Nature and Cognition
   To Be and to Know
   The Thing and the Idea
   The Superabundance of Creation
   The Veracity of Our Cognitions
2. Cognition and Activity
   Objectivity and Activity
   The Fact of Change: First Definition of Action
   The Notion of Immanent Activity
   A Second (Transcendental) Definition of Action
   Third (Transcendental) Definition of Action
   Fourth (Transcendental) Definition of Action
   Action and Quality
   Vitality
3. Experience and Thought
   Experimental Knowledge
   Sensory Experience and the Immanent Act of Knowing
   The Birth of the Idea
   The Internal Expression of Thought
   To Know the Truth
   The Progress of Thought
Appendix: *Habitus* and *Idea*
Index

101 *Critique de la connaissance morale*
Collection ⟨Questions Disputées⟩
Series directed by Charles Journet and Jacques Maritain
Paris: Desclée de Brouwer, 1934. Pp. 166.
   An unpublished translation is available at the Yves R. Simon Institute.

Contents:
1. Pour la notion de connaissance pratique (v. 333)
2. La sagesse pratique (v. 333)
3. L'intelligence disciple de l'amour (v. 333)
4. Les principes premiers de l'ordre pratique (v. 333)
5. Le mouvement de la pensée pratique (v. 333)
6. La philosophie morale (v. 333)
7. La science pratiquement pratiqué (v. 333)
8. Morale chrétienne (v. 333)
9. Philosophie morale et science des faits moraux (v. 333)
10. Pour la notion de science politique. Programme (v. 336)

102  *La campagne d'Éthiopie et la pensée politique française*
Lille: Societé d'Impressions Littéraires, Industrielles, et Commerciales, 1936. Pp. 128.
Contents:
1. Introduction
2. De l'avant-guerre à la Conférence de Stresa
3. Que nous importe l'Éthiopie?
4. La croisade antifasciste
5. Mais cette guerre est-elle juste?
6. Les relations exterieures de l'Éthiopie
7. Le chien enragé
8. La situation intérieure de l'Éthiopie
9. Le Pacte des Nations
10. La politique britannique
11. Intervention des intellectuels
12. Réflexions sur certaines résistances au progrés du droit international
13. Le 7 mars 1936

102.1  *La campagne d'Éthiopie et la pensée politique française*
Collection ⟨Courrier des Îles⟩. Second edition
Paris: Desclée de Brouwer, 1937. Pp. 128.

103  *Trois leçons sur le travail**
Collection ⟨Cours et Documents de Philosophie⟩
Series directed by Yves R. Simon
Paris: Pierre Téqui, 1938. Pp. 72.

Contents:
1. La définition du travail (v. 207, 343, 361)
2. Travail et richesse (v. 362)
3. La culture ouvrière

104 *Nature and Functions of Authority**
The 1940 Aquinas Lecture
Milwaukee: Marquette University Press, 1940. Reprinted 1948. Pp. 75 (v. 219, 365).

This annual lecture series was founded by John O. Riedl in 1937 under the auspices of the Aristotelian Society of Marquette University. The series has continued to the present and has published some of the foremost philosophers of the century. Simon's volume has been widely recognized as a classic work on authority.

105 *La grande crise de la République Française: Observations sur la vie politique des français de 1918 à 1938*
Collection ⟨Problèmes Actuels⟩
Montreal: Éditions de l'Arbre, 1941. Pp. 237.
Contents:
1. La France sous la croix gammée (v. 364)
2. Au lendemain de la victoire
3. Nationalisme et pacifisme
4. Politique et religion
5. Incertitudes françaises
6. Les amis de nos amis sont nos amis
7. Le Front Populaire au pouvoir (v. 215)
8. Les ennemis de nos ennemis sont nos amis
9. Qu'est-ce qu'un traître? (v. 365)
10. La libération du monde

105.1 Revised English edition of 105
*The Road to Vichy: 1918–1938**
Translated by James A. Corbett and George J. McMorrow
New York: Sheed and Ward, 1942. Pp. 207
Ann Arbor, Michigan: Books on Demand, 1980.
Contents:
1. France Under the Swastika (v. 364)
2. The Aftermath of the Victory
3. Nationalism and Pacifism

                4. Politics and Religion
                5. The Twilight of the Myths
                6. Our Friends' Friends Are Our Friends
                7. The People's Front in Power (v. 215)
                8. Our Enemies' Enemies Are Our Friends
                9. What Is a Traitor? (v. 365)
                10. The Deliverance of the World
            Table of Events

105.2   Revised English edition of 105.1
        *The Road to Vichy, 1918–1938* [Revised Edition★]
        Translated by James A. Corbett and George J. McMorrow
        New introduction by John Hellman
        Lanham, Maryland: University Press of America, 1988. Pp. xxxiv + 212. Indexed
        Reprinted 1990.

106     *La marche à la délivrance*
        Collection ⟨Civilisation⟩
        Directed by Jacques Maritain
        New York: Éditions de la Maison Française, 1942. Pp. 126.
        Contents:
            1. L'épreuve de la nuit
            2. L'utopie
            3. La foi des héros
            4. Renaissance de la liberté
            5. Une guerre civile internationale (v. 373)
            6. La libération du monde
            7. L'imposture
            8. La quatrième République
            9. La grande élection

106.1   English translation of 106
        *The March to Liberation*
        Translated by Victor M. Hamm
        Milwaukee: The Tower Press, 1942. Pp. 102.
        Contents:
            1. The Ordeal of Night
            2. Utopia
            3. The Faith of Heroes (v. 376)

4. Rebirth of Freedom
5. An International Civil War
6. The Liberation of the World
7. The Imposture
8. The Fourth Republic (v. 377)
9. The Great Choice

107 *Prévoir et savoir: Études sur l'idée de nécessité dans la pensée scientifique et en philosophie*
Montreal: Éditions de l'Arbre, 1944. Pp. 204.
Contents:
Avant-Propos (v. 411)
1. La théorie du déterminisme
2. Science et systématique (v. 412)
3. L'École de Vienne (v. 413)
4. Le pluralisme épistémologique
5. Remarques sur l'objet de la connaissance physique (v. 410)
6. La connaissance de l'âme (v. 378, 378.1)

107.1 Revised English translation of 107
*Foresight and Knowledge*★
Edited by Ralph Nelson and Anthony O. Simon
New York: Fordham University Press, 1995. Pp. xxii + 153.
Contents:
Introduction
Acknowledgments
Foreword by Yves R. Simon (v. 411)
1. The Theory of Determinism
2. Science and Systematic Knowledge (v. 412)
3. The Vienna Circle (v. 413)
4. Epistemological Pluralism
5. Some Remarks on the Object of Physical Science (v. 410)
6. Knowledge of the Soul (v. 378.1)
Bibliography
Index

108 *Par delà l'expérience du désespoir*
Montreal: Lucien Parizeau, 1945. Pp. 225.

Contents:
Avant-Propos
1. La conquête de la liberté dans la vie quotidienne
2. Sources secrètes du succès de l'idéologie raciste
3. Le pessimisme et la philosophie du progrès

108.1 Revised English edition of 108
*Community of the Free*
Translated by Willard R. Trask
New York: Henry Holt and Company, 1947. Pp. xi + 172.

Chapter 4 was not included in the original edition; it was written in English and added to the English edition.

Contents:
Foreword
1. Freedom in Daily Life (v. 113)
    The Spirit of Freedom and the Spirit of Truth
    The Truth about Timely Issues
    The Love of Truth Is Indivisible
    Freedom and Law
    Slaves and Rebels
    The Community of the Free
    A Universalist Ethics
2. Secret Sources of the Success of the Racist Ideology (v. 212, 337)
    A Pool of Cheap Labor
    Competition and the Quota
    Aristocratic Distinction
    The Age of the Masses
    Scapegoats and Accursed Groups
    Perversion of Religious Feelings
3. Pessimism and the Philosophy of Progress (v. 113)
    The Romantic Philosophy of Progress
    Disillusioned Optimists
    A Pessimistic Theory of Progress
4. Socialism and the Democracy of the Common Man (v. 405)
    The Brotherhood of Men
    Rationalism
    The Withering Away of the State

    Democracy and Totalitarianism
    Problems Worked Out by Socialism
    Utopia and Justice

108.2 Revised edition of 108.1
*The Community of the Free: Revised Edition*★
Translated by Willard R. Trask
Lanham, Maryland: University Press of America, 1984. Pp. 182. Indexed.

109 *Philosophy of Democratic Government*
Charles R. Walgreen Foundation Lectures
Foreword by Jerome G. Kerwin
Chicago: The University of Chicago Press, 1951. Pp. vii + 324
Chicago: Phoenix Books (P–67)/The University of Chicago Press, paperback edition, 1961 Reprinted 1977. Pp. vii + 324 (v. 750).
Contents:
 1. General Theory of Government (v. 213)
   The Paternal Function of Authority
   Authority as Cause for United Action
   The Volition of the Common Good
 2. Democratic Freedom
   Universal Suffrage
   The Rule of the Majority
   The Party System
   The Instruments of Government
   The Democratic Transformation of the State
 3. Authority in Democracy (v. 216)
   The Coach Driver Theory
   Divine Right
   The Transmission Theory
   Sovereignty in Democracy
 4. Democratic Equality
   Equality as Unity of Nature
   Natural Inequality and Structural Inequality
   Equality of Opportunity
   Equality versus Exploitation
 5. Democracy and Technology
   On Technological Society

The Pursuit of Happiness and the Lust for Power
(v. 222)
The Training of Free Men
Common Life versus Individualistic Loneliness
Index

109.1 Revised edition of 109
*Philosophy of Democratic Government*★
Notre Dame, Indiana: University of Notre Dame Press, 1993. Pp. 343.
A detailed index and Simon's corrections to the text have been added.

109.2 Japanese translation of 109
民主政治の原理
The Institute of International Culture
Tokyo: Kokusai Bunka Kenkyujo, 1955. Pp. 294.

109.3 Portuguese translation of 109
*Filosofia do govêrno democrático*
Translated by Edgard Godói da Mata-Machado
Translator's Preface
Rio de Janeiro: Agir Livraria Editora, 1955. Pp. 307.

109.4 German translation of 109
*Philosophische Grundlagen der Demokratie*
Translated by Lotte Piening
Collection ⟨Schriften zur politischen Wissenschaft⟩ No. 1
Meisenheim/Glan: Verlag Anton Hain, 1956. Pp. 327.

109.5 Korean translation of 109
民主政治 原理
Seoul: Bak Yeung Sa, 1960. Pp. 310.

109.6 Italian translation of 109
*Filosofia del governo democratico*★
Translated by Romeo Fabbri
Collana ⟨Scienze Umane e Filosofia⟩ No. 17
Milan: Editrice Massimo, 1983. Pp. 308.

109.7 Polish translation of 109
*Filozofia radu demokratcyznego*★
Translated by Ryszard Legutko

Cracow: Wydawnictwo Arka Press PKU, 1993. Pp. 279.

This edition includes a detailed bibliography of Simon's books entitled "Bibliografia dziel Yves R. Simona," compiled by Anthony O. Simon as an appendix. See pp. 262–275.

110  *Traité du libre arbitre*
Liège: Sciences et Lettres, 1951. Pp. 143.
Contents:
1. Images de désordre
2. Les passions de l'homme
3. L'intelligible
4. Un cas privilégié de nécessité naturelle
5. La conscience de la liberté
6. Libre arbitre, ou jugement libre
7. Le libre arbitre et le principe de causalité
8. Les perfections divines
9. De l'idée d'indétermination
10. La loi et la liberté (v. 403, 403.1)

Index des noms cités

110.1 *Traité du libre arbitre*
Second publication
Paris: Librairie Philosophique Jules Vrin, 1952. Pp. 143.
The text is identical to the first edition.

110.2 Revised Edition of 110
*Traité du libre arbitre*★
Collection ⟨Prémices⟩ directed by Patrick de Laubier
Avant-propos by Patrick de Laubier
Preface by Pierre-Marie Emonet
Fribourg: Éditions Universitaires, 1989. Pp. 143.

110.3 Italian translation of 110
*Trattato del libero arbitrio*
Translated by Franca Zambonini
Collana ⟨Philosophica Saggi⟩ No. 8
Rome: Edizioni Paoline, 1957. Pp. 165
Second Edition, 1963. Pp. 175.

110.4 Revised English edition of 110
*Freedom of Choice*★

Edited by Peter Wolff
Foreword by Mortimer J. Adler
Editor's Preface
New York: Fordham University Press, 1969. Pp. xx + 167
New York: Rose Hill Books/Fordham University Press, paperback edition, 1987. Pp. xx + 167.
    Chapters 8, 9, and 10 of the original were not included in this English translation.
Contents:
1. Introduction
    Images of Disorder
2. The Will
    Voluntariness
    The Passions of Man
    Happiness and the Last End
3. Freedom
    The Consciousness of Freedom
    Freedom of Choice as Freedom of Judgment
    Free Will and the Principle of Causality
Bibliography
Index

111    *A General Theory of Authority*
Introduction by A. Robert Caponigri
Notre Dame, Indiana: University of Notre Dame Press, 1962. Pp. ix + 167.
Contents:
1. The Bad Name of Authority (v. 218, 221)
2. Common Good and Common Action (v. 397)
3. The Search for Truth
4. The Communication of Excellence (v. 218)
5. Afterthoughts on the Bad Name of Authority (v. 218)
Appendix: On the Meaning of Civil Obedience

111.1  *A General Theory of Authority**
Introduction by A. Robert Caponigri
Westport, Connecticut: Greenwood Press, 1973. Pp. ix + 167.

111.2  Revised edition of 111
*A General Theory of Authority*★
New Introduction by Vukan Kuic
Notre Dame, Indiana: University of Notre Dame Press, 1980, 1991 (paperback editions). Pp. 167. Indexed.

112  *The Tradition of Natural Law: A Philosopher's Reflections*★
Edited by Vukan Kuic
Editor's Preface
Foreword by John H. Hallowell
New York: Fordham University Press, 1965, 1967. Pp. xii + 194
Ann Arbor, Michigan: Books on Demand, 1993.
Contents:
Part I
   1. The Problem
       Doctrinal Connections
       Historical Contexts
       Dialectic and History
   2. The History of Natural Law
       Ideology and Philosophy
       Some Examples of Historic Adventures of Natural Law
   3. Some Theoretical Questions
       The Concept of Nature
       Necessity and Contingency
       Free Choice
       Reason versus Will
       God
Part II
   4. The Definition of Law
       The Rational Nature of Law
       The Common Good
   5. Natural Law
       From Positive Law to Natural Law
       The Divisions of Natural Law
       On the Knowledge of Natural Law
       On Obligation of Natural Law
       The Variations of Natural Law
   6. The Future of Natural Law

Notes
Index

112.1 Revised Edition of 112
*The Tradition of Natural Law: A Philosopher's Reflections*★
New Introduction by Russell Hittinger
New York: Fordham University Press, 1992 (paperback edition). Pp. xxxii + 194.

112.2 Spanish translation of 112
*La tradición de la ley natural: Reflexiones de un filósofo*
Translated by Ignacio de Despujol
Prologo by John H. Hallowell
Collection ⟨Biblioteca de Filosofía y Pedagogía⟩
Madrid: Editorial Razón y Fe, S.A., 1968. Pp. 210.

113 *Freedom and Community*★
Edited by Charles P. O'Donnell
Editor's Preface
New York: Fordham University Press, 1968. Pp. xxii + 201
Ann Arbor, Michigan: Books on Demand, 1993.
Contents:
  1. Freedom in Daily Life (v. 108.1)
      The Spirit of Freedom and the Spirit of Truth
      The Truth About Timely Issues
      The Love of Truth Is Indivisible
      Freedom and Autonomy
      Slaves and Rebels
      The Community of the Free
      A Universalist Ethics
  2. Liberty and Authority (v. 360)
      The Meaning of Liberty
      Authority and Liberty
      Totalitarianism and Liberty
  3. Freedom and Community
      Alienation versus Integration
      Servitude
      Exploitation Integration
  4. Autonomy and Authority
      The Imperialistic Tendency of Authority

Freedom and Law
Freedom and Organization
Society and Contemplation
5. Political Society
Coercion as a Characteristic of Political Society
Political Society Defined
6. Pessimism and the Philosophy of Progress (v. 108.1)
The Romantic Philosophy of Progress
Disillusioned Optimists
A Pessimistic Theory of Progress
Bibliography
Index

114 *The Great Dialogue of Nature and Space**
Edited by Gerard J. Dalcourt
Editor's Preface
Albany, New York: Magi Books, 1970 (paperback edition). Pp. xvii + 206
Albany, New York: Magi Books, 1973 (hardbound edition). Pp. xvii + 206.
Contents:
1. The Great Dialogue of Nature and Space
2. How We Explain Nature
3. The Science and Philosophy of Inertia
4. The Philosophy of Change
5. The Real and the Ideal in Nature
6. Place and Space
7. Time
8. Philosophers and Facts (v. 332)
9. Science, Scientism and Realism, (v. 200, 341)
10. Chance and Determinism in Philosophy and Science (v. 107, 107.1, 201)

115 *Work, Society, and Culture**
Edited by Vukan Kuic
Appendix: Yves R. Simon / A Bibliography, 1923–1970, compiled by Anthony O. Simon
New York: Fordham University Press, 1971. Pp. xvi + 234
New York: Fordham University Press, paperback edition, 1987. Pp. xvi + 192.

The paperback edition deleted the original Simon bibliography.
Contents:
Editor's Preface
1. The Concept of Work
    Manual Work
    The Works of the Mind
    Irksomeness of Work
2. Work and Society
    Service to Society
    The Ethics of the Worker
    Useful Activity and Modern Social Thought
    The Sociological Concept of the Working Man
3. Man at Work
    The Psychology of the Worker
    Work, Joy, and Love
    The Sociability of the Worker
    Family as a Working Unit
    Slavery and Alienation
4. The Working Class
    Historical Origins
    Social Orders and Social Classes
    The Proletariat
    The Ideology of the Working Class
5. Work and Wealth
    Service and the Profit of Work
    Work as a Commodity
    Distribution According to Needs
6. Work and Culture
    Historic Aspects
    Culture and Civilization
    The Hard Core of Culture
    The Plenitude of Culture
    Man's Art
    Leisure, Work, and Culture
Appendix: Yves R. Simon / A Bibliography, 1923–1970, compiled by Anthony O. Simon
Index

115.1 Spanish translation of 115
*Trabajo, sociedad y cultura*★

Translated by Gloria Brigé de Sucre and Loló Gil de Yánes
Caracas: IFEDEC, 1988. Pp. 167.

116   *Jacques Maritain: Homage in Words and Pictures*
By John Howard Griffin and Yves R. Simon
Edited with a Foreword by Anthony O. Simon
Albany, New York: Magi Books, 1974. Pp. xii + 64.
Contents:
  1. Foreword by Anthony O. Simon
  2. Homage in Words by Yves R. Simon (v. 217, 408)
  3. Homage in Pictures by John Howard Griffin
      Princeton
      Fort Worth
      Kolbsheim
      Toulouse
  4. Epilogue 1973

116.1   Italian translation of 116
*Omagio a Jacques Maritain: Parole e immagini*★
Translated by Maria Silvia Serafini
Presentazione by Roberto Papini
Prefazione by Anthony O. Simon
Milan: Editrice Massimo, 1981. Pp. 95

117   *The Definition of Moral Virtue*★
Edited by Vukan Kuic
New York: Fordham University Press, 1986. Pp. xiv + 137
New York: Rose Hill Books/Fordham University Press, paperback edition, 1986). Reprinted 1989. Pp. xiv + 137.
Contents:
  Editor's Preface
  Yves R. Simon (1903–1961): A Bio-Bibliography by Marie-Vincent Leroy
  1. The Modern Substitutes for Virtue
      Natural Goodness
      Social Engineering
      Psycho-technology
  2. Clearing Up Some Confusions
      Nature and Use

>     Spontaneity and Reason
>     Forms of Sociability
>  3. Further Necessary Distinctions
>     Habit
>     Habitus
>     Opinion
>  4. Virtue Is Not Science
>     Readiness
>     Disposition
>  5. The Definition of Moral Virtue
>     Traditional Moral Values
>     The Definition
>     How Do We Know Right From Wrong?
>     Virtue and Objectivity
>  6. The Interdependence of Virtues
>  Index

118 *Practical Knowledge*\*
Edited by Robert J. Mulvaney
New York: Fordham University Press, 1991. Pp. xiii + 163
New York: Rose Hill Books/Fordham University Press, paperback edition, 1991. Pp. xiii + 163.
Contents:
> Editor's Note
>  1. The Ultimate Practical Judgment (v. 226, 398)
>     Practical Judgment as the Form of Action
>     The Synthesis of Practical Judgment
>     Nature and Use
>     The Truth of Practical Judgment
>     Judgment by Inclination
>     The Incommunicability of the Ultimate Practical Judgment
>     Fulfillment and Explanation
>  2. On Moral Philosophy
>     Moral Science in Socrates and Aristotle
>     Moral Philosophy as a Theoretical Study
>     Moral Philosophy as Intrinsically Practical
>     Truth and Communication
>  3. Disputed Questions
>     The Problem of Practically Practical Science

Ethics and Christian Philosophy
The Timely Need for Moral Philosophy
Appendix: Extracts from Correspondence of Yves R. Simon and Jacques Maritain
4. From the Science of Nature to the Science of Society (v. 391)
The Emergence of Social Science
Practical Knowledge of Social Science
Nature and Use in Social Science
From Social Science to the Philosophy of Science
5. Christian Humanism: A Way to World Order (v. 211)
The Illusions of Social Science
The Conflict Between Humanism and Christianity
Humanism and Christianity: A Possible Synthesis
Index

## II
### Translations

150 *Commentaire de St. Thomas sur l'oraison dominicale*
French translation of: *Expositio Orationis Dominicae*
Translated by Yves R. Simon and Pierre Péguy
In:
*La Vie Spirituelle* [Paris],
Vol. XX (1929), 342–352, 451–458, 545–551
Vol. XXI (1929–1930), 212–216
Vol. XXII (1930), 83–88, 282–287
Vol. XXIII (1930), 73–88.

151 *Le prolétariat industriel*
French translation by Yves R. Simon of Goetz A. Briefs,
   *Das gewerbliche Proletariat*
Collection ⟨La Lumière Ouvrière⟩
Préface by Jacques Maritain
Paris: Desclée de Brouwer, 1936. Pp. xii + 302.

The preface is reprinted in *Jacques et Raïssa Maritain: Œuvres Complètes*. VI. *1935–1938*.★ Fribourg: Éditions Universitaires—Fribourg; Paris: Éditions Saint-Paul, 1984. Pp. 1257–1260.

152 *Saint Thomas d'Aquin—Pages choisies*★
Edited and translated by Yves R. Simon
Préface by Jacques Maritain
Collection ⟨Catholique⟩ directed by André David
Paris: Librairie Gallimard, 1939. Pp. 93.

153 *Entia Rationis and Second Intentions*
John of St. Thomas
*Ars logica,* Pars II, q. 11, aa. 1–2
Edited and translated by Yves R. Simon, John J. Glanville, and G. Donald Hollenhorst
In:
*The New Scholasticism* [Washington, D.C.]
Vol. XXIII, No. 4 (October 1949), 395–413.
Reprinted and later published in *The Material Logic of John of St. Thomas* as pp. 60–76 (v. 155).

154 *La civilisation américaine*
Introduction by Yves R. Simon (v. 208)
Edited and translated by Yves R. Simon
In collaboration with:
John Cort
Willis D. Nutting
John H. Sheehan
Waldemar Gurian
Aaron I. Abell
Leo R. Ward
Benjamin T. Crawford
Matthew A. Fitzsimons
Alvan S. Ryan
Frank O'Malley
Collection ⟨Questions Disputées⟩
Paris: Desclée de Brouwer, 1950. Pp. 270.

154.1 Italian translation of 154
*Civiltà americana*
Translated by Liana Bortolon
Milan: Vita e Pensiero, 1953. Pp. 288 (v. 208.1).

155 *The Material Logic of John of St. Thomas: Basic Treatises*
Edited and translated by Yves R. Simon, John J. Glanville, and G. Donald Hollenhorst

Preface by Jacques Maritain
Foreword by Yves R. Simon
Chicago: The University of Chicago Press, 1955. Reprinted 1965. Pp. xxxiv + 638 (v. 153, 156, 210).

156  *On the Universal*
John of St. Thomas
*Ars logica*, Pars II, q. 3, aa. 1–5
Translated by Yves R. Simon, John J. Glanville, and G. Donald Hollenhorst
Extracts from *The Material Logic of John of St. Thomas*, pp. 89–130
In:
*Readings in Logic*
Edited by Roland Houde
Dubuque, Iowa: William C. Brown, 1958. Pp. 3–40 (v. 155).

### III
### Parts of Books

200  La science moderne de la nature et la philosophie
in:
*Philosophie et science*
Le Saulchoir: Kain, 1935. Pp. 92–114 (v. 341, 114).
    Proceedings volume of a symposium sponsored by the Société Thomiste and the Société Philosophique Internationale de Louvain convened at Louvain's Institut Supérieur de Philosophie.

201  Travaux d'approche pour une théorie du déterminisme
in:
*Études Philosophiques*
Contributors:
    Yves R. Simon          Étienne Borne
    Gaston Bachelard       Eugène Dupréel
    René Le Senne          Louis Lavelle
    Gabriel Marcel         Vladimir Jankélévitch
    Marcel de Corte
Annales de l'École des Hautes Études de Gand III

Ghent: École des Hautes Études de Gand, 1939. Pp. 186–236 (v. 107, 107.1, 114).

202   Thomism and Democracy
in:
*Science, Philosophy, and Religion*
Second Symposium, Vol. II
Edited by Louis Finkelstein and Lyman Bryson
New York: The Conference on Science, Philosophy, and Religion in Their Relations to the Democratic Way of Life, Inc., 1942. Pp. 258–272.

203   Beyond the Crisis of Liberalism
in:
*Essays in Thomism*
Edited by Robert E. Brennan
Contributors:
    Robert E. Brennan    Jacques Maritain
    Charles O'Neill    Rudolf Allers
    Mortimer J. Adler    Vernon J. Bourke
    Yves R. Simon    John K. Ryan
    Walter Farrell    Hilary Carpenter
    John A. Ryan    John O. Riedl
    Robert J. Slavin    Anton C. Pegis
    Immanuel Chapman    Herbert T. Schwartz
New York: Sheed and Ward, 1942. Pp. 261–286; notes, pp. 411–414.

203.1   Beyond the Crisis of Liberalism
in:
*Essays in Thomism*
Edited by Robert E. Brennan
Reprinted: Freeport, New York: Books for Libraries Press 1972. Pp. 261–286; notes, pp. 411–414.

203.2   Spanish Translation
Mas allá de la crisis del liberalismo
in:
*Ensayos sobre el tomismo*
⟨Colección Jordán⟩
Translated by Efrén Villacorta

Edited by Marcos Fernández Manzanedo
Madrid: Ediciones Morata, 1963. Pp. 345–373.

204 Prólogo
in:
*Propedeutica filosófica*
Edited by Oswaldo Robles
Mexico City: Librería de Porrúa Hnos y Cía, 1943. Pp. xiii–xv.

205 Maritain's Philosophy of the Sciences
in:
*The Maritain Volume of the Thomist*
*The Thomist*
Vol. 5 (1943)
New York: Sheed and Ward, 1943 Pp. 85–102 (v. 375, 375.1).

205.1 Maritain's Philosophy of the Sciences
in:
*The Maritain Volume of the Thomist*
*The Thomist*
Vol. 5 (1943)
Reprinted: New York: Kraus Reprint Corporation, 1969. Pp. 85–102 (v. 375, 375.1).

205.2 Maritain's Philosophy of the Sciences
in:
*The Maritain Volume of the Thomist*
*The Thomist*
Vol. 5 (1943)
Reprinted: Great Neck, New York: Core Collection Books, 1978. Pp. 85–102 (v. 375, 375.1).

205.3 Maritain's Philosophy of the Sciences
Reprinted in:
*The Philosophy of Nature*
By Jacques Maritain
New York: Philosophical Library, 1951. Pp. 157–182 (v. 375, 375.1).

205.4 Maritain's Philosophy of the Sciences
Revised and reprinted in:

*The Philosophy of Physics*
Edited by Vincent E. Smith
Collection ⟨St. John's University Studies, Philosophical Studies⟩ No. 2
New York: St. John's University Press, 1961. Pp. 25–39 (v. 375, 375.1).

206   Yves R. Simon
in:
*The Book of Catholic Authors* (Third Series)
Edited by Walter Romig
Detroit: Walter Romig Company, 1945. Pp. 262–270 (v. 835).
　　An autobiographical essay.

207   The Concept of Work
in:
*The Works of the Mind*
Edited by Robert B. Heywood
Preface by John U. Nef
Contributors:
　　Yves R. Simon　　　　S. Chandrasekhar
　　Marc Chagall　　　　 Heinrich Brüning
　　J. W. Fulbright　　　 Frank Lloyd Wright
　　Arnold Schoenberg　　John von Newman
　　C. H. McIlwain　　　 Robert M. Hutchins
　　Alfeo Faggi　　　　　Mortimer J. Adler
Chicago: The University of Chicago Press, 1947. Pp. 3–17
Chicago: Phoenix Books (P–239)/The University of Chicago Press, revised paperback edition, 1966. Pp, 3–17.
　　The paperback edition contained a new preface by John U. Nef.

208   Introduction
in:
*La civilisation américaine*
Paris: Desclée de Brouwer, 1950. Pp. 7–20 (v. 154).

208.1 Premessa
Italian translation of 208

in:
*Civiltà americana*
Translated by Liana Bortolon
Milan: Vita e Pensiero, 1953. Pp. 7–21 (v. 154).

209  The Doctrinal Issue Between the Church and Democracy
in:
*The Catholic Church in World Affairs*
Edited by Waldemar Gurian and Matthew A. Fitzsimons
Contributors:
| | |
|---|---|
| Yves R. Simon | M. F. Sciacca |
| John Courtney Murray | Thomas T. McAvoy |
| Edward L. Heston | Rafael Calvo Serer |
| Harry Koenig | Otto B. Roegele |
| Oskar Bauhofer | Aron I. Able |
| Heinrich Rommen | M. A. Fitzsimons |

Notre Dame, Indiana: University of Notre Dame Press, 1954. Pp. 87–114.
   The distribution of this volume was halted, shortly after its release, by the direct intervention of Vatican authorities.

210  Foreword
in:
*The Material Logic of John of St. Thomas*
Chicago: The University of Chicago Press, 1955. Pp. v–xxxiv (v. 155).

211  Christian Humanism: A Way to World Order
in:
*From Disorder to World Order*
75th Anniversary Conference of Marquette University
Edited with an Introduction by John O. Riedl
Milwaukee: Marquette University Press, 1956. Pp. 185–208
Reprinted as Chapter 5 in Yves R. Simon, *Practical Knowledge*
New York: Fordham University Press, 1991. Pp. 137–156 (v. 118).

212  Secret Sources of the Success of the Racist Ideology
Translated by Victor M. Hamm

in:
*The Image of Man*
A Review of Politics Reader
Edited by Matthew A. Fitzsimons, Thomas T. McAvoy, and Frank O'Malley
Notre Dame, Indiana: University of Notre Dame Press, 1959. Pp. 192–219 (v. 108, 108.1, 381).

213    The Essential Functions of Authority
in:
*Modern Catholic Thinkers*
Edited by A. Robert Caponigri and revised by Yves R. Simon
Extracts from *Philosophy of Democratic Government*, pp. 19–57 (v. 109)
New York: Harper and Brothers, 1960. Pp. 351–371
Paperback Edition, Vol. II, Harper Torchbooks TB-307H
New York: The Cathedral Library, 1965, Pp. 351–371.

214    An Essay on Sensation
in:
*Philosophy of Knowledge*
Edited by Roland Houde and Joseph Mullally
Philadelphia: J. P. Lippincott, 1960. Pp. 55–95.

215    La grande crise de la République Française
An Extract, pp. 151–159 (v. 105)
Reprinted in:
*France—L'individu et le destin (1918–1960)*
Edited by William C. Holbrook and Robert J. Neiss
Boston: Houghton Mifflin, 1962. Pp. 62–67.

216    The Consent of the Governed
An Extract, pp. 191–194 (v. 109)
Reprinted in:
*The Nature of Politics*
Edited by Michael Curtis
New York: Avon Books, 1962. Pp. 225–228.

217    Jacques Maritain: The Growth of a Christian Philosopher
in:
*Jacques Maritain: The Man and His Achievement*

Edited by Joseph W. Evans
New York: Sheed and Ward, 1963. Pp. 3–24 (v. 116, 116.1, 409).

218 De l'autorité
in:
*Pouvoir et société*
Collection ⟨Recherches et Débats⟩ No. 53
Introduction by Olivier Lacombe
Translated by Paule Simon
Paris: Desclée de Brouwer, 1966. Pp. 72–84
Extracts, from Yves R. Simon, *A General Theory of Authority*, pp. 20–22, 148–156, 157–161 (v. 111).

219 On the Essence of Authority
in:
*The Business System: Readings in Ideas and Concepts* III
Edited by Clarence Walton and Richard Eells
New York: Macmillan, 1967. Pp. 1505–1508.
An extract from Yves R. Simon, *Nature and Functions of Authority*; pp. 7–18 (v. 104).

220 Sovereignty in Democracy
Extracts from Yves R. Simon, *Philosophy of Democratic Government*, pp. 144–160, 176–194 (v. 109)
in:
*In Defense of Sovereignty*
by W. J. Stankiewicz
New York: Oxford University Press, 1969. Pp. 241–272.

221 The Bad Name of Authority
Chapter 1 of *A General Theory of Authority*
in:
*Authority in Social Work*
Edited by Shanker A. Yelaja
Toronto: University of Toronto Press, 1970. Pp. 18–26
Paperback edition: Toronto: University of Toronto Press, paperback edition, 1970. Pp, 18–26 (v. 111).

222 The Pursuit of Happiness and Lust for Power in Technological Society

An extract from Yves R. Simon, *Philosophy of Democratic Government*, pp. 262–296 (v. 109).
in:
*Philosophy and Technology*
Edited by Carl Mitcham and Robert Mackey
New York: The Free Press, 1972. Pp. 171–186; notes, p. 371.
New York: The Free Press, paperback edition, 1983. Pp. 171–186; notes, p. 371.

223  Introduction to the Study of Practical Wisdom
in:
*The Great Ideas Today*
Chicago: Encyclopædia Britannica, 1988. Pp. 382–405 (v. 118, chapter 1 of *Practical Knowledge*, and 398).

224  Lettre de Yves R. Simon à Msgr. A. Jean Chollet [10 Août 1939].
in:
*1939–1940: Les catholiques devant la guerre*
By Paul Christophe
Paris: Les Éditions Ouvrières, 1989. P. 166.

225  A Note on Proudhon's Federalism
in:
*Federalism as Grand Design*
Edited by Daniel J. Elazar
Lanham, Maryland: University Press of America, 1989. Pp. 223–234 (v. 345.1).

## IV
### Articles

300  *L'Atelier: Journal d'ouvriers*
in:
*Les Cahiers Catholiques* [Paris]
No. 91 (25 Juillet 1923), 2353–2361.
    Founded in 1919, *Les Cahiers Catholiques* was a monthly journal of art, literature, and religion edited by Jacques Debout.

301  À propos du VIe centenaire de la canonisation de Saint Thomas d'Aquin
in:
> *La Démocratie* [Paris]
> N.S. Vème Année, Tome I, No. 6 (25 Décembre 1923), 273–274.
>
> *La Démocratie* was founded and directed by Marc Sangnier, the celebrated leader of the *Sillon*. After the papal condemnation of the *Sillon* in 1910, the *Jeune République* [League of the Young Republic] was formed. Yves R. Simon was an active member for about two years during 1923–1925.

302  Libéralisme et démocratie
in:
*La Démocratie* [Paris]
N.S. Vème Année, Tome I, No. 10 (25 Février 1924), 429–433.

303  Visite à Saint-Louis de Vincennes
in:
*Les Cahiers Catholiques* [Paris]
No. 105 (25 Mars 1924), 2821–2822.

304  Les idées artistiques et littéraires de Proudhon
in:
*La Démocratie* [Paris]
N.S. Vème Année, Tome I, No. 12 (25 Mars 1924), 553–562.

305  Le caractère religieux de premier socialisme français
in:
*Les Cahiers Catholiques* [Paris].
Part I: Saint-Simon et les Saint-Simoniens
No. 104 (10 Mars 1924), 2785–2792.
Part II: Buchez et Proudhon
No. 106 (10 Avril 1924), 2870–2874.

306  Les prières de saint Thomas d'Aquin
in:
*Les Cahiers Catholiques* [Paris]
No. 109 (25 Mai 1924), 2973.

307  Notes sur intelligence et la poésie
in:
*Les Cahiers Catholiques* [Paris]
No. 109 (25 Mai 1924), 2974.

308  Le nouveau théâtre chrétien
in:
*La Démocratie* [Paris]
N.S. Vème Année, Tome II, No. 5 (10 Juin 1924), 195–199.

309  En lisant les revues
Ordre et autorité
L'idéal socialiste
L'idée de victoire
Wodan ou Jésus
in:
*La Démocratie* [Paris]
N.S. Vème Année, Tome II, No. 5 (10 Juin 1924), 233–240.

310  Revue des revues
Saint Thomas d'Aquin et le modernisme au treizième siècle
Wodan ou Jésus
L'art de Maurice Denis-Marc
Les trois sortes d'oraison
in:
*Les Cahiers Catholiques* [Paris]
No. 111 (25 Juin 1924), 3036–3038.

311  Revue des revues
Poèmes de l'enfance
Le couvent désaffecté
Le bolshevisme dans l'art
La vivant continuité du symbolisme
in:
*Les Cahiers Catholiques* [Paris]
No. 113 (25 juillet 1924), 3101–3102.

312  En lisant les revues
Le modernisme républicain
Le problème agraire devant les semaines sociales
Une heure avec Frédéric Lefèvre

in:
*La Démocratie* [Paris]
N.S. Vème Année, Tome II, No. 9 (25 septembre 1924), 470–476.

313   Revue de revues
Roma aeterna
Le problème de l'union des églises chrétiennes
La doctrine de la semaine sociale de Rennes
in:
*Les Cahiers Catholiques* [Paris]
No. 116 (10 Octobre 1924), 3196–3198.

314   À propos d'Anatole France: Un entretien avec Maurice Brillant, Yves R. Simon, et Georges Desgrippes
in:
*Les Cahiers Catholiques* [Paris]
No. 118 (10 Novembre 1924), 3237–3239.

315   En lisant les revues
La mort d'Anatole France
Le général Dawes
in:
*La Démocratie* [Paris]
N.S. VIème Année, Tome I, No. 3 (Décembre 1924), 164–170.

316   Un entretien avec Monseigneur Pharès
By Georges Desgrippes and Yves R. Simon
in:
*Les Cahiers Catholiques* [Paris]
No. 120 (10 Décember 1924), 3310–3311.

317   Revue des revues
Pierre de Ronsard
La mort d'Anatole France
Poésies par Fagus
in:
*Les Cahiers Catholiques* [Paris]
No. 120 (10 Décembre 1924), 3321–3323.

318   La semaine des écrivains catholiques
in:
*Les Cahiers Catholiques* [Paris]
No. 121 (25 Décembre 1924), 3339–3340.

319    Un entretien avec M. Henri Massis
in:
*Les Cahiers Catholiques* [Paris]
No. 121 (25 Décembre 1924), 3353–3356.

320    Revues françaises
Les hésitations de l'Allemagne et le danger prussien
L'avenir des relations franco-allemandes
Les progrès du communisme en Grande-Bretagne
Une visite chez Abdel Krim adversaire de l'Espagne
Le mémoire classé premier au concours de la paix
in:
*La Démocratie* [Paris]
N.S. VIème Année, Tome I, No. 4 (Janvier 1925), 227–235.

321    Révolution communiste—Révolution socialiste
in:
*La Démocratie* [Paris]
N.S. VIème Année, Tome I, No. 5 (Février 1925), 265–271.

322    Revues françaises
Fédération nationale catholique et organisations de défense politique et sociale
Samuel Gompers
À propos des élections allemandes
Une témoignage sur la Russie
in:
*La Démocratie* [Paris]
N.S. VIème Année, Tome I, No. 5 (Février 1925), 297–303.

323    Les compagnons de Notre Dame: Théâtre chrétien
in:
*Les Cahiers Catholiques* [Paris]
No. 126 (10 Mars 1925), 3508.

324    Réponse à une enquête: Un chrétien peut-il prendre part à une guerre?
in:
*L'Âme Commune* [Paris]
(1 Mars 1925), 114–115.
   A brief synopsis in German follows on p. 115.

325  Revues françaises
Une application de l'idée coopérative à l'organisation du travail
Allemagne, Russie, et société des nations
Une lettre du professeur Quidde
in:
*La Démocratie* [Paris]
N.S. VIème Année, Tome II, No. 3 (Juin 1925), 186–191.

326  Politique d'Alain
in:
*La Vie Intellectuelle* [Paris]
Part I, Tome I, No. 3 (Décembre 1928), 417–430
Part, II, Tome II, No. 4 (Janvier 1929), 116–135.
   A monthly journal edited by M. V. Bernadot and Étienne Lajeunie, it was published by the French Dominicans at Éditions du Cerf.

326.1  The Politics of Alain
in:
*Interpretation* [New York]
Translated by John M. Dunaway
Vol. 13, No. 2 (May 1985), 215–231.
   A journal of political philosophy, edited by Hilail Gildin and published at Queens College in Flushing, New York.

327  Philosophia perennis
in:
*La Vie Intellectuelle* [Paris].
Tome V, No. 1 (10 Octobre 1929), 52–79.

328  L'objet de l'intelligence
Yves R. Simon and Jacques de Monléon
in:
*Revue de Philosophie* [Paris]
Tome XXXVI, No. 3 (Mai–Juin 1929), 314–335.
   Yves R. Simon was managing editor [Secrétaire Général] of the *Revue de Philosophie* from 1934 to 1938. This bi-monthly journal was founded in 1900 by Émile Peillaube and published by the faculty of philosophy at the Institut Catholique de Paris with support from other

French universities. It was an influential and prestigious journal that ceased publication after the War in 1946. In the fall of 1938, after Simon left to become a Visiting Professor at the University of Notre Dame in Indiana, Albert Sandoz replaced him as managing editor.[1]

329 Statistics des missions
in:
*La Vie Intellectuelle* [Paris]
Tome II, No. 7 (Avril 1929), 746–750.

A discussion of information presented in Robert Streit's book *Les missions catholiques*, published in Paris by Desclée de Brouwer in 1927.

330 Les missions catholiques et l'œuvre de civilisation
in:
*La Vie Intellectuelle* [Paris]
Tome IV, No. 2 (Juillet–Août 1929). 202–208.

331 La philosophie bergsonienne—Étude critique
in:
*Revue de Philosophie* [Paris]
N.S. Tome II, No. 3 (Mai–Juin 1931), 281–290.

332 Les préoccupations expérimentales des philosophes et la notion de fait philosophique
in:
*Revue de Philosophie* [Paris]
N.S. Tome III, No. 3 (Mai–Juin 1932). 267–289 (v. 114).

---

[1] The *Revue de Philosophie* is mislabeled with regard to Tome numbers several times. In addition, the Tome numbers are again mislabeled in the yearly indexes. The errors are as follows. The Tomes for both (New Series) 1930 and 1931 are identified as Tome I in the accumulated yearly bindings. The Tomes for 1933 and 1934 are both labeled as Tome IV; 1935 is labeled Tome V; 1936 as Tome VI; 1937 as Tome VII; 1938 as Tome VII. The correct labeling should be as follows: [1930, Tome I; 1931, Tome II; 1932, Tome III; 1933, Tome IV; 1934, Tome V; 1935, Tome VI; 1936, Tome VII; 1937, Tome VIII; 1938, Tome IX; and 1939, Tome X]. Additionally, the indexes for the years 1934–1938 at the end of the bound yearly volumes are incorrectly identified as XXXV, XXXVI, XXXVI, XXXVII and XXXIII. The corrections are 1934 V, 1935 VI, 1936 VII, 1937 VIII, 1938 IX. The individual unbound issues do not list a tome number and all the *yearly* labelings are correct. In order to avoid any confusion the tome numbers can be eliminated but I have corrected the erroneous labelings.

333 Réflexions sur la connaissance pratique
in:
*Revue de Philosophie* [Paris]
Part I, N.S., Tome III, No. 5 (Septembre–Octobre 1932), 449–473.
Part II, N.S., Tome III, No. 6, (Novembre–Décembre 1932), 531–555.
   This text also appeared in revised form as pp. 7–142 of *Critique de la connaissance morale* (v. 101).

334 Les thèses de M. Pierre Deffontaines
in:
*Les Facultés Catholiques de Lille* [Lille]
22ème Année, No. 10 (Juillet 1932), 258–260.

335 Positions aristotéliciennes concernant le problème de l'activité du sens
in:
*Revue de Philosophie* [Paris]
N.S. Tome IV, No. 3 (Mai–Juin 1933), 229–258.

336 Pour la notion de science politique
in:
*La Vie Intellectuelle* [Paris]
N.S. 5ème Année, Tome XXV, No. 1 (25 Novembre 1933), 55–65 (v. chapter 10 of *Critique de la connaissance morale*, 101).

337 Philosophie chrétienne—Notes complémentaires
in:
*Études Carmélitaines* [Paris]
Tome XIX, Vol. I (Avril 1934), 107–119.
   A journal of theology and mysticism published by Desclée de Brouwer. Yves R. Simon served as an editorial consultant.

338 Le problème de la transcendance et le défi de Proudhon
in:
*Nova et Vetera* [Geneva]
IXème Année, No. 3 (Juillet–Septembre 1934), 225–238 (v. 336.1).
   This journal was founded in Fribourg, Switzerland,

by Charles Journet, later named cardinal by Pope Paul VI. It played a significant role in the Thomistic revival and in promoting the works of Jacques Maritain.

338.1 The Problem of Transcendence and Proudhon's Challenge
Translated by Charles P. O'Donnell and Vukan Kuic
in:
*Thought* [New York].
Vol. LIV, No. 213 (June 1979), 176–185.
    A quarterly formerly published by Fordham University, Bronx, New York.

339 Philosophy of Science—Étude critique
in:
*Revue de Philosophie* [Paris]
N.S., Tome VI, No. 1 (Janvier–Fevrier 1935), 53–64.
    The page numbers are incorrectly label as 51–64 on the issue's cover.

340 Lettre au général Vouillemin [Charles Ernest Vouillemin]—Et réponse
in:
*Revue de Philosophie* [Paris]
N.S. Tome VI, No. 3 (Mai–Juin 1935), 255–265.
    This article also appeared in revised form as pp. 117–121 of *Prévoir et savoir* (v. 107). See also *Foresight and Knowledge* (107.1).

341 La science moderne de la nature et la philosophie
in:
*Revue Néoscolastique de Philosophie* [Louvain, Belgium]
Tome 39, Deuxiéme série, No. 49 (Février 1936), 64–77 (v. 114, 200).
    This quarterly founded in 1894 by Désiré-Joseph Mercier was later renamed *Revue Philosophique de Louvain* and continues to be a distinguished philosophical journal.

342 Le nouvel empiricisme—Étude critique
in:
*Revue de Philosophie* [Paris].

N.S. Tome VII, No. 6 (Novembre–Décembre 1936), 545–552.
    This article later appeared in revised form as pp. 122–135 of 107, *Prévoir et Savoir* (v. 107); see also *Foresight and Knowledge* (107.1).

343   La définition du travail
      in:
      *Revue de Philosophie* [Paris]
      N.S. Tome VII, No. 5 (Septembre–Octobre 1936), 426–441 (v. 103, *Trois leçons sur le travail*).

344   Études sur le communisme
      in:
      *Univers: Bulletin Catholique International* [Paris–Lille]
      3ème Année, No. 20 (Janvier 1937), 5–7.
          *Univers* was the monthly journal of the *Comité Français pour la Justice et la Paix* edited by Paul Catrice and Jean Létourneau.

345   Note sur le fédéralisme proudhonnien
      in:
      *Esprit* [Paris]
      5ème Année, No. 55 (1 Avril 1937), 53–65 (v. 345.1).
          *Esprit* was founded by Emmanuel Mounier (1903–1950) in 1932 with partial financial support from Jacques Maritain. Mounier and Yves R. Simon regularly attended the Cercles Thomistes meetings held at Maritain's home in Meudon, near Paris, together during the 1920s and 1930s. Mounier's "personalism" disappointed Maritain in the direction that *Esprit* took in the late 1930s and reprised after the War. The journal played a notable role in French political, social, and economic thought before and after the War.

345.1 A Note on Proudhon's Federalism
      Translated by Vukan Kuic
      in:
      *Publius* [Philadelphia, Pennsylvania]
      Vol. 3, No. 1 (Spring 1973), 19–30 (v. 225).
          *Publius* was published by the Center for Federalism

and edited by Daniel J. Elazar at Temple University in Philadelphia.

346 [Untitled Editorial Comment] on Émile Callot's book review of Gaston Bachelard's book *L'expérience de l'espace dans la physique contemporaine*, Paris: Alcan, 1937
in:
*Revue de Philosophie* [Paris]
N.S. Tome VIII, No. 4 (Juillet–Août 1937), 355.

347 Note sur la prévision scientifique
in:
*Revue de Philosophie* [Paris].
N.S. Tome VIII, No. 6 (Novembre–Décembre 1937), 508–513.

348 Du travail ou du pain
in:
*Temps Présent* [Paris]
Ier Année, No. 2 (12 Novembre 1937), 1, 6.

Yves R. Simon was one of the founding members of *Temps Présent*. This newspaper was created to fill the void left after the Vatican suppression of the controversial *Sept*. The first issue appeared on November 5, 1937, and listed the distinguished collaborators including Mauriac, Bernanos, Marcel, Maritain, Du Bos, Lacombe, Massignon, Mounier, and Yves R. Simon. The editor, Stanislas Fumet, was also managing editor of Desclée de Brouwer. *Temps Présent* was suppressed early during the German occupation, then revived briefly as *Temps Nouveau*, and finally suppressed by Admiral Jean Darlan and the puppet Vichy government on August 15, 1941.

349 Les mystères du C.S.A.R. [Comité Secret pour l'Action Révolutionaire]
in:
*Temps Présent* [Paris]
2ème Année (4 Février 1938), 1.

350 À propos de la guerre de Chine
in:
*Univers: Bulletin Catholique International* [Paris–Lille]
4ème Année, No. 31 (Mars–Avril 1938), 24–26 (v. 344).

351 Patriotisme
in:
*Temps Présent* [Paris]
2ème Année, No. 23 (8 Avril 1938), 1.

352 De la générosité dans la connaissance et dans l'amour
in:
*La Vie Intellectuelle* [Paris]
Tome LVI, 10ème Année, No. 3 (10 Mai 1938), 325–335.

353 Un homme irréprochable
in:
*Temps Présent* [Paris]
2ème Année (17 Juin 1938), 1.

354 Faire de la politique
in:
*Temps Présent* [Paris]
2ème Année, No. 34 (24 Juin 1938) 3.

355 L'argent et l'ideal
in:
*Temps Présent* [Paris]
2ème Année (8 Juillet 1938), 3.

356 Crimes salutaires
in:
*Temps Présent* [Paris]
2ème Année (22 Juillet 1938), 1.

357 Raison politique
in:
*Temps Présent* [Paris]
2ème Année (29 Juillet 1938), 1.

358 D'Aristote à Marx—Étude critique
in:
*Revue de Philosophie* [Paris]
N.S. Tome IX, No. 1 (Janvier–Février 1938), 71–78.

359 L'opinion américaine et la guerre d'Espagne
in:
*L'Aube* [Paris]
8ème Année, No. 1965 (13 Janvier 1939), 1.

Founded in 1932, *L'Aube* was a political newspaper edited by Gaston Tessier and Francisque Gay.

360 Liberty and Authority
in:
The Problem of Liberty*
*Proceedings of the American Catholic Philosophical Association* [Washington, D.C.].
Vol. XVI (1940), 86–114 (v. 113 and 110)
Reprinted: New York: Johnson Reprint Corporation, 1992.

361 Work and Workman: A Philosophical and Sociological Inquiry
in:
*The Review of Politics* [Notre Dame, Indiana]
Vol. 2, No. 1 (January 1940), 63–86 (v. 103, *Trois leçons sur le travail*; v. 115, *Work, Society, and Culture*).
Reprinted: New York: Kraus Reprint Corporation, 1992.

Yves R. Simon was an advisory editor of *The Review of Politics* during the earlier years of its publication. It was founded by Waldemar Gurian (1902–1954) in 1939. He was Russian-born but German-educated. Gurian, a Francophile, was co-editor of *Deutsche Brief, 1934–1938* [see the two-volume collection edited by Heinz Hürten (Mainz: Mattias-Grunwald Verlag, 1969), vol. I, pp. xxxii + 733, Vol. II, pp. 1186] with Otto Knab in Lucerne, Switzerland. It was an influential anti-Nazi publication despite its limited circulation as a weekly newsletter. Gurian joined the department of political science at the University of Notre Dame in 1937. *The Review of Politics*, a quarterly, quickly received national attention and remains a major journal of cultural, historical, philosophical, and political thought. Gurian and Simon were friends in Germany and in Paris during the 1930s.

362 Work and Wealth
in:
*The Review of Politics* [Notre Dame, Indiana]
Vol. 2, No. 2 (April 1940), 197–217 (v. 103, 115)
Reprinted: New York: Kraus Reprint Corporation, 1992.

363 Résolution
in:
*France Forever* [New York]
Vol. 1, No. 3 (January–February 1941), 3.

Yves R. Simon signed this article with one of his pseudonyms, Antoine Olivier. *France Forever,* a monthly established in 1940, was one of several publications of the Free French in America [France Forever / France Quand Même] which was composed of prominent French exiles and a distinguished American sponsoring committee, headquartered at Rockefeller Plaza in New York. General Charles de Gaulle was an active supporter.

364 France under the Swastika
in:
*The Commonweal* [New York]
Vol. XXXIII, No. 24 (April 4, 1941) 590–592 (v. *The Road to Vichy,* chapter 9, 105.1, 105.2).

An influential American national weekly magazine of lay Catholic thought.

365 The European Crisis and the Downfall of the French Republic
in:
*The Review of Politics* [Notre Dame, Indiana]
Vol. 3, No. 1 (January 1941), 32–64 (v. *The Road to Vichy,* 105.1, 105.2
Reprinted New York: Kraus Reprint Corporation, 1992.

366 Modern Propaganda
in:
*The Catholic World* [New York]
Vol. CLIII (May 1941), 229–230.

This is a brief extract from *Nature and Functions of Authority* (v. 104).

367 La philosophie dans la foi: Extrait des mémoires d'un philosophe français
in:
*La Nouvelle Relève* [Montréal]

Part 1: Vol. I, No. 5 (Février 1942), 257–265 (v. 367.2)
Part 2: Vol. I, No. 6 (Mars 1942), 336–342 (v. 367.1).
    Founded in 1934, *La Nouvelle Relève* was edited by Claude Hurtubise. It published major authors including Georges Bernanos, Yves R. Simon, Luigi Sturzo, Wallace Fowlie, René Schwob, Jacques Maritain, Paul Claudel, Emmanuel Mounier, Stanislas Fumet, and Henri Daniel-Rops. This journal ceased publication shortly after the War.

367.1 Philosophy and Faith: Extracts from the Memoirs of a French Philosopher—Part 2
in:
*Notes et Documents* [Rome]
Simon/Maritain Issue edited by Anthony O. Simon
Translated by Vukan Kuic
Vème Année, No. 14 (Janvier–Mars 1979), 5–8 (v. 367).
    Journal of the Institut International Jacques Maritain in Rome.

367.2 Philosophy and Faith: Extracts from the Memoirs of a French Philosopher—Part 1
in:
*Notes et Documents* [Rome]
Translated and edited by Anthony O. Simon
N.S. XIIIème Année, No. 23 (Septembre–Décembre 1988), 76–82.

368 Chronique des événements internationaux: Saint Pierre et Miquelon
in
*La Nouvelle Relève* [Montréal]
Vol. I, No. 5 (Février 1942), 303–306.

369 La guerre longue et la guerre dure
in:
*La Nouvelle Relève* [Montréal]
Vol. I, No. 6 (Mars, 1942), 354–359.

370 Les evénements internationaux: L'offensive du printemps
in:
*La Nouvelle Relève* [Montréal]
Vol. I, No. 7 (Avril 1942), 428–435.

371    La paix de compromis: Les événements internationaux
in:
*La Nouvelle Relève* [Montréal]
Vol. II, No. 1 (Octobre 1942) 41–47.

372    Pour le soixantième anniversaire de Jacques Maritain
in:
*La Nouvelle Relève* [Montréal]
Vol. II, No. 2 (Décembre 1942), 66–69.

373    Una guerra civil internacional
in:
*Argentina Libre* [Buenos Aires]
24 Décembre 1942 (v. 105).
    This is a Spanish translation, published in an Argentinian newspaper, of chapter 5 of Yves R. Simon, *La march à la délivrance*, New York, 1942, pp; 45–61 (v. 106).

374    France and the United Nations
in:
*The Review of Politics* [Notre Dame, Indiana]
Vol. 5, No. 1 (January 1943), 26–37
Reprinted: New York: Kraus Reprint Corporation, 1992.

375    Maritain's Philosophy of the Sciences
in:
*The Thomist* [Washington, D.C.].
*The Maritain Volume of the Thomist*
Vol. 5 (January 1943), 85–102 (v. 205, 205.1, 205.2, 205.3).
    This philosophical quarterly is published by the Dominican order.

375.1    La philosophie des sciences de Jacques Maritain
in:
*Revue Philosophique de Louvain* [Louvain]
Translated by Paule Simon
IVème Serie, Tome. 70, No. 6 (Mai 1972), 220–236.

376    Heroic Faith
in:
*The Thinker's Digest* [Dallas, Pennsylvania]

Vol. IV, No. 3 (Spring 1943), 11–12, a brief extract from *The March to Liberation*, pp. 14–30 (v. 106.1).
   This brief extract was condensed by Helen Mang.

377   True Functions of Universal Suffrage
in:
*The Catholic World* [New York]
Vol. CLVII (July 1943), 421–422, an extracted from chapter 4 of *The March to Liberation*, pp. 82–86 (v. 106.1).

378   La connaissance de l'âme
in:
*Gants du Ciel* [Montréal]
No. 5 (Septembre 1944), pp. 87–109 (v. 107, 107.1), chapter 6 of *Prévoir et savoir* and *Foresight and Knowledge*.
   A series edited by Guy Sylvestre and published by Édition Fides, Montreal.

378.1   Knowledge of the Soul
in:
*The Thomist* [Washington, D.C.].
Translated by Ralph Nelson
Vol. 54, No. 2 (April 1990), 269–291 (v. 107, 107.1).

379   Internal Policy of Liberated France: A World Problem
in:
*France/Canada* [Ottawa]
English edition: Vol. II, No. 5 (May 1944), 6–7 (v. 334.1).

379.1   La politique intérieure de la France libérée: Problème mondial
in:
*France/Canada* [Ottawa]
French edition: Vol. II, No. 5 (Mai 1944), 6–7 (v. 334).

380   La démocratie et le purisme démocratique
in:
*La République Française* [New York]
Vol. I, No. 7 (Août 1944), 6–9 (v. 380.1, 380.2, 380.3, 380.4).
   One of the monthly publications of France Forever [The Free French in America].

380.1 La démocratie et le purisme démocratique
in:
*Supplément des Nouvelles Catholiques* [Ottawa]
No. 39 (1 Octobre 1944), 1–3.

380.2 Democracy and the Purists
in:
*The Commonweal* [New York]
Vol. XLI, No. 2 (October 27, 1944),. 32–36.

380.3 La democracia y los puristas
in:
*Orden Cristiano* [Buenos Aires]
Año IV, No. 79 (15 Diciembre 1944) 709–712.

380.4 La democracia y los puristas
in:
*Politica y Espiritu* [Santiago de Chile]
Año I, No. 1 (Julio 1945), 7–11.

381 Secret Sources of the Success of the Racist Ideology
Translated by Victor M. Hamm
in:
*The Review of Politics* [Notre Dame, Indiana]
Vol. 7, No. 1 (January 1945), 74–105
Reprinted: New York: Kraus Reprint Corporation, 1992
(v. reprinted in, 108, 108.1, 108.2, and 212).

382 United Nations Conference in San Francisco
in:
*Our Sunday Visitor* [Huntington, Indiana]
May 13, 1945, p. 5.
The O.S.V. is a national Catholic weekly newspaper.

383 Economic Organization in a Democracy
in:
The Philosophy of Democracy*
*Proceedings of the American Catholic Philosophical Association*
[Washington, D.C.].
Vol. XX (1945), 83–108 (v. 108.1)
Reprinted: New York: Johnson Reprint Corporation, 1992.

384   Progress in Metaphysics
      in:
      *The Commonwealth* [New York]
      Vol. XLII, No. 1 (April 20, 1945), 5–6.

385   Saint Thomas
      in:
      *The Commonweal* [New York]
      Vol. XLII, No. 13 (July 13, 1945) 313–314.
         A review article of the two-volume *Basic Writings of Saint Thomas Aquinas*, edited and translated by Anton C. Pegis, 2 vols. (New York: Random House, 1945). Simon's criticism of this landmark edition centered on his objection to Pegis's translation of *habitus* as "habit."

386   The Philosophical Study of Sensation
      Yves R. Simon and J. L. Péghaire
      in:
      *The Modern Schoolman*★ [St. Louis, Missouri]
      Vol. XXIII, No. 3, March, 1946; pp. 111–119.
      Reprinted: A.M.S. Reprint Press, Inc., New York, 1992.
         Published by the School of Science and Philosophy at St. Louis University.

387   Aristotelian Demonstration and Postulational Method
      By Yves R. Simon and Karl Menger
      in:
      *The Modern Schoolman*★ [St. Louis, Missouri]
      Vol. XXV, No. 3 (March 1948) 183–192.
      New York: A. M. S. Reprint Press, 1992.

388   Pacifism
      Letter to the Editor
      in:
      *The Commonweal* [New York]
      Vol. XLVIII, No. 11 (June 25, 1948), 256–257.
         This letter to the editor of *The Commonweal* was in response to an editorial of May 28, 1948, on pacifism. The exchange was prompted by Robert Hovda's letter criticizing Yves R. Simon's positions on the morality of a Just War.

389   On the Foreseeability of Free Acts
      in:
      *The New Scholasticism* [Washington, D.C.]
      Vol. XXII, No. 4 (October 1948), 357–370.
         This journal was later renamed *American Catholic Philosophical Quarterly.*

390   Three Lectures by Yves R. Simon
      Catholic Renascence: Backgrounds and Problems
      Catholic Renascence and Theology
      Catholic Renascence and Temporal Problems
      in:
      *Renascence* [Milwaukee, Wisconsin]
      Vol. 1, No. 1 (Autumn 1948), 35–39.
         These lectures were edited by John Pick, the editor of *Renascence,* a semi-annual journal published by the Renascence Society at Marquette University.

391   From the Science of Nature to the Science of Society
      in:
      *The New Scholasticism* [Washington, D.C.]
      Vol. XXVII, No. 3 (July 1953) 280–304 (v. 118, chapter 4 of *Practical Knowledge*, pp. 115–136).

392   Maritain's Thomism
      in:
      *The Commonweal* [New York]
      Vol. LIX, No. 24 (March 19, 1954), 601.
         A letter to the editor of *The Commonweal* in response to a book review by James V. Mullaney of Charles A. Fecher's *The Philosophy of Jacques Maritain* published in *The Commonweal,* February 26, 1954; pp. 534–536.

393   The Rationality of the Christian Faith
      in:
      *Thought* [New York]
      Vol. XXXI, No. 123 (Winter 1956–57), 495–508.
         Based on a lecture delivered at Hamilton College, New York. *Thought: A Review of Culture and Idea* was a quarterly journal published by Fordham University, Bronx, New York.

394 The Community of Intellects
in:
*Cap and Gown* [Notre Dame, Indiana]
Vol. XXII, No. 1 (December 1957), 5–6 (v. 348.1).
   Yves R. Simon was the feature speaker for the inaugural of the University of Notre Dame's annual Faculty Day.

394.1 Philosophy, Humanities, and Education
Newly titled republication of the article above
in:
*The New Scholasticism* [Washington, D.C.]
Vol. XlII, No. 4 (Autumn 1988), 467–471 (v. 348).

395 The Philosopher's Calling
The 1958 Cardinal Spellman–Aquinas Medalist Address
Delivered at Detroit, Michigan.
in:
Role of the Christian Philosopher*
*Proceedings of the American Catholic Philosophical Association*
   [Washington, D.C.]
Vol. XXXII (1958), 29–34.
Reprinted: New York: Johnson Reprint Corporation, 1992.

396 On Order in Analogical Sets
in:
*The New Scholasticism* [Washington, D.C.]
Vol. XXXIV, No. 1 (January 1960), 1–42.

397 Common Good and Common Action
in:
*The Review of Politics* [Notre Dame, Indiana]
Vol. 22, No. 2 (April 1960), 202–244
Reprinted: Kraus Reprint Corporation, 1992 (v. 111, *A General Theory of Authority*).

398 Introduction to the Study of Practical Wisdom
in:
*The New Scholasticism* [Washington, D.C.]
Vol. XXXV, No. 1 (January 1961), 1–40 (v. 118, chapter

1 of *Practical Knowledge*, pp. 1–26; see also 223, *The Great Ideas Today*, 1988; pp. 382–405).

399 To Be and to Know
in:
*Chicago Review* [Chicago].
Vol. 14, No. 4 (Spring 1961), 83–100.
   A quarterly review published at The University of Chicago.

400 On Art and Morality
in:
*The New Scholasticism* [Washington, D. C.]
Vol. XXXV, No. 3 (July 1961), 338–341.

401 Nature and the Process of Mathematical Abstraction
Edited by Edward D. Simmons
in:
*The Thomist* [Baltimore, Maryland]
Vol. XXIX, No. 2 (April 1965), 117–139.

402 Jacques Maritain
in:
*U.S. Catholic* [Chicago]
Vol. XXXIV, No. 1 (May 1968), 43–44.
   The publication of this address was occasioned by the presentation to Jacques Maritain of the Leo XIII Award for outstanding work in Christian Education by the Sheil School of Social Studies in Chicago on November 28, 1948. This address is part of a letter to the editor by Anthony O. Simon.

402.1 Yves R. Simon on Maritain
in:
*Maritain Newsletter* [San Francisco]
Vol. 1, No. 1 (Fall 1988), 4.
   Reprint of the Sheil School address above.

403 La loi et la liberté
in:
*Nova et Vetera* [Geneva]
XLIVème Année, No. 1 (Janvier–Mars 1969), 42–53 (v. *Traité du libre arbitre*, 110, 110.1, 110.2).

403.1 Law and Liberty
Translated by Peter Wolff
in:
*The Review of Politics* [Notre Dame, Indiana]
Vol. 52, No. 1 (Winter 1990), 107–118 (v. 110, 110.1, 110.2).

404 An Essay on the Classification of Action and the Understanding of Act
in:
*Revue de l'Université d'Ottawa* [Ottawa]
Edited by John N. Deely
Vol. 41, No. 4 (Octobre–Décembre 1971), 518–541.

405 Socialisme et démocratie
in:
*Revue de l'Université d'Ottawa* [Ottawa]
Translated by Paule Simon
Vol. 42, No. 1 (Janvier–Mars 1972), 8–34 (v. chapter 4 of 108.1).

406 A Comment on Censorship
in:
*International Philosophical Quarterly* [New York]
Vol. XVII, No. 1 (March 1977), 33–42.

407 Mes premiers souvenirs de Jacques Maritain
in:
*The New Scholasticism* [Washington, D.C.]
Vol. LVI, No. 2 (Spring 1982), 200–206.

407.1 My First Memories of Jacques Maritain
in:
*Notes et Documents* [Rome]
Translated and edited by Anthony O. Simon
N.S. Nos. 2–3 (Avril–Septembre 1983), pp. 106–110.

407.2 Mis primeros recuerdos de Jacques Maritain
in:
*Notas y Documentos* [Caracas, Venezuela].
Translated by Melena de Sanchez Pelaez
N.S. Año 1, No. 1 (Julio–Septiembre 1984), 74–78

This journal is the South American edition of *Notes et Documents*.

407.3   My First Memories of Jacques Maritain
Translated and edited by Anthony O. Simon
*Maritain Institute Series* [Niagara, New York]
Niagara University, 1985. Pp. 1–5.

408   The First Non-Scholastic Among the Disciples of St. Thomas
in:
*Notes et Documents* [Rome]
The Maritain Centenary Issue
VIIème Année, No. 27 (Avril–Juin 1982), 46–50.
This is a condensed version of 116 and 217.

409   Jacques Maritain
in:
*Cahiers Jacques Maritain* [Kolbsheim, France]
Edited by Anthony O. Simon
No. 11 (Juin 1985), 5–24 (v. *Jacques Maritain: Homage in Words and Pictures*, 116).

410   Some Remarks on the Object of Physical Knowledge
in:
*International Philosophical Quarterly* [New York]
Edited by Ralph Nelson and Anthony O. Simon
Vol. 32, No. 3 (September 1992), 275–283 (v. 107, 107.1, chapter 5 in *Prévoir et savoir* and *Foresight and Knowledge*).

411   Foreword to *Foresight and Knowledge*
in
*American Catholic Philosophical Quarterly* [Washington, D.C.].
Edited by Ralph Nelson and Anthony O. Simon
Vol. LXVI, No. 3 (1992), 322–325 (v. 107, 107.1, The foreword to *Prévoir et savoir* and *Foresight and Knowledge*).

412   Science and Systematic Knowledge
in:
*American Catholic Philosophical Quarterly* [Washington, D.C.]

Edited by Ralph Nelson and Anthony O. Simon
Vol. LXVI, No. 3 (1992), 325–330 (v. 107, 107.1, chapter 2 in *Prévoir et savoir* and *Foresight and Knowledge*).

413 The Vienna Circle: Meaning and Objectivity
Translated and edited by Ralph Nelson and Anthony O. Simon
in:
*Semiotica* [Berlin–New York]
Vol. 102, Nos. 3–4 (November 1994), 279–293 (v. 107, 107.1, chapter 3 of *Prévoir et savoir* and *Foresight and Knowledge*).

This is the Journal of the International Association for Semiotic Studies edited by Thomas A. Sebeok at Indiana University in Bloomington, Indiana.

V

SELECTED BOOK AND ARTICLE REVIEWS

500 Étienne Gilson
*Le thomisme* [Revised edition]
Paris: Jules Vrin, 1922
in:
*Philosophies* [Paris]
No. 1 (15 Mars 1924) 86.

Founded in 1924 by a group of philosophy students at the Sorbonne, this journal was heavily influenced by Max Jacob.

501 Robert Streit
*Les missions catholiques: Statistiques et graphiques des missions catholiques d'après l'exposition missionnaire vaticane*
Paris: Desclée de Brouwer, 1927
in:
*La Vie Intellectuelle* [Paris]
Tome II, No. 7 (Avril 1929) 746–750 (v. 329).

502 Jacques Maritain
*La philosophie bergsonienne*
Paris: Rivière, 1930

in:
*Les Cahiers Thomistes* [Paris]
Tome 6, No. 2 (25 Novembre 1930), 151–153.

503 Raïssa Maritain
Histoire d'Abraham ou la sainteté dans l'état de nature
in:
*Univers* [Lille–Paris]
2ème Année, No. 13 (Mars 1936), 19.
A brief review notice on an article by Raïssa Maritain published in *Nova et Vetera*, No. 3 (1935), 239–266.

504 Roland Dalbiez
*La méthode psychanalytique et la doctrine freudienne*
Bibliothèque de Philosophie Médicale
Paris: Desclée de Brouwer, 1936
in:
*La Vie Intellectuelle* [Paris]
Tome XLIII, No. 3 (25 Juin 1936), 491–493.

505 André Tardieu
*La révolution à refaire*
Paris: Flammarion, 1936
in:
*La Vie Intellectuelle* [Paris]
Tome XLIV, No. 1 (10 Juillet 1936), 104–107.

506 Martin Grabmann
*Saint Thomas d'Aquin*
Paris: Bloud et Gay, 1936
in:
*La Vie Catholique* [Paris]
14ème Anneé, No. 641 (9 Janvier 1937), 9.

507 Pierre-Henri Simon
*Discours sur la guerre possible*
Paris: Editions du Cerf, 1937
in:
*La Vie Catholique* [Paris]
14Vème Année, No. 656 (24 Mars 1937), 19.
This review is signed *Marcel Olivier,* one of the

pseudonyms Yves R. Simon used during the late '30s and '40s.

508   Étienne Borne and François Henry
      *Le travail et l'homme*
      Paris: Desclée de Brouwer, 1937
      in:
      *Revue Thomiste* [Paris]
      Tome XLIV, No. 1 (Janvier 1938), 199–203.

509   André Maurois
      *I Remember, I Remember*
      New York: Harper, 1943
      in:
      *Books on Trial* [Chicago]
      Vol. 1, No. 7 (March 1943), 206.

*REVUE DE PHILOSOPHIE* [Paris]
This journal founded in 1900 by Émile Peillaube. It was published first by Marcel Rivière, then, in 1930, by Pierre Téqui in Paris. Yves R. Simon was its Secrétaire Général from 1934 to 1938, until his departure to the United States for the University of Notre Dame where he became a distinguished Visiting Professor in the fall of 1938. The journal started a nouvelle série (N. S.) beginning with the Tome I (January–February 1930) issue. Items from *Revue de Philosophie* referred to in this bibliography have been corrected to their true tome numbers.

The following tomes of the *Revue de Philosophie* are mislabeled: tome 1931 is mislabeled tome I; 1933 and 1934 as tome IV; 1935 as tome V; 1936 and 1937 as VI; 1938 as tome VII. All the yearly volumes are correctly dated, so pagination can easily be verified in (1930–1938) bound sets. I have corrected all mislabelings.

510   Jules de la Vaissière
      *La théorie psychanalytique de Freud*
      Paris: Beauchesne, 1930
      in:
      N.S. Tome II, No. 6 (Novembre–Décembre 1931), 661–664.

511   Georges Gurvitch
      *Les tendances actuelles de la philosophie allemande*

Paris: Jules Vrin, 1930
in:
N.S. Tome IV, Nos. 4–5 (Juillet–Octobre 1933), 510–513.

512 Ewald Oldekop
*Le principe de hiérarchie dans la nature*
Paris: Jules Vrin, 1933
in:
N.S. Tome V, Nos. 1–2 (Janvier–Avril 1934), 123–127.

513 Gaston Rabeau
*Dieu: Son existence et sa providence*
Paris: Bloud et Gay, 1933
in:
N.S. Tome V, No. 4 (Juillet–Août 1934), 311–313.

514 M. T.-L. Penido
*Dieu dans le bergsonisme*
Paris: Desclée de Brouwer, 1934
in:
N.S. Tome V, No. 4 (Juillet–Août 1934), 313–316.

515 Chanoine Dehove
*La théorie bergsonienne de la morale et de la religion*
Lille: Société d'Impressions Littéraires, Industrielles, et Commerciales, 1933
in:
N.S. Tome V, No. 4 (Juillet–Août 1934), 319–321.

516 Henri Sérouya
*Initiation à la philosophie contemporaine*
Paris: La Renaissance du Livre, 1933
in:
N.S. Tome V, Nos. 5–6 (Septembre–Décembre 1934), 500–501.

517 Gaetan Pirou
*Le corporatisme*
Paris: Sirey, 1934
in:
N.S. Tome VI, No. 3 (Mai–Juin 1935), 276–278.

518 Auguste Pinloche
*Fourier et le socialisme*
Paris: Alcan, 1933
in:
N.S. Tome VI, No. 3 (Mai–Juin 1935), 278–279.

519 Antoine Lemonnyer, A. J. Tonneau, Robert Troude
*Précis de sociologie*
Marseille: Editions Publiroc, 1934
in:
N.S. Tome VII, No. 1 (Janvier–Février 1936), 76–79.

520 Charles Nicolle
*La nature: Conception et morale biologiques*
Paris: Alcan, 1934
in:
N.S. Tome VII, No. 6 (Novembre–Décembre 1936), 544–556.

521 R. S. Lacape
*La notion de liberté et la crise du déterminisme*
Paris: Hermann, 1935
in:
N.S. Tome VII (Novembre–Décembre 1936), 556–557.

522 Louis de Raeymaeker
*Introductio generalis ad philosophiam et ad Thomismum*
Louvain: E. Warny, 1934
in:
N.S. Tome VII (Novembre/Décembre 1936), 564–565.

523 Federigo Enriques
*Signification de l'histoire de la pensée scientifique*
Paris: Hermann, 1934
in:
N.S. Tome VIII (Janvier 1937), 173–174.

524 Georges Urbain and Marcel Boll, eds.
*La science, ses progrès, ses applications* I–II
Paris: Larousse, 1936
in:
N.S. Tome VIII (Janvier 1937), 174–176.

525 Hélène Metzger
*La philosophie de la matière chez Lavoisier*
Paris: Hermann, 1935
in:
N.S. Tome VIII (Janvier 1937), 177–178.

526 Lefebvre des Noettes
*De la marine antique à la marine moderne*
Paris: Masson, 1935
in:
N.S. Tome VIII (Janvier 1937), 182–183.

527 Daniel Lallement
*Principes catholiques d'action civique*
Paris: Desclée de Brouwer, 1935
in:
N.S. Tome VIII (Avril 1937), 267–268.

528 Jacques Paliard
*Le monde des idoles: Connaissance de l'illusion*
Paris: Bloud et Gay, 1936
in:
N.S. Tome VIII (Juillet 1937), 360–362.

529 Célestin Bouglé
*Bilan de la sociologie française contemporaine*
Paris: Alcan, 1935
in:
N.S. Tome IX (Janvier–Février 1938), 79–82.

530 Armand Cuvillier
*Introduction à la sociologie*
Paris: Armand Colin, 1936
in:
N.S. Tome IX (Janvier–Février 1938), 82–85.

531 Raymond Aron
*La sociologie allemande contemporaine*
Paris: Alcan, 1935
in:
N.S. Tome IX (Janvier–Février 1938), 85–88.

532 Arthur Mettler
*Max Weber und die philosophische Problematik in unserer Zeit*

Leipzig: Hirzel, 1934
in:
N.S. Tome IX (Janvier–Février 1938), 88.

533 Armand Cuvillier
*Proudhon*
Paris: Éditions Sociales Internationales, 1937
in:
N.S. Tome IX (Janvier–Février 1938), 88–89.

534 Philipp Frank
*La fin de la physique mécaniste*
Collection ⟨Actualités Scientifiques et Industrielles⟩ No. 414
Paris: Hermann, 1936
in:
N.S. Tome X, No. 1 (Janvier–Février 1939), 79–81 (v. 107, 107.1, *Prévoir et savoir* and *Foresight and Knowledge*).

*THE REVIEW OF POLITICS*
University of Notre Dame, Notre Dame, Indiana
Yves R. Simon reviews, 1939–1947
Reprinted Kraus Reprint Corporation, New York.

535 Élie Halévy
*L'ère des tyrannies*
Paris: Librairie Gallimard, 1938
in:
Vol. I, No. 4 (October 1939), 500–501.

536 Simon Deploige
*The Conflict between Ethics and Sociology*
St. Louis, Missouri: B. Herder Book Company, 1938
in:
Vol. II, No. 1 (January 1940), 131–132.

537 Ross J. S. Hoffman
*The Organic State*
New York: Sheed and Ward, 1940
in:
Vol. II, No. 2 (April 1940), 228–230.

538　Dennis W. Brogan
*France under the Republic (1870–1939)*
New York: Harper and Brothers, 1940
in:
Vol. III, No. 1 (January 1941), 124–125.

539　Hamilton Fish Armstrong
*Chronology of Failure*
New York: Macmillan Company, 1940
in:
Vol. III, No. 1 (January 1941), 125.

540　Edmond Taylor
*The Strategy of Terror*
Boston, Massachusetts: Houghton Mifflin Company, 1940
in:
Vol. III, No. 1 (January 1941), 125–127.

541　André Maurois
*Tragedy in France*
New York: Harper and Brothers, 1940
in:
Vol. III, No. 1 (January 1941), 127–128.

542　André Simone
*J'accuse: The Men Who Betrayed France*
New York: Dial Press, 1940
in:
Vol. III, No. 1 (January 1941), 128.

543　Stanton B. Leeds
*These Rule France*
New York: Bobbs-Merrill Company, 1940
in:
Vol. III, No. 1 (January 1941), 128–129.

544　André Morize
*France: Été 1914*
New York: Éditions de la Maison Française, 1941
in:
Vol. III, No. 4 (October 1941), 500–501.

545　Robert de Saint Jean
*Démocratie, burre, et canons*

New York: Éditions de la Maison Française, 1941
in:
Vol. III, No. 4 (October 1941), 501.

546 Georges Gurvitch
*Sociology of Law*
New York: Philosophical Library, 1942
in:
Vol. IV, No. 3 (July 1942), 361–362.

547 Geoffrey Bruun
*Clémenceau*
Cambridge, Massachusetts: Harvard University Press, 1943
in:
Vol. VI, No. 3 (July 1944), 382–383.

548 Charles De Koninck
"On the Common Good"
*De la primauté du bien commun contre les personalistes*
Québec: Éditions de l'Université Laval, 1943
in:
Vol. VI, No. 4 (October 1944) 530–533.

  This review was one of the important documents involved in "the Common Good" controversy, involving Charles De Koninck, Jacques Maritain, I. Thomas Eschmann, Yves R. Simon, and others, that raged inside philosophical circles during the 1940s (v. 703).

549 Henri de Lubac
*Proudhon et la christianisme*
Paris: Éditions du Seuil, 1945
in:
Vol. IX, No. 2 (April 1947), 258–261.

550 Hans J. Morgenthau
*Scientific Man vs. Power Politics*
Chicago: The University of Chicago Press, 1946
in:
Vol. IX, No. 4 (October 1947), 506–508.

551 Anton C. Pegis
*Basic Writings of Saint Thomas Aquinas*, 2 vols.

Edited and annotated with an Introduction by Anton C. Pegis
New York: Random House, 1945.
in:
*The Commonweal* [New York].
Vol. XLII, No. 13 (July 13, 1945), 313–314 (v. 100.1, 117).

A review article by Yves R. Simon. See the appendix to *An Introduction to Metaphysics of Knowledge* on "Habitus," pp. 159–160, and chapter 3 of *The Definition of Moral Virtue*, pp. 47–58.

## VI
### Series Edited by Yves R. Simon

(A)  Collection: ⟨Cours et Documents de Philosophie⟩ 1934–1938

This series was originally edited by Yves R. Simon and Jacques de Monléon, but within a short time Simon became the sole editor, with the support and collaboration of Étienne Gilson, professor at the College de France, Raymond Simeterre, professor at l'Institut Catholique de Paris, Réginald Garrigou-Lagrange, O.P., professor at the Collège Angélique in Rome, Gaston Rabeau, professor at the Université de Lille, Benoît Lavaud and M. T-L. Penido, professors at the Université de Fribourg, Charles Journet, professor at the Grande Séminaire de Fribourg, Georges Desgrippes, professor at Prytanée Militaire de La Flèche, Gustave Thibon, A.-M. Goichon, and Olivier Lacombe. The series was published by Pierre Téqui in Paris.

600  Jacques Maritain
*Sept leçons sur l'être et les premiers principes de la raison spéculative*, 1934

601  Georges Dwelshauvers
*L'étude de la pensée: Méthodes et résultats*, 1934

602  Georges Desgrippes
*Études sur Pascal: De l'automatisme à la foi*, 1935

603 Émile Peillaube
*Caractère et personnalité*, 1935

604 Jacques Maritain
*La philosophie de la nature: Essai critique sur ses frontières et son objet*, 1935

605 M. T-L. Penido
*La conscience religieuse: Essai systématique suivi d'illustrations*, 1935

606 Étienne Gilson
*Le réalisme méthodique*, 1936

607 Marcel de Corte
*La philosophie de Gabriel Marcel*, 1937

608 Yves R. Simon
*Trois leçons sur le travail*, 1938 (v. 103, 343, 361, 362)

(B) Collection: ⟨Les Beaux Voyages d'Autrefois⟩
    This book series edited by Yves R. Simon and Pierre Deffontaines was also published by Pierre Téqui, Paris. The series was suspended by the collapse of France in 1940.

609 *Odoric de Pordenone: De Venise à Pekin au Moyen Age*, 1938
Preface by René Grousset.

## VII
### Selected Works on Yves R. Simon

700 Mortimer J. Adler
*The Idea of Freedom*
Volume I: Garden City, New York: Doubleday, 1958. Pp. 689.
Volume II: Garden City, New York: Doubleday, 1961. Pp. 754.
    These volumes contain extensive quotes and discussion of Yves R. Simon's concepts of liberty, freedom, and authority.

701 Mortimer J. Adler
Foreword
in:
Yves R. Simon, *Freedom of Choice*
New York: Fordham University Press, 1969. Reprinted 1987, 1992. Pp. vii–xii (v. 110.4).

702 George Anastaplo
in:
*Freedom in the Modern World: Jacques Maritain, Yves R. Simon, Mortimer J. Adler*
Edited by Michael D. Torre
Notre Dame, Indiana: American Maritain Association/ University of Notre Dame Press, 1989. Reprinted 1990. Pp. 79–85.

703 Eugène Babin
Qui sont ces Personnalistes . . . ?
in:
*Le Canada Français* [Québec]
Deuxième série, Vol XXXII, No. 9 (Mai 1945), 711–714.
    One of the major documents involved in the Jacques Maritain, Charles De Koninck, I. Th. Eschmann, and Yves R. Simon controversy "On the Common Good" which raged during the late 1940s. Babin's article was written in response to Simon's review article "On the Common Good" of De Koninck's book, *De la primauté du bien commun contre les personnalistes,* 1943, which appeared in *The Review of Politics*, Vol. VI, No. 4 (October 1944), 530–533 (v. 548).

704 Laurence Berns
Simon on Freedom: À propos of *Freedom of Choice*
in:
*Revue de l'Université d'Ottawa* [Ottawa]
Vol. 42, No. 1 (Janvier–Mars 1972), 35–45 (v. 110.4).

705 Enrico Berti
Yves R. Simon: Philosophe de la démocratie
in:
*Notes et Documents* [Rome]
N.S. Nos. 2–3 (Avril–Septembre 1983), 111–115.

706     Marshall Burtt
I Recall a Summer Walk with Simon
in:
*The Loveland Herald Press* [Loveland, Ohio]
April 12, 1988, p. 2.

707     Virginia Black
Reflections on Natural Law: A Critical Review of the Thought of Yves R. Simon
in:
*Vera Lex* [Pleasantville, New York]
Vol. IX, No. 2 (1989), 10–13.
     Virginia Black is editor of *Vera Lex*, published at Pace University by the Natural Law Society.

708     David B. Burrell
A Note on Analogy
in:
*The New Scholasticism* [Washington, D.C.]
Vol. XXXVI, No. 2 (April 1962), 225–232.

709     John C. Cahalan
Necessary Truth and Philosophical Method: An Examination
Ph.D. Dissertation, Department of Philosophy, University of Notre Dame, Notre Dame, Indiana, 1968. Pp. 262.

710     John C. Cahalan
Analogy and the Disrepute of Metaphysics
in:
*The Thomist* [Washington, D.C.]
Vol. XXXIV, No. 3 (July 1970), 387–422.

711     Diane M. Caplin
*Authority, Freedom, and Community in the Political Philosophy of Yves R. Simon*
M.A. Thesis, Department of Philosophy, St. Louis University, St. Louis, Missouri, 1990. Pp. 97.

712     Diane M. Caplin
Essentially Human: Democracy in the Thought of Yves R. Simon

Ph.D. Dissertation, Department of Philosophy, Marquette University, Milwaukee, Wisconsin, 1993. Pp. 167.

713 Diane M. Caplin
*The Good Citizen and the Demands of Democracy: An Application of the Political Philosophy of Yves R. Simon*
in:
*Freedom, Virtue, and the Common Good*
Edited by Curtis L. Hancock and Anthony O. Simon
Notre Dame, Indiana: American Maritain Association/University of Notre Dame Press, 1995. Pp. 293–306.

714 A. Robert Caponigri
Introduction
in:
Yves R. Simon, *A General Theory of Authority*
Notre Dame, Indiana: University of Notre Dame Press, 1962. Pp. v–ix.
   The paper editions of 1980 and 1991 substituted a new introduction by Vukan Kuic. Reprint edition of original: Westport, Connecticut: Greenwood Press, 1973, pp. v–ix (v. 111).

715 Carolyn A. Chandler
The Concept of Political Authority in the Works of Emile Durkheim and Yves R. Simon
M.A. Thesis, Texas Tech University, Lubbock, Texas, 1983. Pp. 169.

716 Paul Christophe
*1939–1940, Les catholiques devant la guerre*
Paris: Les Éditions Ouvrières, 1989. Pp. 96, 100, 111, 166.

717 Clarke E. Cochran
Authority and Freedom: The Democratic Philosophy of Yves R. Simon
in:
*Interpretation* [New York]
Vol. 6, No. 2 (May 1977), 107–123.

718 Clarke E. Cochran
Authority and Community: The Contributions of Carl Friedrich, Yves R. Simon and Michael Polanyi

in:
*The American Political Science Review* [Washington, D.C.]
Vol. LXXI, No. 2 (June 1977), 546–558.

719 Clarke E. Cochran
Yves R. Simon and "The Common Good": A Note on the Concept
in:
*Ethics* [Chicago]
Vol. 88, No. 3 (1978), 229–239.

720 Clarke E. Cochran
*Character, Community, and Politics*
University, Alabama: University of Alabama Press, 1982. Pp. 195.

This volume contains extensive discussion of Yves R. Simon's political philosophy. See especially chapters 5, "Authority"; 6, "Freedom"; and 7, "Pluralism, and the Common Good."

721 Clarke E. Cochran and Thomas R. Rourke
The Common Good and Economic Justice: Reflections on the Thought of Yves R. Simon
in:
*The Review of Politics* [Notre Dame, Indiana]
Vol. 54, No. 2 (Spring 1992), 231–252.

722 Clarke E. Cochran and Thomas Rourke
Beyond Ideology in Christian Economic Thought: Yves R. Simon and Recent Debates
in:
*Freedom, Virtue, and the Common Good*
Edited by Curtis L. Hancock and Anthony O. Simon
Notre Dame, Indiana: American Maritain Association/ University of Notre Dame Press, 1995. Pp. 307–331.

723 James A. Corbett
Yves R. Simon at Notre Dame
in:
*Notre Dame Alumnus* [Notre Dame, Indiana]
Vol. 49, No. 5 (October 1971), 8–9.

The author, an historian and graduate of the École

de Chartres, was one of Simon's closest friends at the University of Notre Dame.

724  Maurice Cranston
Political Philosophy in Our Time
in:
*The Great Ideas Today*
Chicago: Encyclopædia Britannica, 1975, pp. 102–145.
   See especially pp. 125–128ff. for a treatment of the political philosophy of Yves R. Simon, Bertrand de Jouvenel, and Raymond Aron.

725  Frederick J. Crosson
Introduction to "Law and Liberty" by Yves R. Simon
in:
*The Review of Politics* [Notre Dame, Indiana]
Vol. 52, No. 1 (Winter 1990), 105–106 (v. 110; chapter 10 of *Traité du libre arbitre*).

726  Gerard J. Dalcourt
Editor's Preface
in:
Yves R. Simon, *The Great Dialogue of Nature and Space*
Albany, New York: Magi Books, 1970. Pp. xiii–xv (v. 114).

727  John N. Deely
Editor's Introductory Note
Yves R. Simon, "An Essay on the Classification of Action and the Understanding of Act"
in:
*Revue de l'Université d'Ottawa* [Ottawa]
Vol. 41, No. 4 (Octobre–Décembre 1971), 518–519.

728  Patrick de Laubier
Un ouvrage d'Yves R. Simon sur la loi naturelle
in:
*Nova et Vetera* [Geneva]
LIème Année, No. 2 (Avril–Juin 1976), 155–159.

729  Patrick de Laubier
Avant-Propos

in:
Yves R. Simon, *Traité du libre arbitre* [Revised edition]
Fribourg: Éditions Universitaires, 1989. Pp. 3–4 (v. 110.2).

730  Raymond L. Dennehy
Yves R. Simon's Metaphysics of Action
in:
*Acquaintance with the Absolute: The Philosophy of Yves R. Simon—Essays and Bibliography*
Edited by Anthony O. Simon
New York: Fordham University Press, 1998. Pp. 19–56 (v. 828).

731  Bernard Doering
The Philosophy of Work and the Future of Civilization: Maritain, Weil and Simon
in:
*From Twilight to Dawn: The Cultural Vision of Jacques Maritain*
Edited by Peter A. Redpath
Notre Dame, Indiana: American Maritain Association/ University of Notre Dame Press, 1990. Pp. 49–71.

732  Pierre-Marie Emonet
Préface
in:
Yves R. Simon, *Traité du libre arbitre* [Revised edition]
Fribourg: Éditions Universitaires, 1989. Pp. 5–7 (v. 110.2).

733  Thomas Fay
The Role of Contingency in the Moral Philosophy of Yves R. Simon
in:
*Contemporary Philosophy* [Boulder, Colorado]
Vol. XVI, No. 3 (May–June 1994), 13–16.

734  Desmond J. FitzGerald
Traité du libre arbitre
in:
*Masterpieces of Catholic Literature*

Edited by Frank N. McGill
New York: Harper & Row, 1965. Pp. 986–989 (v. 110).

735  James R. Flynn
Modern Thomism and Democracy
Ph.D. Dissertation, Department of Political Science, The University of Chicago, Chicago, Illinois,1958. Pp. 451.

736  William A. Frank
Authority as Nurse of Freedom and the Common Good
in:
*Faith & Reason* [Front Royal, Virginia]
Vol. XVI, No. 4 (1990), 371–386.

737  Timothy Fuller
Conversational Gambits in Political Theory: Yves R. Simon's Great Dialogue
in:
*Political Theory* [Beverly Hills, California]
Vol. 10, No. 4 (1982), 566–579.

738  Timothy Fuller
Authority and the Individual in Civil Association: Oakeshott, Flathman, Yves R. Simon
in:
*Authority Revisited: Nomos XXIX*
New York: New York University Press, 1987. Pp. 131–151.

739  Donald A. Gallagher
Yves R. Simon
in:
*The Thinker's Digest* [Dallas, Pennsylvania]
Vol. IV, No. 3 (Spring 1943), 9–10.

740  Donald A. Gallagher
Yves R. Simon: Retrospect and Prospect
in:
*Revue de l'Université d'Ottawa* [Ottawa]
Vol. 41, No. 4 (Octobre–Décembre 1971), 237–244.

741  Donald and Idella Gallagher
Introduction

in:
*The Achievement of Jacques and Raïssa Maritain*
Garden City, New York: Doubleday, 1962. Pp. 7–36.
 The Introduction includes a brief historical survey of Simon's participation among French intellectuals in the 1920s and 1930s. The book is dedicated to Yves René Simon.

742 Donald A. Gallagher
Recollections of Three Thinkers, Adler, Simon, Maritain
in:
*Freedom in the Modern World: Jacques Maritain: Jacques Maritain, Yves R. Simon, and Mortimer J. Adler*
Edited by Michael D. Torre
Notre Dame, Indiana: American Maritain Association/ University of Notre Dame Press, 1989. Reprinted 1990. Pp. 13–30.

743 Francis L. Gammon
A Study of the Theory of Authority of Yves R. Simon
M.A. Thesis, Department of Philosophy, St. John's University, Jamaica, New York, 1966. Pp. 95.

744 Francis L. Gammon
*The Philosophical Thought of Yves R. Simon: A Brief Survey*
in:
*Revue de l'Université d'Ottawa* [Ottawa]
Vol. 42, No. 2 (Avril–Juin 1972), 237–244.

745 Gerald Gerhringer
The Concept of Political Liberty According to Mortimer J. Adler and Yves R. Simon
Ph.D. Dissertation, Facultas Philosophiae, Pontificia Universitas Lateranensis, Rome, 1962. Pp. 199.

746 John Baptist Gichuhi Theuri
Democracy and Authority According to Yves R. Simon
M.A. Thesis, Faculty of Philosophy, Roman Athenaeum of the Holy Cross, Rome, 1993. Pp. 81.

747 Edgard Godói da Mata-Machado
Nota Prévia do tradutor

in:
*Yves R. Simon, Filosophia do Govêrno Democrático*
Portuguese translation by Edgar Godói da Mata-Machado
Rio de Janeiro: Livraria Agir Editóra, 1955. Pp. 1–8 (v. 109.3).

748 Catherine Green
The Nature of Moral Action: An Examination of Yves R. Simon's Metaphysics of Morals
M.A. Thesis, School of Philosophy, The Catholic University of America, Washington, D.C., 1987. Pp. 92.

749 Catherine Green
*Freedom and Determination: An Examination of Yves R. Simon's Ontology of Freedom*
in:
*Freedom in the Modern World: Jacques Maritain, Yves R. Simon, Mortimer J. Adler*
Edited by Michael D. Torre
Notre Dame, Indiana: American Maritain Association/ University of Notre Dame Press, 1989. Reprinted 1990. Pp. 89–99.

750 Marc F. Griesbach
Philosophy of Democratic Government
in:
*Masterpieces of Catholic Literature*
Edited by Frank N. Magill
New York: Harper & Row, 1965. Pp. 982–986 (v. 109).

751 John Gueguen
Parallels on Work, Theory, and Practice in Yves R. Simon and John Paul II
in:
*Freedom in the Modern World: Jacques Maritain, Yves R. Simon, Mortimer J. Adler*
Edited by Michael D. Torre
Notre Dame, Indiana: American Maritain Association/ University of Notre Dame Press, 1989. Reprinted 1990. Pp. 153–161.

752   Terry Hall
Civil Association and the Common Good in the Thought of Michael Oakeshott
Ph.D. Dissertation, School of Philosophy, The Catholic University of America, 1989, p. 275.
    See especially chapter 3, pp. 169–231, for a comparison between Michael Oakeshott and Yves R. Simon on the "Common Good."

753   John Hellman
Introduction: Yves R. Simon, Maritain and the Vichy Catholics
in:
Yves R. Simon, *The Road to Vichy, 1918–1938* [Revised edition]
Lanham, Maryland: University Press of America, 1988. Reprinted 1990. Pp. vii–xxxiv (v. 105.2).

753.1   John Hellman
The Road to Vichy: Yves R. Simon's Lonely Fight Against Fascism
in:
*Crisis* [Notre Dame, Indiana]
Vol. 6, No. 5 (May 1988), 30–37.
    The text is identical but retitled.

753.2   John Hellman
The Road to Vichy: Yves R. Simon's Lonely Fight Against Fascism
in:
*Notes et Documents* [Rome]
N.S. Nos. 24–25 (Janvier–Août 1989), 78–91.

754   John Hellman
Maritain, Simon, and Vichy's Elite Schools
in:
*Freedom in the Modern World: Jacques Maritain, Yves R. Simon, Mortimer J. Adler*
Edited by Michael D. Torre
Notre Dame, Indiana: American Maritain Association/University of Notre Dame Press, 1989. Reprinted 1990. Pp. 165–180.

755 John Hellman
World War II and the Anti-Democratic Impulse in Catholicism
in:
*From Twilight to Dawn: The Cultural Vision of Jacques Maritain*
Edited by Peter A. Redpath
Notre Dame, Indiana: American Maritain Association/ University of Notre Dame Press, 1990. Pp. 95–116.

756 John Hellman
The Anti-Democratic Impulse in Catholicism: Jacques Maritain, Yves R. Simon, and Charles de Gaulle During World War II
in:
*Journal of Church and State* [Waco, Texas]
Vol. 33, No. 3 (Summer 1991), 453–471.

757 John Hittinger
Approaches to Democratic Equality, Maritain, Simon, Kolnai
in:
*Freedom in the Modern World: Jacques Maritain, Yves R. Simon, Mortimer J. Adler*
Edited by Michael D. Torre
Notre Dame, Indiana: American Maritain Association/ University of Notre Dame Press, 1989. Reprinted 1990. Pp. 237–252.

758 John Hittinger
Jacques Maritain and Yves R. Simon's Use of Thomas Aquinas in Their Defense of Liberal Democracy
in:
*Thomas Aquinas and His Legacy*
Edited by David Gallagher
Collection ⟨Studies in Philosophy and the History of Philosophy⟩ No. 28.
Washington, D.C.: The Catholic University of America Press, 1994. Pp. 149–172.

759 Russell Hittinger
Introduction

in:
Yves R. Simon, *The Tradition of Natural Law: A Philosopher's Reflections* [Revised edition]
New York: Fordham University Press, 1992. Pp. vii–xxxii (v. 112.1).

760 Russell Hittinger
Yves R. Simon on Law, Nature, and Practical Reason
in:
*Acquaintance with the Absolute: The Philosophy of Yves R. Simon—Essays and Bibliography*
Edited by Anthony O. Simon
New York: Fordham University Press, 1998. Pp. 101–127 (v. 828).

761 Matthew Hoehn
Yves R. Simon
in:
*Catholic Authors: Contemporary Biographical Sketches, 1930–1947*
Edited by Matthew Hoehn
Newark, New Jersey: St. Mary's Abbey, 1948. Pp. 694–695.

762 John H. Hallowell
Foreword
in:
Yves R. Simon, *The Tradition of Natural Law: A Philosopher's Reflections*
New York: Fordham University Press, 1965. Reprinted 1967. Revised edition 1992. Pp. vii–x (v. 112, 112.1, 112.2).

763 Ngozi Anthony Ikeme
The Basic Principles of Democratic Freedom in the Political Philosophy of Yves R. Simon
Ph.D. Dissertation, Faculty of Philosophy, University of Navarra, Pamplona, Spain, 1993. Pp. 233.

764 Frank L. Keegan
Yves R. Simon: Disciple and Master

in:
*The Notre Dame Scholastic* [Notre Dame, Indiana]
Vol. 101, No. 8 (November 20, 1959), 18–19.
    This article was occasioned by Yves R. Simon's famous last public lecture, on Jacques Maritain, delivered at the University of Notre Dame Law School. *The Notre Dame Scholastic* was the University's weekly magazine.

765    John Killoran
A Moral Realist Perspective on Yves R. Simon's Interpretation of *Habitus*
in:
*Freedom, Virtue, and the Common Good*
Edited by Curtis L. Hancock and Anthony O. Simon
Notre Dame, Indiana: American Maritain Association/University of Notre Dame Press, 1995. Pp. 88–103.

766    John F. X. Knasas
Yves R. Simon and the Neo-Thomist Tradition in Epistemology
in:
*Acquaintance with the Absolute: The Philosophy of Yves R. Simon—Essays and Bibliography*
Edited by Anthony O. Simon
New York: Fordham University Press, 1998. Pp. 83–100 (v. 828).

767    David T. Koyzis
*Towards a Christian Democratic Pluralism: A Comparative Study of Neo-Thomist and Neo-Calvinist Political Theories*
Ph.D. Dissertation, Department of Government and International Studies, University of Notre Dame, Notre Dame, Indiana, 1986. Pp. 398.
    This dissertation is a study and contrast of the political and social thought of Yves R. Simon and the Dutch thinker Herman Dooyeweerd.

768    David T. Koyzis
Yves R. Simon's Contribution to Structural Political Pluralism

in:
*Freedom in the Modern World: Jacques Maritain, Yves R. Simon, Mortimer J. Adler*
Edited by Michael D. Torre
Notre Dame, Indiana: American Maritain Association/ University of Notre Dame Press, 1989. Reprinted 1990. Pp. 131–139.

769   Vukan Kuic
Editor's Preface
in:
Yves R. Simon, *The Tradition of Natural Law: A Philosopher's Reflections*
New York: Fordham University Press, 1965. Reprinted 1967. Pp. xi–xii.
New York: Rose Hill Books/Fordham University Press (revised paperback edition), 1992 (v. 112, 112.1).

770   Vukan Kuic
Editor's Preface
in:
Yves R. Simon, *Work, Society, and Culture*
New York: Fordham University Press, 1971. Pp. ix–xvi.
New York: Fordham University Press (paperback edition), 1986. Pp. ix–xvi (v. 115).

771   Vukan Kuic
The Contribution of Yves R. Simon to Political Science
in:
*The Political Science Reviewer* [Bryn Mawr, Pennsylvania]
Vol. IV (Fall 1974), 55–104.

772   Vukan Kuic
*Jacques Maritain and Yves R. Simon on Truth, Liberty and the Role of the Philosopher in Society*
in:
*Notes et Documents* [Rome]
Vème Année, No. 14 (Janvier–Mars 1979), 9–17.

773   Vukan Kuic
*Introduction*

in:
Yves R. Simon, *A General Theory of Authority*
Notre Dame, Indiana: University of Notre Dame Press, paperback edition, 1980. Reprinted 1991. Pp. 5–12 (v. 111.2).

774 Vukan Kuic
Introduction for "The Politics of Alain" by Yves R. Simon
in:
*Interpretation* [New York].
Vol. 13, No. 2 (May 1985), 213–214 (v. 326).

775 Vukan Kuic
Editor's Preface
in:
Yves R. Simon, *The Definition of Moral Virtue*
New York: Fordham University Press, 1986. Pp. vii–viii.
New York: Fordham University Press/Rose Hill Books, paperback edition, 1986. Reprinted 1989. Pp. vii–viii (v. 117).

776 Vukan Kuic
Yves R. Simon, 1903–1961
in:
*Vera Lex* [Pleasantville, New York]
Vol. IX, No. 2 (1989), 8–9.

777 Vukan Kuic and Richard J. Thompson
Translators' Preface
in:
Yves R. Simon, *An Introduction to Metaphysics of Knowledge*
New York: Fordham University Press, 1990. Pp. vii–xii.
New York: Fordham University Press, paperback edition, 1990. Pp. vii–xii. (v. 100.1).

778 Vukan Kuic
Yves R. Simon on Liberty and Authority
in:
*Acquaintance with the Absolute: The Philosophy of Yves R. Simon—Essays and Bibliography*
Edited by Anthony O. Simon

New York: Fordham University Press, 1998. Pp. 128–146 (v. 828).

779 Olivier Lacombe
*De l'autorité*
Textes presented by Olivier Lacombe
in:
*Pouvoir et société: Recherches et Débats, No. 53*
Paris: Desclée de Brouwer, 1966. Pp. 72–73.
    An introduction to collected abstracts from Yves R. Simon, *A General Theory of Authority* (v. 111, 218).

780 Olivier Lacombe
Yves R. Simon
in:
*Revue de l'Université d'Ottawa* [Ottawa]
Vol. 42, No. 1 (Janvier–Mars 1972), 5–7.
    Olivier Lacombe, Dean Emeritus at the Sorbonne, was one of Yves R. Simon's closest friends and colleagues.

781 Marie-Vincent Leroy
Yves R. Simon, 1903–1961
in:
*Revue Thomiste* [Paris]
Vol. LXXIX, No. IV (Octobre–Décembre 1979), 691–693.
    See also 117, 782, 783, and 784, which are updated and translated versions of this original bio-bibliographic article. M. V. Leroy was the longtime editor of the *Revue Thomiste*.

782 Marie-Vincent Leroy
Yves R. Simon, 1903–1961: A Bio-Bibliography
in:
*The New Scholasticism* [Washington, D.C.]
Vol. LIV, No. 4 (Autumn 1980), 512–518.

783 Marie-Vincent Leroy
Un filosofo christiano: Yves R. Simon, 1903–1961
in:
*Revista del Rosario* [Bogotà, Colombia]
No. 517 (Febrero–Abril 1982), 60–65.

784 Marie-Vincent Leroy
Yves R. Simon, 1903–1961: A Bio-Bibliography
in:
Yves R. Simon, *The Definition of Moral Virtue*
New York: Fordham University Press, 1986. Pp. ix–xiv
New York: Rose Hill Books/Fordham University Press, paperback edition, 1986. Reprinted 1989. Pp. ix–xiv
(v. 117.)

785 John A. Lucal
Yves R. Simon's Theory of Authority
M.A. Thesis, Department of Philosophy, Loyola University, Chicago, Illinois, 1961. Pp. 146.

786 Marianne Mahoney
Prudence as the Cornerstone of the Contemporary Thomistic Philosophy of Freedom
in:
*Freedom in the Modern World: Jacques Maritain, Yves R. Simon, Mortimer J. Adler*
Edited by Michael D. Torre
Notre Dame, Indiana: American Maritain Association/University of Notre Dame Press, 1989. Reprinted 1990. Pp. 117–129.

787 Luisa Mariotti
Attività e verità nella filosofia di Yves R. Simon
Ph.D. Dissertation, Facoltà di Lettere e Filosofia, Università Cattolica del Sacro Cuore, Milan, 1981, p. 157.

788 Jacques Maritain
Yves R. Simon
in:
*Jubilee* [New York]
Vol. 9, No. 4 (August 1961), 2–3.

788.1 Jacques Maritain
Yves R. Simon: Mon frère d'armes
in:
*Nova et Vetera* [Geneva]
Translated by Paule Simon
XLVIIIème Année, No. 1 (Janvier–Mars 1973), 43–45.

788.2 Jacques Maritain
Yves R. Simon: Brother-in-Arms
in:
*Notes et Documents* [Rome]
Vème Année, No. 14 (Janvier–Mars 1979), 3–4.

788.3 Jacques Maritain
Yves R. Simon: Mon frère d'armes
in:
*Jacques et Raïssa Maritain: Œuvres complètes*. XII.
Fribourg: Éditions Universitaires; Paris: Éditions Saint-Paul, 1992. Pp. 1207–1210.

789 Jacques Maritain
[Letters to Yves R. Simon]
Maritain à Yves R. Simon, 8 Janvier 1945
Maritain à Yves R. Simon, 29 Janvier 1945
Maritain à Yves R. Simon, 18 Mars 1945
in:
L'ambassade au Vatican (1945–1948)
*Cahiers Jacques Maritain* [Strasbourg]
4/Bis (Juin 1982). Pp. 11, 17, 20.

    The complete Yves R. Simon/Jacques Maritain correspondence (1929–1961) is available in typed transcription at the Yves R. Simon Institute. The editing and publication of parts of this correspondence is a future project of the Institute.

790 Henri Massis
Les idées & les faits: Surnaturalisme
in:
*La Revue Universelle* [Paris]
Vol. LVII, No. 6 (15 Juin 1934), 743–748.

    An attack by Henri Massis on Yves R. Simon's article "Philosophie chrétienne," published in *Études Carmélitaines*, 19ème Année, 1 (Avril 1934), 107–119. Henri Massis was editor of the influential *La Revue Universelle*.

791 Ralph McInerny
On Yves R. Simon as a Moral Philosopher

in:
*Freedom, Virtue, and the Common Good*
Edited by Curtis L. Hancock and Anthony O. Simon
Notre Dame, Indiana: American Maritain Association/ University of Notre Dame Press, 1995. Pp. 76–87.

792    George J. McMorrow
Yves R. Simon
in:
*New Catholic Encyclopaedia*
San Francisco: McGraw-Hill, 1967. Pp. 226–227.

793    Edmond Michelet
Mon ami Yves R. Simon
in:
*Nova et Vetera* [Geneva]
XLIIIème Année, No. 3 (Juillet–Septembre 1968), 208–213.

    A homage by Edmond Michelet, who was French Minister of Culture and held various cabinet positions during de Gaulle's presidency. He was a lifelong friend of Yves R. Simon's.

793.1  Edmond Michelet
Mon ami Yves R. Simon
in:
*Listening Magazine* [Dubuque, Iowa]
Translated by Paule Simon
Vol. 5, Nos. 2–3 (1970), 145–152.

793.2  Edmond Michelet
Mon ami Yves R. Simon
in:
*Association des Anciens et Anciennes Élèves* [Paris]
Décembre 1988, pp. 31–36.

    The article is preceded by brief biographic comments on Yves R. Simon. The journal is published by the Collège de Valognes de l'Institut Saint Paul et des Écoles Catholiques Associées de Cherbourg. Yves R. Simon was a student at l'Institut Saint-Paul in Cherbourg.

794 Robert J. Mulvaney
Freedom and Practical Rationality in the Thought of Yves R. Simon
in:
*Freedom in the Modern World: Jacques Maritain, Yves R. Simon, Mortimer J. Adler*
Edited by Michael D. Torre
Notre Dame, Indiana: American Maritain Association / University of Notre Dame Press, 1989. Reprinted 1990. Pp. 109–116.

795 Robert Mulvaney
Editor's Note
in:
Yves R. Simon, *Practical Knowledge*
New York: Fordham University Press, 1991. Pp. vii–xiii (v. 118).

796 Robert J. Mulvaney
Practical Wisdom in the Thought of Yves R. Simon
in:
*Acquaintance with the Absolute: The Philosophy of Yves R. Simon—Essays and Bibliography*
Edited by Anthony O. Simon
New York: Fordham University Press, 1997. Pp. 147–181 (v. 828).

797 Arthur E. Murphy
An Ambiguity in Professor Simon's *Philosophy of Democratic Government*
in:
*The Philosophical Review* [Ithaca, New York]
Vol. LXI, No. 2 (April 1952), 198–211.
    Yves R. Simon answered Murphy's criticism in the appendix of his sequel to *Philosophy of Democratic Government*, published by the University of Notre Dame Press and entitled *A General Theory of Authority*. See "On the Meaning of Civil Obedience," pp. 163–167 (v. 111).

798 J. Stanley Murphy
Yves R. Simon and the Free World: A Canadian View
in:
*Revue de l'Université d'Ottawa* [Ottawa]

Vol. 42, No. 2 (Avril–Juin 1972), 245–251.

An historical survey of Yves R. Simon's lectures and publications in Canada. J. Stanley Murphy was director of the Christian Culture Series at Assumption University, Windsor, Ontario.

799   John U. Nef
John U. Nef Recalls Yves R. Simon
in:
*The University of Chicago Magazine* [Chicago]
Vol. LXIV, No. 5 (May–June 1972), 37–38.

A homage by John U. Nef, who was a co-founder with chancellor Robert M. Hutchins and first chairman of the graduate Committee on Social Thought at The University of Chicago, where Yves R. Simon taught from 1947 to 1961.

800   Ralph Nelson
Freedom and Economic Organization in a Democracy
in:
*Freedom in the Modern World: Jacques Maritain, Yves R. Simon, Mortimer J. Adler*
Edited by Michael D. Torre
Notre Dame, Indiana: American Maritain Association/ University of Notre Dame Press, 1989. Reprinted 1990. Pp. 141–152.

801   Ralph Nelson
Translator's Foreword
Yves R. Simon, "Knowledge of the Soul"
in:
*The Thomist* [Washington, D.C.]
Vol. 54, No. 2 (April 1990), 269–271 (v. 378.1).

802   Ralph Nelson and Anthony O. Simon
Translators' Introduction
Yves R. Simon, "The Vienna Circle: Meaning and Objectivity"
in:
*Semiotica* [Berlin/New York]
Vol. 102, Nos. 3–4 (1994), 279 (v. 107.1, chapter 3 of *Foresight and Knowledge*).

803 Ralph Nelson
The Scope of Justice
in:
*Freedom, Virtue, and the Common Good*
Edited by Curtis L. Hancock and Anthony O. Simon
Notre Dame, Indiana: American Maritain Association/ University of Notre Dame Press, 1995. Pp. 342–357.

804 Ralph Nelson
Introduction
in:
Yves R. Simon, *Foresight and Knowledge*
Edited by Ralph Nelson and Anthony O. Simon
New York: Fordham University Press, 1995. Pp. vii–xix (v. 107.1).

805 Ralph Nelson
Yves R. Simon's Philosophy of Science
in:
*Acquaintance with the Absolute: The Philosophy of Yves R. Simon—Essays and Bibliography*
Edited by Anthony O. Simon
New York: Fordham University Press, 1998. Pp. 57–82 (v. 828).

806 Michael Novak
Free Persons and the Common Good
Lanham, Maryland: Madison Books, 1989. Pp. 233.
    This volume contains an extensive treatment of Yves R. Simon's political philosophy, especially his concept of "The Common Good."

807 Sean P. O'Connell
A Treatment of Free Choice as Found in the Philosophical Writings of Yves R. Simon
M.A. Thesis, School of Philosophy, The Catholic University of America, Washington, D.C , 1981. Pp. 100.

808 Charles P. O'Donnell
Editor's Preface
in:
Yves R. Simon, *Freedom and Community*

New York: Fordham University Press, 1968. Pp. xi–xx (v. 113).

809 Charles P. O'Donnell
Democracy in the Philosophy of Jacques Maritain and Yves R. Simon
in:
*Notes et Documents* [Rome]
Vol. 5, No. 14 (Janvier–Mars 1979), 18–27.

810 Roberto Papini
Presentazione
in:
*Omaggio a Jacques Maritain: Parole e immagini*
By John Howard Griffin and Yves R. Simon
Milan: Editrice Massimo, 1981. P. 7 (v. 116.1).

811 Christopher James Pollard
The Concept of Virtue as *Habitus* in the Moral Philosophy of Yves R. Simon
M.A. Thesis, School of Philosophy, The Catholic University of America, Washington, D.C., 1994. Pp. 98.

812 Jacques Marie Ramirez
Sur l'organization du savoir moral d'après J. Maritain, Y. Simon, et Th. Deman
in:
*Bulletin Thomiste* [Paris]
Vol. XII, Tome IV, No. 6 (Avril–Juin 1935), 423–432.

813 Patricia Pallasch Radzin
The Development of the Relation Between Authority and Freedom in the Political Philosophy of Yves R. Simon
Ph.D. Dissertation, Department of Philosophy, Marquette University, Milwaukee, Wisconsin, 1995. Pp. 222.

814 Clare Riedl
Yves R. Simon, Philosopher
in:
*Revue de l'Université d'Ottawa* [Ottawa]
Vol. 42, No. 2 (Avril–Juin 1972), 232–236.

815   José Antonio Rivera
      Political Authority and the Good in the Thought of Yves R. Simon and Luis Muñoz Marín
      Ph.D. Dissertation, School of Philosophy, The Catholic University of America, Washington, D.C., 1993. Pp. 239.

816   José Antonio Rivera
      Fundamentos filosóficos del concepto muñocista de la libertad
      in:
      *Diálogos* [San Juan, Puerto Rico]
      Vol. 30, No. 66 (Julio 1995), 137–151.
      This article is based on the author's dissertation; see above.

817   Thomas R. Rourke and Clarke E. Cochran
      The Common Good and Economic Justice: Reflections on the Thought of Yves R. Simon
      in:
      *The Review of Politics* [Notre Dame, Indiana]
      Vol. 52, No. 2 (Spring 1992), 231–252.

818   Thomas R. Rourke
      Yves R. Simon and Contemporary Catholic Neo-Conservatism
      Ph.D. Dissertation, Department of Political Science, Texas Tech University, Lubbock, Texas, 1994. Pp. 265.

819   Thomas R. Rourke and Clarke E. Cochran
      Beyond Ideology in Christian Economic Thought: Yves R. Simon and Recent Debates
      in:
      *Freedom, Virtue, and the Common Good*
      Edited by Curtis L. Hancock and Anthony O. Simon
      Notre Dame, Indiana: American Maritain Association/ University of Notre Dame Press, 1995. Pp. 307–331.

820   Glen N. Schram
      A Neo-Thomist's Defense of Democracy
      in:
      *New Oxford Review* [Berkeley, California]
      Vol. LX, No. 1 (January–February 1993), 13–17 (v. 109).

821   Anthony O. Simon
      Bibliographie de Yves René Simon, 1923–1968
      in:
      *Revue Philosophique de Louvain* [Louvain]
      Tome 67, IIIème Série, No. 94 (Mai 1969), 285–305.

822   Anthony O. Simon
      Bibliographie d'Yves René Simon: Complément, 1969–1974
      in:
      *Revue Philosophique de Louvain* [Louvain]
      Tome 73, IVème Série, No. 18 (Mai 1975), 362–367.

823   Anthony O. Simon
      Yves R. Simon: A Bibliography, 1923–1970
      in:
      Yves R. Simon, *Work, Society, and Culture*
      New York: Fordham University Press, 1971. Pp. 190–228 (v. 115).

824   Anthony O. Simon
      *Yves R. Simon: A Bibliography*
      in:
      *Notes et Documents* [Rome]
      Vème Année, No. 14 (Janvier–Mars 1979), 36–37.

825   Anthony O. Simon
      Foreword
      in:
      *Jacques Maritain: Homage in Words and Pictures*
      By John Howard Griffin and Yves R. Simon
      Albany, New York: Magi Books, 1974. Pp. ix–xii (v. 116. 116.1).

826   Anthony O. Simon
      Foreword
      in:
      *Notes et Documents* [Rome]
      The Yves R. Simon/Jacques Maritain Special Issue
      Edited by Anthony O. Simon
      Vème Année, No. 14 (Janvier–Mars 1979), 1.

827 Anthony O. Simon
Bibliograpfia dziel Yves R. Simon
in:
Yves R. Simon, *Filozofia Rzadu Demokratycznego*
Crakow: Wydawnictwo Arka, 1993. Pp. 262–275 (v. 109.7).
    This bibliography of Simon's books was translated by Ryszard Legutko and included as an appendix to the Polish edition of Yves R. Simon, *Philosophy of Democratic Government*.

828 Anthony O. Simon
*Acquaintance with the Absolute: The Philosophy of Yves R. Simon—Essays and Bibliography*
Edited by Anthony O. Simon
New York: Fordham University Press, 1998.
Contents:
    Editor's Note
    Part I: Essays
        Yves R. Simon's Metaphysics of Action
            Raymond L. Dennehy
        Yves R. Simon's Philosophy of Science
            Ralph Nelson
        Yves R. Simon on Natural Law
            Russell Hittinger
        Yves R. Simon and the Neo-Thomist Tradition in Epistemology
            John F. X. Knasas
        Yves R. Simon on Liberty and Authority
            Vukan Kuic
        Practical Wisdom in the Thought of Yves R. Simon
            Robert J. Mulvaney
    Part II:
        Yves R. Simon: A Definitive Bibliography, 1923–1997
            Compiled and Annotated by Anthony O. Simon
        Indexes

829 Anthony O. Simon
Yves R. Simon : A Definitive Bibliography, 1923–1995

in:
*Acquaintance with the Absolute: The Philosophy of Yves R. Simon—Essays and Bibliography*
Edited by Anthony O. Simon
New York: Fordham University Press, 1998. Pp. 185–305.

830 Paule Yves Simon
The Papers of Yves R. Simon
in:
*The New Scholasticism* [Washington, D.C.]
Vol. XXXII, No. 4 (October 1963), 501–507.

831 Pierre-Henri Simon
Yves R. Simon
in:
*Revue de l'Université d'Ottawa* [Ottawa]
Vol. 42, No. 2 (Avril–Juin 1972), 227–231.

Pierre-Henri Simon (1903–1972), member de l'Académie Française and literary critic of *Le Monde*, was a lifelong friend of Yves R. Simon's. They were students together in Paris and colleagues at Lille. His bibliography and some supplemental articles are contained in *Témoin de l'homme: Hommage à Pierre-Henri Simon*, Fribourg: Éditions Universitaires, 1994, pp. 217.

832 Yves R. Simon
La philosophie dans la foi: Extrait des mémoires d'un philosophe français
in:
*La Nouvelle Relève* [Montréal]
Part I, Vol. I, No. 5 (Février 1942), 257–265 (v. 367)
Part II, Vol. I, No. 6 (Mars 1942), 336–342 (v. 367).

833 Yves R. Simon
Philosophy and Faith: Extract from the Memoirs of a French Philosopher [Part II]
Translated by Vukan Kuic
in:
*Notes et Documents* [Rome]
Vème Année, No. 14 (Janvier–Mars 1979), 5–8 (v. 833).

834  Yves R. Simon
Philosophy and Faith: Extract from the Memoirs of a French Philosopher [Part I]
Edited and translated by Anthony O. Simon
*Notes et Documents* [Rome]
N.S.. XIIIème Année, No. 23 (Septembre–Décembre 1988), 76–82 (v. 833).

835  Yves R. Simon
Autobiographical Essay
in:
*The Book of Catholic Authors* [Third Series]
Edited by Walter Romig
Detroit: Walter Romig Company, 1945. Pp. 262–270 (v. 206).

836  Vincent Edward Smith
Professor Yves R. Simon: A Citation for the 1958 Award of the Spellman-Aquinas Medal
in:
The Role of the Christian Philosopher
*Proceedings of the American Catholic Philosophical Association* [Washington, D.C.]
Vol. 32 (1958), 28–29
Reprinted: New York: Johnson Reprint Corporation, 1991.

837  Gerard Smith
Eulogy for Yves R. Simon
in:
*Renascence* [Milwaukee, Wisconsin]
Vol. XXIV, No. 3 (Spring 1972), 115–118.
   Gerard Smith was chairman of the philosophy department at Marquette University.

838  Robert Speaight
A Frenchman Speaks
in:
*Blackfriars* [London]
Vol. XXIII, No. 262 (January 1942), 15–17.
   Robert Speaight, C.B.E., was an English writer, bi-

ographer, actor, and literary critic. He taught at the University of Notre Dame during 1939–1940 and developed a great friendship with Simon.

839   Robert Speaight
Yves R. Simon: Friend and Ally
in:
*The Catholic World* [New York]
Vol. 211, No. 1266 (September 1970), 268–269.

840   W. J. Stankiewicz
Yves R. Simon's Transmission Theory of Consent
in:
*In Defense of Sovereignty*
New York: Oxford University Press, 1969. Pp. 34–37.

841   W. J. Stankiewicz
In Defense of Yves R. Simon
in:
*Approaches to Democracy: Philosophy of Government at the Close of the Twentieth Century*
New York: St. Martin's Press, 1980. Pp. 228–234.

842   Leo Strauss
Yves R. Simon, *Philosophy of Democratic Government*
in:
*What Is Political Philosophy?*
New York: The Free Press, 1959. Pp. 306–311
Chicago: The University of Chicago Press, 1959. Reprinted 1988. Pp. 306–311
Reprinted: Westport, Connecticut: Greenwood Press, 1973. Pp. 306–311 (v. 109).

Leo Strauss was a German political scientist and a colleague of Simon's who taught at the University of Chicago. He esteemed Simon's philosophical thought and referred his students to Simon's classes at the Committee on Social Thought.

842.1   Leo Strauss
Yves R. Simon, *Philosophy of Democratic Government*
in:
*Qu'est-ce que la philosophie politique?*

French translation by Olivier Sedeyn
Paris: Presses Universitaires de France, 1992. Pp. 290–294
(v. 109).

843 Karen Stadler
Signification de quelques notions clés employées dans la psychanalyse de Sigmund Freud et dans la théologie morale de St. Thomas d'Aquin
M.A. Thesis, Gregorian University, Rome, 1992. Pp. 83.
See chapter 4; pp. 61–80.

844 John Baptist Gichuhi Theuri
Democracy and Authority According to Yves R. Simon
M.A. Thesis, Faculty of Philosophy, Roman Athenaeum of the Holy Cross, Rome, 1993. Pp. 81.

845 Richard J. Thompson and Vukan Kuic
Translators' Preface
in:
Yves R. Simon, *An Introduction to Metaphysics of Knowledge*
New York: Fordham University Press, 1990. Pp. vii–xii
(v. 100.1).

846 Michael D. Torre
Yves R. Simon: The Merit and Limit of Federalism
in:
*Notes et Documents* [Rome]
N.S. No. 35 (Septembre–Décembre 1992), 53–63.

847 Phillip W. Turner
Theological Anthropology and the State: A Study of the Political Ethics of Yves R. Simon and Helmut Thielicke
Ph.D. Dissertation, Princeton University, Princeton, New Jersey, 1978. Pp. 428.
   The author is Dean of the Berkeley Divinity School at Yale University.

848 Sylvanus Iniobong Udoidem
Authority and the Common Good in the Social and Political Philosophy of Yves R. Simon
Ph.D. Dissertation, School of Philosophy, The Catholic

University of America, Washington, D.C., 1985. Pp. 302.

849  Sylvanus Iniobong Udoidem
Authority and the Common Good in Social and Political Philosophy
Lanham, Maryland: University Press of America, 1988. Pp. 139.
   This book is a revised version of the author's dissertation.

850  Sylvanus Iniobong Udoidem
Metaphysical Foundations of Freedom in the Social and Political Thought of Yves R. Simon
in:
*Freedom in the Modern World: Jacques Maritain, Yves R. Simon, Mortimer J. Adler*
Edited by Michael D. Torre
Notre Dame, Indiana: American Maritain Association/ University of Notre Dame Press, 1989. Reprint 1990. Pp. 101–107.

851  Charles Van Doren
*The Idea of Progress*
New York: Frederick A. Praeger, 1967. Pp. 497.
   This volume contains abundant citations of Simon's concepts of liberty and progress.

852  Charles Van Doren
The Idea of Freedom: Part I
The Idea of Freedom: Part II
in:
*The Great Ideas Today*
Chicago: Encyclopædia Britannica, 1972. Pp. 300–392
Chicago: Encyclopædia Britannica, 1973. Pp. 235–300.
   These volumes contain numerous citations and discussion of Simon' concepts of freedom, authority, and liberty.

853  John Van Doren
Editor's Introduction
Yves R. Simon, "Introduction to the Study of Practical Wisdom"

in:
*The Great Ideas Today*
Chicago: Encyclopædia Britannica, 1988. Pp. 383–384 (v. 226).

854 Jaime Vélez-Sáenz
*Eterno retorno del derecho natural*
in:
*Universidad de Santo Tomas* [Bogotà, Colombia]
Vol. IV, No. 11 (Mayo–Agosto 1971), 433–446.

855 Jaime Vélez-Sáenz
Una concepción contemporánea sobre el trabajo
in:
*Revista Arco* [Bogotà, Colombia]
No. 144 (Enero 1973), 68–71.

856 Phillipe Veysset
Situation de la politique dans la pensée de St. Thomas d'Aquin
Paris: Éditions du Cèdre, 1981. Pp. 69–85.

See especially chapter 5, "L'action politique," in reference to Yves R. Simon's *Introduction à l'ontologie du connaître* (v. 100).

857 Paul Vignaux
Yves R. Simon: Par delà l'expérience du désespoir
in:
*Revue Philosophique de Louvain* [Louvain]
Tome 70, Quatrième Série, No. 6 (Mai 1972), 237–239.

Paul Vignaux, director of the École des Hautes Études at the Sorbonne, spent the war years teaching in the United States at the University of Wisconsin and later at the École Libre des Hautes Études (The New School for Social Research) in New York before his return to Paris at war's end.

858 Louise von Simpson
*Happy Exile*
Darmstadt: Roetherdruck, 1981. Pp. 173.

This autobiography privately printed by Mrs. Otto von Simpson contains personal memoirs of Yves R.

Simon during his years at the University of Notre Dame and The University of Chicago's Committee on Social Thought. See especially pp. 107–118. Copies are available at the Loyola University library, Chicago, Illinois; St. Mary's College, Notre Dame, Indiana; and the Yves R. Simon Institute, Mishawaka, Indiana.

859 Edward P. Ward
Authority and Democracy: An Essay on the Political Thought of Yves R. Simon
M.A. Thesis, Department of Political Science, The University of Chicago, Chicago, Illinois, 1968, Pp. 290.

860 Leo R. Ward
Yves R. Simon: Philosopher
in:
*The Commonweal* [New York]
Vol. LXXIV, No. 14 (June 30, 1961), 351–352.
Leo R. Ward, chairman of the philosophy department, and Rev. John O'Hara, president of the University of Notre Dame, were responsible for inviting Yves R. Simon to join the University of Notre Dame as a Distinguished Visiting Professor in the fall of 1938.

861 John Emory Whipple
Some Contemporary Catholic Views of Democracy
M.A. Thesis, Duke University, Durham, North Carolina, 1969. Pp. 133.

862 Brooke Williams
*Mystical Contemplation in the Thought of Yves R. Simon and Jacques Maritain*
in:
*Notes et Documents* [Rome]
The Yves R. Simon/Jacques Maritain Special Issue
Edited by Anthony O. Simon
Vème Année, No. 14 (Janvier–Mars 1979), 28–35.

863 H. E. S. Woldring
Dooyeweerd, Maritain, en Simon: Hun strijd om het behoud van de rechtsstaat

in:
*Christen Democratische Verkenningen* [Amsterdam]
November 1994. Pp. 476–484.

This article treats Dooyeweerd's, Maritain's, and Simon's struggle for the maintenance of government of law.

864 Peter Wolff
Editor's Preface
in:
Yves R. Simon, *Freedom of Choice*
New York: Fordham University Press, 1969. Pp. xiii–xvii
New York: Rose Hill Books/Fordham University Press, paperback edition, 1987. Reprinted 1992. Pp. xiii–xvii (v. 110. 4).

865 Unsigned
Yves René Marie Simon
in:
*The National Cyclopaedia of American Biography, Vol. 50*
New York: James T. White and Company, 1968. Pp. 389–390.

Numerous obituary notices appeared in newspapers such as *The New York Times* (May 12, 1961), *Le Monde* (June 12, 1996, by Stanislas Fumet), and the *Chicago Daily News* (May 12, 1961), as well as in the local newspapers of South Bend, Indiana (*South Bend Tribune* [May 11, 1961]) and Cherbourg, France (*La Presse de la Manche* [May 18, 1961]). They were followed by a variety of magazine and journal tributes.

## VIII
### Addenda and Forthcoming

Joseph Buckley
Logic and Mathematical Abstraction in the Philosophy of Yves R. Simon
in:
*American Catholic Philosophical Quarterly* [Washington, D.C.]
Vol. XLIX, No. 4 (Autumn 1995), 573–583.

Kathleen M. Connelly
Catholic Witness: The Political Activities of Five European Christian Democratic Scholars in Exile in the United States, 1938–1945 [Jacques Maritain, Yves R. Simon, Luigi Sturzo, Waldemar Gurian, and Ferdinand A. Hermans]
Ph.D. Dissertation, Department of History, Boston College, Boston, Massachusetts, 1995. Pp. 212.

Catherine Green
The Intentionality of Knowing and Willing in the Writings of Yves R. Simon
Ph.D. Dissertation, School of Philosophy, The Catholic University of America, Washinton, D.C., 1996. Pp. 284.

John Hittinger
The Achievement of Yves R. Simon
in:
*Crisis* [Washington, D.C.]
Vol. 14 No. 1 (January 1996), 36–40.

Joseph Papin III
Freedom and Solidarity in Sartre and Simon
in:
*The American Catholic Philosophical Quarterly* [Washington, D.C.]
Jean-Paul Sartre Special Issue
Edited by Thomas C. Anderson
Vol. LXX, No. 4 (Autumn 1996), 569–584.

Steven A. Long
Yves R. Simon's Approach to Natural Law
in:
*The Thomist* [Washington, D.C.]
Vol. 59 No. 1 (January 1995), 125–135.

Michael Novak
A "Catholic Whig" Replies
in:
*The Review of Politics* [Notre Dame, Indiana]
Vol. 58, No. 2 (Spring 1996), 259–264.

José Antonio Rivera
La autonomía como principio teológico filósofico

in:
*Cruz Ansata* [Bayamón, Puerto Rico]
Vol. XVII (1995), 213–224.

Thomas R. Rourke
Michael Novak and Yves R. Simon on the Common Good and Capitalism
in:
*The Review of Politics* [Notre Dame, Indiana]
Vol. 58, No. 2 (Spring 1996), 229–258.

Thomas R. Rourke
Response to a "Catholic Whig"
*The Review of Politics* [Notre Dame, Indiana]
Vol. 58, No. 2 (Spring 1996), 265–267.

Thomas R. Rourke
*A Conscience as Large as the World: Yves R. Simon versus the Catholic Neoconservatives*
Lanham, Maryland: Rowman & Littlefield, 1997. Pp. ix + 287.
   Contents:
      Preface
         1. Introduction
         2. Practical Reason
         3. The Political System
         4. The Economic System
         5. The Moral-Cultural System
         6. Conclusion
      Bibliography
      Appendix; Ecclesiastical Documents
      Index

[Forthcoming]
Vukan Kuic
*Democracy with a Human Face: The Contributions of Yves R. Simon to Political Science*
Lanham, Maryland: Rowman & Littlefield.

## IX
### MANIFESTOS AND ALLIED PUBLICATIONS

900   *Pour le bien commun: Les responsabilités du chrétien et le moment présent*

This manifesto was drafted by Jacques Maritain in collaboration with Yves R. Simon, Olivier Lacombe, Maurice de Gandillac, Étienne Borne, and Étienne Gilson. It includes a Foreword dated March 1934. The manifesto was published as a booklet and signed by the following group of distinguished figures: Jacques Arney, compositeur de musique—Paul Bazan—Dr. René Biot, ancien chef de laboratoire à l'Hotel-Dieu de Lyon—Étienne Borne, professeur au lycée de Nevers—Maurice Brillant—Dr. Rémy Collin, professeur à la Faculté de Médecine de Nancy—Jacques Copeau—Jean Dajat—Georges Desvallières, membre de l'Institut—Charles Du Bos—Michel Dufrenne—Roger Dumaine, agrégé de l'Université—Maurice Éblé, secrétaire général du Secrétariat social de Paris—Louis Fliche—Dr. R. de Fresquet—D. V. Fumet, compositeur de musique—Stanislas Fumet—Maurice de Gandillac, agrégé de l'Université—André Garrigou-Lagrange, professeur à la Faculté de Droit Bordeaux—Étienne Gilson, professuer au Collège de France—Bernard Guyon, professeur à l'Institut des Hautes Études de Gand—François Henry, professeur au lycée d'Orléans—Jean Victor-Hugo, artiste-peintre—Pierre Humbert, professeur à la Faculté de Sciences de Montpellier—Emmanuel Jacob, journaliste—Maurice Jaubert, compositeur de musique—René Jaubert, journaliste—Olivier Lacombe, agrégé de l'Université—Jean Lacroix, professeur au lycée de Dijon—Louis Laloy, chargé de cours à l'Institut des Hautes Études Chinoises—Louis Le Fur, professeur de Droit international à l'Université de Paris—Marcel Légaut, professeur à la Faculté des Sciences de Rennes—Olivier Leroy, professeur au lycée de Châteauroux—Jacques Madaule, professeur au lycée Rollin—Gabriel Marcel—Jacques Maritain, professeur à l'Institut Catholique de Paris—Pierre Mesnard, chargé de conférence à l'Université de Poitiers—Achille Mestre, professeur à la Faculté de Droit de Paris—Alfred Michelin, Secrétaire général de la Corporation des Publicistes chrétiens—Emmanuel Mounier, agrégé de l'Université—Dr. J.

Okinczyc, chirurgien des hôpitaux, professeur à la Faculté de Médecine de Paris—Jean-Rémy Palanque, maître de conférences à la Faculté des Lettres de Montpellier—Comte Jean de Pange—Jean Peyraube, agrégé de l'Université—Eugène Primard, Maurice Rey, agrégé de l'Université—Roland-Manuel, compositeur de musique—Pierre-Henri Simon, professeur au Faculté catholique de Lille—Yves R. Simon, chargé de cours aux Facultés catholiques de Lille et de Paris—Maurice Vaussard, publiciste—Joseph Vialatoux, professeur à l'Institut des Chartreux de Lyon—Jean Vignaux, professeur au lycée de Chartres.
Paris: Desclée de Brouwer, April 19, 1934. Pp. 30.

900.1 *Pour le bien commun: Les responsabilitiés du chrétien et le moment présent*
Reprinting of the original manifesto
in:
Jacques Maritain and Raïssa Maritain, *Œuvres complètes*. V. *1932–1935*
Fribourg: Éditions Universitaires; Paris; Éditions Saint-Paul, 1982. Pp. 1022–1041.

900.2 *Un documento fundamental:* ⟨*Por el bien común*⟩
Spanish translation
in:
*Criterio* [Buenos Aires]
7 año, Tome 23, No. 325 (May 24, 1934), 83–87.

900.3 *Per il bene comune: Le responsabilità del cristiano ed il momento presente*
Italian translation
in:
Jacques Maritain, *Scritti e manifesti politici, 1933–1939*
Edited by Giorgio Campanini
Brescia: Morcelliana, 1978. Pp. 201–218.

900.4 *For the Common Good: The Christian's Responsibilities in the Present Crisis*
English translation with an introduction by Bernard Doering

in:
*Notes et Documents* [Rome]
Vème Année, No. 20 (Juillet–Septembre 1980), 1–20.

901   *Un cri d'alarme des catholiques français en faveur de l'Espagne martyre*
in:
*L'Aube/Quotidien du matin* [Paris]
VIème année, No. 1411 (5 Fevrier 1937), 3.
   A manifesto signed by twenty-one French intellectual, political, and cultural figures including Étienne Borne, Stanislas Fumet, Yves R. Simon, Francisque Gay, Jacques Madaule, Jacques Maritain, Emmanuel Mounier, Marc Sangnier, and Paul Vignaux.

901.1  *Un cri d'alarme des catholiques français en faveur de l'Espagne martyre*
in:
*Euzko Deya/La voz de Euzkadi* [The Voice of the Basques] [Paris]
2ème Année, No. 21 (7 Fevrier, 1937) 1.

901.2  *Un appel de catholiques francais* [Revised title]
in:
*La Paix en Espagne* [Paris]
No. 2 (Avril 1937), 4.

901.3  *Un cri d'alarme des catholiques français en faveur de l'Espagne martyre*
Republication of the original manifesto
in:
*Jacques et Raïssa Maritain: Œuvres complètes.* VI.
Fribourg: Éditions Universitaires; Paris: Éditions St. Paul, 1984. Pp. 1178–1179.

902   *Pour la justice et la paix*
in:
*Sept/L'Hebdomadaire du Temps Présent* [Paris]
2ème Année, No. 86 (18 Octobre 1935), 5.

902.1  *Pour la justice et la paix*
in:
*La Vie Catholique* [Paris]
12ème Année, No. 577 (19 Octobre 1935), 3.

902.2　*Pour la justice et la paix*
in:
*L'Aube/Quotidiem du Matin* [Paris]
4ème Année, No. 1029 (19 Octobre 1935), 1.

902.3　*À propos du conflict italo-ethiopien: Manifeste pour la justice et la paix*
in:
*La Croix* [Paris]
56ème année, No. 16157 (19 Octobre 1935), 5.

902.4　*Pour la justice et la paix*
in:
*La Vie Intellectuelle* [Paris]
7ème Année, Tome XXXIII, No. 2 (25 octobre 1935), 261–264.

*Pour la justice et la paix* was also reprinted in its entirety and in part in a number of other newspapers and journals with abbreviated lists of the original signers not including Yves R. Simon (v. *Esprit*, Paris, 3ème année, No. 38 [1935]; *Le Figaro*, Paris, 110ème Année, No. 293, p. 4; and partial publications in *L'Humanité*, Paris, 32ème Année, No. 13454, p. 4; and *Le Populaire*, 18ème Année, No. 4633, p. 2). Yves R. Simon wrote a controversial polemic book on the Ethiopian war, *La campagne d'Èthiopie et la pensée politique française* closely related to these manifestos (v. 102).

903　Pour l'honneur: Un appel d'intellectuels
in:
*L'Aube/Quotidien du Matin* [Paris]
5ème année, No. 1348 (21 Novembre 1936), 1.

Issued by French intellectuals and occasioned by the suicide on November 18, 1936, of Roger Salengro, the Minister of the Interior, which was precipitated by a vicious and calumnious campaign against him by the press. It was signed by Yves R. Simon and a group of intellectuals and political figures including Paul Archambault, Maurice Merleau-Ponty, Maurice de Gandillac, Emmanuel Mounier, Pierre-Henri Simon, Jacques Maritain, Stanislas Fumet, and Pierre van de Meer de Walcheren.

903.1  *Pour l'honneur*
in:
*Jacques et Raïssa Maritain: Œuvres complètes* VI.
Fribourg: Éditions Universitaires; Paris: Éditions Saint-Paul, 1984. Pp. 1176–1177.

904  *Comité français pour la paix civile et religieuse en Espagne*
This is the text and plan of action for the French committee to mediate the Spanish Civil War crisis. The text was edited by Jacques Maritain with the cooperation of Yves R Simon, Gabriel Marcel, Domenico Russo, Étienne Borne, Claude Bourdet, Maurice de Gandillac, Olivier Lacombe, Jacques Madaule, Pierre Van de Meer de Walcheren, and Paul Vignaux.
in:
*Jacques et Raïssa Maritain: Œuvres complètes. VI.*
Fribourg: Éditions Universitaires; Paris: Éditions Saint-Paul, 1984. Pp. 1123–1129.

A version of this text was published in *Esprit*, as "*Déclaration du Comité pour la Paix Civile et Religieuse en Espagne*," 5ème année, No. 58 (1 Juillet 1937), 651–652, but did not include Simon as signator.

904.1  *Appello del ⟨Comitato francese per la pace civile e religiose in Spagna⟩*
Italian translation of the original text
in:
Jacques Maritain, *Scritti e manifesti politici, 1933–1939*
Edited by Giorgio Campanini
Brescia: Morcelliana, 1978. Pp. 219–225.
It includes Simon's name.

905  *Devant la crise mondiale: Manifeste de catholiques européens séjournant en Amérique*
Published as a booklet and signed by: J. A. de Aguirre (Basque), Charles Boyer (France), R. F. Van Cauwelaert (Belgium), M. A. Couturier, O.P. (France), André David (France), J. T. Delos, O.P. (France), J. V. Decattillon (France), Lady Gainsborough (Great Britain), Sir Philip Gibbs (Great Britain), Waldemar Gurian (Germany), Oscar Halecki (Poland), Msgr. Edward Hawks

(Great Britain), Nicolas Higgins, O.F.M. (Great Britain), Dietrich von Hildebrand (Austria), E. Hula (Austria), Hélène Iswolsky (Russia), Henri de Kérillis (France), Otto Michael Knab (Germany ), H. J. A. Koevoets, S.C.J. (Holland), Aurel Kolnai (Austria), Jacques Maritain (France), Raïssa Maritain (France), René de Messières (France), Thomas Michels, O.S.B. (Germany), Peter Mommersteeg (Holland), Joep Nicolas (Holland), Alfred Noyes (Great Britain), John M. Oesterreicher (Austria), L. A. H. Peters (Holland), Stefan de Ropp (Poland), Eva J. Ross (Great Britain), Baudouin Schwarz (Germany), Frank Sheed (Great Britain), Yves R. Simon (France), Charles O. Von Soden (Germany), P. J. de Strycker (Belgium), Don Luigi Sturzo (Italy), Hugh S. Taylor (Great Britain), George Theunis (Belgium), Sigrid Undset (Norway), Auguste Viatte (France), Paul Van Zeeland (Belgium), Guido Zernatto (Austria).

New York: Éditions de la Maison Française: New York, 1942. Pp. 49.

Initially Yves Simon refused to sign an earlier version of this manifesto originally drafted by Auguste Viatte in Montreal but after his revisions and modifications by Jacques Maritain, J. T. Delos, and J. V. Decattillon, Simon gave it his support. A lengthy synopsis review of this manifesto by Guy Sylvestre appeared in *Revue Dominicaine* [Montreal], 47, No. 2 (Octobre 1942), 174–177.

905.1 *In the Face of the World's Crisis: A Manifesto by European Catholics Sojourning in America*
English translation
in:
*The Commonweal* [New York]
Vol. 36, No. 18 (August 21, 1942), 414–421.

905.2 *In Face of the World's Crisis: Manifesto of European Catholics Resident in North America*
A newly translated English edition
in:
*The Dublin Review* [London]
Vol. 211, No. 423 (October–December 1942) 105–115.

905.3 *Catholics Face the World Crisis: An International Catholic Manifesto*
Republication of *The Dublin Review* translation printed as a pamphlet by *The Sword of the Spirit* (London, 1943), i–iii + 1–13.

905.4 *Devant la crise mondiale: Positions catholiques* [Revised version]
in:
*Cahiers du Témoignage Chrétien* [Lyon]
Nos. XV–XVI, *Les voiles se déchirent* (Août 1943), 269–272.

905.5 *Devant la crise mondiale: Positions catholiques* [Revised version]
in
*Cahiers du Témoignage* [Paris]
Décembre 1943, pp. 21–24

905.6 *In the Face of the World's Crisis: A Manifesto by European Catholics Sojourning in America*
Republication of the original manifesto
in:
*Notes et Documents* [Rome]
No. 15 (Avril–Juin 1979), 1–10.
   This quarterly is published by the Institut International Jacques Maritain in Rome.

905.7 *Devant la crise mondiale: Positions catholiques*
in:
*Témoignage Chrétien, 1941–1944: Cahiers et Courriers* [Facsimile collection]
Paris: Les Éditions Ouvrières, 1980. Pp. 269–272.

## X
### Archival Materials

The Yves R. Simon Institute is the repository of many Simon manuscripts including those from his projected twenty-one-volume *Philosophical Encyclopedia* on which he was working at the time of his death. In addition, the Institute houses the complete transcribed correspondence between Yves R. Simon and Jacques Maritain as well as letters from a host of other friends and colleagues including Étienne Gilson, Emmanuel Mounier, Olivier Lacombe, Edmond Michelet, and Robert Speaight. Also available at the Institute are the originals or copies of all the items listed in this bibliography and extensive biographic and countless other materials.

By virtue of a donation by the Yves R. Simon estate, the Jacques Maritain Center in the Hesburgh Library at the University of Notre Dame is the custodian of vast Simon manuscripts and unpublished materials, correspondence, notes, and lectures. A portion of the original collection, including extensive tapes of Simon's graduate courses at the Committee on Social Thought lectures at The University of Chicago, were retained by the Simon estate and remain available at the Institute.

The following is a brief list of the Simon collection as donated in 1961. These materials and hundreds of subdivisions have now been carefully catalogued at the Jacques Maritain Center and are available for perusal by interested parties. The center was also the recipient via a donation from Anthony O. Simon of the originals of Jacques Maritain's letters (1927–1961) to Yves R. Simon.

1. Action Française
2. Alain [Émile A. Chartier].
3. Ancient Philosophy
4. Ancient Philosophy—Pre-Socratics—Socratics—Plato
5. American Democracy
6. Analogy—Analogy—Fundamentals
7. Anti-Predicaments and Universals
8. Authority
9. Causality I
10. Causality II
11. Causality III—Determinism
12. Causality IV—Chance
13. Causality V—Laws—Probability
14. Connaissance scientifique—Sciences morales
15. Critique of Scientific Knowledge—[Courses]
16. Critique of Practical Knowledge I
17. Critique of Practical Knowledge II
18. Critique of Practical Knowledge III

19. Democracy
20. Demonstration
21. Descartes
22. Dialectics
23. Doctrines socialistes
24. Eighteenth Century
25. Ethics I—Last End—Morality
26. Ethics II—Habitus and Virtues
27. Ethics III—Laws
28. Ethics—Marriage
29. Existence and Nature of God
30. Economique—Richesses
31. Fascisme et National Socialisme
32. Papers on Freedom and Authority
33. Daniel Lallement—Sociologie général
33. Formal Logic—First Operation of the Mind
34. Formal Logic—Second Operation of the Mind
35. Formal Logic—Third Operation of the Mind
36. History of Logic
37. Immanent Action
38. La Liberté
39. Logic Categories I
40. Logic Categories II
41. Logic Demonstration
42. Logic-Predicables—Signs
43. Logic Proemialis I
44. Logic Proemialis II
45. Mathematics—Fundamental Concepts
46. Métaphysique
47. Metaphysics of Knowledge I
48. Metaphysics of Knowledge II
49. Metaphysics of Knowledge III
50. Metaphysics—Unity and Truth
51. Metaphysics—Being and Transcendentals
52. Metaphysics—Good—Evil—Beautiful
53. Metaphysics—General Theory of Being
54. Metaphysics of Love I
55. Metaphysics of Love II
56. Metaphysics of Love III [Courses, 1934–1943–1956].

57. Miscellaneous
58. Philosophie Moderne I
59. Philosophie Moderne II
60. Moral Psychology
61. Morale—[Courses, Paris 1934–1935].
62. Philosophie de la Nature
63. Philosophie de la Nature—Psychologie Philosophique
64. Philosophie de la Nature—Psychologie Philosophique
65. Philosophie de la Nature I
66. Philosophie de la Nature II
67. Philosophy of Nature
68. Philosophy of Nature—Philosophical Psychology I
69. Philosophy of Nature—Philosophical Psychology II
70. Philosophy of Nature—Finality
71. Philosophy of Nature—Life and Soul
72. Philosophy of Nature—Nature, Unity, Plurality
73. Philosophy of Nature—Change
74. Philosophy of Nature—Quantity—Place—Time—Continuum—Void—Infinity
75. Philosophy of Nature—Psychology
76. Philosophy of Nature—Psychology—Power of Motion I
77. Philosophy of Nature—Psychology—Power of Motion II
78. Philosophy of Nature
79. Philosophy of Nature
80. Philosophy of Nature
81. Philosophy of Nature
82. Philosophy of Nature
83. Philosophy of Nature—Life
84. Philosophy of Nature—Will
85. Philosophical Inquiries—Love
86. Philosophical Psychology—Internal Senses
87. Philosophical Psychology—Sens Enternes
88. Philosophical Psychology—Sens Enternes
89. Philosophical Psychology—Memory
90. Philosophical Systems
91. Politics I
92. Politics II
93. Politics III
94. Pierre-Joseph Proudhon

95. Pierre-Joseph Proudhon—Anti-théisme de Proudhon
96. Pierre-Joseph Proudhon—Esprit et l'Absolu
97. Pierre-Joseph Proudhon
98. Pierre-Joseph Proudhon—Divers
99. Pierre-Joseph Proudhon—Life and Works of Proudhon
100. Pierre-Joseph Proudhon—Les Idées Religieuses de Proudhon
101. Pierre-Joseph Proudhon—l'État
102. Pierre-Joseph Proudhon
103. Psychologie Philosophique—Intelligence
104. Psychology
105. Philosophy of Nature—Psychologie philosophique—Memory—Freedom of Choice
106. Saint-Simonist
107. Scientific Knowledge—Abstraction
108. Scientific Knowledge—General Characteristics
109. Scientific Knowledge—Math
110. Scientific Knowledge—Math
111. Scientific Knowledge—Math
112. Scientific Knowledge—Math
113. Scientific Knowledge—Math
114. Scientific Knowledge—Math
115. Scientific Knowledge—Science and Common Thought
116. Scientific Knowledge
117. Social Science—Fundamentals
118. Critique of Scientific Knowledge
119. La Vérité et la Communauté
120. Vie Affective
121. Work I
122. Work II

# BIBLIOGRAPHIC INDEX[1]

Abell, Aron I., 154, 209
Abraham, 503
Académie Française, 831
*Achievement of Jacques and Raïssa Maritain, The*, 741
*Acquaintance with the Absolute*, 730, 760, 766, 778, 796, 829
Action Française, *290*
Adler, Mortimer J., 110.4, 203, 207, 700, 701, 742, 745, 749, 751, 850
Aguirre, José Antonio de, 905
Alain [Émile A. Chartier], 326, 326.1, 774, *290*
Allemagne, 320, 322, 325
Allers, Rudolf, 203
*L'Âme Commune*, 324
America, 905.6
*American Catholic Philosophical Quarterly*, 389, 411, 412
*American Political Science Review, The*, 718
Analogical sets, 396
Analogy, 396, 708, 710
Anastaplo, George, 702
Anderson, Thomas C., *281*
*Annales de l'École des Hautes Études de Gand*, 201
d'Aquin, *see* Aquinas
Aquinas, St. Thomas, 150, 152, 301, 306, 310, 506, 551, 758, 843, 856
Archambault, Paul, 903, 905
*Argentina Libre*, 373
Aristotle, 118, 335, 358, 387
Aristotelian Society of Marquette University, 104
Armstrong, Hamilton Fish, 539
Arney, Jacques, 900
Aron, Raymond, 531, 724
*Ars logica*, 153, 156

Art, 400
Association des Anciens et Anciennes Élèves, 793.2
*L'Atelier*, 300
*L'Aube*, 359, 901, 902.2, 903
Authority, 109, 109.1–109.7, 111–111.2, 213, 218, 219, 221, 360, 397, 711, 714, 715, 717, 718, 720, 738, 743, 746, 773, 778, 779, 785, 813, 815, 828, 844, 848, 849, 859, *290*
*Authority in Social Work*, 221
*Authority Revisited: Nomos XXIX*, 738
Autonomy, 104, 108, 108.1, 108.2, 109, 113, 360, 397, 403, 403.1, 700, 702, 711, 717, 720, 745, 749, 778, 800, 808, 813, 828, 850, 852, 859

Babin, Eugène, 703
Bachelard, Gaston, 201, 346
*Basic Writings of Saint Thomas Aquinas*, 385
Bauhofer, Oskar, 209
Bazan, Paul, 900
*Les Beaux Voyages d'Autrefois*, *609*
Bergson, Henri, 114, 331, 332, 502, 514, 515
Bernadot, M. V., 326
Bernanos, Georges, 348, 367
Berns, Lawrence, 704
Berti, Enrico, 705
*Bibliografia dziel Yves R. Simona*, 109.7
Bibliography (Simon) 109.7, 821, 822, 823, 824, 828
Bibliothèque Française de Philosophie, 100
Biot, René, 900
Black, Virginia, 707
*Blackfriars*, 838

---

[1] *Italicized* index numbers refer to pages, all other numbers refer to specific bibliography items.

Boll, Marcel, 524
Bolshevism, 311
*Book of Catholic Authors, The*, 206, 835
*Books on Trial*, 509
Borne, Étienne, 201, 509, 900, 901, 904
Bortolon, Liana, 154.1, 208.1
Bouglé, Célestin, 529
Bourdet, Claude, 904
Bourke, Vernon J., 203
Boyer, Charles, 905
Brennan, Robert E., 202
Briefs, Goetz A., 151
Brigé de Sucre, Gloria, 115.1
Brillant, Maurice, 314, 900
Brogan, Dennis W., 538
Brown, William C., 100, 156
Brüning, Heinrich, 207
Bruun, Geoffrey, 547
Bryson, Lyman, 202
Buchez, Philippe Joseph Benjamin, 305
Buckley, Joseph, *280*
*Bulletin Thomiste*, 812
Burrell, David B., 708
Burtt, Marshall, 706
*Business System, The*, 219

C.S.A.R. (Comité Secret pour l'Action Révolutionnaire), 349
Cahalan, John C., 709
*Cahiers Jacques Maritain*, 409, 789
*Les Cahiers Catholiques*, 300, 303, 305, 306, 307, 310, 311, 313, 314, 316, 317, 318, 319, 323
*Les Cahiers Thomistes*, 502
*Cahiers du Témoignage Chrétien*, 905.4, 905.5
Callot, Émile, 346
*La campagne d'Éthiopie et la pensée politique française*, 102, 102.1, 902.4
Campanini, Giorgio, 900.3, 904.1
*Le Canada Français*, 703
*Cap and Gown*, 394
Caplin, Diane, 711, 712
Caponigri, A. Robert, 111, 111.1, 213, 714
Carpenter, Hilary, 203
*Catholic Church in World Affairs, The*, 209

Catholic University of America, The, 748, 752, 811, 815, 848
Catholic Whig, *281*
*Catholic World, The* 366, 377, 839
*Catholic Authors*, 761
Catholic missions, 329, 330
*Les catholiques devant la guerre*, 224
Catrice, Paul, 344
Censorship, 406
Cercles Thomistes, 345
Chagall, Marc, 207
Chandrasekhar, S. Subrahmanyan, 207
Chapman, Immanuel, 203
*Character, Community, and Politics*, 720
Charles R. Walgreen Foundation, 109
*Chicago Review*, 399
*Chicago Daily News*, 865
China, 350
Christ (Jesus), 309, 310
Christian, 308, 393
Christophe, Paul, 224, 716
*La Civilisation Américaine*, 154
*Civiltà Americana*, 208.1
Claudel, Paul, 367
Clémenceau, Georges, 547
Cochran, Clarke E., 717, 718, 719, 720, 721, 722
Coleccion Jordán, 203.2
Collana Philosophica Saggi, 110.3
Collection Catholique, 152
Collection Biblioteca de Filosofia y Pedagogia, 112.2
Collection Civilisation, 106
Collection Courrier des Îles, 102.1
Collection La Lumière Ouvrière, 151
Collection Prémices, 110.2
Collection Problèmes Actuels, 105
Collection Questions Disputées, 154
Collin, Rémy, 900
Comité française pour la justice et la paix, 344
Comité française pour la paix civile et religieuse en Espagne, 904
Committee on Social Thought, 842, 858
Common good, 397, 713, 752, 848, 900, 900.1
*Commonweal, The*, 364, 380.2, 384, 385, 388, 392, 551, 860, 905.1
Communism, 320, 344
Community, 711, 718, 720

*Community of the Free*, 108.1 108.2
*Contemporary Philosophy*, 733
Contingency, 733
Copeau, Jacques, 900
Corbett, James A., 105.1, 723
Cort, John, 154
Corte, Marcel de, 201, 607
Couturier, Marie-Alain, 905
Cranston, Maurice, 724
Crawford, Benjamin T., 154
*Crisis*, 753.1, *281*
*Criterio*, 900.2
*Critique de la connaissance morale*, 101, 336
*La Croix*, 902.3
Crosson, Frederick J., 725
Curtis, Michael, 216
Cuvillier, Armand, 533

Dajat, Jean, 900
Dalbiez, Roland, 504
Dalcourt, Gerard J., 114, 726
Daniel-Rops, Henri Petiot dit, 367
Darlan, Admiral Jean, 348
David, André, 152, 905
Dawes, Général Rufus F., 315
de Gaulle, *see* Gaulle
*De la primauté du bien commun contre les personnalistes*, 703
Debout, Jacques, 300
Decattillon, Joseph Vincent, 905
Deely, John N., 404, 727
Deffontaines, Pierre, 334, 609
*Definition of Moral Virtue, The*, 117, 551, 775, 784
Dehove, Chanoine, 515
De Koninck, Charles, 548, 703
Delos, Joseph Thomas, 905
Deman, Thomas, 812
Democracy, 106, 106.1, 108, 108.1, 108.2, 109–109.7, 202, 209, 216, 220, 302, 377, 380–380.4, 405, 711, 712, 713, 717, 735, 746, 750, 755, 756, 757, 758, 763, 767, 797, 800, 809, 841, 842, 842.1, 844, 859, 861
*La Démocratie*, 301, 302, 304, 308, 309, 312, 315, 320, 321, 322, 325
Denis-Marc, Maurice, 310
Dennehy, Raymond L., 730, 828
Deploige, Simon, 536
Descartes, René, *291*

Desgrippes, Georges, 314, 316, 602
Despujol, Ignacio de, 112.2
Desvallières, Georges, 900
*Deutsche Brief (1934–1938)*, 361
*Devant la crise mondiale* (manifesto), 905
*Dialogos*, 816
Doering, Bernard, 731, 900.4
Dominicans, 326
Dooyeweerd, Herman, 767, 863
Du Bos, Charles, 348, 900
*Dublin Review, The*, 905.2, 905.3
Dufrenne, Michel, 900
Duke University, 861
Dumaine, Roger, 900
Dunaway, John M., 326.1
Dupréel, Eugène, 201
Durkheim, Émile, 715
Dwelshauvers, Georges, 602, *00*

Éblé, Maurice, 900
École des Hautes Études de Gand, 201
École Libre des Hautes Études, 857
Economics, 103, 108, 108.1, 108.2 109–109.7, 115, 115.1, 151, 207, 223, 305, 321, 325, 343, 344, 348, 355, 361, 362, 383, 405, 508, 517, 518, 721, 722, 731, 770, 800, 806, 817, 818, 819, 855
Éditions de la Maison Française, 106, 905
Éditions du Cerf, 326
Eells, Richard, 219
Elazar, Daniel J., 225, 345.1
Emonet, Pierre-Marie, 110.2, 732
Enriques, Federigo, 523
Epistemology, *see* Metaphysics of knowledge
Eschmann, I. Th. (Theodore), 548, 703
Espagne, 359
*Esprit*, 345, 902.4, 904
*Essays in Thomism*, 203, 203.1
*Ethics*, 719
Ethics, *see* Moral philosophy
Ethiopia, 102, 102.1
*Études Carmélitaines*, 337, 790
*Études Philosophiques*, 201
*Euzko Deya*, 901.1
Evans, Joseph W., 217
*L'expérience de l'espace dans la physique contemporaine*, 346

Les Facultés Catholiques de Lille, 334
Faggi, Alfeo, 207
Fagus (Georges Faillet), 317
*Faith & Reason*, 736
Farrell, Walter, 203
Fascism, 753.1
Fay, Thomas, 733
Fecher, Charles A., 392
Federalism, 345, 345.1
Fernández Manzanedo, Marcos, 203.2
*Le Figaro*, 902.4
*Filosofia do govêrno democrático*, 109.3, 747
*Filozofia rzadu demokratycznego*, 109.7, 827
Finkelstein, Louis, 202
FitzGerald, Desmond, 734
Fitzsimons, Matthew A., 154, 209, 212
Flathman, Richard E., 738
Fliche, Louis, 900
Flynn, James R., 735
Fordham University Press, 755, 777, 778
*Foresight and Knowledge*, 107.1, 340, 378, 410, 411, 412, 413, 534, 804
Fourier, François, 518
Fowlie, Wallace, 367
France, 105, 105.1, 105.2, 106, 106.1, 215, 320, 364, 365, 368, 374, 379, 509, 538, 541, 542, 543, 544, 547, 753, 753.1, 753.2, 754, 755, 756
*France/Canada*, 379, 379.1
*France Forever*, 363, 380
France Quand Même, 363
France, Anatole, 315, 317
*France—L'individu et le destin*, 215
Franco-Allemandes, 320
Frank, Philipp, 534
Frank, William A., 736
Free choice, 110–110.4, 112, 389, 700, 701, 702, 704, 729, 734, 742, 807, 852, 864
Free French in America, 363
*Free Persons and the Common Good*, 806
Freedom, 700, 701, 702, 704, 713, 717, 754
*Freedom and Community*, 113, 808
*Freedom in the Modern World*, 702, 754, 757, 768, 786, 850
Freedom of autonomy, *see* autonomy
*Freedom of Choice*, 110.4, 701, 864

*Freedom, Virtue, and the Common Good*, 713, 722, 765, 791, 819
Fresquet, Raymond de, 900
Freud, Sigmund, 504, 510, 843
*From Disorder to World Order*, 211
*From Twilight to Dawn*, 731, 755
Fulbright, J. W., 207
Fuller, Timothy, 737, 738
Fumet, D. V., 900
Fumet, Stanislas, 348, 367, 865, 900, 901, 903

Gainsborough, Lady (Alice Mary), Countess of, 905
Gallagher, David, 758
Gallagher, Donald A., 69
Gallagher, Idella, 741
Gammon, Francis L., 744
Gandillac, Maurice de, 900, 903, 904
*Gants du Ciel*, 378
Garrigou-Lagrange, André, 900
Garrigou-Lagrange, Réginald, *245*
Gaulle, Charles de, 363, 756
Gay, Francisque, 359, 901
*General Theory of Authority, A*, 111, 111.1, 111.2, 218, 221, 397, 714, 773, 779
Gerhringer, Gerald, 745
Gibbs, Sir John, 905
Gichuhi Theuri, John Baptist, 746
Gildin, Hilail, 326.1
Gilson, Étienne, 500, 606, 900, *245*
Glanville, John J., 153, 155, 156
Godói da Mata-Machado, Edgard, 109.3, 747
Goichon, A.-M., *245*
Gompers, Samuel, 322
Grabmann, Martin, 506
*La grande crise de la République Française*, 105
Great Britain, 320
*Great Dialogue of Nature and Space, The*, 114, 726
*Great Ideas Today, The*, 223, 398, 724, 852, 853
Green, Catherine, 748, 749
Gregorian University, 843
Griesbach, Marc F., 750
Griffin, John Howard, 116
Grousset, René, 609
Gueguen, John, 751

Gurian, Waldemar, 154, 209, 361, 905
Gurvitch, Georges, 511, 546
Guyon, Bernard, 900

Habit, 385, 117
Habitus, 100.1, 117, 385, 765
Halecki, Oscar, 905
Halévy, Élie, 535
Hall, Terry, 752
Hallowell, John H., 112, 112.1, 112.2, 762
Hamilton College, 393
Hamm, Victor M., 106.1, 212, 381
Hancock, Curtis L., 713, 722, 765, 791, 819
*Happy Exile*, 858
Hawks, Msgr. Edward, 905
Hellman, John, 753, 753.1, 753.2, 754, 755, 756
Henry, François, 508, 900
Hesburgh Library, *290*
Heston, Edward L., 209
Heywood, Robert B., 207
Higgins, Nicolas, 905
Hildebrand, Dietrich von, 905
Hittinger, John, 757, 758, addenda
Hittinger, Russell, 112.1, 759, 760
Hoehn, Matthew, 761
Hoffman, Ross J. S., 537
Holbrook, William C., 215
Hollenhorst, G. Donald, 153, 155
Houde, Roland, 156, 214
Hovda, Robert, 388
Hula, Erich, 905
*L'Humanité*, 902.4
Humbert, Pierre, 900
Hurtubise, Claude, 367
Hutchins, Robert M., 207

*Idea of Freedom, The*, 852
*Idea of Progress, The*, 851
Ikeme, Ngozi Anthony, 763
*Image of Man, The*, 212
*In Defense of Sovereignty*, 220, 840
*In the Face of the World's Crisis*, 905.1
  905.2, 905.6 (manifesto)
Iniobong Udoidem, Sylvanus, 848, 849, 850
Institut International Jacques Maritain, 367.1, 905.6
Institut Supérieur de Philosophie, 200

*International Philosophical Quarterly*, 406, 410
*Interpretation*, 326.1, 717, 774
*Introduction à l'ontologie du connaître*, 100, 856
*Introduction to Metaphysics of Knowledge, An*, 100.1, 551, 777, 845
Iswolsky, Hélène, 905

Jacob, Emmanuel, 900
Jacob, Max, 500
Jacques Maritain Center, *290*
*Jacques Maritain: Homage in Words and Pictures*, 116, 409, 825
*Jacques Maritain: The Man and His Achievement*, 217
Jankélévitch, Vladimir, 201
Jaubert, Maurice, 900
Jaubert, René, 900
Jeune République, 301
John of St. Thomas (John Poinsot), 153, 155, 156
John Paul II (Pope), 751
*Journal of Church and State*, 756
Journet, Charles Cardinal, 101, 338, *245*
Jouvenel, Bertrand de, 724
*Jubilee*, 778

Keegan, Frank L., 74
Kérillis, Henri de, 905
Kerwin, Jerome G., 109
Killoran, John, 765
Knab, Otto Michael, 905
Knasas, John F. X., 766, 828
Knowledge, *see* Metaphysics
Koenig, Harry, 209
Koevoets, H. J. A., 905
Kolnai, Aurel, 757, 905
Koyzis, David T., 767, 768
Krim, Abdel, 320
Kuic, Vukan, 100.1, 112, 115, 117, 338.1, 345.1, 833, *282*

Lacape, R. S., 521
Lacombe, Olivier, 218, 348, 779, 780, 900, 904, 905, *245*
Lacroix, Jean, 900
Lajeunie, Étienne, 326
Lallement, Daniel J., 527, *291*
Laloy, Louis, 900

Laubier, Patrick de, 728
Lavaud, Benoit, *245*
Lavelle, Louis, 201
Lavoisier, Antoine, 525
Law, Natural, *see* Natural law
Le Fur, Louis, 900
Le Senne, René, 201
Leeds, Stanton, B., 543
Lefèvre, Frédéric, 312
Légaut, Marcel, 900
Legutko, Ryszard, 827
Lemonnyer, Antoine, 519
Leo XIII Award, 402
Leroy, Marie-Vincent, 117, 781, 782, 783, 784
Leroy, Olivier, 900
Létourneau, Jean, 37
Liberalism, 203, 203.1, 203.2, 302, 738, 800
Liberty, 360, 725
*Listening Magazine*, 793.1
Long, Steven A., *281*
*Loveland Herald Press, The*, 706
Loyola University, 785, 858
Lubac, Henri de, 549
Lucal, John A., 785

Mackey, Robert, 222
Madaule, Jacques, 900, 901, 904
Magill, Frank N., 750
Mahoney, Marianne, 786
Mang, Helen, 376
Marcel, Gabriel, 201, 348, 607, 900, 904, 905
*March to Liberation, The*, 106.1, 377
*La marche à la délivrance*, 106, 373
Mariotti, Luisa, 787
Maritain, Jacques, 101, 106, 116, 116.1, 118, 151, 155, 203, 205, 205.1, 205.2, 205.3, 205.4, 217, 338, 345, 348, 367, 367.1, 372, 375, 375.1,392, 402, 402.1, 407, 407.1, 407.2, 407.3, 408, 409, 502, 548, 702, 703, 731, 741, 742, 754, 756, 757, 758, 789, 810, 812, 862, 900, 903, 900.3, 901, 905
 *Œuvres complètes: Jacques et Raïssa Maritain*, 151, 788.3, 900.1, 901.3, 903.1, 904
Maritain Institute Series, 407.3
Maritain Newsletter, 402.1

*Maritain Volume of the Thomist, The*, 205, 205.1, 205.2, 375
Maritain, Raïssa, 503, 741, 905; *see also* Maritain, *Œuvres Complètes*
Marquette University, 712, 813
Marx, Karl, 358
Massignon, Louis, 348
Massis, Henri, 319, 790
*Masterpieces of Catholic Literature*, 734, 750
Material logic, 153, 155, 156, 210, 708, 710
*Material Logic of John of St. Thomas, The*, 153, 155, 156, 210
Mathematical abstraction, 401
Mauriac, François, 348
Maurois, André, 509, 541
McAvoy, Thomas I., 209, 212
McGill, Frank N., 734
McIlwain, Charles H., 207
McInerny, Ralph, 791
McMorrow, George J., 105.1, 105.2, 792
Mémoires (Simon), 367, 367.1 367.2, 832, 833, 834
Menger, Karl, 387
Mercier, Désiré-Joseph, 341
Merleau-Ponty, Maurice, 903
Mesnard, Pierre, 900
Messières, René de, 905
Mestre, Archille, 900
Metaphysics, 100, 100.1, 101, 107, 384, 709, 710, 730, 828
Metaphysics of knowledge, 100, 100.1, 101, 118, 200, 214, 266, 327, 328, 332, 333, 341, 399, 766, 777, 828, 845
Mettler, Arthur, 532
Metzger, Hélène, 525
Michelet, Edmond, 793, 793.1, 793.2, *290*
Michelin, Alfred, 900
Michels, Thomas, 905
Mitcham, Carl, 222
*Modern Catholic Thinkers*, 213
*Modern Schoolman, The*, 386, 387
Mommersteeg, Peter J. M. H., 905
*Le Monde*, 831, 865
Monléon, Jacques de, 328, *245*
Moral philosophy, 101, 110–110.4, 112, 112.1, 112.2, 118, 226, 333,

389, 391, 398, 400, 701, 704, 725, 729, 733, 734, 748, 765, 791, 794, 796, 807, 811, 812, 828
Moral virtue, 117, 118, 765, 775, 786, 796, 803, 811
Morgenthau, Hans J., 550
Morize, André, 544
Mounier, Emmanuel, 345, 348, 367, 900, 901, 903, *290*
Mullally, Joseph, 214
Mullaney, James V., 392
Mulvaney, Robert J., 118, 794, 828
Muñoz Marin, Luis, 815
Murphy, Arthur E., 797
Murphy, J. Stanley, 798
Murray, John Courtney, 209

*National Cyclopaedia of American Biography, The*, 865
Natural law, 112, 112.1, 112.2, 707, 728, 759, 760, 762, 769, 828, 854, 863, *281*
*Nature and Functions of Authority*, 104, 219, 366
*Nature of Politics, The*, 216
Nef, John U., 207, 799
Neiss, Robert J., 215
Nelson, Ralph, 107.1, 378.1, 410, 411, 412, 413, 800, 801, 802, 803, 804
Neo-Calvinist, 767
Neo-Conservatism, 818
Neo-Thomist, 767, 820
*New Catholic Encyclopaedia*, 792
*New Oxford Review*, 820
*New Scholasticism, The*, 153, 389, 391, 400, 407, 708, 782, 830
*New York Times, The*, 865
Newman, John von, 207
Nicolas, Joep, 905
Nicolle, Charles, 520
Noëttes, Lefebvre des, 526
*Notes et Documents* (Rome), 367.1, 367.2, 407.1, 705, 753.2, 772, 788.2, 809, 824, 833, 862, 900.4, 905.6
*Notre Dame Alumnus*, 723
*Notre Dame Scholastic, The*, 764
*La Nouvelle Relève*, 367, 368, 369, 370, 371, 372, 832
*Nouvelles Catholiques, Supplément des*, 380.1

*Nova et Vetera*, 338, 403, 503, 728, 788.1, 793
Novak, Michael, 806, *281*
Noyes, Alfred, 905
Nutting, Willis D., 154

Oakeshott, Michael, 738, 752
O'Connell, Sean P., 807
O'Donnell, Charles P., 113, 338.1, 808, 809
Odoric de Pordenone, 609
O'Hara, John Cardinal, 860
Okinczyc, Dr. Joseph, 900
Oldekop, Ewald, 512
Olivier, Antoine, 363
Olivier, Marcel, 507
*Omaggio a Jacques Maritain*, 116.1, 810
O'Malley, Frank, 154, 212
O'Neill, Charles, 203
*Orden Cristiano*, 380.3
*Our Sunday Visitor*, 382
Oxford University Press, 840

Pacifism, 388
Palanque, Jean-Rémy, 900
Paliard, Jacques, 528
Pange, Comte Jean de, 900
Papini, Roberto, 116.1, 810
Pappin, Joseph, III, *281*
*Par delà l'expérience du désespoir*, 108
Pascal, Blaise, 602
Patriotisme, 351
Paul VI (Pope), 338
Péghaire, J. L., 386
Pegis, Anton C., 203, 385, 551
Péguy, Pierre, 150
Peillaube, Émile, 328, 603, *54*
Penido, M. T.-L., 245, 514, 605
Personalism, 345
Peters, L. A. H., 905
Peyraube, Jean, 900
Pharès, Msgr. Emmanuel, 316
Philosophia perennis, 327
*Philosophical Encyclopedia*, *289*
*Philosophical Review, The*, 797
*Philosophie et sience*, 200
Philosophie chrétienne, 337
*Philosophies*, 52
*Philosophische Grundlagen der Demokratie*, 109.4
Philosophy, *see* Moral philosophy

*Philosophy and Technology*, 222
*Philosophy of Democracy, The*, 383
*Philosophy of Jacques Maritain, The*, 392
*Philosophy of Knowledge*, 214
Philosophy of logic, 153, 155, 156, 210, 396, 708, 710
Philosophy of nature, 107, 114, 200, 201, 205.1, 205.2, 205.3, 205.4, 332, 335, 339, 341,347, 375, 375.1, 386, 387, 401, 410, 411, 412, 413, 520, 523, 524, 525, 726, 802, 804, 805, 828
*Philosophy of Nature*, 205.3
*Philosophy of Physics, The*, 205.4
Philosophy of science, 101, 107, 107.1, 114, 200, 201, 205, 205.4, 214, 332, 335, 339, 340, 341, 342, 346, 347, 375, 375.1 378, 378.1, 386, 387, 391, 398, 401, 410, 411, 412, 413, 519, 520, 523, 524, 525, 529, 531, 534, 536, 726, 800, 802, 804, 805, 828
Pick, John, 390
Piening, Lotte, 109.4
Pinloche, Auguste, 518
Pirou, Gaetan, 517
Plato, *290*
Poinsot, John, *see* John of St. Thomas
Polanyi, Michael, 718
*Politica y Espiritu*, 380.4
Political commentary, 102, 102.1, 105, 105.1, 105.2, 106, 106.1 215, 309, 312, 315, 320, 321, 322, 325, 344, 350, 351, 354, 359, 363, 364, 365, 366, 368, 369, 370, 371, 373, 374, 379, 379.1, 380–380.4, 382
Political philosophy, 101, 105, 109–109.7, 118, 202, 391, 550, 724, 771, 842, 842.1, 856
*Political Science Reviewer, The*, 771
Political theory, 737
Pollard, Christopher J., 811
Pontificia Universitas Lateranensis, 745
*Le Populaire*, 902.4
*Pour la justice et la paix* (manifesto), 902, 902.1, 902.2, 902.3, 902.4
*Pour le bien commun* (manifesto), 900
*Pour l'honneur* (manifesto), 903
*Pouvoir et société*, 218, 779
Practical knowledge, 101, 118, 223, 226, 333, 391, 398, 794, 795, 796, 828, 853

*Practical Knowledge*, 118, 795
Pre-Socratics, *290*
*La Presse de la Manche*, 865
*Prévoir et savoir*, 107, 340, 378, 410, 411, 412, 413
Primard, Eugène, 900
Princeton University, 847
*Proceedings of the American Catholic Philosophical Association*, 360, 383, 395, 836
*Le prolétariat industriel*, 151
*Propedeutica Filosofica*, 204
Proudhon, Pierre-Joseph, 225, 304, 305, 338, 338.1, 345, 345.1 533, 549, *292*, *293*
Prussia, 322, 325
Psychology, 107, 107.1, 110–110.4, 214, 378, 378.1, 386, 389, 391, 404, 504, 510, 701, 734
Publius, 345.1

*Qu'est-ce que la philosophie politique?*, 842.1
Quidde, Ludwig, 325

Rabeau, Gaston, 513, *245*
Radzin, Patricia P., 813
Raeymaeker, Louis de, 522
Ramirez, Jacques Marie, 812
Redpath, Peter A., 755
*Renascence*, 390, 837
Renascence Society, 390
Rennes, 313
*La République Française*, 380
*Review of Politics, The*, 361, 362, 365, 374, 381, 397, 403.1; 703, 817, 725, *281*, *282*
Book reviews by Simon in, 535–550
*Revista Arco*, 855
*Revista del Rosario*, 783
*Révolution communiste*, 321
*Révolution socialiste*, 321
*Revue de l'Université d'Ottawa*, 404, 704, 727, 740, 798, 814, 831
*Revue de Philosophie*, 328, 331, 332, 333, 335, 339, 340, 342, 346, 347, 358; book reviews by Simon in, 510–534
*Revue Dominicaine*, 905
*Revue Néoscolastique de Philosophie*, 341

*Revue Philosophique de Louvain*, 341, 375.1, 821, 857
*Revue Thomiste*, 508, 781
*La Revue Universelle*, 790
Rey, Maurice, 900
Riedl, Clare, 814
Riedl, John O., 104, 203, 211
Rivera, José Antonio, 515, 816, *281*
Rivière, Marcel, *238*
*Road to Vichy, The*, 105.1, 105.2, 365, 753, 753.1
Robles, Oswaldo, 204
Roegele, Otto B., 25
Roland-Manuel, Levy dit, 900
*Role of the Christian Philosopher, The*, 395
Roman Athenaeum of the Holy Cross, 746, 844
Romig, Walter, 206, 835
Rommen, Heinrich A., 209
Ronsard, Pierre de, 317
Ropp, Stefan de, 905
Ross, Eva J., 905
Rourke, Thomas R., 721, 817, *282*
Russia, 322, 325
Russo, Domenico, 904
Ryan, Alvin S., 154
Ryan, John A., 203
Ryan, John K., 203

Saint Jean, Robert de, 545
Saint Pierre and Miquelon, 368
Saint-Simon, Comte de, 305
Saint-Simoniens, 305
Saint-Simonist, *293*
*Saint Thomas d'Aquin—Pages choisies*, 152
Saint-Louis de Vincennes, 303
Salengro, Roger, 903
Sanchez Pelaez, Melena de, 407.2
Sandoz, Albert, 328
Sangnier, Marc, 301, 901
Sartre, Jean-Paul, *281*
Schoenberg, Arnold, 207
Schram, Glen N., 820
Schwarz, Baudouin, 905
Schwartz, Herbert T., 203
Schwob, René, 367
Sciacca, M. F., 209
*Science, Philosophy, and Religion*, 202
*Scritti e manifesti politici*, 900.3, 904.1

Sebeok, Thomas A. 413
Sedeyn, Olivier, 842.1
*Semiotica*, 413, 802
*Sept*, 348, 902
Serafini, Maria Silvia, 116.1
Serer, Rafael Calvo, 209
Sérouya, Henri, 516
Sheed, Frank J., 905
Sheehan, John H., 154
Sheil School of Social Studies, 402
*Sillon*, 301
Simeterre, Raymond, *245*
Simmons, Edward D., 401
Simon, Anthony O., 107.1, 109.7, 115, 116, 116.1, 367.2, 402, 407.1, 407.3, 409, 410, 411, 412, 413, 796, 819, 821, 822, 823, 824, 825, 826, 827, 828, 829, *290*
Simon, Paule, 218, 405, 375.1, 788.1, 793.1, 830
Simon, Pierre-Henri, 507, 831, 900, 903
Simon, Yves R., 103, 107.1, 115, 116, 118, 150, 151, 152, 153, 154, 155, 156, 201, 206, 207, 209, 213, 218, 219, 220, 222, 224, 328, 337, 361, 363, 367, 367.1, 367.2, 385, 386, 387, 388, 390, 394, 548, 551, 608, 700, 703, 705, 706, 707, 711, 713, 714, 715, 717, 718, 719, 720, 721, 722, 723, 724, 725, 726, 727, 728, 729, 730, 731, 732, 733, 737, 738, 739, 740, 741, 742, 743, 744, 745, 746, 747, 748, 749, 751, 752, 753, 753.1, 753.2, 754, 756, 757, 758, 759, 760, 761, 762, 763, 764, 765, 766, 767, 768, 769, 770, 771, 772, 773, 774, 775, 776, 777, 778, 779, 780, 781, 782, 783, 784, 785, 786, 787, 788, 788.1, 788.2, 788.3, 789, 790, 791, 792, 793, 793.1, 793.2, 794, 795, 796, 797, 798, 799, 800, 801, 804, 805, 806, 807, 808, 809, 810, 811, 812, 814, 815, 817, 818, 819, 821, 822, 823, 824, 825, 826, 827, 828, 829, 830, 831, 832, 833, 834, 835, 836, 837, 838, 839, 840, 841, 842, 842.1, 844, 845, 846, 847, 848, 850, 851, 852, 853, 856, 857, 858, 859, 860, 862, 863, 864, 865, 900, 901, 903, 905

Simone, André, 542
Simpson, Louise von, 858
Simpson, Otto von, 858
Slavin, Robert J., 203
Smith, Vincent E., 205.4
Socialism, 105, 105.1, 108, 108.1, 115, 115.1, 151, 309, 321, 344, 361, 405, 508, 518, 525, 800
Société Philosophique Internationale de Louvain, 200
Société Thomiste, 22
Sociology, 105, 105.1, 105.2, 108, 108.1, 115, 115.1, 118, 151, 391, 519, 529, 530, 531, 536, 546
Socratics, 118, *290*
Soden, Charles O. von, 905
*South Bend Tribune*, 94
Speaight, Robert, 838, 839, *290*
St. Thomas, *see* Aquinas
St. John's University (New York), 743
St. Louis University, 711
St. Mary's College (Indiana), 858
Stadler, Karen, 843
Stankiewicz, W. J., 220, 840, 841
Strauss, Leo, 842.1, 842.2
Streit, Robert, 329, 501
Strycker, P. J. de, 905
Sturzo, Luigi, 367, 905
*Sword of the Spirit, The*, 905.3
Sylvestre, Guy, 378, 905

Tardieu, André, 505
Taylor, Edmond, 540
Taylor, Hugh S., 905
*Témoignage Chrétien*, 905.7
*Témoin de l'homme: Hommage à Pierre-Henri Simon*, 831
Temple University, 345.1
*Temps Nouveau*, 348
*Temps Présent*, 348, 349, 351, 353, 354, 355, 356, 357
Téqui, Pierre, *238, 245, 246*
Tessier, Gaston, 359
Texas Tech University, 818
Théâtre chrétien, 308
Theological anthropology, 847
Theunis, George, 905
Thibon, Gustave, *245*
Thielicke, Helmut, 847
*Thinker's Digest, The*, 376, 739
*Thomas Aquinas and His Legacy*, 758

Thomism, 150, 152, 202, 301, 306, 310, 392, 408, 500, 522, 548, 551, 735, 820
*Le Thomisme*, 500
*Thomist, The*, 205, 205.1, 205.2, 375, 378.1, 401, 710, 801
Thompson, Richard J., 101.1, 777, 845
*Thought*, 338.1, 393
Tonneau, A. J., 519
Torre, Michael D., 702, 742, 749, 751, 754, 757, 768, 786, 794, 800, 846
*Trabajo, sociedad, y cultura*,115.1
*La tradición de la ley natural*, 112.2
*Tradition of Natural Law, The*, 112, 112.1, 759, 762, 769
*Traité du libre arbitre*, 110, 110.1, 110.2, 729, 732
Trask, Willard R., 108.1, 108.2
*Trattato del libero arbitrio*, 110.3
*Trois leçons sur le travail*, 103, 343, 361
Troude, Robert, 519
Turner, Phillip W., 847

*U.S. Catholic*, 402
*Un cri d'alarme* (manifesto), 901, 901.1, 901.2, 901.3
Undset, Sigrid, 905
United Nations, 374, 382
United States, 154, 154.1, 208, 208.1
*Univers*, 344, 350, 503
*Universidad de Santo Tomas*, 854
Università Cattolica del Sacro Cuore, 787
University of Notre Dame, 331, 723, 764, *54, 238, 290*
University Press of America, 753
University of Chicago, The, 735, 859
*University of Chicago Magazine The*, 799
University of Navarra, 763
Urbain, Georges, 524

Vaissière, Jules de la, 510
Van Cauwelaert, Franz J., 905
Van der Meer de Walcheren, Pierre, 903, 904
Van Doren, Charles, 852
Van Doren, John, 3, 853
Van Zeeland, Paul, 905
Vaussard, Maurice, 900
Vélez-Sáenz, Jaime, 854, 855
*Vera Lex*, 707, 776

Veysset, Phillipe, 856
Vialatoux, Joseph, 900
Viatte, Auguste, 905
Vichy, 105.1, 105.2, 348, 753, 753.1
Victor-Hugo, Jean, 900
*La Vie Catholique*, 506, 902.1
*La Vie Intellectuelle*, 326, 327, 329, 330, 336, 352, 501, 505, 902.4
*La Vie Spirituelle*, 150
Vienna Circle, 413, 802
Vignaux, Jean, 900
Vignaux, Paul, 857, 901, 904
Villacorta, Efren, 203.2
*Les voiles se déchirent*, 905.4
Vouillemin, Général Charles Ernest, 340

Walton, Clarence, 219
War, 102, 102.1, 105, 105.2, 106, 106.1, 223, 309, 350, 359, 363, 364, 365, 368, 369, 370, 371, 373, 374, 379, 379.1, 388, 507, 509, 541, 542, 545, 716, 755, 838

Ward, Edward P., 859
Ward, Leo R., 154, 860
Weber, Max, 532
Weil, Simone, 731
*What Is Political Philosophy?* 842
Whipple, John Emory, 861
Williams, Brooke, 862
Wodan, 310
Woldring, H. E. S., 863
Wolff, Peter, 110.4, 403.1, 864
Work, 103, 115, 115.1, 207, 325, 343, 348, 361, 362, 508, 731, 751, 770, 800
*Work, Society, and Culture*, 115, 361, 770, 823
*Works of the Mind, The*, 207
Wright, Frank Lloyd, 207

Yánes, Loló Gil de, 115.1
Yelaja, Shanker A., 221
Yves R. Simon Institute, 789, 858, *289*

Zambonini, Franca, 110.3
Zernatto, Guido, 905

# INDEX

abortion, 109–110
absolute, 60
  experimental, 74
  particular things as way to, 4
abstraction, 22
  presupposing its object, 96
  universal in the particular, 95
absurdity: denial of obvious fact, 27, 39
action (activity), 6, 7, 20, 38
active life, 20, 44
  all premises of, as laws, 124
  analogue of God's perfection, 53
  authority compared with, 120
  change, 42, 43, 50
  command and, 166, 168
  command as form of, 159
  definition(s), 46, 48
  dependence on external being, 47
  deliberative acts, 152
  determination of, 157
  divine premonition, 52
  efficient causality, 43, 47
  emanation, 46
  flow-chart, 54
  freedom as self-delusion, 130
  harmony, 122
  immanent, 43–44
  judgment and command at moment of, 176
  judgment and rule of, 156
  law and, 160
  metaphysics of, 40, 42, 53
  moral, and modern science, 176
  objectives, 114
  perfect form of, 53
  positive laws as premises of, 115, 116
  practical; speculative, 53
  practical wisdom, 150
  prior premises (natural law), 112
  prudential rules of, 122
  relation between acts and ends, 120
  right reason and law-making, 117
  self-identical with the agent, 47–48
  terminal act, 44–45
  theoretical goals of, 174
  theoretical science and, 176
  thought and, 166, 167, 175
  transcendental definition, 44
  transitive and immanent, 44, 46, 48–49
  unity of, 120
  wisdom determined by, 162–163
  *see also* human acts
actuality:
  change, 52
  knowledge of source of, 43
  vitality, 51
Adler, Mortimer J., 129, 144
adultery: Aristotle on, 113$n$34
*Aeterni Patris* (1879), 83, 84
alienation, 134
American Founders, 145
amplitude (the word), 97
analogy, 44
  logic of, 125, 126
analysis of data, 38
angels, 51–52, 138
animals: change and, 51
Anscombe, G. E. M., 79
appetite, 167, 174
  role in rational life, 151
  wisdom, 159
Arendt, Hannah, 144
argumentation, 172, 173
Aristotle, 1, 2, 5, 6, 10, 15, 27, 39, 40, 87, 89, 90, 92, 96, 99, 104$n$6, 121, 132, 135, 147, 154, 160, 162, 163, 164, 170, 171, 172, 174, 176
  on adultery, 113$n$34
  on wisdom, 149–151
Aron, Raymond, 65$n$34

art, 181
  external products, 161
  political wisdom, 161
  practical wisdom, 150, 152, 167
  prudence and, 160–161
  virtue, 161
Ashley, Benedict M., 68$n$41
assent, 115
atheism, 39
Athens, 7
attachment: to things inferior to man, 180
Augustine, Saint, 151
authority, 128, 131, 174
  autonomy and, 135, 157
  choosing between two courses, 140
  coercion and (Hayek), 133$n$11
  command, 159
  complementary with liberty, 131, 136, 141, 142, 144
  deciding among choices, 4, 178
  deficiency theory, 135–136
  definition, 155
  expansion, with liberty also expanding, 144
  governance by, 121
  governing personnel, 137–138
  ideal conditions, 141, 144
  inheres only in self-governing people, 144
  judicial office, 121
  law and, 120–121
  law distinct from, 159
  legitimate political functions, 136
  liberty and, 155
  Marxism, 136
  need: examples, 4
  parental, 137
  practical living, 2–3
  practical wisdom, 153
  protection of individual liberties, 141
  prudential requirements, 9
  reason protected by, 15
  science and society, 36
  social groups, 156
  substitutional functions, 156
  transmission theory, 8–9
  unanimity and, 5, 120
  understanding meaning of, 145
  united action and, 121, 140
  wisdom and, 155

autonomy, 135, 157
Averroës, 100
awareness, 95$n$25

Baccalauréat-ès-Lettres, xvii
Bachelard, Gaston, 63, 74
Bay, Christian, 133
beauty: loss of, and love, 7
Beaux Voyages d'Autrefois, Les, xviii
becoming, 26
beginning and end: nature, 29
behavior, 176
  determined (Toynbee), 141$n$28
  disorderly, 38
  science applied to, 65
being, 20
  abstract/simple notion of, 44
  act and potency, 44
  finite, 45
  formal object of investigation, 45
  identification of "to be" and "to think," 34, 35
  intuitive perception, 95
  knowledge of being as being, 42
  knowledge of sensible being, 43
  laws governing, 43
  life in a living thing, 51
  limited capacities for, 41
  notion from abstraction, 88
  object of sensation and, 94
  perfection of, 43
  primary datum of intellect, 74
  principles of, 40
beings of reason (*entia rationis*), 64
Bellarmine, Robert, Saint, 8, 9, 10
Benrubi, Isaac, 58–59
Bentham, Jeremy, 131
Bergson, Henri, 61$n$17, 78
Berlin, Isaiah, 129
Biden, Senator Joseph, 109
Bill of Rights, 145
biologists, 28
Blanche, F. A., xviii
Blankenhagen, Peter H. von, xi
Boethius: definition of a person, 6
Bork, Robert, 109$n$21
botany, 26, 30
Bouglé, Célestin, xvii
brotherhood, 38

Cahalan, John C., 95$n$25
Cajetan, Thomas de Vio, 8

Carnap, Rudolf, 76
*Casey* decision, 14
Cassinelli, C. W., 132
Cassirer, Ernst, 74
cause(s); causality:
　explanation, 73
　free will and, 177
　infinite regress, 35
　social sciences, 139
　substitutes for causal explanation, 70
　*see also* efficient cause; final cause; first cause; etc.
certainty, 156, 168, 172, 173, 174, 175
Certificat d'Etudes Physiques, Chimiques, et Naturelles, xvii
chance, 70, 177
change:
　action and, 42, 43
　activity and, 50
　efficient causality, 42
　form's capacity to receive, 41
　immanent activity, 51
　imperfection, 50
　living beings, 51, 52
　physical reality, 73
　practical knowledge, 150
　source of, 42
　sufficient reason for, 42
character: virtue, 130–131
chastity: habit of, 114n37
checks and balances, 162
Cherbourg, ix
Chicago, 29
choice [free choice], 70, 156, 167, 178
choosing, 48
　example: equally suitable ways, 139
　factors related to widening, 140
　final movement of the mind, 151
　judgment of, 175
　knowledge specifies, 158
　opposite of indetermination, 130
　picking best option, 138–139
　reason and authority, 4–5, 158
　restricted by deficiencies, 140
　superdetermination, 128, 131
　virtues and choosing wrongly, 131
　wisdom commands (individual and social), 152
Christianity: humanism and, 179
Church Fathers, 83
Cicero, 5

city: good of the, 132
civilization, 2, 29–31, 135, 180
clarity, 4
　laws, 115, 122
coercion:
　authority and (Hayek), 133n11
　Marxism, 136
　practical wisdom, 156
cognition, *see* knowledge
college: faculty as governing board, 142
command:
　action and, 166
　ambiguous concept, 159
　authority, 156
　choice, 158
　definition, 175
　fulfillment, 169, 173
　intelligibility, 175
　last practical judgment, 175
　law and, 152
　moment of action, 176
　practical wisdom, 152, 157
　ultimate practical judgment, 166
　wisdom, 168
Committee on Social Thought, xi
common good, 1, 2, 10, 16, 132, 169
　community more directed, more free, 144
　deficiencies and, 140
　end of society, 141
　formal and material intention, 142–143, 146
　free choice related to, 140
　good of the individual, 133
　greater than individual good, 135
　nominalist denial of reality of, 133
　particular goods essential for, 143
　Plato's *Republic* as false, 132
　self-government essential for, 135
　unanimity and, 120
　unity in diversity, 142
common sense, 61, 72
community (political):
　free people, 135
　intelligence and will in, 160
　particularized commands, 121
　perfect; decision-making, 137–138
　political; ideally governed, 161
　self-governing, 142
　unanimity, 120
　wholeness (political), 135

compromise:
  politics and natural law, 107, 110–111
Comte, Auguste, 74, 75
concept(s), 153
  abstracted from judgment, 172
  judgment has priority over, 172
  ontological or empiriological inquiry, 73
  sensation as source of, 87
conditioning, 73
conduct: guide, 155, 171
conscience, 8
consent, 115
  freely given, 141
Constitution (U.S.), 145
contemplation, 50, 53, 54
  contemplative life, 15, 44
  highest/noblest activity, 40
  most perfect activity, 20
  mystery, 56
contingency, 178
  law and authority, 121
  practical reason, 111, 122
  practical syllogism, 150
  reduction of, 158
  science and society, 37
cooperation, 38
Copleston, Frederick C., 63n23
cosmology, 68, 69
counsel, 166
courage, 164, 171
Cours et Documents de Philosophie, xviii
Cranston, Maurice, xii
creation:
  efficient action, 43
  radical dependence on God, 153
creature: God's conserving action, 43
culture, 135, 180
  final causality and, 36–40
  freedom from work, 55
  grand work, 163
  humanistic, 37
  understanding, 162

Davis, Jefferson, 108n18
De veritate, 96
death, 130
death rate: poorest people, 25

decision-making, 48, 164, 165, 167
  analogy: the practical syllogism, 150
  authority in society, 36, 178
  human right, 110
  perfect community, 137–38
  practical wisdom, 153
  virtue and, 173
  will and, 158
  wisdom has last word in, 162
Declaration of Independence, 23, 108
Deely, John, 66n35
deficiencies: choices restricted by, 140
Degrees of Knowledge, The, 58, 60, 62, 92
deism, 32
deliberation, 158, 166
  will and, 151
democracy, x, 8, 128, 162
  coach–driver theory, 11, 12
  deciding public issues, 9
  defended; definition of man, 144
  evolution of, 10
  formal organization, 11
  natural form of rule, 8, 9, 10
  natural law, 13
  principle: all men are created equal, 21, 25
  protecting liberty and authority in, 145
  Simon's enthusiasm for, 161
  state absolutism and, 145
  transmissible powers, 11
  word implications, 11
Dennehy, Raymond L., 15, 19–56
Dent, N. J. H., 79
Derrida, Jacques, 72
Descartes, René, 26, 27, 65, 147, 172
desire, 50, 168
despotism: natural law and, 105
determinism, 37, 176
  three systems, 73
  various meanings, 70
differentiation thesis, 68
dignity, 141
Diploma Cooperationis Causa, xviii
Diplôme d'Études Supérieures de Philosophie, xvii
direct democracy, 11, 12, 13
disposition, 49, 50
dissertation, Ph.D. (Simon's), xvii, xviii

divine right, 128
divorce, 176
Doctorat de Philosophie, xviii
doubt, 61n14
Dromard, Paule (Mrs. Yves R. Simon), xviii
Duhem, Pierre, 75
duty:
   final causality: moral obligation, 31–36, 53
   major premise (syllogism), 150
Dwelshauvers, Georges, xviii
dynamism, 30

eclecticism, 68
École de Medécine, xvii
École Libre des Hautes Études, xviii
École Normale Supérieure, xv
economics, 29, 176
   natural law and, 105
Eddington, Sir Arthur, 75
education:
   humanistic, 37
   moral law and, 24
effect, 47, 48, 49
efficiency: transitive activity, 48
efficient cause, 53
   acts on all beings, 43
   change and, 42
   direct emanation, 48
   immanent action, 44
   nature; freedom, 48
   relation in every activity, 47
egalitarian dynamism, 25
election, 11
Eliade, Mircea, xi
emanation, 46–47
empiricism, 76
end, 54, 119
   acts and, 120
engineering, 80, 81
entities:
   law of progression, 26, 27
   natural; essences, 26
   potency, 30
   see also being
epistemology, 15
   moral, 155, 162
   science of psychology and, 78
   seventeenth-century revolution in, 147
   Simon's neo-Thomist tradition, 83–100
equality:
   democratic, 21
   egalitarian tendency, 24
Erasmus, 37
error: defense against, 56
essence:
   existence adds nothing to, 45–46
   metaphysical theory of, 23, 24
   natural entities, 26
   things lacking, 28
   universals, 21–22
ethics, 19, 20, 54, 64, 79, 181
   epistemology of, 148
   knowledge in, 170
   manifesto: "For the Common Good," x
   moral philosophy as directive, 170–171
   objects of, 154
   philosophy of science and, 82
   ultimate goal of moral knowledge, 154
Eucharistic transubstantiation, 42
exemplary cause, 54
existence:
   adds nothing to essence, 45–46
   dependence on a necessary being, 47
   existential modalities, 22
   objects treated mathematically, 39
   physical, existing intentionally, 88
   terminal act, 44–45
existentialism, 40, 107, 178
experience:
   arguments from causes, 34
   normative, 177
   philosophical facts, 61–62
   thought, 46
explanation, 81
   final cause and, 176
   Meyerson, 75
   moral action, 169
   predictivist account of, 76
   providing reasons or causes, 73
Eyselé, Charles, xviii

fact(s):
   demonstration of, 27
   general theory of, 60

principle, 60–61
scientific, 61
faith, 91
  authority in, 2
  natural law and, 180
  religious freedom, 12
  study of philosophy and, 83n2
family:
  example of authority, 4
  prudential rules, 122
  Fascism, 136
  *Federalist, The*, 145
  final cause, 28, 53, 153, 157
  culture and, 36–40
  explanation and, 176
  importance, 40
  moral obligation, 31–36, 53
  rejection of, 39
finality, *see* teleology
finite being: potency and act, 45
first cause, 33, 34
Flathman, Richard E., 132
forecasting, 76
form:
  capacity to receive change, 41
  knower receives form of the known, 97, 98
formal cause, 157, 158
formal explanation, 167
Frank, Philip, 75
free choice, *see* choice
free will, *see* will
freedom, 181
  absolute, 143
  community protected from disunity, 144
  having one's way at all costs, 140
  indeterminism, 130, 146
  knowledge of truth and, 146
  main conceptions of (Adler), 129
  maximization, 133
  personal, 129
  protecting individual liberties, 141
  science of society, 139
  Simon charged with restricted idea of, 146
  superdetermination, 131, 146
  unconditional, 43
  understanding idea of, 145
  unpredictability as measure of, 129
  *see also* liberty

freedom of the press, 145–146
French philosophy, 58
Freud, Sigmund, 78
friendship, 3, 6–7
  Aristotle on, 6

Garrigou-Lagrange, Réginald, 93
generosity, 134
Germany, 57
Geyer, Georgie Anne, 12
gift: proceeding by way of, 5, 6
Gilson, Étienne, 1, 14, 84n3, 85, 95
giving: use of human accomplishments, 134
God:
  being and thinking (distinctions in), 35
  creative self-knowledge, 54
  distinctions of [our] reason and, 35
  divine infinity, 53
  effects of: to be, to live, to understand, 114n38
  existence of divine intelligence, 32, 33, 34
  existence: controversy over, 32
  first cause, 34
  First Intelligence, 34
  idea of perfect being leads to God, 45
  immutability, 27
  infinite actualization, 51, 52
  life itself, 52
  limitation not found in, 45
  natural law and, 123
  omniscience, 42
  perfect immanence, 54
  perfections of, 52, 53
  pure actuality of, 40
  stability of the universe, 27
good of society, 128, 132, 134
goodness:
  acting in accord with, 112
  capacity in each created person, 7
  desirability, 7
  divine love as cause of, 7
  knowledge of, by argument, 114
  mathematical entities, 39
  nature tends to desire, 52
  tripartite: to be, to live, to know, 114, 119
  use, 168

government:
  consent of the governed, 140–141
  deficiency theory, 135–137
  governance by law; by authority, 121
  parental function, 137
gratuitous act, 129
greatest man or woman, 135
Grene, David, xi
Gurwitsch, Aron, 74

habit:
  character, 131
  cognition from, 114
Hahn, Hans, 76
Hamlet, 130
happiness, 5, 176
harmony of action, 122
Hart, H. L. A., 105
Hayek, Friedrich A., xi, 133
health, 24, 125
heart, 50, 161, 163, 180
Hegel, G. W. F., 132
Heiligkreuz-Neisse, Nordost (Germany), xvii
Heisenberg, Werner, 75
Held, Virginia, 131–132
Heraclitus, 27
Henle, Robert J., 96n27
Henry, Patrick, 130
heroes, 130n5, 132
Hittinger, Russell, 13–14, 101–127
Hobbes, Thomas, 29, 131
  denial of natural law, 104
Hodgson, Marshall, xi
human acts:
  conditioned; practical syllogism, 150–151
  solicitude at moment of action, 153
  subject to rational principle, 151
  Thomas Aquinas on, 151
  virtuous man as rule of, 113n36
human beings:
  activity from interiority, 51
  authority and rationality, 5
  defined in philosophy and in zoology, 67
  definition: ontological or empiriological, 73
  democratic equality, 21
  determinations; cause, 51
  essential features, 24
  essentially identical, 23
  exploitation of, 36
  fulfillment; natural striving, 31
  manipulation of, 81, 176
  rational agents, 31
  spirit and flesh, 56
  unique creatures, 52
  universality (concept), 22
  wholistic approach to, 38
human condition, 178
  Maritain on, 56
  political authority, 137
human nature:
  change in human condition, 9
  ground for loving without measure, 7
  moral law grounded in, 23
  objective study of, 65
  philosophy, 178
  reality of unity of, 23, 25
humanism:
  attitude, 37
  Christianity and, 179
  culture, 37
  science and, 36–40
  secularized, 179
humanistic studies, 180–181
Hume, David, 131
Hutchins, Robert M., xi, xix
hylomorphic body, 97

idea(s):
  abstraction from the sensible real, 95
  analogy: religious faith, 91
  external sense (Aristotle), 90n19
  intentional existence, 89
  memory image compared with, 90, 96
  objectivity, 92
  reality; likeness, 89
  representative things, 91n22
  self-validation, 91, 92, 96, 100
  two-sided notion of, 91, 92, 100
idealism, 28, 57, 62, 63, 74, 94, 164
identity, 30, 53
  dynamism toward completion, 30
  efficient act and imminent act, 48
  knower and known, 96
  principle of, 88, 89
  subjectivity, 94

certitude, 93
  drawn from existing things, 93
  realities united, 43
  universal nature, 22
ideology: natural law and, 107
ignorance: social disunity, 36
image of God, 6
imagination, 23
immanent action, 43–44, 53
  change and, 51
  efficient cause of, 47
  freedom of, 56
  intimate to the agent acting, 47
  knowing as, 49–50
  mobility, 50
  proceeds from its subject, 48
inanimate life, 52–53
inclinations: seeds of law and virtue, 114, 115
indeterminacy, principle of, 70
indeterminism: freedom, 130, 146
individualism: misreading human needs, 134
individuality, 22, 24
ineluctability, 94
inequality, 23
infinite:
  being, 45, 53
  knowledge as opening upon, 41
  regress, 35
  series: first cause, 33
injustice: natural law and, 105
Institut Catholique de Lille, x
Institut Catholique de Paris, ix
intellect, 32
  antecedent, 53
  being as primary datum of, 74
  discursive thinking, 50–51
  material object of, 52
  ordered to the intelligible, 53
  principle of identity, 93
  pure condition for learning, 88
  Transcendental Thomism, 88
  truth and, 50
  will and, 48
  *see also* mind
intelligence:
  authority and making choices, 4–5
  divine, 32, 33, 34
  moral obligation and, 34
  political community, 160

intentionality: objectivity, 90
intuition, 168

Jerusalem, 7
Jesus Christ: divine and human, 179
John of Saint Thomas (John Poinsot), 1, 22, 66*n*35, 154
John Paul II, Pope, 113*n*33
joy, 50
judgment(s), 64
  authoritarian directives, 121–122
  communication; secret, 157
  definition, 172
  habit of virtue and, 113*n*36
  logic, 159
  moment of action, 176
  practical wisdom, 150
  primacy of, 153
  priority over concept, 172
  prudential, 168–169
  prudential; singular, 154
  rational; divine providence, 116*n*48
  rectitude of, 114*n*37
  singularity, 154
  social and individual aspects, 175
  ultimate practical judgment, 155, 166, 167, 168, 175
  understanding and, 160
  unity of, 120
  wisdom and, 163, 164
jurisprudence: law in realm of necessity, 112
justice:
  acts contrary to nature, 113
  all moral norms as conventional (Hobbes), 104
  animate (Aristotle), 121
  Aristotle on, 104*n*6
  artifactual, 104
  egalitarian, 23
  essence of, 24
  modern appeals against authority, 108
  perfect, 24–25
  Thomas Aquinas on, 103

Kant, Immanuel, 28, 59, 64, 85, 172
Kennedy, Anthony (Justice), 14
Kierkegaard, Søren, 165, 169
killing: intrinsic evil, 25
Knasas, John F. X., 15, 83–100

Knight, Frank H., xi
knot (metaphor: virtues), 165
knowing, 49–52
knowledge, 181
   *a priori* mediating factor, 86
   affective, 157
   amplitude of knower's form, 97
   connatural and reasoned out, 114
   critique of, 62, 69, 94
   development of Simon's thought, 153–165
   existentially becoming what one cannot be, 41
   existing physical object, 88
   external realities, 88
   first the thing, then the idea, 91
   formal amplitude of the knower, 100
   formal reception of form, 97–98
   idea as object of, 89
   immateriality, 97, 99
   infused (angels), 52
   knower becomes the other (cognition), 41
   known is some way in the knower, 96, 97
   laws of being as being, 42
   legislative process, 160
   metaphysical foundations of, 40–41
   moral science as, 154
   natural law, 101
   objective, 41, 95
   opening upon the infinite, 41
   passivity; contradiction, 42
   perfection of one thing is in another, 97
   physical, 66, 67, 77
   practical, 80, 165–181
   scientific, 156
   sensation and material reality, 84
   sense experience, 43
   separation from matter, 97
   social and political areas, 159
   theoretical and practical, 150, 153–154
   truth as its end, 156
   two ways of knowing, 113–114
   virtue; identity, 170
   wisdom (practical), 149
Kuic, Vukan, 14, 62n20, 79, 158

labor unions: right to strike, 146
Lallement, Daniel J., xviii

Laski, Harold, 133
law(s), 181
   authority and, 120–121, 159
   clarity in law-making, 112
   commands of sovereign, 104
   Constitution (U.S.), 108
   definition (Aquinas), 123
   deliberative acts and, 152
   essential and statistical, 73
   eternal; positive; natural, 13
   general rules for individual actions, 118
   history: reform of penal laws, 105
   human decree as source, 1056
   inclinations as seeds of, 114
   inherently changeable, 106
   instilled law (Aquinas), 114–115
   last word belonging to things, 127
   *see also* justice; natural law
   morality:
      acts wrong by essence, 113
      consensus, 110, 111
      existence of God and, 123
      likelihood of dispute, 110
      making or changing laws, 105
      order of knowledge, 124
      order of naming, 126
      premise: act in accord with the good, 112
      separation thesis, 105
   natural to divine, 32, 34
   pervasiveness re human conduct, 106
   positive:
      autonomy of, 104
      conclusions in, 115
      consensus and, 115
      contrast between nature and convention, 106
      conventions, 104
      definition of law (Aquinas), 123
      determinate, 124
      justice in the human mind, 104n6
      moral norms, 125
      morality and, 104
      natural law overlap, 118
      natural right to immunity, 110
      prior moral premises, 126
      proper predication of law, 125
      slavery and, 108
      traffic laws and, 117, 124

unanimity of action, 110
valid regardless of moral aspects, 104
private law, 106
qualities in character of, 112, 121
right reason in contingent matters of action, 117
role in directing practical reason, 111–112
Stoic tradition, 152
temporal and divine (Aquinas), 125n72
Thomism, 152
universality and necessity, 160
unqualifiedly immutable laws, 112
work of reason, 160
learning, 2
Lector Philosophiae, xvii
legalism, 116
legislation:
clarity in communication, 112
practical knowledge and, 160
leisure, 55, 163
Leo XIII, Pope, 83
Lévy-Bruhl, Lucien, 64–65
liberalism, 10, 11, 14
liberty, xi, 25, 128, 131
absence of authority, 135
authority and, 155
complementary with authority, 131, 136, 141, 142, 144
concern for individual well-being, 134
expansion, with authority also expanding, 144
how much a democracy can afford, 141
political, 129
social sciences, 139
Supreme Court opinion, 109
see also freedom; self-government
Licence-ès-Lettres, xvii
Licentiate, xvii
life:
artistic product, 161
capacity to impose change on itself, 51
cognitive; vegetative; inanimate, 52
knowledge of goodness of, 114
radical threats to common life, 107
unique meaning in God, 52
vitality, 51

likeness: reality, 89n16
limitation: passivity, 41
literary criticism: philosophers and, 72
logic:
inductive and deductive, 70
order of being, 126
practical judgment, 159
reflection on (metaphysics), 69
logical positivism, 70, 71, 76
Lonergan, Bernard, 85, 86
Louvain School, 68–69
love, 5
act of a perfect subject, 51
disinterested, 134
gift of self, 6
heart does not cease loving, 50
human nature as ground for, 7
person as object of, 6–7
person loved without measure, 7
qualities of one loved, 6–7
sharing in common, 3
use: give of it freely, 134
Lycée Louis-le-Grand, ix, xvii

MacIntyre, Alasdaire, 19
Madison, James, 12, 136
Maine de Biran, 78
man:
defined as rational, political animal, 144
philosophy of man, 80
universality (concept), 22
see also human being
Maréchal, Joseph, 85, 86
Maritain, Jacques, ix, xviii, 56, 57, 59, 62, 63, 64, 66, 67, 72, 80n78, 85, 94, 95, 100, 154, 173, 175, 181
Marx, Karl, 132
Marxism, 136
mathematics, 26, 29
objects, 28
textbooks, 84
matter: form received by the knower, 97, 98
McCoy, Charles N. R., 9, 10, 11–12
meaning: new empiricism, 76
measurement, 67
mechanism, 26, 28, 39
medieval civilization, 180
Mémoire sur Charles Dunoyer, xvii
memory, 61n7, 89–91, 96

Mercier, Désiré-Joseph Cardinal, 68
Merleau-Ponty, Maurice, 78
metaphysics, 8, 16, 19, 20, 34, 40, 56, 66, 77
　common experience and, 62
　practical metaphysics, 20, 21–40
　scientific thinking, 71
　special, 69
　speculative, 40–54
　Van Steenberghen's divisions, 68–69
Meyerson, Émile, 59, 63, 74, 75
Middle Ages, 84n3
Mill, John Stuart, 65
mind, 22, 26–27, 64
　becoming all things, 3
　choice as final movement of, 151
　measured measure, 116
　order of propositions in, 125
　values and, 28
misanthropy, 38
modernity: closed to inquiry re first things, 127
Monet, Claude, 89, 90
monism, 26, 27, 76
moral law, 23, 31, 33
moral obligation: intelligence and, 34
moral order: natural theology, 32
moral philosophy, 65
　analytic and synthetic, 171
　communicability, 173
　moral theology and, 174
　normative judgments, 171
　science of the moralist, 173–74
　theoretically-practical knowledge, 66
　truth, 172
　*see also* ethics
moral science:
　science and, 173
　the term, 65
　theoretically-practical knowledge, 65, 66
moral theology, 174–175
moralists, 174
morality:
　contingency of moral action, 153
　first premises and, 115, 116
　judgment and virtue, 163
　law and, *see* law
　practical intuition, 164
　provisional, 65
　prudential objectivity, 164
　reduction of authority, 107
　responsible choices, 109
　science of the soul, 77
　value-free facts, 177
Morgenthau, Hans J., xi
motion: physics and laws of, 27
motionless activity, 50
Mulvaney, Robert J., 14, 147–181
murder, 23–24
　absolute freedom, 129
　natural law, 112
mystery: relation to, 55
mysticism: Christian, 181

nations: rich and poor; options, 139
natural (definition), 10
natural law, 177, 179, 180
　Catholic tradition, 14
　causality and practical reason, 101
　common principles, 112
　concept of, as Janus-faced, 115
　conclusions, 112
　conditions to be "law," 124, 126
　contingencies of human action, 122
　definition, 126
　democracy, 13
　diversity of doctrinal contexts, 101, 102
　divine lawgiver, 102
　effectiveness, 116
　eternal return of, 105
　existing in things, 31–33
　extra-philosophical difficulties, 102
　facts of obligation, 35, 53
　first premises not always clear, 115
　first principles always reasoned from, 115
　Hobbes's denial of, 104
　ideology and, 102, 107
　inclination before cognition, 113
　inferences from premises, 113
　inherently multifaceted, 102
　irrepressible idea, 103
　law (the word), 123
　laws of nature and, 127
　legality of, 127
　mathematized view of the universe and, 28

metaphysical ground of theory, 25–31, 53
moral obligation, 53
necessities expressed by first precepts, 113
negative precepts (John Paul II), 113n33
ontological existence prior to rational, 126
order of discovery, 32, 34, 123, 125
order of practical cognition, 101
order of reality, 32
participation in eternal law, 116, 125
philosophical issues submerged, 111
prior premises of action, 112
proposition in the mind, 32–33, 125
prudence and first premises, 118, 122
reason for opposing, 32
reduced to practical tool, 102
relation of acts and ends, 118
rhetoric; insinuation, 111
right and wrong actions, 126
right by nature; by contract, 103
skepticism or caution, 111
source for positive law, 118
tripartite: to be, to live, to know, 114, 119
untainted by human will and compromise, 107
what nature teaches all animals, 119
natural right, *see* right(s)
natural science, *see* science
nature:
    beginning and end, 29
    finalistic aspects, 177
    identification of "to be" and "to think," 35, 53
    imposed by divine intelligence, 33
    inanimate things, 53
    man's power over, 38
    mathematical analysis of, 28, 39, 176
    metaphysical analysis of concept, 25–26
    metaphysical unity of, 21, 22
    natural fulfillment, 30
    philosophy of, 61–62
        cosmology and psychology, 68–69
        metaphysics and, 77
        obsolescence, 66–67
        science of nature and, 67, 77, 80
    plurality, 26–27, 30
    potency of an entity, 30
    recognition of author of, 32
    science of, 36
    science; intelligibility, 67
    state of accomplishment, 29
    teleology, 28
    uncorrupted (Pascal), 179
    universal, 21–22
need(s), 134, 162
Nef, John U., xi
Nelson, Ralph, 14–15, 57–82
Neo-Thomism, 83–100, passim
    opposition considered by, 84n3
New Philosophers of Science, 70
New School for Social Research, xviii
Newton, Isaac, 66
nominalism, 23
non-contradiction, principle of, 44, 87
Normandy, xvii
nothing(ness), 27, 45
notion, *see* idea
nuclear bomb, 29

obedience: civil, 11
objects:
    mathematical, 39
    sensing or imagining, 74n63
obligation: meaning (law), 31
ontology, *see* being
optimism, 179, 180
    eighteenth-century, 37
order, 38, 55, 181
original sin, 179
Owens, Joseph, 97n31, 98n32

Paine, Thomas, 136
painting: memory image and, 89–90
Parmenides, 26, 27
particular goods, 7, 143
particulars: teaching through, 4
Pascal, Blaise, 179
passivity, 41
peace, 36
Peillaube, Émile, xviii
Peirce, Charles Sanders, 61
perception, 77
    critique of knowledge, 94, 95

perfection, 163
  counsels of, 181
performative self-contradiction defense, 86
person(s):
  definition (Boethius), 6
  object of love, 6–7
  wholes, 38
personalism, 163
personality, 6
persuasion:
  consensus re laws, 115
  practical wisdom, 156
pessimism: disappointed optimism, 179
phenomenology, 74
philosophers:
  literary criticism, 72
  principal figures treated by Benrubi, 59
  use only terms reducable to being, 74
philosophy:
  each defining his own, 14
  faith and study of, 83n2
  humanistic studies, 38
  literary, 72
  modern mind, 2
  of nature, see nature
  practical philosophy, 19, 20, 54, 64, 65
  reduced to interpretation, 72
  relations with other disciplines, 174
  scientific forms in, 55
  see science
physical science, see science
physics, 27, 39, 57, 176
Piaget, Jean, 78
Planck, Max, 75
plants (botany), 26, 51
Plato, 132, 172
Platonism, 22
plurality, 26–27, 135
Poincaré, Henri, 75
Poinsot, John, see John of St. Thomas
policy options, 139
political philosophy, 19, 20, 30
  liberty and authority, 128, 131
politicians, 132
politics:
  highest activity (Aristotle), 15

political society, 30
transmission of power, 10
see also authority; government; law; natural law
Pontifical Academy of St. Thomas Aquinas, xviii
positive scientists: use of observable data, 74
positivism: reform of penal laws, 105
potency, 45, 46
potentiality, 41, 49
poverty:
  death rate of the poor, 25
  spirit; decisive virtue, 180
practical, see knowledge; reason; wisdom; etc.
pragmatism, 61
prediction: function in science, 75–76
principle: fact as, 60–61
probabilities, 70, 158
progress, 38, 177
  illusion of, 178, 179
properties, 24
Protagoras, 127
providence:
  knowledge of things for an end, 116
  rational judgment and, 116n48
prudence, 80, 107, 108, 110–111, 122, 152, 162, 172, 174, 181
  art and, 160–161
  contradictory judgments, 156
  creative, 116
  decision-making, 165
  effects, 131
  first premises, 116, 118
  generality; and in singular matters, 117
  harmony of action, 122
  individual; familial; political, 122
  knowledge of things for an end, 116
  legislative, 118
  objectivity in moral situations, 164
  practical wisdom, 162, 164
  rectitude of, 119
  species of, 116
  sphere of the contingent, 111, 122
  traits not associated with law-making, 117
  vice; pseudo-virtue, 149
  virtues knotted together by, 165
  wisdom and, 169
psyche: disposition of, 91

psychology, 68, 171
  applied and moral, 78, 79
  confusion in, 77
  epistemology and, 78
  ethical neutrality, 80
  moral philosophy and, 171
  philosophy and physical science, 171
  science of nature, 79
  study of, 81
punishment, 31

quality: immanent action, 49
Quine, Willard Van Orman, 72

race, 24
Rahner, Karl, 85, 86
rationalism, 116
rationality, 6
Rawls, John, 79
realism, 15
  conformity of thought to reality, 87
  critical realism, 62, 74
  direct, 88, 89, 90
  epistemological, 84
  moderate, 24
  retorsion, 86
  revival of, 57
  scientific thought, 64
  unity of thing and thought, 93
realists, 63
reality, 1–2, 16
  authority and, 5
  critique of knowledge, 69
  Descartes on, 27
  known mediately, 85
  nature of the real, 87
  participation in existence, 45
  thought grasping, 64
reason(ing), 7, 14, 51
  causes and, 35
  choices and, 4–5
  element of choice, 158
  imperative function, 152
  law and deliverative rationality, 152
  legislative and practical, 117, 122
  measured by things, 31
  practical reason, 13, 15
    cardinal virtues, 111
    instilled law, 114–115
    measures as laws, 118

  reduction to natural or social science, 161
  technical reasoning, 81
  truth and, 168
  wisdom and perfection of, 167
Redfield, James M., xi
religion: society and, 12
religious freedom, 12
Renaissance, 39, 180
*respublica*, 10
responsibility:
  law and, 106
  moral choices, 109
retorsion, 86, 87, 94
revelation, 7, 42
*Revue de philosophie*, x, 60
rich nations: more options for, 139
right(s):
  artifactual, 105
  natural right, 103
  positive right, 103
  Simon's list of, 145
  things owed by nature, 108
right and wrong, 169
  intuition, 164
  nature and convention, 116
  wisdom and, 162
Roman positive law, 119
Rorty, Richard, 72
Rousseau, Jean-Jacques, 11, 13, 29, 131
rule: good forms of, 9
ruler (crooked), 86

sacrifice: disinterested, 134
*Sagesse et illusions de la philosophie*, 78
Saint-Simon, Claude Henri, Conte de, 36
saints: freedom, 130n5
Sangnier, Marc, x
Sartre, Jean-Paul, 78
savagery, 29
Schall, James V., S.J., 1–16
Scholastics, 37
Schrödinger, Erwin, 75
science, 178, 181
  contingency and, 37
  crisis; indeterminacy, 70
  critique of, 57, 58
  human action and (Aristotle), 149
  humanism and, 36–40

intellectual background, 14
  limitation, 38
  mathematics in, 26
  of nature: social engineering, 80, 81
  philosophy of, 57–82
  practically practical science, 174
  theoretical, 174, 181
science and philosophy:
  explanation and prediction in, 73, 75–76
  French reflection on, 75
  metaphysics and, 71, 77
  philosophy as derived from science, 72
  scientific research, 71
  Simon and, 71–72
  wrong track(s) in use of terms, 74
scientific knowledge: construction in, 75
scientific method, 36, 38, 39
scientific research, 61
Searle, John, 139
seed, 30
self, 6
self-actualization, 51
self-determination:
  freedom, 129
  natural right, 108n18
self-government:
  authority inheres only in, 144
  common good, 135
  free choice, 131
  model, 137–138, 142
  parents teach children, 137
  political liberty, 140
self-perfection: freedom, 129
selfishness, 5
semiotics, 66n35, 76
sensation, 74
  direct realism, 89, 90
  form united to its subject, 99
  intentionality, 90
  knowledge of material reality, 84
  most difficult part of philosophy of, 96n28
  numerical identity of received form, 100
  objectivity of ideas of, 94
  principle of identity, 88
  objectivity of, 86
  realism, 100

source of concepts, 87
truth of, 88
validation issue, 92, 100
senses:
  form received without the matter, 99
  indefectible, 88
*Sept*, xi
sex: Roman positive law, 119
Sheen, Fulton J., 62n18
Shils, Edward A., xi
sign, 50, 76
Simon, Auguste, xvii
Simon, Berthe Porquet dit la Féronnière, xvii
Simon, Paule Dromard, xvii
Simon, Yves R.:
  acknowledgments to Maritain, 57
  chronology, xvii–xix
  defender of liberty, 146
  defender of speculative life, 13
  focus of his energy, 56
  medical studies, 71
  political writings, x
  works:
    books written during World War II, xi
    *Critique de la connaissance morale*, 62, 153, 155
    *Critique of Moral Knowledge*, ix, 64
    *Definition of Moral Virtue*, 19, 77, 79, 163
    *Foresight and Knowledge*, 58, 60, 69, 70, 74, 75, 81
    *Freedom and Community*, 146, 161
    *Freedom of Choice*, 157
    *General Theory of Authority*, 2, 121, 155, 158, 159, 175
    *An Introduction to Metaphysics of Knowledge*, ix, xii, 62, 83
    *March to Liberation, The*, 71
    *Nature and Functions of Authority*, 155, 169
    "Philosophers and Facts," 60
    *Philosophy of Democratic Government*, xii, 8, 11, 128, 155, 157, 158
    *Philosophy of Knowledge*, 4
    posthumous works and reprints, xii
    *Practical Knowledge*, 66, 79, 148,

149, 152, 155, 165, 166, 176, 181
*Prévoir et savoir*, 73, 74
*Réflexions sur l'intelligence et sur sa vie propre*, 59
*Tradition of Natural Law, The*, 106, 160
*Traité du libre arbitre*, 157
*Work, Society, and Culture*, 162
writing style, 3–4
Simon Frères, xvii
Simpson, Otto von, xi
Simpson (O. J.) trial, 90, 92
singular actions, 154, 155
singularization, 99
Skinner, B. F., 78, 141n28
slavery, 108
Smith, Vincent E., 67n36
social conditions: science and human progress, 37
  Darwinism, 177
  engineering, 80, 81, 141n28
  groups: authority in, 156
  justice: natural law, 102
  knowledge: critique of, 82
  life: immanent in the souls of men, 1
  order, 36
social science(s), 66
  beginnings, 147
  bondage to natural science, 139
  choosing among options, 138–139
  Christian humanism, 36
  Comtean conception of, 65
  critique of, 162
  epistemology, 80
  knowledge acquired in, 81
  limitations of, 176
  model for, 79
  moral philosophy and, 82
  progress and perfectibility, 178
  shortcomings, 178
  value-free, 176
  wisdom and, 170
Société des Sciences de Lille, La, xviii
society: plurality, 135
Socrates, 160, 170, 173
Sokolowski, Robert, 15
solicitude: human actions, 153
solipsism, 90, 91
soul:

efficient cause of cognitive activity, 48
  knowledge of, 77
  life of (Aristotle), 150
sovereignty, 128
space: pure extension (Descartes), 27, 39
*species* (the word), 98
speculative metaphysics, 20
Spragens, Thomas A., 146
state:
  absolutism, 145
  evil, 136
  Marxism: withering away, 136
  model, 132
statesmanship, 7
stealing, 172
Strauss, Leo, 7, 8, 9, 10, 11–12, 80
strike, right to, 146
Suarez, Francisco, 8, 11
subjectivism, 55
  moral values, 28–29
  subjectivity: passivity, 41
Supreme Being, 35
Supreme Court: opinion on abortion, 109, 110
syllogism:
  command and, 159
  first premise, 116
  theoretical and practical, 150

Taney, Roger B. (Justice), 108
taxation: coercion, 133
teaching, 2, 3
technology, 9, 176, 181
  culture and, 38
  modern civilization, 180
Téqui, Pierre, x, xviii
teleology, 25, 30
  finality, 32, 35, 39, 172, 178
  natural stages, 29
*Temps Présent*, x–xi
terminal act, 44–45, 53
theology:
  humanistic studies, 38
  philosophy and, 174
theory and practice, 181
things:
  intelligibility of, 40
  natural law, 31
  wholes, 38

thinking, *see* thought and thinking
Thomas Aquinas, x, 1, 2, 3, 8, 21, 23, 33, 40, 51, 79, 83, 87, 89, 92, 94, 96–100, 103, 104n6, 113, 118, 119, 124–125, 147, 154, 160, 177
  Aristotle and, 151
  on connatural knowledge, 114
  definition of law, 123
  laws (two kinds), 125n72
  on providence and rational judgment, 116n48
  Transcendental Thomists and, 86
  treatise on law, 152
  on wisdom, 151–153
Thomas, Clarence (Justice), 109
Thomism (or Thomists), x, 8, 24, 57, 58, 59, 66, 67, 68, 74, 77, 79
thought and thinking:
  action and, 166, 167, 175
  determined by the real, 87
  discursive, 50–51
  discursiveness of, 158
  experience, 46
  grasping reality, 64
  highest form of, 7
  law of completeness, 167
  object of, 93
Tocqueville, Alexis de, 21
totalitarian state, 38, 136, 143
Toulmin, Stephen, 76
Toynbee, Arnold, 141n28
tradition: breakdown of, 107n16
traffic code: positive law and, 117, 124
Transcendental Thomism:
  intellect and, 88
  realistic sensation, 85
  retorsion, 94
  Thomas Aquinas and, 86–87
transitive action, 50, 53, 56
triangle, 30
Trinity, 6, 47
truth, 13, 15, 50, 55, 64, 76, 170, 172
  conformity with right desire, 172
  critique of knowledge, 69
  end of knowledge, 156
  freedom and, 146
  moral; measurement, 180
  practical decisions and good will, 177
  practical reason, 168
  quest for, 7
  shared: teacher and student, 3
  thinker pointing out mistakes, 2
  ultimate practical judgment, 168
twentieth century, 37

unanimity:
  common good, 120
  decision-making, 137–138
  logically impossible, 138
understanding, 32, 37, 81, 170, 173
  failure, 138
  final judgments, 160
  practical wisdom, 150
  priority over fulfillment, 169
  technology and culture, 38
  will and, 154, 157
United States: justice, 108
unity:
  act identical with its product, 49
  authority and, 140
  community action, 159
  sense level; intellectual level, 94
universality, 23
universals, 21–22
  object of science, 154
universe, 177
  Cartesian; stability, 27
  extension, 26, 39
  mathematized view of, 28, 29
  order in, 35
  views of: as nature or as space, 40
Universidad Nacional de México, xviii
Université de Paris (Sorbonne), ix, xvii
University of Notre Dame, x, xviii
unpredictability: measure of freedom, 129
use: goodness, 168

vacation: example of choosing, 139
value judgments, 64n32
values, 176, 177, 178
  Christian, 179
  economic, 29
  philosophical basis of, 28
  subjectivism, 28–29
  virtues, 177
Van Steenberghen, Fernand, 68–69
Vatican Council II, 84
vegetative life, 52–53

*Veritatis Splendor*, 113n33
Vienna Circle, 71, 76
virtue(s):
  art, 161
  certitude necessary for, 154
  character, 130–131
  contingencies of action, 121
  decision-making and, 173
  ethics of, 163
  guarantee their own performance, 131
  habit of, and right judgment, 113n36, 114
  inclinations as seeds of, 114
  incomplete without wisdom, 165
  intellectual (Aristotle), 162
  interconnection, 152–153, 159, 164, 165, 174
  keep us from choosing wrongly, 131
  knotted together, 165
  knowledge and, 170
  political wisdom, 161
  practical reason, 111
  practical wisdom, 181
  public role, 153
  spirit of poverty, 180
  values as, 177
  virtuous inclinations, 173
  will and, 151
vitality, 51
voluntarism: in democracies, 13

war, 36
  natural law and, 105
Weber, Max, 80
Whitehead, Alfred North, 75
will, 32, 37, 156, 163, 164, 167, 168, 178
  causality and, 177
  command and, 175
  decisions, 158
  determinant of action, 151
  failure to act, 138
  intellect and, 48
  limitations of reason and, 153
  moral psychology, 152
  ordered to the good, 53
  political community, 160
  practical decisions and, 177
  practical understanding and, 157
  rectitude of, 119
  rule of conduct, 155
  syllogism's conclusion, 151
  terminating deliberation, 158
  virtuous inclination of, 157
  well-ordered, 154, 159
wisdom, 30, 78, 165
  act as determinant of, 162–163
  action through command, 168
  ancient, practical virtue, 147
  Aristotle on, 149–151
  art, 167
  authority and, 155
  coercion and persuasion, 156
  decisive, 157
  development of Simon's thought on, 149ff.
  fulfillment of commands, 169
  human perfection, 163
  human thinking; practical syllogism, 150
  hylemorphic virtue, 151
  judgment and, 163, 164
  last word in decision-making, 162
  making poor use of, 168
  moral virtue incomplete without, 165
  perfection of practical reason, 167
  political and individual, 159
  political dimension, 155
  political; moral virtues, 161
  practical knowledge and, 149
  prudent person, 169
  public and private virtue, 152
  right reason in things done, 150
  role in a wide range of problems (Simon), 147
  science and, 151
  science and technique leading to, 37–38
  Simon's concern in all his major writings, 148
  social sciences and, 170
  sociopolitical dimension, 152
  theory of virtue and law, 181
  Thomas Aquinas on, 151–153
  virtue, 157
work:
  culture and, 55
  importance of, 54
  practical wisdom, 163

world:
  change in, 150
  mathematical reading of, 39
  multiplicity and complexity, 44
  regulated by divine providence, 125

World War II, 13
worth, 161

zoology, 67

# NOTES ON THE CONTRIBUTORS

RAYMOND L. DENNEHY is Professor of Philosophy at the University of San Francisco. He did graduate work at the University of California at Berkeley and received his Ph.D. at the University of Toronto. He is the author of a number of works including *Reason and Dignity*; has published widely in such journals as the *University of California, Davis, Law Review, Studies,* the *American Catholic Philosophical Quarterly, The Thomist, Vera Lex, Thought,* and the *New Oxford Review*; and is a frequent contributor to edited volumes. He is much in demand as a campus lecturer and television resource commentator on ethical and social issues.

RUSSELL HITTINGER holds the Warren Chair of Catholic Studies at the University of Tulsa where he is also Research Professor of Law. In addition to having taught at Princeton, Fordham, and the Catholic University of America, he has been a research fellow at the American Enterprise Institute. His books and articles have been published by Oxford University Press, the University of Notre Dame Press, *The Review of Politics, International Philosophical Quarterly, The Review of Metaphysics,* and several law journals. His *Critique of the New Natural Law Theory* (1987) is widely regarded as a major contribution. His introduction to the revised edition of Yves R. Simon's *The Tradition of Natural Law* appeared in 1992.

JOHN F. X. KNASAS is Professor of Philosophy in the Center for Thomistic Studies at the University of St. Thomas, Houston. He is the author of *The Preface to Thomistic Metaphysics: A Contribution to the Neo-Thomist Debate on the Start of Metaphysics*. In addition, he is a frequent contributor to *The Thomist* and the *American Catholic Philosophical Quarterly,* and has published in *The Modern Schoolman, Divus Thomas, Doctor Communis,* and *Angelicum*. He is editor of *Jacques Maritain: The Man and His Metaphysics* and, more recently, of *Thomistic Papers VI,* which contains assessments of Gerald McCool's *From Unity to Pluralism*.

VUKAN KUIC is Professor Emeritus of Government and International Studies at the University of South Carolina. He has taught at the University of Alabama and is a former Visiting Fellow at the Center for the Study of Democratic Institutions and the Center for the Study of Federalism. Kuic earned his Ph.D. from The University of Chicago and has edited a series of Yves R. Simon's manuscripts, including *The Tradition of Natural Law, Work, Society, and Culture,* and *The Definition of Moral Virtue.* With Richard J. Thompson Kuic has also translated Simon's *An Introduction to Metaphysics of Knowledge.* Currently he is writing a book on Yves R. Simon's contributions to political science for Rowman & Littlefield's Twentieth Century Political Thinkers Series.

ROBERT J. MULVANEY is Professor of Philosophy and Comparative Literature at the University of South Carolina. He writes on the history of philosophy—particularly, Leibniz and the seventeenth century, the ethics of Thomas Aquinas, American philosophy and the philosophy of education. His recent publications include articles and reviews in *Educational Studies, The Personalist Forum, Idealistic Studies,* and *The Modern Schoolman.* He is currently preparing a new translation of Leibniz's *Theodicy.* His work on Yves R. Simon includes editing *Practical Knowledge* (1991).

RALPH NELSON has taught philosophy and political science at the University of Windsor since 1961, and is now Professor Emeritus. His research and publications are in the areas of French moral, social, and political philosophy and in democratic theory. Author of numerous articles on Yves R. Simon and Jacques Maritain, he has published in such journals as *Semiotica, Canadian Journal of Political Science, Comparative Politics, Publius, Science et Esprit,* and *International Philosophical Quarterly.* He is co-editor of Yves R. Simon's *Foresight and Knowledge* (1996) and co-author of *Introduction to Canadian Government and Politics* (sixth edition, 1994) and *Decision-Making Analysis of Canadian Confederation.*

JAMES V. SCHALL, S.J., is Professor in the Department of Government at Georgetown University. He was formerly on the Faculty of the University of San Francisco and the Gregorian University in Rome. He has authored some twenty volumes, including *At* the Limits of Political Philosophy (1996), *Does Catholicism Still Exist?* (1994), *Reason, Revelation, and the Foundation of Political Philosophy* (1987), and *Church and State in the Thought of John Paul II* (1982). He has co-edited *On the Intelligibility of Political Philosophy: Essays of Charles N. McCoy* and *Essays in Christianity and Political Philosophy*. He is well known for his monthly columns in *Crisis* and the *Midwest Chesterton News*.

ANTHONY O. SIMON is Director of the Yves R. Simon Institute and Secretary of the American Maritain Association. He formerly taught at Indiana University. The General Editor of the Association's publications, he has published in a variety of journals, including the *Revue Philosophique de Louvain, Cross Currents, Cahiers Jacques Maritain, Notes et Documents*, and has contributed to a number of edited collections. Recently he co-edited *Freedom, Virtue, and the Common Good* (1995) with Curtis L. Hancock and Yves R. Simon's *Foresight and Knowledge* (1996) with Ralph Nelson.

www.ingramcontent.com/pod-product-compliance
Lightning Source LLC
Chambersburg PA
CBHW031231290426
44109CB00012B/246